Fodor's

WASHINGTON, D.C.

T0049429

Welcome to Washington, D.C.

With its neoclassical buildings and broad avenues, Washington, D.C. looks its part as America's capital. Majestic monuments and memorials honor our nation's history, but D.C. also lives in the present; new restaurants and bars continually emerge, upping the hipness factor from Capitol Hill to U Street. Fun museums and tree-shaded parks make it a terrific place for families. You may come for the official sites, but you'll remember D.C.'s local flavor, too. As you plan your visit, let us know when we need to make updates by writing to us at editors@fodors.com.

TOP REASONS TO GO

★ **Cherry Blossoms:** For a few weeks in spring, D.C. is awash in glorious pink blooms.

★ **The White House:** 1600 Pennsylvania Avenue may be the best-known address in the U.S.

★ **Memorials:** The lives of soldiers, presidents, and political figures are commemorated.

★ **Museums:** For every taste—whether you like spies, airplanes, history, or art.

★ **Globe-trotting Cuisine:** Diverse cultures support restaurants with authentic flavors.

★ **The Mall:** Ground zero for museums, picnics, festivals, and performances.

Contents

Fodor's Features

Chapter 1

EXPERIENCE
WASHINGTON, D.C.

26 ULTIMATE EXPERIENCES

Washington, D.C., offers terrific experiences that should be on every traveler's list. Here are Fodor's top picks for a memorable trip.

1 Cherry Blossom Festival

Every spring Washington is blanketed with pink and white flowers, heralding the three-week-long National Cherry Blossom Festival. Many of the original trees (a gift from Japan in the early 1900s) stand around the Tidal Basin; come early to avoid the crowds. *(Ch. 3)*

2 The NMAAHC

The museum chronicles the African American experience, from the history of slavery through the Civil War to the Jim Crow era and up to today. *(Ch. 3)*

3 The White House

The White House is located at 1600 Pennsylvania Avenue; opposite nearby Jackson Square, the Black Lives Matter Plaza reminds us to fight injustice. *(Ch. 6)*

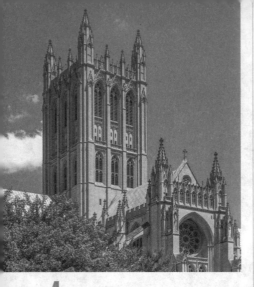

4 National Cathedral

With a prominent spot on the city's skyline, this stone church is built in a soaring, 14th-century English Gothic style and is the site of state funerals for presidents of every faith. *(Ch. 11)*

5 The Wharf

One of D.C.'s newest neighborhoods opened to acclaim in 2017, with a mix of residences and businesses along the Potomac Southwest Waterfront. *(Ch. 12)*

6 Georgetown

One of Washington's ritziest enclaves, Georgetown marries old-world charm with upscale dining and shopping, as well as a soupçon of college nightlife via Georgetown University. *(Ch. 7)*

7 14th Street and U Street

Historically, U Street was the focal point of early-20th-century African American culture in D.C. *(Ch. 10)*

8 Smithsonian Museums

What do ruby slippers, astronauts, and postage stamps have in common? They all make up the dizzying array of offerings at the Smithsonian's 19 museums. *(Ch. 3, 4, 11)*

9 Nationals Park

Even before the Nationals won the 2019 World Series, Nats games were one of the top things to do, with a waterfront setting, affordable tickets, and friendly fans. *(Ch. 12)*

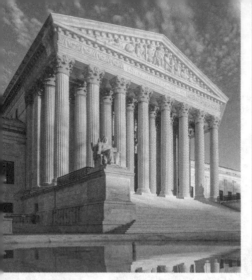

10 Supreme Court

The highest court in the country—and home of the third branch of government—is housed in a neoclassical white building a block from the U.S. Capitol. Oral arguments are open to the public. *(Ch. 5)*

11 Union Market and Eastern Market

D.C.'s markets set a high bar for discerning shoppers. Eastern Market is better known and more historic; Union Market offers high-end brands, while nearby La Cosecha celebrates Latinx culture. *(Ch. 5)*

12 Kennedy Center

The pinnacle of performing arts in Washington has a prominent perch on the banks of the Potomac. It's worth a visit just for the views—and the new state-of-the-art REACH expansion. *(Ch. 6)*

13 Mount Vernon

George Washington's colonial plantation home, 10 miles south of Alexandria, is a place to learn about American history, including the lives of enslaved people in the 18th century. *(Ch. 14)*

14 Monuments and Memorials

If there's one place in Washington you need to visit, it's the National Mall. The 2-mile lawn between the Lincoln Memorial and the U.S. Capitol is home to most of the city's monuments and museums. *(Ch. 3)*

15 Smithsonian's National Zoo

The famous giant pandas are sadly leaving at the end of 2023, but there are plenty of other engaging animals to visit, including Komodo dragons, clouded leopards, and endangered Bornean orangutans. *(Ch. 11)*

16 Dupont Circle

Dupont has a little bit of everything: a mix of shops, restaurants, embassies, and museums, including the Phillips Collection and the Heurich House Museum. It's also a popular residential area. *(Ch. 8)*

17 Potomac River

It won't attract swimmers or win "clean water" accolades anytime soon, but the Potomac swarms with kayakers, stand-up paddleboarders, rowers, and sightseeing cruises. *(Ch. 12)*

18 Arlington National Cemetery

A quick trip across the Memorial Bridge brings you to this 624-acre plot in Virginia that is the final resting place of two presidents and more than 400,000 American veterans. *(Ch. 13)*

19 Shaw

This neighborhood is booming with artisan bars, restaurants, and boutiques. Beer drinkers have plenty to cheer about, as do foodies looking for D.C. hot spots. *(Ch. 10)*

20 U.S. Capitol

The seat of legislative power for the United States anchors one end of the Mall with a soaring dome, one of the tallest structures in the city. *(Ch. 5)*

21 The Food Scene

D.C.'s restaurants are among the nation's most vibrant and creative, embracing global flavors and Michelin-worthy flair.

22 Holocaust Museum

You can't leave here without being moved. The brilliant museum educates visitors about Nazi-era Germany and the horrific events of the Holocaust. *(Ch. 3)*

23 Historic Hotels

The Watergate has been restored, while the Mayflower, the Hay Adams, and the Willard InterContinental have hosted everyone from Mark Twain to Martin Luther King Jr. *(Ch. 4, 6)*

24 H Street NE

A tad isolated, the artsy H Street Corridor, also called the Atlas District, is home to many bars and restaurants. *(Ch. 5)*

25 Tidal Basin

One of the most photographed spots in Washington, this serene inlet lined with monuments, memorials, and cherry trees is just south of the National Mall. *(Ch. 3)*

26 Library of Congress

The world's largest library has about 838 miles of bookshelves. The catch: you can't actually check them out, but you can join a free tour of the grand building. *(Ch. 5)*

WHAT'S WHERE

1 **The National Mall and Federal Triangle.** The expanse of green stretching from the Capitol to the Lincoln Memorial is lined by famous museums and monuments.

2 **Downtown, China-town, and Penn Quarter.** The area north of the Mall has hotels, bars, restaurants, museums, and galleries, and the Capitol One Arena.

3 **Capitol Hill and Northeast.** The Capitol, Supreme Court, and Library of Congress dominate this area; northeast is the ever-growing H Street Corridor.

4 **Foggy Bottom, the West End, and the White House.** The world's most famous house sits at the eastern end of this area. To the west are hotels, restaurants, museums, the Kennedy Center, and the Watergate.

5 **Georgetown.** One of the capital's wealthiest neighborhoods is great for strolling and shopping.

6 **Dupont Circle and Kalorama.** This hub of fashionable restaurants, shops, and embassies remains at the heart of gay culture.

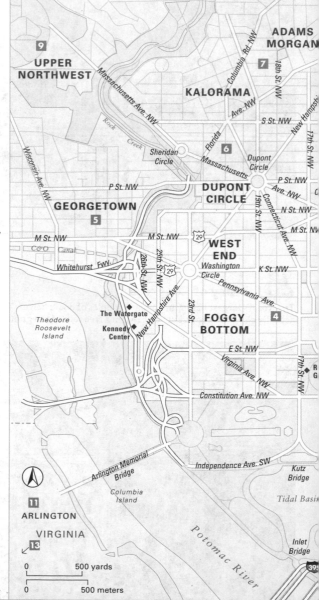

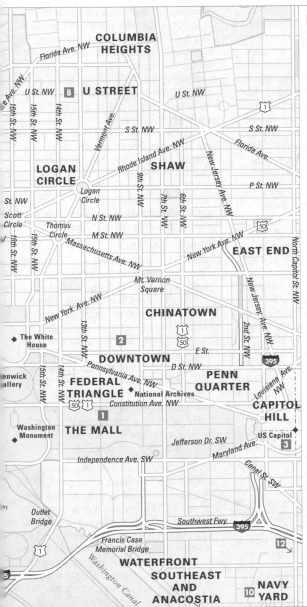

7 Adams Morgan. The ethnically diverse area has offbeat restaurants and shops, happening nightlife, and grand 19th-century apartment buildings and row houses.

8 U Street Corridor, Logan Circle, Shaw, and Columbia Heights. Revitalization has brought trendy boutiques and hip eateries to the area around 14th and U, while Shaw gets busier and trendier every year.

9 Upper Northwest. This mostly residential swath of D.C. has the National Cathedral and the Smithsonian's National Zoo.

10 D.C. Waterfront. The newly developing Waterfront district is one of D.C.'s liveliest new areas.

11 Arlington. Just across the Potomac, this area is home to the Pentagon and Arlington National Cemetery.

12 Side Trips to Maryland. Enjoy the views of the city from National Harbor or fresh crabs in Baltimore.

13 Side Trips to Virginia. Wineries, excellent restaurants, and historical architecture dominate Virginia.

Washington, D.C., Today

POLITICS

President Joseph Biden was welcomed to town when he took office in January 2021, though his era ushered in hardships including war with Ukraine, inflation, and the overturning of Roe v. Wade. Top that off with the ever-present underlying discontent of Washingtonians not having voting representation in Congress—hence the display on their license plates: Taxation without Representation. Let's just say, there's always a protest to attend, and conversation in the bars around town can be very interesting.

SPORTS

First and foremost, this is a football town, as the hordes of loyal Commanders (formerly known as the Redskins) fans demonstrate each fall Sunday at the city's many sports bars. Still, the team has struggled under billionaire owner Danny Snyder, who has shelled out big bucks to attract top players but has yet to return the team to the Super Bowl under his watch. Frustrated fans have noticed, and tickets are much easier to come by than they once were (though they still aren't cheap). Filling the void, the Nationals baseball team won the World Series in 2019 after a series of disheartening playoffs through the years, and even though they're in the process of rebuilding after trading away their all-star talents, it's always fun to go to a game. If that's not enough, the Capitals hockey team, led by perennial all-star Alex Ovechkin, finally snatched the long-evasive Stanley Cup in 2018. The DC United soccer team, spearheaded by manager Wayne Rooney, one of the biggest names to play in the MLS, has a sparkling new stadium. The Wizards basketball team reached a peak in 2016 when it joined the playoff ranks, though they haven't been able to muster much since then; while the Washington Mystics women's basketball team went all out and won the WNBA finals in 2019.

CANNABIS

D.C. has been on the cutting edge of the growing national movement to legalize marijuana, but with some complications. In 2014, D.C. voters overwhelmingly approved a measure permitting those over 21 to possess up to 2 ounces of marijuana, grow a small number of cannabis plants in their homes, and transfer up to an ounce of the drug to another adult—if no money accompanies the exchange. The law means you can smoke pot in private places, but you cannot buy it legally, which doesn't allow the pot tourism seen in states like Colorado. Still, that nuance has not dissuaded faithful users, and visitors should not be surprised if, on occasion, they encounter a whiff of pot smoke in the air.

DEMOGRAPHICS

After a resurgence in city dwellers during a pre-pandemic economic boom, Washington lost one in seven people after COVID-19 arrived in D.C., according to the *Washington Post*. Reasons included reevaluation of lifestyles, wanting to be closer to family, and loss of jobs—as well as the ability to work remotely. Nevertheless, people are beginning to come back. While many office workers have returned to their physical offices, the pandemic forever changed the nature of the workspace, and some remain working from home. One bright side has been less traffic (though it's all relative).

An unfortunate pandemic result was a rise in the number of unhoused people—more than 20 percent by some estimates. The city saw a proliferation of tent villages on city streets and in parks. City officials have worked hard to find a solution, including implementing affordable housing mandates and replacing the dilapidated D.C. General shelter with smaller facilities throughout the city.

Gentrification continues to be an issue. Heightened by enormous stadium projects like National Parks and the development of the Southwest waterfront, gentrification has reached deep into traditionally Black areas, stirring resentment, driving up costs, and pricing many longtime residents out of their childhood homes. Indeed, D.C. has one of the widest income gaps between rich and poor in the country, leaving local officials to seek ways to strengthen commercial interests without sacrificing community and culture.

FOOD

As everywhere, the pandemic hit restaurants hard, but they are coming back strong. One fun outcome has been the introduction of more outdoor dining spaces—some of them very creative, such as Bethesda Crab House's brown-paper-covered tables; Barcelona Wine Bar's chic, industrial vibe; and Iron Gate's wisteria-shaded secret garden—which remain a fixture.

Jeremiah Langhorne aims to put mid-Atlantic cuisine back on the culinary map with The Dabney, with most of its cooking done on a central wood-burning hearth. Marjorie Meek-Bradley, a *Top Chef* alum, has made her mark with Roofers Union, featuring American fare, in Adams Morgan. It's no surprise that Italian chef Fabio Trabocchi wows with his Italian-flavored Fiola and Fiola Mare, but he has set a whole new course with the impeccable, coastal-Spain-inspired Del Mar at the District Wharf.

These relative newcomers join D.C. pioneers like Robert Wiedmaier, whose Belgian roots are on full display at the award-winning Marcel's in Foggy Bottom, and award-winning chef–turned-humanitarian José Andrés, the culinary powerhouse behind Zaytinya, Oyamel, Jaleo, and the Michelin-starred minibar, all near Chinatown.

Food hall fever has infiltrated the District, with 14 to date including the original food hall—the historic Eastern Market on Capitol Hill—along with Union Market in NoMa, the neighboring Latin-American Cosecha; Western Market in Foggy Bottom; Tastemakers, a restaurant incubator in Brookland; and Spice Village, an all-halal food hall in the suburb of Herndon.

FITNESS

The ACSM American Fitness Index recently ranked D.C. as one of the nation's top five fittest cities. Quite aside from the numerous gyms popping up all over the city—and ignoring, for a moment, the countless joggers constantly circling the Mall—residents have adopted a slew of activities to get outside and stay in shape. Like to play kickball? There are teams all over the city. Enjoy Ultimate Frisbee (and/or Frisbee Golf)? There's a league for that, too. Rugby? Got it. Softball? Check. Volleyball? The Mall's open-air courts on a Saturday should give you a sense of its popularity. Little by little, even pickleball is picking up steam.

The District's many parks and green spaces cater perfectly to that game of pickup football (or *fútbol*), and the city's wild embrace of bike sharing has been complemented by the creation of bike-only lanes on some of its most traveled thoroughfares. Add a long list of burgeoning indoor crazes to the mix—everything from yoga and Pilates to Zumba and CrossFit—and you've got a city intent on shedding its wonks-only reputation.

What to Buy

A PLUSH PANDA
Perhaps there's no animal more beloved at the Smithsonian's National Zoo than the giant pandas—Mei Xiang, Tian Tian, and their new baby. Many visitors will want to take one home, even if it's a facsimile.

A UNIQUE MUSEUM GIFT
One thing the District has in abundance is spectacular museums—and along with museums come museum gift shops. These are some of the most underrated places for a shopping spree, with seriously curated wares including designer clothes, hangable art, coffee-table books, weird technology, and more. A few singular museum shops to check out are: the Renwick Gallery (contemporary American pottery, clothing, and jewelry), National Gallery of Art (books, clothes, and housewares featuring famous artworks), National Air and Space Museum (a favorite: astronaut ice cream), and the International Spy Museum (supercool decoder rings or a pen camcorder).

LOCAL FOOD PRODUCTS
D.C. has a lively food culture based on fresh ingredients, and local producers make delicious honey, jam, granola, beer, and more. Shop Made in D.C. at the Wharf and several other locations has a fabulous selection of items (as well as art, clothing, and other locally made items) and primo signature gift boxes. Union Market in NoMa is another option. Salt & Sundry has foodie gifts as well jewelry, knits, and other works by local artists. And everywhere you go, keep an eye out for D.C.'s most iconic condiment: the sweet and tangy Capital City Mambo Sauce.

A REAL-LIFE CHERRY TREE
Crowds flock to D.C. to view the ephemeral cherry blossoms, a traditional spring pilgrimage since the Japanese presented 3,000 of them as a gift to the capital city in 1912. If you'd like one of your own, you can order it through the DC Gift Shop; they'll spare you the trouble of having to shuffle it aboard the plane by sending it straight to your house. If a standard-size cherry tree just isn't practical, what about a gemstone cherry blossom bonsai instead? Or a bloom-emblazoned cap? The DC Gift Shop sells those, too.

LOCAL DESIGNER CLOTHING
Once upon a time (and not that long ago), the District was mostly about three-piece suits, with beach-sand tan being the most audacious color. These days, local fashion designers have quietly blossomed, creating and selling a variety of stunningly unique fashions that you won't find anywhere else. Mimi Miller, Amanda Casarez, and Maven Women by Rebecca Ballard are great places to start, but most don't have their own storefronts—yet.

BOOKS, BOOKS, AND MORE BOOKS
In a city with such integral ties to American history, you can bet your tricorn hat that you'll find a cornucopia of books covering every aspect of Americana. You'll

Books, books, and more books

find them in the shops of every museum and attraction—the shops at the Library of Congress, the National Building Museum, and the National Museum of American History are especially good. And while you're at it, there are several beloved independent bookstores with a local bent that are worth a peek as well, including Kramers and the legendary Politics and Prose.

HANDCRAFTED SUNDRIES

Eastern Market on Capitol Hill has been a buzzing local market since 1873. It's still a viable food market, but these days there's more. On weekends, artists and crafters take over the surrounding streets and the plaza, purveying colorful ceramic pitchers, aromatherapy soaps, funky fashion jewelry, cloth dolls, batik wall hangings, and a long list of other beautifully crafted items. Shop Made in

D.C. and Union Market are other places you'll find the work of local makers.

A STYLIZED, GRAPHIC PRINT OF YOUR FAVORITE D.C. NEIGHBORHOOD

Washington, D.C. is a mosaic of vibrant and diverse neighborhoods. Victory Dance Creative's bold-color, hand-screen-printed neighborhood prints—50-some to choose from—are the perfect reminder to hang on your wall back home.

LOCALS SPORTS GEAR

D.C. has some serious sports teams, including the Nationals (baseball), Wizards (basketball), Capitals (ice hockey), D.C. United (soccer), and Commanders (football). You can find good selections of caps, jerseys, T-shirts, and more at the stadiums themselves if you happen to be there for a game or match. Or stop by any

DICK'S Sporting Goods, Modell's Sporting Goods, even Target in the District.

DISTRICT-THEMED HOUSEWARES

You'll find one-of-a-kind boutiques selling super-original items for your home, including artsy tea towels with D.C. motifs, D.C.-shaped cutting boards, and printed hand-drawn maps of D.C. neighborhoods. You can even find cookie cutters in the shape of the District. Check out Terratorie and Hill's Kitchen for starters.

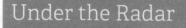

Under the Radar

KENILWORTH AQUATIC GARDENS

Breathtaking water lilies and lotus flowers abound here. Spring and summer are the best times to visit, when the flowers and trees are in bloom. But fall at the park also has its charm, with leaves changing on cypress trees, calm waters, and lower temperatures. Stop by the gardens in July for the annual Lotus and Water Lily Festival. *(Ch. 12)*

LINCOLN COTTAGE

Lincoln and his family lived in this cottage during the Civil War, and it's since become a museum and cultural center. Visitors can take self-guided tours through permanent exhibits that cover the history of the Civil War and the Lincoln family as well as frequent special exhibits. *(Ch. 11)*

PEACOCK ROOM

Painted by American expatriate artist James McNeill Whistler, the Freer Gallery's most famous room's blue-and-gold-hued walls immediately catch visitors' eyes. Walk around the room to browse an extensive collection of Middle Eastern and Asian porcelain and to study the exquisite paintings of dueling peacocks and the "princess from the land of porcelain." *(Ch. 3)*

PHILLIPS COLLECTION

Most visitors flock to the National Mall for art museums, but Dupont Circle's Phillips Collection offers a nice change of pace. Tucked away on a quiet residential street, America's first modern art museum showcases more than 3,000 works, including French Impressionist paintings and American prints. Watch for blockbuster special exhibitions. *(Ch. 8)*

WASHINGTON NATIONAL CATHEDRAL

Take in Gothic-style architecture, stained-glass windows, and gargoyles in Northwest D.C. Book a ticket in advance to climb 333 steps up the cathedral's central tower, the city's highest point. A crypt level inside the cathedral holds the ashes of Helen Keller, her lifelong companion Anne Sullivan, and Matthew Shepard. *(Ch. 11)*

HILLWOOD ESTATE

Once the home of a D.C. socialite, Hillwood now holds collections of Russian imperial and French decorative art. Browse the Georgian-style mansion or roam its lush gardens. A Japanese-style garden includes trickling streams and stone paths. *(Ch. 11)*

U.S. BOTANIC GARDEN

Often overlooked, the inside garden is a hidden gem, one of the oldest in the United States. It's home to a variety of rare and endangered plants. Don't miss Bartholdi Park, across the street from the main conservatory—it features colorful plants, flowers, and a photogenic fountain. *(Ch. 5)*

MERIDIAN HILL PARK

In Columbia Heights, the park, also known as Malcolm X Park, is a good place to stop for a picnic or midafternoon stroll. Designed as an Italian garden, it has cascading water fountains, winding stone staircases, and plenty of green spaces. *(Ch. 9)*

SPANISH STEPS

Named for the famous staircase in Rome, D.C.'s steps, next to Embassy Row, aren't quite as grand, but they do provide a tranquil reprieve from the hustle and bustle of the city. *(Ch. 8)*

THEODORE ROOSEVELT ISLAND

Cross Key Bridge to get to Roosevelt Island, an 88-acre oasis in the middle of the Potomac River. Lush woods and miles of hiking trails offer views of Georgetown and the harbor. *(Ch. 6)*

MARY MCLEOD BETHUNE COUNCIL HOUSE

The African-American educator, philanthropist, and civil rights activist who founded the National Council of Negro Women in 1935, Mary McLeod Bethune's house looks nearly as she left it. *(Ch. 10)*

Free Things to Do in D.C.

OLD POST OFFICE TOWER
Everyone knows about the views from atop the Washington Monument, but you can get just as impressive vistas from the observation deck 270 feet up the Old Post Office Tower. Tours begin every five minutes from the elevator lobby on the stage level of the Old Post Office Pavilion. *(Ch. 3)*

C&O CANAL
The historic Chesapeake & Ohio Canal runs 184.5 miles from Georgetown to Cumberland, Maryland, but you only need to walk a little bit to enjoy its supreme beauty alongside the Potomac River. Keep your eyes peeled for deer, heron, and bald eagles, and, in springtime, fields of bluebells. *(Ch. 7)*

U STREET
The birthplace of Duke Ellington and an important hub of African American culture is known primarily for its theaters and live-music venues. Miles Davis, Ella Fitzgerald, and Louis Armstrong all frequented the area, which is still full of restaurants, boutiques, nightlife—as well as colorful street murals. *(Ch. 10)*

SMITHSONIAN MUSEUMS
Thanks in large part to the Smithsonian Institution, Washington is absolutely stuffed with museums, 16 of which are connected with the institution endowed by James Smithson in 1846 (17 if you count the National Zoo). But that's not all. Other free museums include the National Gallery of Art and the United States Holocaust Memorial Museum. *(Ch. 3)*

THE MEMORIALS
Forming the spine of the city, the National Mall is anchored by the Lincoln Memorial on the west, the Washington Monument in the middle, and the U.S. Capitol on the east. Other famous memorials remember Vietnam veterans, World War II, FDR, and Martin Luther King Jr. *(Ch. 3)*

JOHN F. KENNEDY CENTER FOR THE PERFORMING ARTS
Opened in 1971, the Kennedy Center is one of the largest U.S. performing arts facilities, staging roughly 2,000 performances a year, with the adjacent REACH expansion adding on more indoor-outdoor performance space. Free tours include a stop at an exhibit about Kennedy's life and presidency and a walk through several of the main theaters. On your way out, catch a glimpse of the famous Watergate complex, just to the north. *(Ch. 6)*

National Gallery of Art

THE PENTAGON
A building so big it requires six zip codes, the Pentagon houses the headquarters of the Department of Defense. At its widest point, the Pentagon is almost as wide as the Empire State Building is tall. Construction began in September 1941 and was finished in a remarkably quick 16 months. Tours are free but require advance reservations; check the Pentagon's website for details. *(Ch. 13)*

OLD STONE HOUSE
This Georgetown house is the oldest unaltered building in the District. Christopher and Rachel Layman purchased the property in 1764, building the house the following year. Now a museum and public garden,

it was turned over to the National Park Service in 1953. *(Ch. 7)*

ROCK CREEK PARK
Rock Creek Park became the third national park ever created, signed into law by President Harrison in 1890. Just a 20-minute drive from the center of the city, it offers 1,754 quiet, beautiful acres for roaming, horseback riding, cycling, and inline skating. *(Ch. 11)*

EASTERN MARKET
Thomas Jefferson established the first market in 1805, and it was moved to its current location in 1873, where it has remained for the last 149 years. Weathering the storm of competition from grocery store chains, Eastern Market has become a community staple and is a great place to stock up or simply window-shop for food, crafts, or antiques. Weekends feature live music and local artists, as well as the farmers' market. *(Ch. 5)*

SMITHSONIAN'S NATIONAL ZOO
An act of Congress created the National Zoo in 1889. Designed by Frederick Law Olmsted, the 163-acre facility is home to more than 360 animal species, including some of the world's most endangered or vulnerable. Sadly, the giant pandas are departing in late 2023. *(Ch. 11)*

What to Read and Watch

MINORITY REPORT
Based on a short story by Philip K. Dick, this Steven Spielberg blockbuster takes place in the year 2054, blending genres of sci-fi, action, and thriller. It's chock-full of dramatic chase scenes throughout a futuristic D.C., as a "pre-crime" police force—backed by a team of surreal psychics—arrests people for crimes they're destined to commit in the future. It has all the special effects and over-the-top action sequences you could desire from a Tom Cruise protagonist and a Steven Spielberg budget.

DEAF U
This docuseries from 2020, full of drama and gossip, follows the lives of a tight-knit group of students at Gallaudet University, a private college in Washington, D.C. that caters to the deaf and hard of hearing. It's noted for its excellent casting and the chance to get to know students whom the outside world often labels as having a disability.

ALL THE PRESIDENT'S MEN
This Academy Award–winning film follows Carl Bernstein and Bob Woodward—the two young *Washington Post* journalists responsible for the incredible investigation of the Watergate scandal—through their meetings with clandestine informant Deep Throat, the discovery of President Nixon's tapes, and the process of exposing it all to the American public. While a little less studly without the young Dustin Hoffman–Robert Redford combination, the nonfiction book of the same name (written by the journalists themselves) delves deeper into the details of a political detective story almost too good for fiction.

ADVISE AND CONSENT
Allen Drury's 1959 political thriller, following the tumultuous nomination process of a secretary of state with a Communist background, was both a *New York Times* bestseller and Pulitzer prize winner—a rare occurrence for any novel. Credited with creating a realistic yet racy tale about a could-be-boring political process, the book became a series and was followed by five sequels. The 1962 movie stars Henry Fonda, with many of the scenes shot in and around key Washington landmarks.

SEVEN DAYS IN MAY
Kirk Douglas, Burt Lancaster, Frederic March, and Ava Gardner star in this 1964 film, where the Cold War hysteria of the times is condensed into a weeklong attempted takeover of the United States government. The 1962 *New York Times* best-selling book (by Fletcher Knebel and Charles W. Bailey II) served as the movie's inspiration. Both film and book follow the same structure, split into day-by-day chapters as the week's events unfurl.

MR. SMITH GOES TO WASHINGTON
In this 1939 black-and-white classic, a baby-faced, idealistic Jimmy Stewart comes to the nation's capital and is soon wrapped up in the unscrupulousness of the U.S. Senate. Stewart's scene orating against greed and corruption on the floor of the Senate is still one of the most iconic cinematic performances ever about D.C. politics.

DESIGNATED SURVIVOR
What happens when the Capitol is blown up in a terrorist attack—killing the president, vice president, his cabinet, and all of Congress? In this three-season political thriller that originally aired on ABC, Kiefer Sutherland plays the man chosen to stay away from the State of the Union and becomes the inexperienced sole survivor, suddenly responsible for piecing the government back together. It's not so easy, he finds, when shadowy forces are up to no good, threatening national—and personal—security at every turn.

WEST WING

Follow President Josiah Bartlet through his two terms in this epic political drama that delves into the lives of staffers of the White House's West Wing. On the air for seven seasons beginning in 1999, it's a feel-good reminder of what politics can be when run by good people.

VEEP

This HBO political comedy satirizes the personalities that make up American policy and power, with an Emmy-winning performance by Julia Louis-Dreyfus as the Veep (vice president, and on-again, off-again president hopeful) and a hilarious, hapless cast of political staffers. Scenes take you in and out of political press conferences, conspiratorial meetings in the VP's back rooms, the Oval Office, the halls of Congress, and many a limo drive through the streets of Washington.

SCANDAL

In this political thriller full of plot twists, Olivia Pope, played by Kerry Washington, is D.C.'s ultimate fixer. She is based loosely on George H.W. Bush's administrative press aide, Judy Smith, who started her own crisis management firm. The series ran seven seasons, from 2012 to 2018.

LONG DISTANCE LIFE BY MARITA GOLDEN

Marita Golden's novel centers on one family's experience living in D.C. throughout the 20th century, but she vividly fills in the background with the complex history of Black America as a whole. Naomi Johnson, the family's matriarch (and first-person narrator of many chapters) moves from North Carolina to D.C. in 1926, and the novel continues from there to tell the hardships and joys of Naomi's family throughout generations in the capital city.

THE BEAUTIFUL THINGS THAT HEAVEN BRINGS BY DINAW MENGESTU

A refreshing break from the political circus of Capitol Hill, Dinaw Mengestu's 2007 novel exists instead within the stores, restaurants, and homes of Northwest D.C.'s Logan Circle neighborhood. In a city of monuments and memorials to America's (often constructed, embellished) past, and in a neighborhood on the brink of gentrification, Sepha, an Ethiopian refugee, moves through the daily grind of being an American while haunted by memories of his home country. Through Sepha's long talks and friendships with refugees from other African countries, Mengestu creates a gentle, moving portrait of the African diaspora in Washington.

GO-GO LIVE: THE MUSICAL LIFE AND DEATH OF A CHOCOLATE CITY BY NATALIE HOPKINSON

The story of Black Washington, written by activist and cultural scholar Natalie Hopkinson and published in 2012, is told against the backdrop of the rise of go-go music, the conga-drum-infused mix of blues, church, and Latino sounds that D.C. native Chuck Brown—the godfather of go-go—created in the '70s.

THE CONTENDER

This 2000 thriller combines political process and sex-driven scandal, when the Republican opposition digs into the past and private life of a female candidate for vice president. Joan Allen, Jeff Bridges, Christian Slater, and Sam Elliott play characters ranging from affable to immoral. The political sexism, cutthroat party alliances, and invasion of privacy nod to the Clinton–Lewinsky scandal of the time—but the story still rings plenty true today.

D.C. with Kids

D.C. is filled with kid-friendly attractions. These sights are sure winners:

PLANET WORD

Kids have tons of fun at the world's first voice-activated museum—and immerse themselves in the power of language in the process. Among the imaginative exhibits are a speaking willow tree; a wall of words that delves into the story of the English language; and a magical library filled with literary secrets.

U.S. BOTANIC GARDEN

A huge jungle beneath a glass roof, a seasonal children's garden, and children's programs help kids explore the fascinating world of plants just steps from the U.S. Capitol.

INTERNATIONAL SPY MUSEUM

This museum takes the art of espionage to new levels for junior James Bonds and Nancy Drews. Even the most cynical preteens and teenagers are usually enthralled with all the cool gadgetry. This museum is best for older tweens and teens—if you bring along a younger sibling, you could be in for a workout: there aren't many places to sit down, and large strollers aren't allowed in the museum. Also, there is an entrance fee. The museum moved to its more capacious L'Enfant Plaza in 2019.

NATIONAL AIR AND SPACE MUSEUM

There's a good reason why this place is one of the most popular museums in the world: kids love it. The 23 galleries here—being reimagined in a massive renovation, with 1,400 new objects on display—tell the story of aviation and space from the earliest human attempts at flight. The museum store sells ever-popular freeze-dried astronaut food—not as tasty as what we eat on Earth, but it doesn't melt or drip.

NATIONAL MUSEUM OF AMERICAN HISTORY

Oh, say, you can see … the flag that inspired "The Star-Spangled Banner," Oscar the Grouch, the ruby slippers from *The Wizard of Oz*, an impressive collection of trains, and more Americana than anyone can digest in a day.

NATIONAL MUSEUM OF NATURAL HISTORY

Say hello to Henry. One of the largest elephants ever found in the wild, this stuffed beast has greeted generations of kids in the rotunda of this huge museum dedicated to natural wonders. Take your kid to the O. Orkin Insect Zoo, home to live ants, bees, centipedes, tarantulas, roaches, and other bugs. Did we mention the dinosaurs?

SMITHSONIAN'S NATIONAL ZOO

Known more for its political animals than its real animals, D.C. nevertheless has one of the world's foremost zoos. If your child is crazy about animals, this is an absolute must—it's huge.

NATIONAL CHILDREN'S MUSEUM

You enter this relatively new museum in Downtown D.C. via cloud-inspired dream machine, going on to enjoy a slime pavilion, data science alley, a green screen in which body movements create weather, and more—all of which slip in STEAM educational principles.

PADDLEBOAT THE TIDAL BASIN

How better to see the Jefferson Memorial and the world-famous cherry trees—gifts from Japan—than from the waters of the Tidal Basin? The paddleboats get the kids and you off your feet and into the sun!

Chapter 2

TRAVEL SMART

Updated by
Barbara Noe Kennedy

★ **CAPITAL:**
Washington

👤 **POPULATION:**
718,355

💬 **LANGUAGE:**
English

$ **CURRENCY:**
U.S. Dollar

☎ **AREA CODE:**
202

⚠ **EMERGENCIES:**
911

🚗 **DRIVING:**
On the right

⚡ **ELECTRICITY:**
120–220 v/60 cycles;
plugs have two or three
rectangular prongs

🕐 **TIME:**
Same as New York

🌐 **WEB RESOURCES:**
www.washington.org;
www.nps.gov; www.si.edu

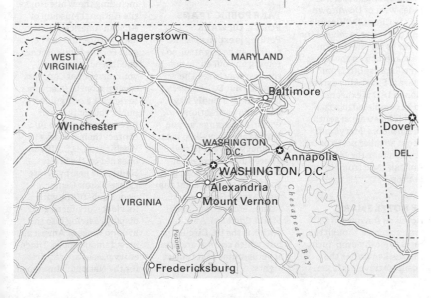

Know Before You Go

When is the best time to visit our nation's capital? What times should you avoid? Which airport should you fly into? Where should you stay? You may have some important questions before your trip to Washington, D.C. We've got the answers and a few tips to help you make the most of your visit.

BE AIRPORT SAVVY

D.C. has three airports: Ronald Reagan Washington National (DCA), Dulles International (IAD), and Baltimore/Washington International–Thurgood Marshall Airport (BWI). DCA, located in Arlington, Virginia, about 4 miles from Downtown D.C., is the closest and most convenient; it has its own Metro stop. It only serves shorter domestic flights (and some flights to the Caribbean and Canada). IAD is the main international airport, 25 miles west of Downtown D.C. in Chantilly, Virginia. You can take the Silver Line as far as Wiehle–Reston East and hop on the Silver Line Express Bus from there (a Silver Line extension to IAD is expected to be completed in 2022). BWI is located just south of Baltimore, Maryland, about 30 miles north of D.C. You can take the MARC or Amtrak train from Union Station.

BE HOTEL SMART

Hotels in Downtown D.C. are expensive, though the rates typically drop during the weekend, after the business travelers leave. Arlington, Alexandria, and Bethesda are relatively nearby and may have better deals than Downtown D.C. One thing to remember: Fairfax, Gaithersburg, and Vienna are not near Downtown D.C., as some hotel advertising will have you thinking they are. The short of it: before you book, study the map to ensure you're staying relatively near the attractions you want to visit. And be sure to book a hotel near the Metro line if you don't have a car.

TAKE PUBLIC TRANSPORT ... OR WALK

Parking is expensive, and traffic can be frightful, so relying on your car is not the best way to see the District. But D.C. is a very pedestrian-friendly city, with many attractions within close range, so you may be able to walk to most of what you want to see. There's also an excellent Metro system that can get you to most major sights as well (except Georgetown, Adams Morgan, and the H Street Corridor). Another option is the DC Circulator bus, which costs $1 and has several routes past tourist sights.

KNOW WHAT STUFF IS FREE ... AND WHAT'S NOT AND STILL WORTHWHILE

One beloved aspect of D.C. is that so many of its remarkable sights are free, including the Smithsonian museums and the national monuments and memorials. Even the blockbuster shows that sometimes stop by the National Gallery of Art are free. Check Destination DC or individual websites for free shows, concerts, lectures, and guided tours, especially at the National Gallery of Art and Library of Congress. That said, keep in mind that some of the city's best museums do come at a price but are still well worth your while, including the Phillips Collection and International Spy Museum.

THE EARLY BIRD CATCHES THE POPULAR SIGHT TICKETS

Get your tickets for popular sights long before your trip, including the White House, the National Museum of African American History and Culture, and the Pentagon. For the White House, you'll need to contact your member of Congress several months in advance to request a self-guided public tour (citizens of foreign countries should contact their embassy in Washington, D.C.). If you miss out on the White House, the nearby White House Visitor Center is a good substitute, with its videos, artifacts, and displays delving into the life and times of America's most famous house. Timed-entry passes are required for the National Museum of

African American History and Culture; you can obtain them up to 30 days in advance on the museum website; same-day passes are released beginning at 8:15 am. Limited tours are offered at the Pentagon, for U.S. citizens with a maximum of five individuals per group. Tours must be scheduled at least two weeks in advance, and all guests must be cleared by the Pentagon.

BE A CAPITOL VIP
Get a VIP Capitol staff–led tour by contacting your representative or senator up to 90 days in advance. Even if you miss out on the VIP tour, you can still visit the Capitol by making your own advance reservation online.

BEAT THE CROWDS AT STAR-STUDDED NSO PERFORMANCES
The nation's capital celebrates July 4th and Memorial Day with world-class performances starring the National Symphony Orchestra, which air around the world on PBS. Thousands of guests are invited to sit on the West Lawn of the Capitol and enjoy these spectacular concerts in person for free (bring a picnic—no alcohol allowed). But therein lies the problem—the thousands of people all vying to get in, requiring you to arrive hours early to stake your space on the grass (and possibly be turned away). You can see exactly the same shows (minus the fireworks) by attending the dress rehearsals in advance. "A Capitol Fourth" practices the evening before, normally at 8 pm, while the "National Memorial Day Concert" rehearsal takes place at 3:30 pm on the Sunday before Memorial Day. The host may be a tad improvisational, and might not get all the lines on the first try, but the shows are enjoyable nonetheless. There's also a Labor Day concert on the Capitol's West Lawn showcasing the NSO (which is not aired on TV).

THINK SMALL
Although the Smithsonian museums get all the glory, remember that there are scores of excellent smaller museums, including the Clara Barton Missing Soldiers Office Museum, the President Woodrow Wilson House, Anderson House, and the National Museum of Women in the Arts. Plan ahead to know which ones suit your interests.

SAVE AT THE THEATER BOX OFFICE
Washington, D.C. is a theater town, with well-reviewed theaters both large (Kennedy Center, Warner Theatre, The National Theatre) and small (Woolly Mammoth Theatre Company, Shakespeare Theatre Company). Save on tickets by using a discount broker such as Goldstar, Groupon, and the TodayTix app. Also keep in mind that some theaters offer same-day tickets at a reduced price, including Shakespeare Theatre Company and Folger Shakespeare Theatre, while others offer pay-what-you-can-afford tickets, including Woolly Mammoth, Round House, and Constellation Theatre (arrive early and bring cash). Arena Stage offers a pay-your-age program for the 30-and-under crowd.

KNOW YOUR SEASONS
Spring and fall have the best weather, with the added bonus of the famous cherry blossoms in spring and colorful changing foliage in fall. The holidays are another time when the nation's capital shines, with special events including the National Christmas Tree Lighting, ZooLights at Smithsonian's National Zoo, and the Downtown Holiday Market. House museums offer special candlelit tours that showcase Colonial-era decorations, including Mount Vernon. D.C. also puts on an extravaganza of festivals, offering another reason to visit at a specific time of year. Some of the most popular include Day of Service on Martin Luther King Jr.'s birthday in January; St. Patrick's Day in March, with a parade down Constitution Avenue; and Passport DC in May, when dozens of embassies open their doors to visitors. But if you simply want to visit at a time with sunny weather and fewer crowds, early November is often prime.

Getting Here and Around

Air

A flight to D.C. from New York takes a little less than an hour. It's about 1½ hours from Chicago, 3 hours from Denver or Dallas, and 5 hours from San Francisco. Passengers flying from London should expect a trip of about 6 hours. From Sydney it's an 18-hour flight. Most major airlines fly into one of D.C.'s three major airports, but only Dulles and Baltimore airports are served by international carriers (DCA services some flights to and from Canada and the Caribbean).

AIRPORTS

Ronald Reagan Washington National Airport (DCA) is in Virginia, 4 miles south of Downtown Washington.

Dulles International Airport (IAD) is in Virginia, 25 miles west of Washington, D.C.

Baltimore/Washington International–Thurgood Marshall Airport (BWI) is in Maryland, about 30 miles to the northeast.

Reagan National Airport is closest to Downtown D.C. and has a Metro stop connected to the terminal. East Coast shuttles and shorter flights tend to fly in and out of this airport. Dulles is configured primarily for long-haul flights, although as a United hub, it's also well-connected regionally. The Metro Silver Line now serves Dulles for easy access into the city. BWI offers blended service, with its many gates for Southwest Airlines, as well as international flights. Although Metro trains don't serve BWI, there is affordable and convenient public transportation to and from each airport. Be aware that the mid-Atlantic region is prone to quirky weather that can snarl air traffic, especially on stormy summer afternoons.

AIRPORT TRANSFERS

Ronald Reagan Washington National Airport, located across the Potomac River in Arlington, Virginia, is the only regional airport reachable by the District's Metro system, a ride that takes about 20 minutes and costs between $2.15 and $6 (you must pay with a plastic SmarTrip card, available from machines in all stations). The Metro station is within easy walking distance of Terminals B and C, and a free airport bus shuttles between the station and Terminal A. Driving typically takes longer than the Metro (about 20 to 30 minutes, depending on traffic and where you start). A taxi will cost between $15 and $25 to Downtown, plus a $3 airport surcharge. Ride-share services like Uber and Lyft are allowed to pick up on the arrivals level.

Dulles International Airport is 25 miles west of Downtown; the ride takes 45 minutes but can be considerably longer when traffic is heavy. Public transit will typically take an hour or more. Take the Metro's Silver Line to the Wiehle–Reston East station (6 am to 10:20 pm); the 15-minute Silver Line Express bus ride from the station to the airport (every 15 to 20 minutes) is $5, payable with cash or credit card at the ticket counter in the Arrivals area. The Washington Metropolitan Area Transit Authority (WMATA) operates express bus service (5A) between Dulles and several stops in Downtown D.C., including the L'Enfant Plaza Metro station and Rosslyn Metro station in Arlington, Virginia, for $7.50 (every hour between 6:35 am and 10:10 pm); exact fare or a SmarTrip card is required. Taxi fare to Washington, D.C. from Dulles is about $55 to $65 plus tip, depending on traffic, and takes about 45 minutes. Ride-share services like Uber and Lyft are allowed to pick up at a pickup curb accessible from baggage claim using doors 2, 4, and 6.

Baltimore/Washington International–Thurgood Marshall Airport is about 30 miles northeast of Downtown; the ride takes 50 to 60 minutes but can be considerably longer when traffic is heavy. Both Amtrak and Maryland Rail Commuter Service (MARC) trains run between BWI and Washington, D.C.'s Union Station from around 4:30 am to 10 pm; the ride takes 30 minutes and costs between $15 and $45 on Amtrak, $8 on MARC's Penn Line. A free shuttle bus connects the airline terminals and the train station (which is in a distant parking lot). WMATA operates express bus service (Bus No. B30) between BWI and the Greenbelt Metro station from approximately 6 am to 10 pm on weekdays for $7.50. The taxi fare from Downtown to BWI is about $90 plus tip. Ride-share services like Uber and Lyft are allowed to pick up at the departures level.

🚍 Bus

Most of the sightseeing neighborhoods (the Mall, Capitol Hill, Downtown, Dupont Circle) are near Metro rail stations, but a few (Georgetown, Adams Morgan) are more easily reached via Metrobus ($2 per ride, exact change payable in bills or coins or with a SmarTrip card; you can also buy a seven-day pass for $15). Bus No. 42 travels from the Dupont Circle Metro stop to and through Adams Morgan.

The DC Circulator has six routes ($1). The Eastern Market–L'Enfant Plaza, Woodley Park–Adams Morgan–McPherson Sq., and Congress Heights–Union Station routes cut a path from north to south; the Georgetown–Union Station and Rosslyn–Georgetown–Dupont Circle routes go west to east. And the National Mall route, which operates on an extended schedule in summer and reduced schedule in winter, stops at major sightseeing destinations around the Mall.

Several bus lines run between New York City and the Washington, D.C. area, including BestBus, FlixBus, Megabus, Peter Pan Bus Lines, TripperBus, Vamoose, Washington Deluxe, and the first-class Jet. Tripper and Vamoose routes run between NYC and Metro stations in Bethesda, Maryland, and Arlington, Virginia. All the buses are clean, the service satisfactory, and the price can't be beat. Believe it or not, with advance planning, you might be able to get a round-trip ticket for just $2. Several of the bus lines offer power outlets, Wi-Fi, and a frequent-rider loyalty program.

🚗 Car

A car is often a drawback in Washington, D.C. Traffic is frightful, especially at rush hour, and driving is often confusing, with many lanes and some entire streets changing direction at the beginning and end of rush hour. Most traffic lights stand at the side of intersections (instead of hanging suspended over them), and the streets often are dotted with giant potholes. The city's most popular sights are all within a short walk of a Metro station, so do yourself a favor and leave your car at the hotel. If you're visiting sights in Maryland or Virginia or need a car because of reduced mobility, time your trips to avoid D.C. rush hours, 7–10 am and 3–7 pm.

With Zipcar, an urban car-rental membership service, you can rent a car for a couple of hours or a couple of days from convenient Downtown parking lots. A one-time application fee of $25, an annual membership fee of $90 (or $9 per

Getting Here and Around

month with a monthly plan option), plus hourly rates starting at $11, or $91.50 per day, buys you gas, insurance, parking, and satellite radio. Reserve online or by phone.

Another option is Free2Move, a car-sharing program featuring white Chevrolets. Rates are $0.47 a minute, $19.99 an hour, or $99.99 a day (they also have 5-day and 7-day rentals). There is no additional cost for insurance, gas, or parking. One advantage of Free2Move is that you can pick up and end rentals in on-street public parking spots.

Like the comfort of a car but don't want to drive? Uber is your answer. You can request a ride through the mobile app or the Uber website. Drivers are available seven days a week, 24 hours a day. Once you request your ride, you'll be able to see exactly where the driver is and how long you'll have to wait, as well as what your fare is. Options include UberX and Comfort, the economy choices; UberXL for up to 5 people; Black (sedan), which can be rented by the hour with professional drivers; and Black SUV. After registering, your credit card information is kept on file and your card is charged upon completion of your ride. When demand is high due to weather, holidays, or special events, rates can be considerably higher. There's a cancellation fee of $5. Other ride-sharing apps like Lyft offer similar options.

PARKING

Parking in D.C. is a question of supply and demand—little of the former, too much of the latter. The police are quick to ticket, tow away, or boot any vehicle parked illegally, so check complicated parking signs, and feed the meter before you go. If you find you've been towed from a city street, call ☎ *311* or the Department of Public Works Customer

Service Center at ☎ *202/673–6833*. Be sure you know the license-plate number, make, model, and color of the car before you call.

Most of the outlying, suburban Metro stations have parking lots (for a fee), though these fill quickly with city-bound commuters. If you plan to park in one of these lots, arrive early.

Downtown private parking lots often charge around $9–$10 an hour and up to $40 or more a day. Most of the streets along the Mall have metered parking. There is no parking at the Lincoln or Roosevelt memorials. If you don't find street parking nearby, try along Ohio Drive SW and in three lots in East Potomac Park, south of the 14th Street Bridge.

RULES OF THE ROAD

You may turn right at a red light after stopping if there's no oncoming traffic and no signs indicate otherwise, but D.C. has many such signs and one-way streets. When in doubt, wait for the green. The speed limit in D.C. is 25 mph. Beware of High-Occupancy-Vehicle (HOV) express lanes on major highways during rush hours (you need an E-ZPass to use them, and if you don't have the allotted number of occupants, tolls can be high).

Ⓜ Metro/Public Transport

The Metro is a convenient way to get around the city—if you're staying near a Metro stop. It operates from 5 am weekdays, 7 am Saturday and Sunday; it shuts down at 12 am Monday through Thursday and Sunday, and 1 am Friday and Saturday. Keep in mind that service disruptions for weekend work are common. The Metro's base fare is $2 but can be much higher depending on the time of day and the distance traveled. All rides now require a SmarTrip card, a rechargeable fare card that can be used throughout the Metro, bus, and parking system. Buy your SmarTrip card at a vending machine in any station; they accept cash and credit cards or debit cards. You can buy one-day passes for $13, three-day passes for $28, and seven-day passes for $58.

🚗 Ride-Sharing

Both Uber and Lyft operate in Washington, D.C. and may or may not be cheaper than a regular taxi depending on the time of day and distance traveled. For a group of four or five people, however, a rideshare can be cheaper than the Metro for a short trip.

🚕 Taxi

Taxis are easy to hail in commercial districts, less so in residential ones. If you don't see one after a few minutes, walk to a busier street. If you call, make sure to have an address—not just an intersection—and be prepared to wait, especially at night. The base rate for the first one-eighth mile is $3.50. Each additional mile is $2.16, and each minute stopped or traveling less than 10 mph is $25 an hour ($0.40 per minute). A charge of $1 is tacked on for additional passengers, regardless how many. The telephone dispatch fee is $2. During D.C.-declared snow emergencies, there is an additional $15 fee. Cab rates in Virginia differ by county, but immediately surrounding D.C., riders should expect to pay $2–$4 for the first one-tenth mile and $0.25 for each additional one-tenth mile.

🚆 Train

More than 80 trains a day arrive at Washington, D.C.'s Union Station. Amtrak's regular service runs from D.C. to New York in 3¼–3¾ hours and from D.C. to Boston in 7¾–8 hours. Acela, Amtrak's high-speed service, travels from D.C. to New York in 2¾–3 hours and from D.C. to Boston in 6½ hours, but can cost as much as a flight. Two commuter lines—Maryland Rail Commuter Service (MARC) and Virginia Railway Express (VRE)—run to the nearby suburbs. They're cheaper than Amtrak, but the VRE doesn't run on weekends or federal holidays. MARC's Penn Line does run on weekends, offering service to Baltimore for $9 each way.

Essentials

🏃 Activities

Visitors to Washington can enjoy a wealth of outdoor attractions. Rock Creek Park is one of the city's treasures, with miles of wooded trails and paths for bikers, runners, and walkers that extend to almost every part of the city. The National Mall connects the Lincoln Memorial and the Capitol and is one of the most scenic green spaces in the world. Around the Tidal Basin you can run, bike, tour the monuments, and rent paddleboats. Theodore Roosevelt Island, a wildlife sanctuary, has several paths for hiking and enjoyable spots for picnics. Kayaking and stand-up paddleboarding are popular in the Potomac and Washington Channel. And these places are just a few among dozens.

BIKING

The numerous trails in the District and its surrounding areas are well maintained and clearly marked. Washington's large parks are also popular with cyclists. Plus, bike lanes are on all major roads. The Capital Bikeshare scheme, with 480 stations around Washington, Arlington, and Alexandria, is also a great way to get around town.

SPECTATOR SPORTS

Washington, D.C. has several professional sports teams, some with world-champion status.

★ D.C. United

SOCCER | One of the best Major League Soccer teams has a huge fan base in the nation's capital, finding many of its fans in the international crowds who miss the big matches at home, as well as families whose kids play soccer. Matches are played March through October in the state-of-the-art, 20,000-seat Audi Field in Southwest's Buzzard Point. You can buy tickets at the ticket office or through the team's website, which offers special youth pricing. Talon, the team mascot, entertains the crowd, along with enthusiastic, horn-blowing fans. ⊠ *Audi Field, 100 Potomac Ave. SW, Southwest* ⊕ *audifielddc.com* 🎫 *From $29* Ⓜ *Navy Yard–Ballpark or Waterfront–SEU.*

Washington Capitals

HOCKEY | Stanley Cup winners in 2018, the Washington Capitals play loud and exciting home games October through April at Capital One Arena. The team is led by one of hockey's superstars, Alex Ovechkin, and enjoys a huge, devoted fan base. Tickets are difficult to find but can be purchased at the Capital One Arena box office, Ticketmaster, or NHL Ticket Exchange. ⊠ *Capital One Arena, 601 F St. NW, Penn Quarter* 🕿 *202/628–3200* ⊕ *washcaps.com* 🎫 *From $25* Ⓜ *Gallery Pl.–Chinatown.*

Washington Commanders

FOOTBALL | The perennially popular Washington Commanders (formerly the Redskins) continue to play football in the Maryland suburbs at 82,000-seat FedEx Field. Individual game-day tickets can be hard to come by when the team is enjoying a strong season. Your best bet is to check out StubHub or Ticketmaster. ⊠ *FedExField, 1600 Fedex Way, Landover* 🕿 *301/276–6037 FedExField* ⊕ *www.commanders.com* 🎫 *From $60.*

Washington Mystics

BASKETBALL | This WNBA team plays at the Capital One Arena in Downtown Washington and perennially leads the WNBA in attendance, at long last capturing their first championship in 2019. The games are loud, boisterous events. You can buy Mystics tickets at the Capital One Arena box office, StubHub (⊕ *www.stubhub.com*), or Ticketmaster (⊕ *www.ticketmaster.com*). The women's season runs from late May to August. ⊠ *Capital*

One Arena, 601 F St. NW, Penn Quarter ☎ *877/324–6671, 202/628–3200 Capital One Arena* ⊕ *washingtonmystics.com* ✉ *From $15* Ⓜ *Gallery Pl.–Chinatown.*

★ Washington Nationals

BASEBALL & SOFTBALL | The 2019 World Champion Nationals have taken Washingtonians on a wild ride, finally clinching the apex title after several heart-wrenching seasons. The team has changed since then, but it's always fun to hang out in the modern ballpark, eating some of D.C.'s most iconic foods (including half-smokes from Ben's Chili Bowl), admiring a view off to the Capitol and Washington Monument in the distance. Buy tickets directly at the ballpark or through StubHub or Ticketmaster. ✉ *Nats Park, 1500 S. Capitol St. SE, Southeast* ☎ *202/675–6287* ⊕ *www.mlb.com* Ⓜ *Navy Yard–Ballpark.*

Washington Wizards

BASKETBALL | From October to April the NBA's Washington Wizards play at the Capital One Arena and featuring NBA All-Stars Kristaps Porzingis and Bradley Beal. For showtime entertainment look for G-Wiz, G-Man, the Wiz Kids, and the Wizard Dancers. Buy tickets from the Capital One Arena box office, the Wizards online, StubHub, or Ticketmaster. ✉ *Capital One Arena, 601 F St. NW, Penn Quarter* ☎ *202/661–5100 Tickets and membership, 202/628–3200 Capital One Arena* ⊕ *www.nba.com/wizards* ✉ *From $12 (average is $54)* Ⓜ *Gallery Pl.–Chinatown.*

⬤ Addresses

Although it may not appear so at first glance, there's a system to addresses in D.C., albeit one that's a bit confusing for newcomers. The city is divided into the four quadrants of a compass (NW, NE, SE, SW), with the U.S. Capitol at the center. Because the Capitol doesn't sit in the exact center of the city (and because Virginia took back its lands that originally were part of the District in 1847), Northwest is the largest quadrant. Northwest also has most of the important landmarks, although Northeast and Southwest have their fair share. The boundaries are North Capitol Street, East Capitol Street, South Capitol Street, and the National Mall.

If someone tells you to meet them at 6th and G, ask them to specify the quadrant, because there are actually four different 6th and G intersections (one per quadrant). Within each quadrant, numbered streets run north to south, and lettered streets run east to west (the letter *J* was omitted to avoid confusion with the letter *I*). The streets form a fairly simple grid—for instance, 900 G Street NW is the intersection of 9th and G Streets in the NW quadrant of the city. Likewise, if you count the letters of the alphabet, skipping *J*, you can get a good approximation of an address for a numbered street. For instance, 1600 16th Street NW is close to Q Street, Q being the 16th letter of the alphabet if you skip *J*.

As if all this weren't confusing enough, Major Pierre L'Enfant, the Frenchman who originally designed the city, threw in diagonal avenues recalling those of Paris. Most of D.C.'s avenues are named after U.S. states. You can find addresses on avenues the same way you find those on numbered streets, so 1200 Connecticut Avenue NW is close to M Street, because *M* is the 12th letter of the alphabet when you skip *J*.

Essentials

Dining

D.C. has always had a wide variety of international restaurants, but in recent times, the city has come to the forefront of good eating.

DISCOUNTS AND DEALS

If you eat early or late you may be able to take advantage of prix-fixe deals not offered at peak hours. Many upscale restaurants offer great lunch deals with special menus at cut-rate prices designed to give customers a true taste of the place. At high-end restaurants, ask for tap water to avoid paying high rates for bottled water.

PAYING

Most restaurants take credit cards, but some smaller places do not. It's worth asking. Waiters expect a 20% tip at high-end restaurants; some add an automatic gratuity for groups of six or more.

RESERVATIONS AND DRESS

Always make a reservation at an upscale restaurant when you can. Some are booked weeks in advance, but some popular restaurants don't accept reservations. As unfair as it is, the way you look can influence how you're treated—and where you're seated. Generally speaking, jeans and a button-down shirt will suffice at most restaurants, but some pricier restaurants require jackets, and some insist on ties. In reviews, we mention dress only where men are required to wear a jacket or a jacket and tie. If you have doubts, call the restaurant and ask.

MEALS AND MEALTIMES

Washington has less of an around-the-clock mentality than other big cities, with many big-name restaurants shutting down between lunch and dinner and closing by 11 pm. Many Downtown chain eateries close on weekends. For late-night dining, your best bets are restaurants near Dupont Circle and the U Street Corridor; for a late lunch, look for smaller places in Penn Quarter.

PRICES

Prices in the reviews are the average cost of a main course at dinner or, if dinner is not served, at lunch. Restaurant reviews have been shortened. For full information, visit Fodors.com.

What it Costs in U.S. Dollars			
$	$$	$$$	$$$$
AT DINNER			
under $17	$17–$26	$27–$35	over $35

✚ Health

COVID-19

A novel coronavirus brought all travel to a virtual standstill in 2020. Although the illness is mild in most people, some experience severe and even life-threatening complications. Once travel started up again, albeit slowly and cautiously, travelers were asked to be particularly careful about hygiene and to avoid any unnecessary travel, especially if they are sick. Older adults, especially those over 65, have a greater chance of having severe complications from COVID-19. The same is true for people with weaker immune systems or those living with some types of medical conditions, including diabetes, asthma, heart disease, cancer, HIV/AIDS, kidney disease, and liver disease. Starting two weeks before a trip, anyone planning to travel should be on the lookout for some of the following symptoms: cough, fever, chills, trouble breathing, muscle pain, sore throat, new loss of smell or taste. If you experience any of these symptoms, you should not travel at all.

And to protect yourself during travel, do your best to avoid contact with people showing symptoms. Wash your hands often with soap and water. Limit your time in public places, and, when you are out and about, wear a cloth face mask that covers your nose and mouth. Indeed, a mask may be required in some places, such as in a confined space like a theater, where you share the space with a lot of people. You may wish to bring extra supplies, such as disinfecting wipes, hand sanitizer, and a first-aid kit with a thermometer.

Given how abruptly travel was curtailed in March 2020, it is wise to consider protecting yourself by purchasing a travel insurance policy that will reimburse you for any costs related to COVID-19 related cancellations. Not all travel insurance policies protect against pandemic-related cancellations, so always read the fine print.

🛏 Lodging

The District has some great hotels, but in general, rates are very high, especially on weekdays.

RESERVATIONS
Always make a reservation in D.C. Hotels often fill up, and rooms can be particularly hard to come by in late March or early April during the Cherry Blossom Festival, and in May, when students at the many local colleges graduate. Late October's Marine Corps Marathon also increases demand for rooms.

FACILITIES
You can assume that all rooms have private baths, phones, TVs, and air-conditioning, unless otherwise indicated. Breakfast is noted when it is included in the rate, but it's not a typical perk at most Washington hotels. There are a few hotels with pools, though some are indoors.

PARKING
Parking in D.C. is very expensive, and hotel parking fees can exceed $50. Independent garages may be slightly cheaper. Street parking is free after 6:30 pm and Sunday (after 10 pm in some neighborhoods), but parking rules can be confusing, and tickets are expensive.

PRICES
Rates drop in August (during the Congressional recess) and in late December and January, except around inaugurations. Weekends are also more affordable. Travelers on a budget may find cheaper lodging in Virginia and Maryland suburbs, so long as the hotel is near a Metro line.

Prices are for a standard double room in high season, excluding room tax (14.95% in D.C., 7% in Maryland, and 8.5–9% plus additional fees in some cities in Virginia). Hotel reviews have been shortened. For full information, visit Fodors. com.

What it Costs in U.S. Dollars			
$	$$	$$$	$$$$
FOR TWO PEOPLE			
under $210	$210–$295	$296–$400	over $400

Where Should I Stay?

	NEIGHBORHOOD VIBE	PROS	CONS
The West End	Pleasant residential and office area along Pennsylvania Avenue, with excellent restaurant choices. Stately early-20th-century buildings.	Safe area; close to Downtown's commercial sites and to halls of government, and the Mall.	Parking is always difficult and lots of traffic; luxury hotels with few budget rates.
Foggy Bottom	Bustling with college students most of the year. Its 18th- and 19th-century homes make for pleasant views.	Safe area; walking distance to Georgetown and the Kennedy Center; good Metro access.	Somewhat removed from other areas of city; paltry dining options.
Capitol Hill and Northeast D.C.	Charming residential blocks of Victorian row houses on Capitol Hill populated by members of Congress and their staffers.	Convenient to Union Station and Capitol. Stylish (if not cheap) hotels. Fine assortment of restaurants and shops.	Some streets iffy at night; parking takes some work; hotels are pricey. Blocks around Capitol and Union Station are chock-full of tourists.
Downtown	A vibrant, bustling, modern mix of commercial and residential properties, packed during the day and rowdy in places at night.	Right in the heart of the Metro system; easy access to the White House. Large selection of hotels, shops, and restaurants.	Crowded; busy; daytime street parking is nearly impossible.
Georgetown	Wealthy neighborhood bordered by the Potomac and a world-class university. Filled with students, upscale shops, and eateries.	Safe area. Historic charm on every tree-lined street. Wonderful walking paths along river.	Crowded; no nearby Metro access; lots of traffic. Almost no parking. Lodging options are charming but tend to be expensive.
Dupont Circle	Cosmopolitan, lively neighborhood filled with bars and restaurants; beautiful city sights.	Plenty of modern hotels; easy Metro access; good selection of bars and restaurants.	Few budget hotel options; very limited street parking; crowded in summer months.
Adams Morgan	The center of late-night activity; eclectic and down-to-earth; languages galore.	Fabulous selection of ethnic bars and restaurants; vibrant, hip nightlife.	Few lodging options; 10-minute walk to Metro; very hard to park.
Upper Northwest	A pleasant residential neighborhood with a lively strip of good restaurants.	Safe, quiet; easy walk to zoo, Metro, restaurants; street parking easier than Downtown.	A long ride to attractions other than the zoo; feels like an inner suburb. Few new hotels.

$ Money

Washington is an expensive city, comparable to New York for hotels and restaurant prices. On the other hand, many attractions, including most of the museums, are free, though some can cost upward of $20 or more. Prices in this guide are given for adults. Substantially reduced fees are almost always available for children, students, and senior citizens.

🍸 Nightlife

The District has a surprisingly busy nightlife scene. Georgetown, the U Street Corridor, and Adams Morgan are popular destinations, but the Penn Quarter and Shaw are growing in popularity. Good happy hours abound during the week. Last call in D.C. is 3 am on weekends.

💼 Packing

A pair of comfortable walking shoes is your must-pack item. This is a walking town, and if you fail to pack for it, your feet will pay. Business attire tends to be fairly conservative, but around college campuses and in hip neighborhoods like U Street Corridor, H Street, NoMa, or Adams Morgan, styles are more eclectic. While you shouldn't show up at upscale restaurants in a Hawaiian shirt and flip-flops, the dress code takes in a wide range of the spectrum. Even at the Kennedy Center you'll see a mix of sparkly long dresses and jeans.

Winters are cold, with nighttime temperatures in the 20s and 30s and daytime highs in the 40s and 50s. Although the city doesn't normally get much snow, when it does, many streets won't be plowed for days, so if you're planning a visit for winter bring a warm coat and hat and shoes that won't be ruined by snow and salt. Summers are muggy and very hot, with temperatures in the 80s and 90s and high humidity. Plan on cool, breathable fabrics, a hat for the sun, a sweater for overzealous air-conditioning, and an umbrella for afternoon thunderstorms. Fall and spring are the most enjoyable, with temperatures in the 60s and occasional showers. Pants, lightweight sweaters, and light coats are appropriate.

🎟 Performing Arts

Whatever you are looking for, Washington, D.C. has some of the most exciting and thought-provoking entertainment in the country. Since the opening of the John F. Kennedy Center for the Performing Arts in 1971, the city's performing arts culture has grown steadily. Washington now hosts one of the largest theater scenes in the country, as well as a rich offering of nightly music opportunities featuring local, national, and international talent, and so much more. For up-to-date information, look for the *Washington City Paper* (🌐 *www.washingtoncitypaper.com*) or the *Washington Post*'s *Going Out Guide* (🌐 *www.washingtonpost.com/goingoutguide*).

✚ Safety

Washington, D.C. is a fairly safe city, but as with any major metropolitan area, it's best to stay alert. Keep an eye on purses and backpacks, and be aware of your surroundings before you use an ATM, especially one that is outdoors. Assaults are rare, but they do happen,

Essentials

Tipping Guides for Washington, D.C.

Bartender	$1–$5 per round of drinks, depending on the number of drinks
Bellhop	$2–$5 per bag, depending on the level of the hotel
Coat Check	$2 per coat
Hotel Concierge	$5 or more, depending on the service
Hotel Door Staff	$1–$5 for help with bags or hailing a cab
Hotel Room Service Waiter	15%–20% tip if service charge not included; $1–$2 per delivery if service charge included
Housekeeping	$3–$5 a day (in cash, preferably daily since cleaning staff may be different each day you stay)
Porter at Airport or Train Station	$1 per bag
Restroom Attendants	$1 or small change
Skycap at Airport	$1–$3 per bag checked
Spa Personnel	15%–20% of the cost of your service
Taxi Driver	15%–20%
Tour Guide	10%–15% of the cost of the tour, per person; $10–$20 per person if it's a free tour; no tips are allowed to park rangers, Capitol tour leaders, or other federal employees.
Valet Parking Attendant	$2–$5, each time your car is brought to you
Waiter	15%–20%, with 20% being the norm at high-end restaurants; nothing additional if a service charge is added to the bill

especially late at night in Adams Morgan, Capitol Hill, Northeast D.C., and U Street Corridor. Public transportation is quite safe, but late at night, choose bus stops on busy streets over those on quiet ones. If someone threatens you with violence, it's best to hand over your money and seek help from police later. Also be careful with smartphones and other electronics, as it's not uncommon for thieves to snatch those devices straight from the hands of unsuspecting pedestrians and Metro riders.

Shopping

Beyond the typical museum gift shops on the Mall, smaller one-of-a-kind shops, designer boutiques, and interesting specialty collections add to Washington's shopping scene alongside stores that have been part of the landscape for generations. Weekdays, Downtown street vendors add to the mix by offering funky jewelry; brightly patterned ties; buyer-beware watches; sunglasses; and African-inspired clothing, accessories, and art. Discerning shoppers will find satisfaction at upscale malls on the city's outskirts. Not surprisingly, T-shirts and Capital City souvenirs are in plentiful supply. Stores that cater to Downtown office workers may close on weekends, while stores in Georgetown, Adams Morgan, and the U Street Corridor may stay open late.

Taxes

Washington's hotel tax is a whopping 14.95%. Maryland and Virginia charge hotel taxes of 7%–9% plus additional fees in some cities. The effective sales tax is 5.75% in D.C., and 6% in Maryland and Northern Virginia.

D.C.'s Top Festivals

For a look at yearly events, visit ⊕ *www.washington.org*, the website of the tourism bureau.

WINTER

National Christmas Tree Lighting/Pageant of Peace (☎ *202/796–2500, Dec.*). Each year in early December, the president lights the tree at dusk on the Ellipse, with a G-scale model railway running around the tree's base and smaller decorated trees representing the states and territories providing a festive setting. Concerts are held through the month.

Restaurant Week (*Jan. and Aug.*). Dozens of top restaurants in D.C. and the surrounding region offer lunch and dinner menus for around $25 and $40–$55, respectively—often a steal.

Washington Auto Show (*Jan. and Feb.*). Held at the convention center, this yearly event showcases the latest offerings from the world of automobiles.

SPRING

National Cherry Blossom Festival (☎ *877/442–5666, mid-Mar.–mid Apr.*). D.C.'s most eye-catching annual festival opens with an evening of world-class traditional and contemporary performances at the historic Warner Theater.

Georgetown French Market (☎ *202/298–9222* ⊕ *www.georgetownfrenchmarketdc.com, late Apr.*). Shop, eat, wander, and enjoy strolling mimes and live musicians in one of D.C.'s most beautiful neighborhoods.

National Cathedral Flower Mart (⊕ *allhallowsguild.org* or ⊕ *www.cathedral.org, late Apr.–early May*). This long-standing free event on the cathedral grounds features food, music, kids' activities, and, of course, flowers.

SUMMER

Capital Pride (☎ *202/719–5304* ⊕ *www.capitalpride.org, June*). A parade through the Georgetown and Logan Circle neighborhoods and food, music, and fun on Pennsylvania Avenue celebrate LGBTQ+ citizens.

Independence Day Celebration (☎ *800/395–2036* ⊕ *July4thparade.com* or *www.nps.gov, July*). A parade sashays down Constitution Avenue, fireworks fly over the Washington Monument, and the NSO plays on the Capitol's West Lawn.

National Symphony Orchestra Labor Day Concert (☎ *202/416–8114* ⊕ *www.aoc.gov, Labor Day weekend*). This free concert is held on the grounds of the U.S. Capitol.

FALL

National Book Festival (☎ *202/707–5000* ⊕ *www.loc.gov, early Sept.*). This Saturday event attracts some of the world's top authors and poets to the Convention Center, where visitors can listen to readings and discussions and get books signed.

Washington International Horse Show (☎ *202/525–3679* ⊕ *wihs.org, late Oct.*). Held at Capital One Arena, this annual show features jumping, dressage, barrel racing, and more.

Veterans Day (☎ *877/907-8585 for Cemetery Visitor Center or 202/426-6841 for National Park Service, Nov. 11*). Services are held at Arlington National Cemetery, the Vietnam Veterans Memorial, the World War II Memorial, and the U.S. Navy Memorial, with a wreath-laying at 11 am at the Tomb of the Unknowns.

Great Itineraries

One Day in D.C.

If you have a day or less in D.C., your sightseeing strategy is simple: Take the Metro to the Smithsonian stop and explore the area around the National Mall. You'll be at the heart of the city—a beautiful setting where you'll find America's greatest collection of museums, with the city's monuments and the halls of government a stone's throw away.

Facing the Capitol, to your left are the **National Museum of African American History and Culture, National Museum of American History, National Museum of Natural History,** and **National Gallery of Art.** To your right are the **National Museum of Asian Art,** the **National Museum of African Art,** the **Hirshhorn Museum and Sculpture Garden,** the **National Air and Space Museum,** and more. Head in the other direction, toward the **Washington Monument,** and you're also on your way to the **National World War II Memorial,** the **Lincoln Memorial,** the **Vietnam Veterans Memorial,** and more monuments to America's presidents and its past. A lover of American history and culture could spend a thoroughly happy month, much less a day, wandering the Mall and its surroundings.

If you're here first thing in the morning: You can hit monuments and memorials early. They're open 24 hours a day and staffed beginning at 9:30 am. The sculpture garden at the Hirshhorn opens at 10 am, and the Smithsonian Institution Building ("the Castle") opens at 8:30. In the Castle, you can grab a cup of coffee, consult in-house experts on what to see and do, and view examples of objects from many of the Smithsonian's 19 museums and galleries.

If you have only a few hours in the evening: Experience the beauty of the monuments at dusk and after dark. Many people think they're even more striking when the sun goes down. National Park Service rangers staff most monuments until 10 pm.

Three Days in D.C.

DAY 1

With more time, you have a chance both to see the sights and to get to know the city. A guided bus tour is a good way to get oriented; a hop-on, hop-off tour will give you genuine insights without a lot of tourist hokum.

Because you can get on and off wherever you like, it's a good idea to use a bus tour to explore **Georgetown** and the **Washington National Cathedral,** neither of which is easily accessible by Metro. This is a good opportunity to visit **Arlington National Cemetery** as well.

In the afternoon, visit the **Smithsonian American Art Museum** and/or the **National Portrait Gallery** in Penn Quarter; the **International Spy Museum,** recently expanded at its new L'Enfant Plaza location, is another option.

DAY 2

Devote your next day to the National Mall, where you can check out the museums and monuments that were probably your prime motivation for visiting D.C. in the first place. There's no way you can do it all in one day, so just play favorites, and save the rest for next time. Try visiting the monuments in the evening: they remain open long after the museums are closed and are dramatically lit after dark.

Keep in mind that the **National Museum of Natural History** and the **National Air and Space Museum** are among the world's most visited museums, and the **National Gallery of Art** and the **National Museum of American History** aren't far behind; plan for crowds almost any time you visit. If you visit the **United States Holocaust Memorial Museum,** plan on spending two to three hours. The **National Museum of African American History and Culture,** which opened in 2016, is the newest museum on the Mall. If you're with kids on the Mall, take a break by riding the carousel.

Cafés and cafeterias within the museums are your best option for lunch. Three excellent picks are the Cascade Café at the **National Gallery of Art**; the Mitsitam Café at the **National Museum of the American Indian,** where they serve creative dishes inspired by indigenous cultures; and Sweet Water Café at the **National Museum of African American History and Culture,** showcasing the rich traditions of African American cuisine.

If the weather permits—and you're not already weary—consider the healthy walk from the **Washington Monument** to the **Lincoln Memorial** and around the **Tidal Basin,** where you can see the **Jefferson Memorial,** the **Franklin Delano Roosevelt Memorial,** and the **Martin Luther King Jr. Memorial.** Nearby, nestled north of the Mall's reflecting pool, is the **Vietnam Veterans Memorial,** "The Wall," a sobering black granite monolith commemorating the 58,318 Americans who died in service of the Vietnam War—a design that's "not so much a tombstone or a monument as a grave," in the somber words of writer Michael Ventura.

DAY 3

Start your day on **Capitol Hill,** where you'll have the option of visiting the **Capitol** (reserve passes ahead), the **U.S. Botanic Garden,** the **Library of Congress,** the **Supreme Court,** and the **Folger Shakespeare Library.**

Call your senator or congressional representative in advance of your trip for passes to see Congress in session. International visitors can ask about gallery passes at the House and Senate Appointment Desks on the upper level of the Capitol Visitor Center. You can also venture into one of the congressional office buildings adjacent to the Capitol, where congressional hearings are almost always open to the public. Likewise, check the Supreme Court's website (⊕ *www.supremecourt.gov*) for dates of oral arguments. If you arrive early enough, you might gain admission for either a short (three-minute) visit or the full morning session.

In the afternoon, hop on the Metro to bustling **Dupont Circle** for lunch, then visit the renowned **Phillips Collection** or head farther north on Connecticut Avenue to the **Smithsonian's National Zoo** to take a stroll past lions, tigers, and bears.

Washington, D.C., Black History Walk

A walk along U Street and the eastern rim of Adams Morgan gives a taste of D.C. that most tourists never get. This tour through "Black Broadway" bounces from lively commercial streets brimming with hip bars, cafés, and boutiques to quiet, tree-lined, residential blocks.

"BLACK BROADWAY"— U STREET CORRIDOR

The Howard Theatre at T Street and Florida Avenue is a good place to start. Opened in 1910, this landmark of Black culture found its way onto the National Register of Historic Places for hosting some of the greatest musical acts of the last century—a list that includes such notables as Ella Fitzgerald and native son Duke Ellington in the 1930s and, more recently, Lena Horne, James Brown, and Marvin Gaye. All but destroyed in 1968, following the assassination of Martin Luther King Jr., the theater was renovated beautifully in 2012 and now features live acts almost nightly. A short hike west, at Vermont and U Streets, sits the **African American Civil War Memorial,** where the names of more than 200,000 Black soldiers who fought for their freedom are inscribed. The adjacent **African American Civil War Memorial Museum** features wonderful photographs from the era and an extensive on-site database for searching individual soldiers. A block west at 2000 11th Street is **Washington Industrial Bank,** which thrived by offering African Americans a service that others in the city wouldn't: the option to borrow money. Next, grab a half-smoke at **Ben's Chili Bowl**. This D.C. landmark refused to close its doors during the fierce riots that followed King's assassination. While most of U Street was being destroyed, Ben's fed the police officers and Black activists trying to keep order. Next door is the **Lincoln Theater,** another exceptional jazz

Washington, D.C., Black History Walk

HIGHLIGHTS:
U Street was the center of Black culture before Harlem was Harlem. See where Duke Ellington played, indulge in a half-smoke at Ben's Chili Bowl, and learn a bit about African American history along the way.

WHERE TO START:
Howard Theatre, just east of Metro's U Street/African American Civil War Memorial/Cardozo stop on the Green or Yellow lines

LENGTH:
About 1½ miles; 1–2 hours, with window-shopping

WHERE TO STOP:
All Souls Unitarian Church. The S2 or S4 bus lines on 16th Street will whisk you back Downtown.

BEST TIME TO GO:
While the sun is up, though the nightlife on U Street is an attraction in itself.

WORST TIME TO GO:
Avoid walking through Meridian Hill Park after dark.

SHOPPING DETOUR:
Check out the sprawling Miss Pixie's (✉ 1626 14th St. NW) for handpicked collectibles, vintage furniture, and fun home decor, and browse Zawadi African Art Gallery and Gift Shop (✉ 1524 U St.) for African clothes, home goods, and more.

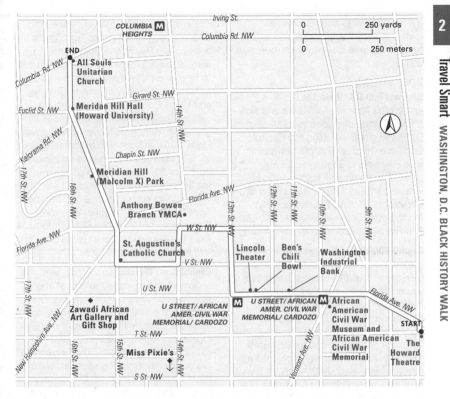

venue and, from 1922 until desegregation, one of the largest and most elegant historically Black theaters. Two blocks north up 13th Street NW and a quick left on W Street will bring you to the **Anthony Bowen Branch YMCA,** the oldest Black Y in the country (1853), recently completely overhauled.

NORTH OF U STREET

Venture a block southwest to 15th and V to marvel at **St. Augustine's Catholic Church**—a gorgeous, two-tower cathedral now home to a Black congregation that seceded from its segregated church (St. Matthews) in 1858. Feel free to walk inside to glimpse the striking stained-glass portrait of a Black St. Augustine and

St. Monica. A block north on 15th Street awaits sprawling **Meridian Hill** (or **Malcolm X**) **Park,** where a number of civil rights marches have originated over the years. Just north of the park, you'll spot **Meridian Hill Hall,** Howard University's first coed dorm. Alumni of the elite African American school include Thurgood Marshall and Toni Morrison. Continuing north, you'll find **All Souls Unitarian Church** at 1500 Harvard Street NW. Its pastor in the 1940s, Reverend A. Powell Davies, led the push to desegregate D.C. schools.

Best Tours in D.C.

It's pretty easy to do D.C. on your own, but consider one of the following options if you're looking for chaperoned convenience.

BIKE TOURS

Bike and Roll DC. Based at L'Enfant Plaza, just off the National Mall, Bike and Roll offers a series of guided tours through D.C.'s top sites, including the Capitol, Supreme Court, and WWII Memorial. Bike rentals and Segway tours are also offered, and self-guided options stretch as far as Mount Vernon and even Pittsburgh. ✉ *955 L'Enfant Plaza SW, North Bldg., Southwest* ☎ *202/842–2453* ⊕ *www.bikeandrolldc.com* ✉ *From $49.*

Capital Bikeshare. A great way to see the memorials and monuments at your own pace, this bike-share scheme lets you rent bikes by the hour and return them to any of the 600-plus stations throughout the city. There are also stations in Alexandria and Arlington, VA, neighboring Montgomery County, MD, and more, if you want to venture farther afield. ☎ *877/430–2453* ⊕ *www. capitalbikeshare.com* ✉ *Single trip ($1 unlock plus.05/min.), day passes ($8), and longer-term membership packages are available.*

Fat Tire Tours. Yet another option for touring the monuments, Fat Tire Tours offers guided day tours, Segway rentals, and private tours. A typical tour is three hours of easy peddling. E-bikes are also available. ✉ *998 Maine Ave. SW, Southwest* ☎ *866/614–6218, 202/842–2453* ⊕ *www. fattiretours.com* ✉ *From $44* Ⓜ *L'Enfant Plaza.*

BOAT TOURS

Boating in D.C. Rent your own canoe, kayak, or stand-up paddleboard from a variety of different boathouses along the Potomac and Washington Channel and take your own scenic tour. Among the choices are Thompson Boat Center in Georgetown, where you can paddle over to Roosevelt Island for a picnic; the Wharf Boathouse, along Washington Channel and Hains Point; and National Harbor, to explore the wilds of the Potomac. A single kayak rents for $18 per hour, a double kayak $25 per hour, while a canoe goes for $28 per hour and a stand-up paddleboard for $22 per hour. Sculls are also available for certified rowers. Check the website for more locations. ✉ *Thompson Boat Center, 2900 Virginia Ave., NW, Georgetown* ☎ *202/337–9642 Thompson Boat Center* ⊕ *boatingindc.com* ✉ *From $18 for a single kayak.*

Capitol River Cruises. This small, family-owned and-operated tour boat agency has been cruising on the Potomac River for more than 30 years. Sightseeing tours lasting 45 minutes are aboard the *Nightingale* and *Nightingale II*, former Great Lakes boats from the 1950s. Departures are hourly, noon through sunset, out of the Washington Harbor in Georgetown. During blossom season, you'll see cherry blooms from the river. ✉ *Washington Harbor, 3050 K St. NW, Georgetown* ☎ *301/460–7447* ⊕ *www.capitolrivercruises.com* ✉ *$25* ◷ *No tours Nov.–Mar.*

City Experiences. Among the different ways to explore D.C. from the Potomac are an elegant dinner cruise aboard the magnificent *Odyssey*; a buffet dinner with a live DJ on the *Spirit of Washington*; and a sail to Mount Vernon aboard the *Spirit of Mount Vernon*. The cruises depart from the District Wharf. ✉ *580 Water St. SW, Pier 4, D.C. Waterfront* ☎ *703/684–0580, 866/404–8439* ⊕ *www. cityexperiences.com* ✉ *From $60 for lunch, $120 for dinner* Ⓜ *Waterfront–SEU.*

BUS TOURS

Big Bus Tours. Brightly painted, red-and-yellow, open-top, double-decker buses provide a hop-on, hop-off service with different city loops. A super helpful app tracks buses in real time and helps locate stops more easily. Discount tickets are sometimes offered online. Contact them with questions via online chat. ⊕ *www.bigbustours.com* ✉ *From $49* ☞ *No active phone lines; contact a representative via chat feature on website.*

City Sights. This bus tour offers double-decker fun for those seeking to take advantage of warmer weather and get an elevated view of Washington. The group runs multiple loops around the city, some of which extend well beyond the Mall to include Georgetown, the National Cathedral, and Arlington National Cemetery. All trips offer hop-on, hop-off convenience, and several multiday options are available for those on longer stays. City Sights also offers boat trips and guided bike tours. ☎ *202/650–5444, 866/723–4400* ⊕ *www.citysightsdc.com* ✉ *From $55.*

SEGWAY AND SCOOTER TOURS

Rest your feet and glide by the monuments, museums, and major attractions aboard a Segway. Guided tours usually last between two and three hours. D.C. city ordinance requires that riders be at least 16 years old; some tour companies have weight restrictions of 250 pounds. Tours, limited to 6 to 10 people, begin with an instruction session.

Capital Segway. More than 20 historic sights are included on this company's Segway tours, including the White House, U.S. Capitol, Smithsonian museums, and more. ✉ *818 Connecticut Ave. NW* ☎ *202/682–1980* ⊕ *www.capitalsegway.com* ✉ *From $65* Ⓜ *McPherson Sq.*

Scootaround Inc. This company rents mobility scooters and wheelchairs for self-guided tours. ✉ *Washington* ☎ *888/441–7575* ⊕ *www.scootaround.com* ✉ *Scooters from $65 per day; wheelchairs from $25 per day.*

SPECIALTY TOURS

DC Metro Food Tours. Some 20 tours, each lasting 3½ hours and conducted on weekends year-round, explore the culinary heritage of different neighborhoods in D.C. and nearby Virginia. Private tours can be arranged. ☎ *202/851–2268* ⊕ *www.dcmetrofoodtours.com* ✉ *From $65.*

Smithsonian Associates. Experience D.C.'s art, history, and culture through the lens of the Smithsonian Associates. Tours of Arlington National Cemetery, nearby Civil War battlefields, Nationals Park, and Old Town's African American history are some of the excursions on offer. ☎ *202/633–3030* ⊕ *www.smithsonianassociates.org* ✉ *From $45.*

A Tour de Force. Local historian and author Jeanne Fogle will escort you via custom-designed tours, by limo or on foot, of historic homes, diplomatic buildings, and off-the-beaten-path sites. You can opt for half-day, full-day, multiday, or evening tours. ☎ *703/525–2948* ⊕ *www.atourdeforce.com* ✉ *From $69.*

Washington Photo Safari. Founder E. David Luria promises opportunities for photographers of all skill levels (even camera phones are fine) on his half-day and full-day "Monuments and Memorials" workshops. Special themed tours, led by a team of professional photographers, are held on selected weekends. ☎ *202/669–8468* ⊕ *www.washingtonphotosafari.com* ✉ *From $89.*

Best Tours in D.C.

WALKING TOURS

Capitol Historical Society. This group leads guided tours around the grounds of the Capitol weekdays at 5:30 pm, March through Memorial Day, 7 pm Memorial Day through September 30, and 5:30 pm October 1 through November 30. The two-hour tour starts at Garfield Circle, at the intersection of First Street and Maryland Avenue SW. Reservations must be made at least 48 hours in advance. ☎ *800/887–9318, 202/525–2790* ⊕ *www. uschs.org* ✉ *$30.*

Cultural Tourism DC. This nonprofit group has 18 self-guided Neighborhood Heritage Trails, plus a citywide African American Heritage Trail, War of 1812 Heritage Trail, and Japanese and Mexican Heritage Trails, all of which are highlighted with historic markers. All the tours can be downloaded from its website. You can also check out other cultural events happening around the city, many free, on the website. ☎ *202/355–4280* ⊕ *www. culturaltourismdc.org* ✉ *Free.*

DC Walkabout. Download a tour to any mobile device, and set off in your own time and at your own pace, guided by a narration, historical recordings, and even music and sound effects. Tours, ranging from 1 to 2 miles, include "American Scandal," "Capitol Hill," "Georgetown Ghost," "Haunted History," "Lincoln Assassination," "National Mall," and "Tidal Basin." ✉ *Washington* ⊕ *www. dcwalkabout.com* ✉ *$9.*

Free Tours By Foot. Dozens of tours, including the Tidal Basin and National Mall, Arlington National Cemetery, and Capitol Hill are led by guides who work for tips, guaranteeing a highly entertaining experience. Other tours, including "Historic Georgetown," "Lincoln Assassination," and "Ghosts of Georgetown," charge a fee but are just as entertaining. Tours last two to four hours and are available year-round, but days and times vary by season, and advance reservations are required. ☎ *202/370–1830* ⊕ *www. freetoursbyfoot.com* ✉ *One some tours, guides work for tips; others are from $20 per person.*

Washington Walks. The wide range of tours offered by Washington Walks includes "Hamilton's D.C." and "Women Who Changed America." ☎ *202/484– 1565* ⊕ *www.washingtonwalks.com* ✉ *$35.*

Contacts

✈ Air

AIRLINE CONTACTS
American Airlines/American Eagle. ☎ *800/433–7300* ⊕ *www.aa.com.* **Delta Airlines.** ☎ *800/221–1212* ⊕ *www.delta.com.* **JetBlue.** ☎ *800/538–2583* ⊕ *www.jetblue.com.* **Southwest Airlines.** ☎ *800/435–9792* ⊕ *www.southwest.com.* **United Airlines.** ☎ *800/864–8331* ⊕ *www.united.com.*

AIRPORTS Baltimore/ Washington International– Thurgood Marshall Airport. (*BWI*). ☎ *800/435–9294, 410/859–7111* ⊕ *www.bwiairport.com.* **Dulles International Airport.** (*IAD*). ☎ *703/572–2700* ⊕ *www.flydulles.com.* **Ronald Reagan Washington National Airport.** (*DCA*). ☎ *703/417–8000* ⊕ *www.flyreagan.com.*

REAGAN NATIONAL (DCA) AIRPORT TRANSFERS
Taxicab Commission. ☎ *311, 202/645–6018* ⊕ *www.dfhv.dc.gov.* **Washington Metropolitan Area Transit Authority.** ☎ *202/637– 7000, 202/962–2033 TTY* ⊕ *www.wmata.com.*

BALTIMORE/WASHING-TON (BWI) AIRPORT TRANSFERS Amtrak. ☎ *800/872–7245* ⊕ *www.amtrak.com.* **Maryland Rail Commuter Service.** ☎ *410/539–5000, 410/539–3497 TTY,*

866/743–3682 ⊕ *www.mta.maryland.gov.* **Washington Metropolitan Area Transit Authority.** ☎ *202/637–7000, 202/962–2033 TTY* ⊕ *www.wmata.com.*

DULLES (IAD) AIRPORT TRANSFERS Washington Flyer. ☎ *703/572–8294* ⊕ *www.flydulles.com.* **Washington Metropolitan Area Transit Authority.** ☎ *202/637–7000, 202/962–2033 TTY* ⊕ *www.wmata.com.*

🚌 Bus

D.C. CITY BUSES DC Circulator. ☎ *202/671–2020* ⊕ *www.dccirculator.com.* **Washington Metropolitan Area Transit Authority.** ☎ *202/637–7000, 202/962–2033 TTY* ⊕ *www.wmata.com.*

REGIONAL BUSES
BestBus. ☎ *202/332–2691, 888/838–3269* ⊕ *www.bestbus.com.* **Megabus.** ☎ *877/462–6342* ⊕ *us.megabus.com.* **Peter Pan Bus Lines.** ☎ *800/343–9999* ⊕ *www.peterpanbus.com.* **Tripper Bus.** ☎ *718/834–9214, 877/826–3874* ⊕ *www.tripperbus.com.* **Vamoose.** ☎ *212/695–6766, 301/718–0036* ⊕ *www.vamoosebus.com.* **Washington Deluxe.** ☎ *866/287–6932* ⊕ *www.washny.com.*

🚗 Car

CAR RENTAL COMPANIES
Alamo. ☎ *844/354–6962 reservations, 844/357–5138 customer service* ⊕ *www.alamo.com.* **Avis.** ☎ *800/230–4898* ⊕ *www.avis.com.* **Budget.** ☎ *800/404–8033* ⊕ *www.budget.com.* **Hertz.** ☎ *800/977–5771 TTY, 800/654–3131* ⊕ *www.hertz.com.* **National Car Rental.** ☎ *844/393–9989 customer service, 844/382–6875 reservations* ⊕ *www.nationalcar.com.*

Ⓜ Metro/ Public Transport

METRO INFORMATION
Washington Metropolitan Area Transit Authority. (*WMATA*). ☎ *202/637–7000, 202/962–1196 lost and found, 888/762–7874 SmarTrip* ⊕ *www.wmata.com.*

🚘 Ride-Sharing

RIDE SHARES
Lyft. ☎ *855/865–9553* ⊕ *www.lyft.com.* **Uber.** ⊕ *www.uber.com.* **Zipcar.** ☎ *866/494–7227* ⊕ *www.zipcar.com.*

Contacts

🚕 Taxi

TAXI COMPANIES
Barwood. ☎ *301/984–1900*
⊕ *www.barwoodtaxi.com.*
Diamond Transportation.
☎ *202/387–6200* ⊕ *nellc.
com/diamondtranspor-
tation.* **Red Top Cab of
Arlington.** ☎ *703/522–3333*
⊕ *www.redtopcab.
com.* **Taxi Transportation.**
☎ *202/398–0500* ⊕ *www.
dctaxionline.com.* **Yellow.**
☎ *202/544–1212* ⊕ *dcyel-
lowcab.com.*

🚆 Train

TRAIN CONTACTS Amtrak.
☎ *800/872–7245* ⊕ *www.
amtrak.com.* **Maryland
Rail Commuter Service.**
(*MARC*). ☎ *866/743–3682,
410/539–5000* ⊕ *www.
mta.maryland.gov.* **Union
Station.** ✉ *50 Massachusetts Ave. NE, Washington*
☎ *202/289–1908* ⊕ *www.
unionstationdc.com.*
Virginia Railway Express.
(*VRE*). ☎ *703/684–1001
customer service,
800/743–3873* ⊕ *www.
vre.org.*

📍 Visitor Information

**EVENTS National Park
Service.** ☎ *202/208–6843*
⊕ *www.nps.gov.* **Smith-
sonian.** ☎ *202/633–1000*
⊕ *www.si.edu.* **White
House Visitor Center.**
✉ *1450 Pennsylvania
Ave. NW, Washington*
☎ *202/208–1631* ⊕ *www.
nps.gov/whho.*

**THE DISTRICT Destination
DC.** ✉ *901 7th St. NW, 4th
fl., Downtown* ☎ *202/789–
7000, 800/422–8644*
⊕ *www.washington.org.*

**VIRGINIA AND
MARYLAND State of
Maryland.** ☎ *866/639–3526*
⊕ *www.visitmaryland.org.*
**Virginia Tourism Corpo-
ration.** ☎ *804/545–5500*
⊕ *www.virginia.org.*

Chapter 3

THE NATIONAL MALL

3

Updated by
Jessica van Dop DeJesus

👁 Sights	🍴 Restaurants	🛏 Hotels	🛍 Shopping	🍸 Nightlife
★★★★★	★★☆☆☆	★☆☆☆☆	★★☆☆☆	★☆☆☆☆

NEIGHBORHOOD SNAPSHOT

TOP EXPERIENCES

Monuments at night: For a unique (and less-crowded) historical experience, tour the many monuments after dark, when they are lit and beautiful.

National Air and Space Museum: Touch a moon rock, see the original *Spirit of St. Louis* and Apollo Lunar Module.

National Archives: Stand in awe as you read the Declaration of Independence, Constitution, Bill of Rights, and a 1297 Magna Carta.

National Museum of African American History and Culture: D.C.'s newest museum is also the most moving. Learn about the history of the arrival of enslaved people to the Americas, and celebrate the many artists, writers, actors, and cultural leaders who have contributed to our country's history.

National Gallery of Art: Two massive buildings offer an extensive collection ranging from classics to modern art. Don't miss the only Leonardo da Vinci in the United States, the renowned *Ginevra de' Benci,* and an extensive collection of the Dutch Masters.

The Holocaust Museum: This museum serves as a monument to those lost in the Holocaust and offers perspective on genocide effects worldwide and throughout time.

GETTING HERE

Federal Triangle (Blue and Orange lines) is convenient to the Natural History and American History museums. Smithsonian (Blue, Orange, and Silver lines) is close to the Holocaust Memorial Museum and Hirshhorn Museum. Archives–Navy Memorial–Penn Quarter (Yellow and Green lines) takes you to the National Gallery of Art. L'Enfant Plaza (Blue, Orange, Yellow, Silver, and Green lines) is the best stop for the Hirshhorn and Air and Space Museum. Many visitors take advantage of the DC Circulator National Mall Route buses that cost just $1 and run daily up and down the Mall.

PLANNING YOUR TIME

With 12 museums spread out along 11 city blocks, it's virtually impossible to see everything in one day. We recommend picking museums whose exhibits are most interesting to you and your travel companions. Most Smithsonian museums are large, and it takes at least half a day for a comprehensive tour. Exploring the National Mall, monuments, and memorials takes at least two days. Also, take into consideration the time of year. Summers in Washington, D.C. tend to be very hot and humid; therefore, work some air-conditioned museum breaks into your trip.

The National Mall, the heart of almost every visitor's trip to Washington, has influenced life in the United States more than any other park. Although the length is 2 miles, there's plenty to keep visitors busy for several days.

The National Mall is a picnicking park, jogging path, and outdoor stage for festivals and fireworks. People come here from around the world to tour the renowned Smithsonian museums, celebrate special events, or rally over the day's hot-button issues.

Also, nearly all the museums and memorials are free to the public, making the National Mall an affordable place to explore in the nation's capital.

⊙ Sights

Bureau of Engraving and Printing

GOVERNMENT BUILDING | FAMILY | Bureau of Engraving and Printing has printed paper money since 1914 when the bureau relocated from the redbrick-towered Auditors Building at the corner of 14th Street and Independence Avenue. They also print military certificates and presidential invitations. Unfortunately, visits are impossible as the building canceled tours in 2020 and has no definite date to resume them. Check the website for updates on the reopening of tours. ⊠ *14th and C Sts. SW, The Mall* ☎ *202/874–2330, 866/874–2330 tour information* ⊕ *www. bep.gov* ⊠ *Free* ☉ *Closed until further notice* Ⓜ *Smithsonian.*

Constitution Gardens

GARDEN | Many ideas were proposed to develop this 52-acre site near the Reflecting Pool and the Vietnam Veterans Memorial. Winding paths along tree groves and a 1-acre island on the lake pay tribute to the signers of the Declaration of Independence, with all of their 56 signatures carved into a low stone wall. This spot is charming in the fall, with vibrant red colors, and it's a quieter part of the Mall for picnics. You can get hot dogs, potato chips, candy bars, and soft drinks at the circular snack bar just west of the lake. ⊠ *Constitution Ave., between 17th and 23rd Sts. NW, The Mall* ⊕ *www.nps. gov/coga* ⊠ *Free* Ⓜ *Farragut W or Foggy Bottom–GWU.*

District of Columbia War Memorial

GARDEN | Despite its location and age, visitors often overlook this memorial on the National Mall, though it's a favorite with locals for wedding and engagement photos. President Herbert Hoover dedicated this monument in 1931, and unlike the neighboring memorials on the Mall, this relatively small structure isn't a national memorial. The 47-foot-high, circular, domed, columned temple is dedicated to the 26,000 residents from Washington, D.C. who served in the Great War and the 499 men and women (military and civilian) who died in service.

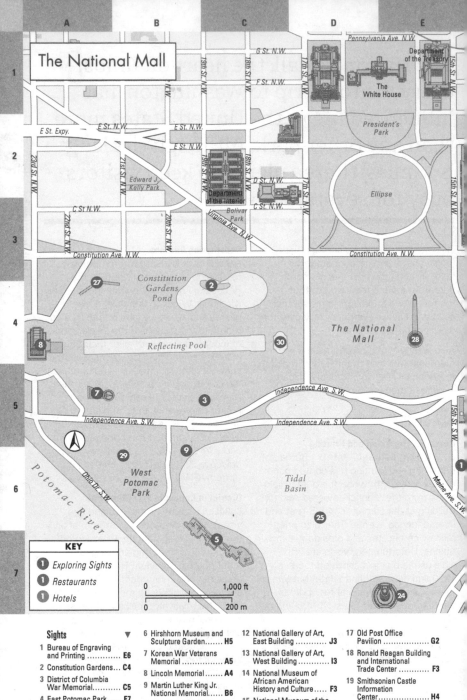

The National Mall

KEY
- Exploring Sights
- Restaurants
- Hotels

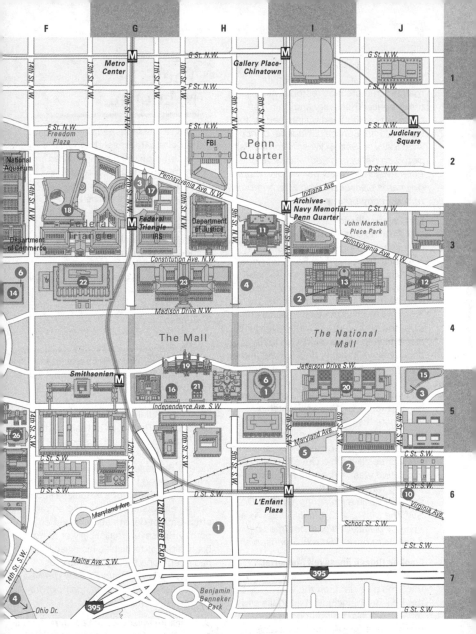

Restaurants ▼

Hotels ▼

Unofficially referred to as the "World War I Memorial" in the District, its marble structure was restored through the American Recovery and Reinvestment Act of 2009 and maintained by the National Park Service. ⊠ *Independence Ave. SW, The Mall* ✢ *West Potomac Park, between Reflecting Pool and Independence Ave.* ☎ *202/426–6841* ⊕ *www.nps. gov/nama/planyourvisit/dc-war-memorial. htm* Ⓜ *Foggy Bottom–GWU.*

East Potomac Park

CITY PARK | FAMILY | This 328-acre finger of land extends south of the Jefferson Memorial from the Tidal Basin, between the Washington Channel and the new Southwest Waterfront redevelopment neighborhood to the east and the Potomac River to the west. Locals consider the park a retreat with playgrounds, picnic tables, tennis courts, swimming pools, a driving range, one 18-hole and two 9-hole golf courses, and miniature golf. There's also a scenic riverfront trail that winds around the park's perimeter. It's a fantastic spot for bird-watching, with more than 250 species identified at the park. If you're lucky, you may spot a bald eagle. Double-blossoming Japanese cherry trees line Ohio Drive and bloom about two weeks after the single-blossoming variety that attracts crowds to the Tidal Basin each spring. ⊠ *Ohio Dr. SW, The Mall* ☎ *202/426–6841* ⊕ *www. nps.gov/places/000/east-potomac-park-hains-point.htm* ▦ *Free* Ⓜ *Smithsonian.*

Franklin Delano Roosevelt Memorial

MONUMENT | This 7½-acre memorial to the 32nd president, on the west side of the Tidal Basin, includes waterfalls and reflecting pools, four outdoor gallery rooms—one for each of Roosevelt's presidential terms (1933 to 1945)—and 10 bronze sculptures. You can find some of Roosevelt's famous statements, including "The only thing we have to fear is fear itself," engraved on the granite megaliths connecting the galleries. A bronze statue

The FDR Memorial ⊙

Congress established the Franklin Delano Roosevelt Memorial Commission in 1955 and invited prospective designers to look to "the character and work of Roosevelt to give us the theme of a memorial." Several decades passed before Lawrence Halprin's design for a "walking environmental experience" was selected. It incorporates work by artists Leonard Baskin, Neil Estern, Robert Graham, Thomas Hardy, and George Segal, and master stone carver John Benson.

of First Lady Eleanor Roosevelt stands in front of the United Nations symbol in the fourth room. She was a vocal spokesperson for human rights and one of the most influential women of her time. Considering Roosevelt's disability, this was the first memorial designed to be wheelchair-accessible, and several pillars include Braille lettering. The memorial was dedicated in 1997, but it wasn't until 2001 that a statue of a wheelchair-bound Roosevelt was added near the entrance after years of debate about whether to portray Roosevelt realistically or to honor his desire not to display his disability, as had been done throughout his presidency. ⊠ *400 W. Basin Dr. SW, The Mall* ☎ *202/426–6841* ⊕ *www.nps.gov/fdr* ▦ *Free* Ⓜ *Smithsonian.*

★ Hirshhorn Museum and Sculpture Garden

ART MUSEUM | Conceived as the nation's museum of modern and contemporary art, the Hirshhorn is home to nearly 12,000 works by masters who include Alexander Calder, Andy Warhol, and Louise Bourgeois, as well as contemporary

The view from inside the Lincoln Memorial captures its reflecting pool and the iconic Washington Monument.

superstars Anish Kapoor and Yinka Shonibare. The art is displayed in a circular poured-concrete building designed by Gordon Bunshaft, dubbed the "Doughnut on the Mall" when it was built in 1974. The museum's founder, Joseph H. Hirshhorn, a Latvian immigrant who made his fortune in uranium mines, bequeathed most of the initial collection.

The sculpture collection has masterpieces by Henry Moore, Alberto Giacometti, and Constantin Brancusi. Outside, sculptures dot a grass-and-granite garden. Among them is Yoko Ono's *Wish Tree for Washington, DC*. On the plaza stands a 32-foot-tall yellow cartoon sculpture by pop-art iconographer Roy Lichtenstein that has become a beloved local landmark.

The third level's outer ring is the place to see thought-provoking conceptual art from the museum's permanent collection. Inside the third level, you can see dramatic postwar art from the museum's permanent collection, displayed

thematically, with works by artists such as Joseph Cornell, Isa Genzken, Alighiero e Boetti, and Sol LeWitt. Check out Cornell's *Untitled (Aviary with Yellow Birds)* and Yoko Ono's *Sky TV for Washington, DC*. Large-scale text works by conceptual artist Lawrence Weiner round out the space.

The second level houses exhibits that rotate about three times a year, curated by museum staff and devoted to particular artists or themes. The lower level houses recent and experimental works from the permanent collection, while the sculpture garden makes an inspiring spot for a picnic. Dolcezza, a popular local coffee and gelato brand, set up a small café at the museum, perfect for a coffee break. ⊠ *Independence Ave. and 7th St. SW, The Mall* ☎ *202/633–4674* ⊕ *www. hirshhorn.si.edu* 🖃 *Free* ⛵ *Reservations may be required for certain exhibitions* Ⓜ *Smithsonian or L'Enfant Plaza (Maryland Ave. exit).*

Introduction to the Smithsonian

Be amazed by the history of air and space travel, then explore the 1903 *Wright Flyer* that Wilbur and Orville Wright piloted over the sands of Kitty Hawk, North Carolina, in the National Air and Space Museum. Imagine yourself as Thomas Jefferson composing documents at his "writing box" or as Julia Child cooking in her perfect kitchen—both are on display at the National Museum of American History.

Thought-provoking modern art is on view at the constantly changing Hirshhorn Museum. You'll see Roy Lichtenstein's 32-foot yellow cartoon sculpture in the outdoor sculpture garden and Yoko Ono's *Sky TV for Washington, DC* inside the museum. You can also view the only Leonardo da Vinci painting in the United States at the National Gallery of Art West Building.

The best part of all these experiences: they are free, as the Smithsonian museums do not charge an admission fee, making art and history accessible to all.

Visiting the Smithsonian

Most of the 19 Smithsonian museums are open daily between 10 am and 5:30 pm (with at least four or five closed days per year for major holidays), and all are free, though there are sometimes charges for special exhibits. During the spring and summer, many of the museums offer extended hours, closing as late as 7:30 pm. To get oriented, start with a visit to the Smithsonian building—aka the "Castle," for its towers-and-turrets architecture—which has information on all the museums. The museum also has a free app to help you explore the collections and buildings, but it has limited functionality.

Special Events

Smithsonian museums regularly host an incredible spectrum of special events, from evenings of jazz and dance nights to food and wine tastings, films, lectures, and events for families and kids. Popular events include live jazz on Friday evenings in summer at the National Gallery of Art sculpture garden and Take Five performances every third Thursday at the Smithsonian American Art Museum. The National Museum of the American Indian often holds weekend festivals that showcase the history and culture of indigenous peoples from the around the world, complete with workshops, film screenings, hands-on activities for all ages, craft shows, and cooking demonstrations.

Korean War Veterans Memorial

MONUMENT | At the west end of the National Mall, this memorial to the 5.8 million United States men and women who served in the Korean War (1950–53) highlights the cost of freedom. Often referred to as the "forgotten war," nearly 37,000 Americans died on the Korean peninsula, 8,000 were missing in action, and more than 103,000 were wounded. The privately funded memorial was dedicated on July 27, 1995, the 42nd anniversary of the Korean War Armistice.

In the *Field of Service,* 19 oversize stainless-steel soldiers trudge through rugged terrain toward an American flag; look beneath the helmets to see their weary faces. The reflection in the black granite wall to their right doubles their number to 38, symbolic of the 38th parallel, the latitude established as the border between North and South Korea in 1953, as well as the 38 months of the war.

Unlike many memorials, this one contains few words. The 164-foot-long granite wall etched with the faces of 2,400 unnamed servicemen and servicewomen says, "Freedom is not free." The plaque at the flagpole base reads, "Our nation honors her sons and daughters who answered the call to defend a country they never knew and a people they never met." The only other words are the names of 22 countries that volunteered forces or medical support, including Great Britain, France, Greece, and Turkey. The adjacent circular Pool of Remembrance honors all who were killed, captured, wounded, or lost in action; it's a quiet spot for contemplation. ⊠ *Daniel French Dr. SW and Independence Ave. SW, The Mall* ☎ *202/426–6841* ⊕ *www.nps.gov/kowa* ⊠ *Free* Ⓜ *Foggy Bottom–GWU.*

★ **Lincoln Memorial**
MONUMENT | Daniel Chester French's statue of the seated president gazing out over the Reflecting Pool may be the most iconic sculpture on the Mall. The 19-foot-high sculpture is made of 28 pieces of Georgia marble. The surrounding white Colorado-marble memorial was designed by Henry Bacon and completed in 1922. The 36 Doric columns represent the 36 states in the Union at the time of Lincoln's death; their names appear on the frieze above the columns. Over the frieze are the names of the 48 states in existence when the memorial was dedicated. At night the memorial is illuminated, creating a striking play of light and shadow across Lincoln's face. Photography enthusiasts will find great light during dawn and dusk. Given the afternoon crowds, sunrise may be a great bet. Two of Lincoln's great speeches—the second

inaugural address and the Gettysburg Address—are carved on the north and south walls. Above each is a Jules Guerin mural: the south wall has an angel of truth freeing an enslaved person; the unity of North and South is opposite. The memorial's powerful symbolism makes it a popular gathering place. In its shadow, Americans marched for integrated schools in 1958, rallied for an end to the Vietnam War in 1967, and laid wreaths in a ceremony honoring the Iranian hostages in 1979. It may be best known, though, as the site of Martin Luther King Jr.'s "I Have a Dream" speech. ⊠ *2 Lincoln Memorial Circle NW, The Mall* ⚓ *West end of Mall* ☎ *202/426–6841* ⊕ *www.nps.gov/linc* ⊠ *Free* Ⓜ *Foggy Bottom–GWU.*

★ **Martin Luther King Jr. National Memorial**
MONUMENT | One of the most iconic American figures, Martin Luther King Jr., stands among the presidents on the National Mall. For his dedication on October 16, 2011, President Barack Obama said, "This is a day that would not be denied." The memorial opened on August 22, 2011, 15 years after Congress approved it in 1996 and 82 years after the famed civil rights leader was born in 1929. Located strategically between the Lincoln and Jefferson memorials and adjacent to the FDR Memorial, the crescent-shaped King Memorial sits on a 4-acre site on the curved bank of the Tidal Basin. There are two main ways to enter the memorial. From West Basin Drive, walk through a center walkway cut out of a huge boulder, the *Mountain of Despair*. From the Tidal Basin entrance, a 28-foot-tall granite structure shows a likeness of King looking out toward Jefferson's statue. King's words explain the symbolism of the mountain and stone: "With this faith, we will be able to hew out of the mountain of despair a stone of hope." Chinese sculptor Lei Yixin carved the centerpiece stone; his design won the commission among more than

900 entries in an international competition. Fittingly, Yixin first read about King's "I Have a Dream" speech at age 10 while visiting the Lincoln Memorial. The themes of democracy, justice, hope, and love are reflected through quotes on the south and north walls and the *Stone of Hope*. The quotes reflect King's speeches, sermons, and writings from 1955 through 1968. Waterfalls in the memorial reflect King's use of the biblical quote: "Let justice roll down like waters and righteousness like a mighty stream." ✉ *1964 Independence Ave. SW, The Mall* ☎ *202/426–6841* ⊕ *www.nps. gov/mlkm* 🎫 *Free* Ⓜ *Smithsonian.*

Museum of the Bible

HISTORY MUSEUM | Seven floors encompassing more than 430,000 square feet are all dedicated to the history, narrative, and impact of the Bible on the world. The *IllumiNations* exhibit displays Bibles in more than 2,000 languages, and visitors can touch, read, and explore them and other illuminated manuscripts. The museum includes exhibits focused on modern films, speakers, fashion, and technology to tell the story of the Bible's continuing influence today. Here you can also see the papyrus featuring early copies of the New Testament, biblically inspired designer clothing, and even Elvis Presley's Bible. Stop by the Manna restaurant for biblically themed foods and other Mediterranean-inspired meals. ✉ *400 4th St. SW, The Mall* ☎ *866/430–6682* ⊕ *www.museumofthebible.org* 🎫 *$25* Ⓜ *Smithsonian.*

★ National Archives Museum

HISTORY MUSEUM | **FAMILY** | Monument, museum, and the nation's memory, the National Archives, headquartered in a grand marble edifice on Constitution Avenue, preserves more than 13 billion paper records dating from as far back as 1774, more than 40 million photographs, and billions of recent electronic records. The National Archives and Records Administration is charged with preserving and archiving the most historically significant U.S. government records at its centers nationwide and in presidential libraries. Admission is free, but reservations are recommended during the busy summer months and cost a nonrefundable $1. Head to ⊕ *recreation.gov* at least six weeks in advance of your visit.

Charters of Freedom—the Declaration of Independence, the Constitution, and the Bill of Rights—are the star attractions. They are housed in the archives' cathedral-like rotunda, each on a marble platform and surrounded by argon gas within cases that have gold-plated titanium frames and bulletproof protective glass.

On display at the entrance to the David M. Rubenstein Gallery's *Records of Rights* exhibit is a 1297 Magna Carta, the document of English common law whose language inspired the Constitution. This Magna Carta, one of four remaining originals, sets the stage for interactive exhibits that trace the civil rights struggles of African Americans, women, and immigrants. Highlights include the discharge papers of an enslaved person who fought in the Revolutionary War to gain his freedom; the mark-up copy of the 1964 Civil Rights Act; and letters to the president from children who questioned segregation.

The Public Vaults convey the sense of going deep into the stacks. You can find records that give a glimpse into federal investigations, from the Lincoln assassination to Watergate. Watch films of flying saucers, used as evidence in congressional UFO hearings, and listen to the Nuremberg trials or Congress debating Prohibition. Reservations to visit the archives are highly recommended; those for guided tours or timed-visit entries

Continued on page 74

THE MALL
AMERICA'S TOWN GREEN

It could be said that the Mall—the heart of almost every visitor's trip to Washington—has influenced life in the U.S. more than any other expanse of lawn. The Mall is a picnicking park, a jogging path, and an outdoor stage for festivals and fireworks. People come here from around the globe to tour the illustrious Smithsonian museums, celebrate special events, or rally to make the world a better place.

The AIDS Memorial Quilt on the Mall in 1996.

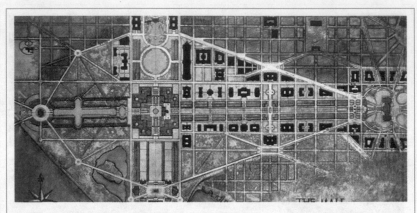

McMillan Plan for the Mall, Washington, D.C., 1902

FROM TRASH HEAP TO TOURIST ATTRACTION: A BRIEF HISTORY OF THE MALL

Even before becoming the birthplace of American political protest, the Mall was a hotly contested piece of real estate. More than a century of setbacks and debate resulted not in Pierre L'Enfant's vision of a house-lined boulevard, but rather the premier green space you see today.

In 1791, Pierre Charles L'Enfant designed Washington, D.C., with a mile-long Grand Avenue running west from the Congress building. According to his plan, the boulevard would be lined with homes for statesmen and open green spaces, including a central garden bordered by a dense grove of trees.

L'Enfant's grandiose plan took more than 100 years to become a reality. By 1850, the area we now know as the Mall had not become a park, but was used instead as a storage area for lumber, firewood, and trash. With President Fillmore's permission, a group of businessmen hired landscape designer Andrew Jackson Downing to plan a national park featuring natural-style gardening. Sadly, Downing was killed in 1852, and his plan was never fully implemented.

Despite this setback, progress continued. The first Smithsonian museum on the Mall, the National Museum (now the Arts and Industries Building),

opened to the public in 1881, and after 35 years of construction, the Washington Monument was completed in 1884.

A victory for the Mall occurred in 1901, when the Senate Park Commission, or McMillan Commission, was created to redesign the Mall as the city's ceremonial center. The McMillan plan embraced L'Enfant's vision of formal, public spaces and civic art, but replaced his Grand Avenue with a 300-foot expanse of grass bordered by American elms. It also called for cultural and educational institutions to line the Mall. Finally, a modified version of L'Enfant's great open space would become a reality.

The National Park Service assumed management of the Mall in 1933. In the latter half of the twentieth century and into the twenty-first, new museums and monuments have opened on the Mall to create the public gathering place, tourist attraction, and tribute to our nation's heroes that we know today.

Top, Martin Luther King Jr. delivers his "I Have a Dream" speech. Center, Vietnam War Veterans protest. Bottom, Million Man March.

HISTORIC RALLIES ON THE MALL

1894: Coxey's Army, a group of unemployed workers from Ohio, stage the first-ever protest march on Washington.

1939: Contralto Marian Anderson gives an Easter Sunday concert on the grounds of the Lincoln Memorial after the Daughters of the American Revolution bar her from performing at their headquarters.

1963: The Lincoln Memorial is the site of Martin Luther King Jr.'s inspirational I Have a Dream speech.

1971: The Vietnam Veterans Against the War camp out on the Mall to persuade Congress to end military actions in Southeast Asia.

1972: The first Earth Day is celebrated on April 22.

1987: The AIDS Memorial Quilt is displayed for the first time in its entirety. It returns to the Mall in 1988, 1989, 1992, and 1996.

1995: Nearly 400,000 African-American men fill the Mall, from the Capitol to the Washington Monument, during the Million Man March.

2009: The inauguration of President Barack Obama brings a record two million onlookers to the Mall.

2017: The Women's March on January 21, 2017, the day after President Donald Trump's inauguration, was the largest single-day protest in U.S. history.

WHAT ABOUT THE MONUMENTS?

Visitors often confuse the Mall with the similarly named National Mall. The Mall is the expanse of lawn between 3rd and 14th Streets, while the National Mall is the national park that spans from the Capitol to the Potomac, including the Mall, the monuments, and the Tidal Basin. To reach the monuments, head west from the Mall or south from the White House and be prepared for a long walk. To visit all the monuments in one day requires marathon-level stamina and good walking shoes. You're better off choosing your top priorities. Better may be to take a guided coach tour, or one at night.

TOP 15 THINGS
TO DO ON THE MALL

1. Ride the old-fashioned carousel in front of the Smithsonian Castle.

2. Watch the fireworks on the Fourth of July.

3. See the original Spirit of St. Louis, and then learn how things fly at the National Air and Space Museum.

4. Gross out your friends at the Natural History Museum's Insect Zoo.

5. Gawk at Dorothy's ruby slippers, Julia Child's kitchen, Abraham Lincoln's top hat, and Lewis and Clark's compass at the American History Museum.

6. Twirl around the ice skating rink in the National Gallery of Art's sculpture garden.

7. View astonishing wooden masks at the Museum of African Art.

8. Taste North, South, and Central American dishes at the National Museum of the American Indian's Mitsitam Café.

9. Exercise your First Amendment rights by joining a rally or protest.

10. Peek at the many-armed and elephant-headed statues of Hindu gods at the Sackler Gallery.

11. Pose with sculptures by Auguste Rodin and Henry Moore at the Hirshhorn Sculpture Garden.

12. Learn how to make money—literally—at the Bureau of Engraving and Printing.

13. Follow the lives of the people who lived and died in Nazi Germany at the Holocaust Memorial Museum.

14. Visit the newest museum, the National Museum of African American History and Culture.

15. Picnic and people-watch on the lawn after a hard day of sightseeing.

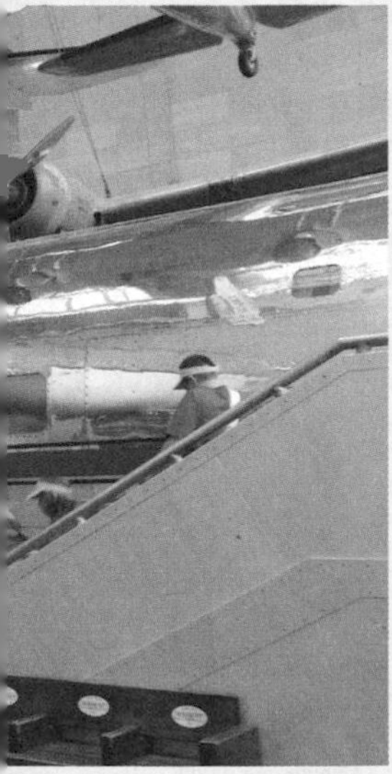

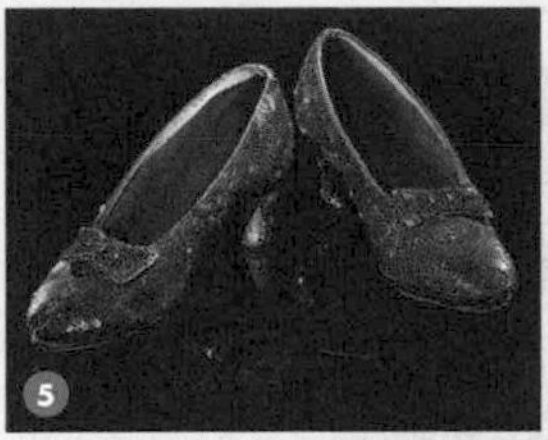
5

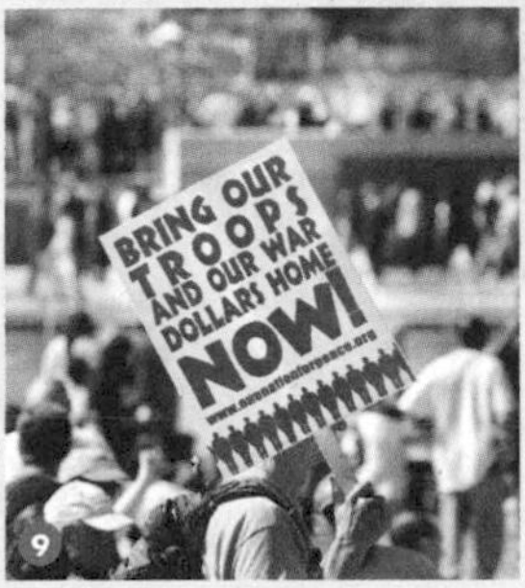
BRING OUR
TROOPS
AND OUR WAR
DOLLARS HOME
NOW!
9

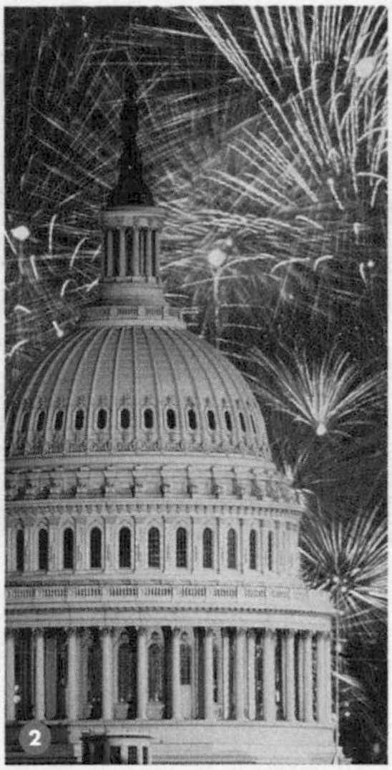
2

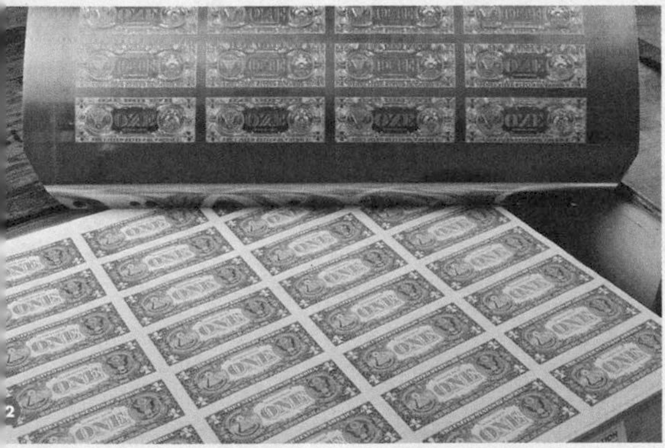

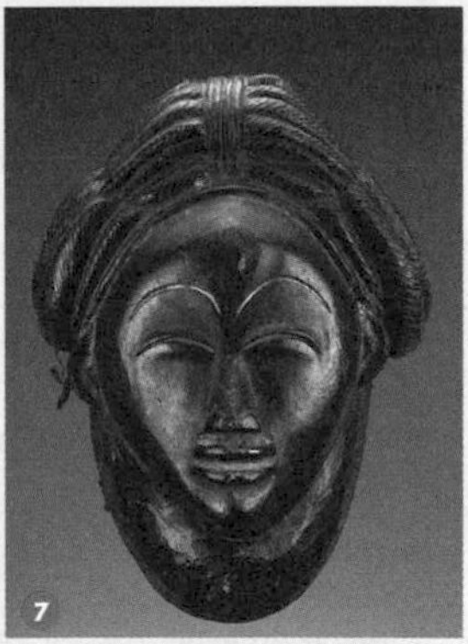
7

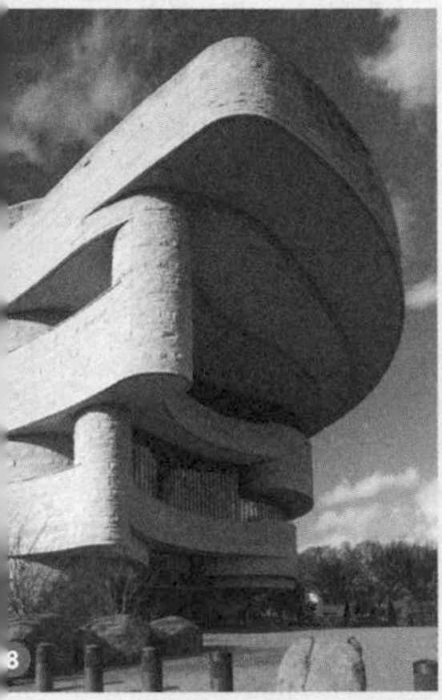
8

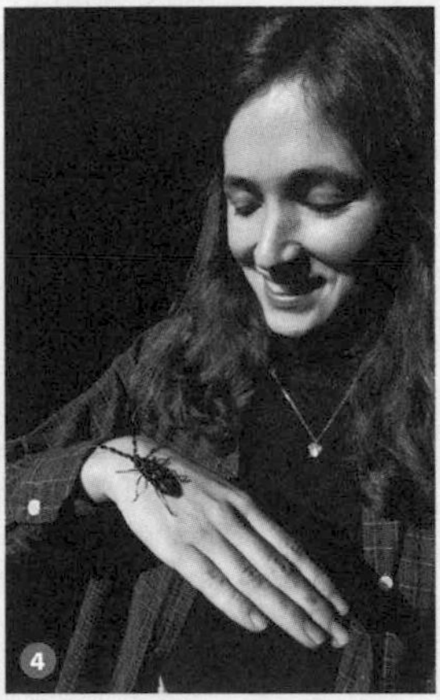
4

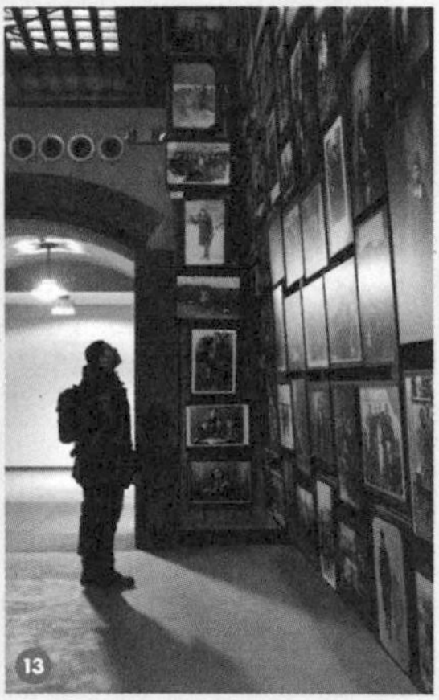
13

VISITING THE MUSEUMS ON THE MALL

MAKE THE MOST OF YOUR TIME

With 13 museums spread out along 11 city blocks, you can't expect to see everything in one day. Few people have the stamina for more than half a day of museum- or gallery-hopping at a time; children definitely don't. To avoid mental and physical exhaustion, try to devote at least two days to the Mall and use these itineraries to make the best use of your time.

Historical Appeal: For a day devoted to history and culture, start with the **National Archives,** grabbing lunch at its café. After refueling, the next stop is the **National Museum of American History.** Or, visit the **National Museum of the American Indian** or the **United States Holocaust Memorial Museum.** It takes planning, but a trip to the **National Museum of African American History and Culture** is a don't-miss experience.

Art Start: To fill a day with paintings and sculptures, begin at the **National Gallery of Art.** Enjoy the museum's sculptures while you dine in the garden's outdoor café. You'll find a second sculpture garden directly across the Mall at the **Hirshhorn.** If you like the avant-garde, visit the Hirshhorn's indoor galleries; for a cosmopolitan collection of Asian and African art and artifacts, head instead to the **Sackler Gallery** and **Museum of African Art.**

Taking the Kids: The most kid-friendly museum of them all, the **National Air and Space Museum** is a must-see for the young and young-at-heart. There's only fast food in the museum, but the **Museum of the American Indian** next door has healthier options. If your young bunch can handle two museums in a day, cross the lawn to the **Natural History Museum.** This itinerary works well for science buffs, too.

THE BEST IN A DAY

Got one day and want to see the best of the Smithsonian? Start at the **Air and Space Museum,** then skip to the side-by-side **Natural History** and **American History Museums.** Picnic on the Mall or hit the museum cafeterias.

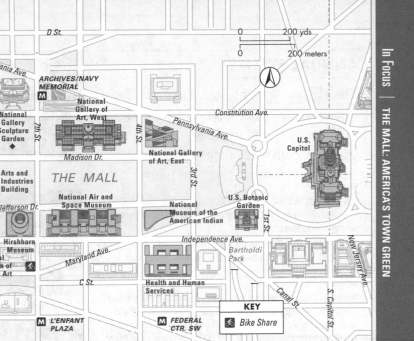

KEY

🚲 Bike Share

NOT ANOTHER HOT DOG! A Survival Guide to Eating Well on the Mall

Even locals wonder where to grab a decent bite to eat when touring the Smithsonian Museums. Hot dogs, soft pretzels, and ice cream from a cart don't make for a nutritious lunch. On a weekday, the streets north of Constitution Avenue offer easy-to-find lunch spots, but virtually all are closed on weekends.

Here are some places for better dining by the Mall, though several require a few blocks' walk.

On the Fly food carts offer eco-friendly, often organic snacks. Find one by the Sackler Gallery.

Museum of the American Indian: The Mitsitam Café—the name means "let's eat" in the language of the Delaware and Piscataway people—is one of the best museum cafeterias on the Mall. Food stations serve native-inspired sandwiches, entrees, soups, and desserts from five regions of the western hemisphere.

Pavilion Café: Located in the **National Gallery's Sculpture Garden,** this eatery offers indoor and outdoor seating with views of the artwork and fountain/ice rink outside. The menu includes salads, sandwiches, and pizzas. You'll also find more food options inside the National Gallery.

Pennsylvania Avenue SE: If lunchtime finds you on the east end of the Mall, head past the Capitol to Pennsylvania Avenue SE. Between Second and Fourth Streets, you'll find plenty of pubs, cafés, and sandwich shops. It's a bit of a hike, but well worth the shoe leather.

National Museum of Natural History: Three high-quality restaurants focus on healthy, seasonal food, drinks, and desserts.

National Museum of African American History and Culture: Sweet Home Cafe, which serves diverse regional American cuisine, is among the best places to eat on the Mall.

ANNUAL EVENTS

The Mall's spacious lawn is ideal for all kinds of outdoor festivals. These annual events are local favorites and definitely worth a stop if you're in town while they're happening.

St. Patrick's Day Parade

WINTER

Ice Skating: Whirl and twirl at the outdoor ice rink in the National Gallery of Art's Sculpture Garden. *Mid-November through mid-March.*

St. Patrick's Day Parade: Dancers, bands, and bagpipes celebrate all things Irish along Constitution Avenue. *Mid-March.*

SPRING

National Cherry Blossom Festival: When the cherry trees burst into bloom, you know that spring has arrived. Fly a kite, watch a parade, and learn about Japanese culture in a setting sprinkled with pink and white flowers. *Late March through early April.*

Cherry Blossom Festival

SUMMER

Smithsonian Folklife Festival: Performers, cooks, farmers, and craftsmen demonstrate cultural traditions from around the world. *Around July 4.*

Independence Day: What better place to celebrate the birth of our nation than in the capital city? Enjoy concerts and parades on the Mall, then watch the fireworks explode over the Washington Monument. *July 4.*

Screen on the Green: Film favorites are shown on a gigantic movie screen on Monday nights. Bring a blanket and picnic dinner to better enjoy the warm summer evenings. *Mid-July through mid-August.*

Smithsonian Folklife Festival

FALL

Black Family Reunion: D.C. celebrates African-American family values. Pavilions showcase businesses owned by African-Americans and events and performances feature black entertainers, celebrities, and experts. *September.*

National Book Festival: Meet your favorite author in person at the Library of Congress' annual literary festival. Over 70 writers and illustrators participate in readings, live interviews, and events for kids. *September.*

Marine Corps Marathon: The "Marathon of the Monuments" starts in Virginia but winds its way around the entire National Mall. It's as fun to cheer as it is to run. *Late October.*

Independence Day Reenactment

Marine Corps Marathon

PLANNING YOUR VISIT

National Cherry Blossom Festival Parade

KEEP IN MIND

■ All of the museums on the Mall are free to the public.

■ Since September 11, 2001 security has increased, and visitors will need to go through screenings and bag checks, which create long lines during peak tourist season.

■ Two museums require timed-entry passes: the Holocaust Museum from March through August, and the Bureau of Printing and Engraving. If you've got a jam-packed day planned, it's best to get your tickets early in the morning or in advance.

GETTING HERE AND AROUND

Metro: You can access the Mall from several Metro stations. On the Blue and Orange lines, the Federal Triangle stop is convenient to the Natural History and American History museums, and the Smithsonian stop is close to the Holocaust Memorial Museum and Sackler Gallery. On the Yellow and Green lines, Archives/Navy Memorial takes you to the National Gallery of Art. The L'Enfant Plaza stop, accessible from the Blue, Orange, Yellow, and Green lines, is the best exit for the Hirshhorn and Air and Space Museum.

Bus: Walking from the Holocaust Memorial Museum to the National Gallery of Art is quite a trek. Many visitors take advantage of the D.C. Circulator National Mall Route buses that cost just $1 and run daily.

Car: Parking is hard to find along the Mall. You can find private parking garages north of the Mall in the Downtown area, where you'll have to pay to leave your car. If you're willing to walk, limited free parking is available on Ohio Drive SW near the Jefferson Memorial and East Potomac Park.

HELP, THERE'S A PROTEST ON THE MALL!

Since the 1890s, protesters have gathered on the Mall to make their opinions known. If you're not in a rallying mood, you don't have to let First Amendment activities prevent you from visiting the Smithsonian museums or enjoying a visit to the Mall.

■ **Use the back door:** All of the Smithsonian museums have entrances on Constitution or Independence Avenues, which do not border the Mall's lawn. Use these doors to gain admission without crossing the Mall itself.

■ **Know you're protected:** The Mall is a national park, just like Yosemite or Yellowstone. The National Park Service has a responsibility to visitors to make sure they can safely view park attractions. To this end, demonstrators are often required to keep main streets open.

■ **Avoid the crowds:** Even the biggest rallies don't cover the entire National Mall. If the crowd is by the Capitol, head west to visit the Lincoln Memorial. If protestors are gathered around the Washington Monument, visit the Jefferson Memorial on the opposite side of the Tidal Basin. There's plenty to see.

should be made at least six weeks in advance. ✉ *Constitution Ave., between 7th and 9th Sts., Washington* ☎ *866/272–6272, 877/444–6777 tours and reservations* ⊕ *www.archives.gov* ▦ *Free; $1 fee for reservations* Ⓜ *Archives–Navy Memorial–Penn Quarter.*

★ **National Gallery of Art, East Building**

ART GALLERY | The East Building opened in 1978 in response to the changing needs of the National Gallery, mainly to house a growing collection of modern and contemporary art. The building itself is a modern masterpiece. The site's trapezoidal shape prompted architect I.M. Pei's dramatic approach: two interlocking spaces shaped like triangles provide room for a library, galleries, auditoriums, and administrative offices. Inside the ax-blade-like southwest corner, a colorful, 76-foot-long Alexander Calder mobile dominates the sunlight atrium. Visitors can view a dynamic 500-piece collection of photography, paintings, sculpture, works on paper, and media arts in thought-provoking chronological, thematic, and stylistic arrangements.

Highlights include galleries devoted to Mark Rothko's giant, glowing canvases; Barnett Newman's 14 stark black, gray, and white canvas paintings from *The Stations of the Cross, 1958–1966;* and several colorful and whimsical Alexander Calder mobiles and sculptures. You can't miss Katharina Fritsch's *Hahn/Cock, 2013,* a tall blue rooster that appears to stand guard over the street and federal buildings from the roof terrace, which also offers views of the Capitol. The upper-level gallery showcases modern art from 1910 to 1980, including masterpieces by Constantin Brancusi, Marcel Duchamp, Sam Gilliam, Henri Matisse, Joan Miró, Piet Mondrian, Jackson Pollock, and Andy Warhol. Ground-level galleries are devoted to American art from 1900 to 1950, including pieces by

George Bellows, Edward Hopper, Georgia O'Keeffe, Charles Sheeler, and Alfred Stieglitz. The concourse level is reserved for rotating special exhibitions.

The East Building Shop is on the concourse level, and the Terrace Café looks out over the atrium from the upper level. You can access an audio tour on your mobile device, and docent-led tours are available most days. Check the website for times and themes. ✉ *Constitution Ave., between 3rd and 4th Sts. NW, The Mall* ☎ *202/737–4215* ⊕ *www.nga.gov* ▦ *Free* Ⓜ *Archives–Navy Memorial–Penn Quarter.*

★ **National Gallery of Art, West Building**

ART MUSEUM | The two buildings of the National Gallery hold one of the world's foremost art collections, with paintings, sculptures, and graphics dating from the 13th to the 21st centuries. Opened in 1941, the museum was a gift to the nation from Secretary of the Treasury Andrew W. Mellon. The rotunda, with marble columns surrounding a fountain, sets the stage for the masterpieces on display in more than 100 galleries.

Ginevra de' Benci, the only painting by Leonardo da Vinci on display in the Americas, is the centerpiece of the collection's comprehensive survey of Italian Renaissance paintings and sculpture. Rembrandt van Rijn and Johannes Vermeer, masters of painting light, anchor the magnificent collection of Dutch and Flemish works. The 19th-century French Galleries house gorgeous impressionist masterworks by such superstars as Vincent van Gogh, Paul Cézanne, Claude Monet, Auguste Renoir, and Edgar Degas.

Walk beneath flowering trees in the sculpture garden on the Mall between 7th and 9th Streets. Granite walkways guide you through a shaded landscape featuring works from the gallery's

TO WORK AND FIGH
OWN LIKE WATER AND
A MIGHTY STREAM

KING JR 1955

I CHERISH MY OWN FREEDOM DEARLY,
BUT I CARE EVEN MORE FOR YOUR FREEDO

NELSON MANDELA 1990

Did You Know?

You'll find a collection
of the country's most
moving and power-
ful exhibits within the
National Museum of
African American History
and Culture. If neces-
sary, you can emotion-
ally recharge within the
Reflection Room, where
a glass structure called
the oculus allows light in
from above, and a water-
fall effect offers a quiet
space for contemplation.

growing collection and loans for special exhibitions.

There are many free docent-led tours every day, and a recorded tour of highlights of the collection is available free on the main floor adjacent to the rotunda. The Information Room maintains a database of more than 1,700 works of art from the collection. ⊠ *4th St. and Constitution Ave. NW, The Mall* ☏ *202/737–4215* ⊕ *www.nga.gov* ⊠ *Free* Ⓜ *Archives–Navy Memorial–Penn Quarter.*

★ **National Museum of African American History and Culture**

HISTORY MUSEUM | One of the most popular museums in the nation's capital is perhaps best summed up with a quote by founding director Lonnie Bunch: "The African American experience is the lens through which we understand what it is to be an American." The museum serves as that lens, thanks to more than a dozen exhibitions that display nearly 3,000 historical artifacts, documents, photographs, memorabilia, and media.

The building's structure resembles nothing else on the Mall. The shape of its bronze-color corona was inspired by a Nigerian artist's carving, prominently displayed in one of the galleries. The corona's filigree design was patterned after railings made by enslaved 19th-century craftsmen. The museum's three tiers are hung at the same angle as the Washington Monument's capstone (it makes for a dramatic photo). Powerful quotes from African Americans are strategically placed throughout the space. The museum divides into two parts: 60% is underground, and the remaining 40% is aboveground. Lower-level exhibits showcase a somber and wrenching historical timeline from slavery through civil rights. Aboveground galleries celebrate the cultural contributions of African Americans.

To best experience this museum, start at the underground Concourse History Galleries. Here you'll see a portion of a slave ship that broke apart off Cape Town, South Africa, in a 1794 shipwreck that drowned 212 people; a 19th-century, Edisto Island, South Carolina, slave cabin that was occupied until 1980; the original casket of 14-year-old Emmett Till, who was murdered in Mississippi in 1955 for allegedly flirting with a white woman; a railcar with its very different first-class and "colored" sections; and a biplane used to train the Tuskegee Airmen who fought in WWII. Also on the main concourse level is the 350-seat Oprah Winfrey Theater, which hosts musical performances, lectures and discussions, film presentations, and other programming. The Center for African American Media Arts is on the second floor, where visitors can research their families in a genealogy center.

The third- and fourth-floor galleries explore the achievements of African Americans. Highlights include sports memorabilia like Jesse Owens's cleats, Michael Jordan's 1996 jersey, Joe Louis's gloves, Muhammad Ali's robe, Gabby Douglas's leotard, and nine Olympic medals won by Carl Lewis. Other of the collection's many gems include a lobby card from the 1967 movie *Guess Who's Coming to Dinner,* Louis Armstrong's trumpet, Michael Jackson's sequined jacket, and the jacket and skirt that Marian Anderson wore when she performed a 1939 concert from the Lincoln Memorial.

You must have a timed pass to enter the museum. Same-day timed passes are available online daily beginning at 6:30 am. A limited number of walk-up passes are given out weekdays beginning at 1 pm, but they go fast. Download the NMAAHC mobile app to further enhance your visiting experience. ⊠ *1400 Constitution Ave. NW, The Mall* ⊹ *14th and Constitution Ave. NW* ☏ *202/633–1000, 844/750–3012 for timed-entry passes only* ⊕ *www.nmaahc.si.edu* ⊠ *Free*

🔊 *Must reserve in advance online*
Ⓜ *Smithsonian or Federal Triangle.*

National Museum of Asian Art

ART MUSEUM | Formerly known as the Freer/Sackler, the National Museum of Asian Art formally rebranded to its current name in 2019. The museum opened in 1923 as the Freer Gallery of Art to showcase the collection of American industrialist and donor Charles Lang Freer. The Arthur M. Sackler Gallery was built next door in 1987 after Sackler donated 1,000 objects and $4 million for a museum to house them. With its commitment to preserving Asian art, the museum counts more than 44,000 items in its permanent collection hailing from countries like China, Japan, and Korea, also expanding into Southwest and Southeast Asia. One of the most popular rooms is the Peacock Room, which has dazzled guests at the Freer Gallery of Art since 1923. Initially designed by artist James McNeill Whistler to showcase a Chinese blue-and-white porcelain collection, the room marries its avian motif with a striking use of color inspired by the arts of East Asia. ✉ *1050 Independence Ave. SW, The Mall* ☎ *202/633–4880* ⊕ *www.asia.si.edu* ✉ *Free* Ⓜ *Smithsonian.*

★ National Museum of the American Indian

HISTORY MUSEUM | FAMILY | Visually and conceptually, the National Museum of the American Indian stands apart from the other cultural institutions on the Mall. The exterior, clad in Minnesota limestone, evokes a sense that wind and water carved the building. Inside, four floors of galleries cover 10,000 years of history of the western hemisphere's indigenous tribes. Nevertheless, only a small portion of the museum's holdings are on display at any time. Live music, dance, theater, and storytelling are central to experiencing this museum. Tribal groups stage performances in the Rasmuson Theater and sunlit Potomac atrium. *Americans,* a permanent exhibition, reveals how Native Americans exist in unexpected ways in the history, pop culture, and identity of the United States. Other rotating exhibits explore the many indigenous groups throughout the Americas.

Visit between 11 and 2 on a sunny day to see the Potomac atrium awash in rainbows created by the light refracted through the southern wall's prisms, which are aligned to show the passage of time with specific patterns marking the equinoxes and solstices. The museum's family-friendly imagiNATIONS Activity Center includes hands-on activities throughout the year. For those looking for a quick bite, check out their award-winning restaurant, whose menu takes you from Canada to South America, exploring the diverse cuisine of the indigenous groups. It's a favorite lunch spot for many locals working in the area. ✉ *4th St. and Independence Ave. SW, The Mall* ☎ *202/633–1000* ⊕ *www.americanindian. si.edu* ✉ *Free* Ⓜ *L'Enfant Plaza.*

Old Post Office Pavilion

CLOCK | Although the building is now the Waldorf Astoria Washington, D.C., the Old Post Office Tower (within the hotel) is still open for public tours through the National Park Service. The building, a symbol of the modern American spirit when constructed in 1899, was the first government tower to have its own electric power plant. Now, tourists can see the 360-degree view from the top of the tower, the second-tallest building in D.C. Tours (from 9 am to 4 pm daily) are free, but tour guests must enter through a specified entrance for the general public. ✉ *Trump International Hotel, 1100 Pennsylvania Ave. NW, The Mall* ☎ *202/289–4224* ⊕ *www.nps.gov/thingstodo/old-post-office-tower.htm* ✉ *Free* 🕐 *Closed Christmas and Thanksgiving* Ⓜ *Federal Triangle.*

3

The National Mall

Ronald Reagan Building and International Trade Center

GOVERNMENT BUILDING | At more than 3 million square feet, this is the largest federal building in Washington and the only property dedicated to government and private entities. A blend of classical and modern architecture, the center welcomes over a million visitors annually and is officially the World Trade Center, Washington, D.C. The Ronald Reagan Building, which hosts special events throughout the year, is home to a permanent art collection—one that includes a section of the Berlin Wall—and the Woodrow Wilson Presidential Memorial Exhibit and Learning Center. It's also a popular place to get married, thanks to its fantastic views over the city. If you're hungry, pick up something from one of the 17 eateries in the spacious food court on the concourse level. In summer, check out Live!, a free concert series, performed daily (weekdays) from noon to 1:30. A farmers' market takes over the plaza on Friday from 11 pm to 3 pm from spring to fall. ⊠ *1300 Pennsylvania Ave. NW, Washington* ☎ *202/312–1300* ⊕ *www. rrbitc.com* ✉ *Free* Ⓜ *Federal Triangle.*

Smithsonian Castle Information Center

ART MUSEUM | The original home of the Smithsonian Institution is an excellent first stop on the Mall to help you get your bearings and plan your exploration of the museums. Built of red sandstone, this Medieval Revival–style building, better known as the "Castle," was designed by James Renwick Jr., the architect of St. Patrick's Cathedral in New York City. Although British scientist and founder James Smithson never visited America, his will stipulated that, should his nephew, Henry James Hungerford, die without an heir, Smithson's entire fortune would go to the United States, "to found at Washington, under the name of the Smithsonian Institution, an establishment for the increase and diffusion of knowledge." The museums on the Mall are the Smithsonian's most visible example of this ideal, but the organization also sponsors traveling exhibitions and maintains research posts in the Chesapeake Bay area and the tropics of Panama.

A 10-minute video gives an overview of the museums and the National Zoo, and *The Smithsonian Institution: America's Treasure Chest* exhibition features objects representing all the museums, revealing the breadth and depth of the collections. James Smithson's crypt is in a small chapel-like room here. The Castle also has *Views from the Tall Tower*—an exhibit demonstrating how the Washington skyline has changed since 1863—a good café, brochures in several languages, and a museum store. Kids appreciate the historic carousel at the north entrance; at the south entrance, you'll find the beautifully manicured Haupt Garden and copper-domed kiosk called the S. Dillon Ripley Center, which houses the Discovery Theater (delightful and affordable live, family-oriented shows on selected weekday mornings—usually geared for kids 2–12—are held here). ⊠ *1000 Jefferson Dr. SW, The Mall* ☎ *202/633–1000* ⊕ *www.si.edu* ✉ *Free* Ⓜ *Smithsonian.*

★ Smithsonian National Air and Space Museum

SCIENCE MUSEUM | FAMILY | This is one of the country's most visited museums. Between its two buildings, it attracts 6 to 8 million people annually to the world's largest collection of historic aircraft and spacecraft. More than 20 galleries tell the story of aviation—from the earliest human attempts at flight to supersonic jets and spacecraft. The museum reopened in late 2022 after undergoing a series of renovations, and more are currently in the works. The renovated museum features hundreds of new artifacts to the building, such as the WR-3 air racer built by Neal Loving, the first African

American certified to race airplanes; a T-38 flown by Jackie Cochran, the first woman to break the sound barrier; and Sean Tucker's custom-built aerobatic biplane, and the Aviation Specialties Unlimited Challenger III.

Buy IMAX theater and planetarium tickets up to two weeks in advance or as soon as you arrive (times and prices vary); then tour the museum. Museum tickets are free, but visitors must reserve tickets in advance for every member of their group, regardless of age.

The three-story museum store is the largest (and one of the best) in all the Smithsonian museums. You'll find souvenirs, clothing, books and movies, kites, and many collector items. It is closed during construction, but two satellite stores are available. ✉ *Independence Ave. at 6th St. SW, The Mall* ☎ *202/633–1000, 866/868–7774 movie information* ⊕ *www.airandspace.si.edu* ✉ *Free; IMAX or planetarium are an extra fee, must reserve in advance* Ⓜ *Smithsonian.*

Smithsonian National Museum of African Art

ART MUSEUM | FAMILY | This unique underground building houses stunning galleries, a library, photographic archives, and educational facilities dedicated to collecting, conserving, and studying Africa's arts and culture from different perspectives. The rotating exhibits illuminate African visual arts, including sculpture, textiles, photography, archaeology, and modern art. *Currents: Water in African Art* showcases the power of art through pieces like intricately carved wooden masks and figures paying tribute to water spirits and deities. The museum's educational programs for children and adults include films with contemporary perspectives on African life, storytelling programs, and festivals, including Community Day. The hands-on workshops, such as traditional basket weaving, bring Africa's oral and cultural traditions to life. Workshops and demonstrations by African and African American artists offer a chance to meet and talk to practicing artists. ✉ *950 Independence Ave. SW, The Mall* ☎ *202/633–4600* ⊕ *africa.si.edu* ✉ *Free* Ⓜ *Smithsonian.*

★ Smithsonian National Museum of American History

HISTORY MUSEUM | FAMILY | The 3 million artifacts and archival materials in the country's largest American history museum explore America's cultural, political, and scientific past. The centerpiece of the Star-Spangled Banner gallery is the banner that in 1814 was hoisted to show that Fort McHenry had survived 25 hours of British rocket attacks and inspired Francis Scott Key to write the lyrics that became the national anthem. Exhibits also explore food history, innovation, and the different cultural groups in the United States. ✉ *Constitution Ave. and 14th St. NW, The Mall* ☎ *202/633–1000* ⊕ *www.americanhistory.si.edu* ✉ *Free* Ⓜ *Smithsonian or Federal Triangle.*

Smithsonian National Museum of Natural History

HISTORY MUSEUM | FAMILY | One of the world's great natural history museums offers 20 exhibition halls—including a fully renovated Dinosaur and Fossil Hall, filled with not only fossils, but also glittering gems, creepy-crawly insects, and other natural wonders. There are more than 145 million specimens in the collection. Marvel at the enormous African bush elephant, which greets you in the rotunda, and learn about elephant behavior and conservation efforts. Discover Q?rius, a state-of-the-art discovery space for all ages featuring 6,000 objects, on-site experts, and an array of digital tools that focus on the natural world. Walk among hundreds of live butterflies in the Butterfly Pavilion ($8 adults, $7 children/seniors). Check out giant millipedes and furry tarantulas in the O. Orkin Insect

Zoo (don't miss the daily live tarantula feedings). See perfectly preserved giant squids, a jaw-dropping replica of a whale, and the ecosystem of a living coral reef in the Sant Ocean Hall. Watch as paleo-biologists study some of the museum's collection of 46 million fossils, which includes the nation's *T. rex* found in Montana in 1988. ⊠ *Constitution Ave. and 10th St. NW, The Mall* ☎ *202/633–1000* ⊕ *www.mnh.si.edu* ✉ *Free; Butterfly Pavilion $8 (free Tues.)* ⚴ *Must reserve for Butterfly Pavilion in advance* Ⓜ *Smithsonian or Federal Triangle.*

★ Thomas Jefferson Memorial

MONUMENT | In the 1930s, Congress decided to build a monument to Thomas Jefferson as prominent as the Washington and Lincoln memorials. Workers scooped and moved tons of the river bottom to create dry land for the spot due south of the White House. Jefferson had always admired the Pantheon in Rome, so the memorial's architect, John Russell Pope, drew on it for inspiration. His finished work was dedicated on April 13, 1943, the bicentennial of Jefferson's birth. The bronze statue of Jefferson stands on a 6-foot granite pedestal. Surrounding the statue are his writings about freedom, which have since come under scrutiny for their inherent hypocrisy, as Jefferson owned many enslaved people in his lifetime. The Smithsonian National Museum of African American History and Culture delves into Jefferson's transgressions in its Monticello exhibit *Paradox of Liberty.* ⊠ *Tidal Basin, south bank, off Ohio Dr. SW, The Mall* ☎ *202/426–6841* ⊕ *www.nps.gov/thje* ✉ *Free* Ⓜ *Smithsonian.*

★ Tidal Basin

NATURE SIGHT | **FAMILY** | The Tidal Basin, a partially man-made reservoir between the Potomac and the Washington Channel, is part of West Potomac Park, adjacent to the Mall. It's the setting for memorials to Thomas Jefferson, Franklin Delano Roosevelt, Martin Luther King Jr., and George Mason. Two gargoyles on the sides of the Inlet Bridge can be seen as you walk along the sidewalk hugging the basin. The inside walls of the bridge also feature two other sculptures: bronze, human-headed fish that once spouted water from their mouths. Sculptor Constantin Sephralis, who also worked on the National Cathedral, made them in honor of John Fish, the park's chief, who was retiring at the time. Once you cross the bridge, continue along the Tidal Basin to the right. This route is incredibly scenic when the famous cherry trees are in bloom. The trees, a gift from the Japanese during the administration of William Howard Taft, are the Tidal Basin's most iconic feature beyond the memorials. ⊠ *Bordered by Independence and Maine Aves., The Mall* ⊕ *www.nps.gov/articles/dctidalbasin.htm* ✉ *Free* Ⓜ *Smithsonian.*

★ United States Holocaust Memorial Museum

HISTORY MUSEUM | This museum asks you to consider how the Holocaust was made possible by the choices of individuals, institutions, and governments and what lessons they hold for us today. The permanent exhibition, *The Holocaust,* tells the stories of the millions of Jews, Romani, Jehovah's Witnesses, homosexuals, political prisoners, the mentally ill, and others killed by the Nazis between 1933 and 1945. The exhibitions are detailed and sometimes graphic but powerful.

Upon arrival, you are issued an "identity card" containing biographical information on a real person from the Holocaust. As you move through the museum, you read sequential updates on your card. In the early exhibits, Hitler's rise to power and the spread of European anti-Semitism are thoroughly documented with films of Nazi rallies, posters, newspaper articles, and recordings of Hitler's speeches, immersing you in the world that led to

The United States Holocaust Memorial Museum is the country's official memorial remembering those lost in the Holocaust.

the Holocaust. Exhibits include footage of scientific experiments done on Jews, artifacts such as a freight car like those used to transport Jews to concentration camps, and oral testimonies from Auschwitz survivors. Rotating exhibitions highlight how genocide is still a real worldwide issue, featuring the stories of current survivors.

After this powerful experience, the *Hall of Remembrance*, filled with candles, provides a much-needed space for quiet reflection.

Tickets are required for entry into the museum. For up-to-date information about hours, tickets, and exhibitions, visit their website. ⊠ *100 Raoul Wallenberg Pl. SW, at 14th St. SW, The Mall* ☎ *202/488–0400, 800/400–9373 for tickets* ⊕ *www.ushmm.org* 🎟 *Free; $1 per ticket service fee for advance online reservations* ⊙ *Closed Sun.* ⚜ *Must reserve in advance* Ⓜ *Smithsonian.*

★ **Vietnam Veterans Memorial**
MONUMENT | "The Wall," as it's commonly called, is one of the most visited sites in Washington, D.C. The names of more than 58,000 Americans who died in the Vietnam War are etched in its black granite panels, creating a powerful memorial. Jan Scruggs, a corporal who served in Vietnam, conceived the memorial, and Maya Lin, a then-21-year-old architecture student at Yale, designed the landmark.

Thousands of offerings are left on the wall each year; many people leave flowers, and others leave soldiers' uniform items or letters of thanks.

In 1984, Frederick Hart's statue of three soldiers and a flagpole was erected to the south of the wall, with the goal of winning over veterans who considered the memorial a "black gash of shame." In 2004, a plaque was added to honor veterans who died after the war as a direct result of injuries in Vietnam, but who fall outside Department of Defense guidelines for remembrance at the wall.

DC's Famed Cherry Blossoms

The first batch of ornamental cherry trees arrived from Japan in 1909 but were infected with insects and fungus, and the Department of Agriculture ordered them destroyed. A diplomatic crisis was averted when the United States politely asked the Japanese for another batch, and in 1912, First Lady Helen Taft planted the first tree. The wife of the Japanese ambassador, Viscountess Chinda, planted the second one. There are 3,750 total trees around the Tidal Basin, some of which are considered original from 1912.

The trees are now the centerpiece of Washington's three-week **National Cherry Blossom Festival**, held each spring since 1935. The festivities begin with the lighting of a ceremonial Japanese lantern, which rests on the north shore of the Tidal Basin, not far from where the first tree was planted. The celebration has grown over the years to include concerts, a running race, a kite festival, and a parade. The trees bloom for about 12 days in late March or early April, with locals and travelers anxiously waiting for the blooms. When winter does not release its grip, the parade and festival take place without the presence of blossoms.

The Vietnam Women's Memorial was dedicated in 1993. Glenna Goodacre's bronze sculpture depicts two women caring for a wounded soldier while a third kneels nearby; eight trees around the plaza commemorate the eight women in the military who died in Vietnam. Names on the wall are ordered by the date of death. To find a name, consult the alphabetical lists at either end of the wall. You can get assistance locating a name at the white kiosk with the brown roof near the entrance. At the wall, rangers and volunteers wearing yellow caps can look up the names and supply you with paper and pencils for making rubbings. Every name on the memorial is preceded (on the west wall) or followed (on the east wall) by a symbol designating status. A diamond indicates "KIA." A plus sign (found by a small percentage of names) indicates "MIA." ✉ *Constitution Gardens, 23rd St. NW and Constitution Ave. NW, The Mall* ☎ *202/426–6841* ⊕ *www.nps. gov/vive* 🖪 *Free* Ⓜ *Foggy Bottom–GWU.*

★ Washington Monument

MONUMENT | FAMILY | The top of the Washington Monument is perhaps the best, most breathtaking place to see the city and get a good idea of its layout.

The 555-foot, 5⅛-inch monument, which punctuates the capital like a huge exclamation point, was part of Pierre L'Enfant's plan for Washington, but his intended location proved to be so marshy that the structure was moved 100 yards southeast. Construction began in 1848 and continued until 1884. Upon completion, the monument was the world's tallest structure and weighed more than 81,000 tons. Six years into construction, members of the anti-Catholic Know-Nothing Party stole and smashed a block of marble donated by Pope Pius IX. This action, combined with funding shortages and the onset of the Civil War, brought construction to a halt. After the war, building finally resumed, and though the new marble came from the same Maryland quarry as the old, it was taken

Every Memorial Day, thousands flock to the Vietnam Veterans Memorial to pay their respects to those lost in the conflict.

from a different stratum with a slightly different shade. Inserted into the walls of the monument are 193 memorial stones from around the world. The monument reopened in spring 2019 after an elevator modernization project. Up to six tickets can be requested for just $1 per person at ⊕ *recreation.gov*. ✉ *15th St. NW, between Constitution Ave. NW and Independence Ave. SW, The Mall* ☎ *202/426–6841, 877/444–6777 for reservations* ⊕ *www.nps.gov/wamo* ✉ *Free, but $1 if reserved in advance* Ⓜ *Smithsonian.*

West Potomac Park

CITY PARK | FAMILY | Between the Potomac and the Tidal Basin, this park is known for its flowering cherry trees, which bloom for two weeks in late March or early April. It also includes a slew of memorials, including those honoring Abraham Lincoln, Martin Luther King Jr., Franklin Delano Roosevelt, Thomas Jefferson, and George Mason, as well as the World War II, Korean War, and Vietnam War Veterans memorials. It's a nice place to play ball, picnic, or just relax while admiring the water views. ✉ *Bounded by Constitution Ave., 17th St., and Independence Ave., The Mall* ⊕ *www.npca.org.*

★ World War II Memorial

MONUMENT | This symmetrically designed monument, in a parklike setting between the Washington Monument and Lincoln Memorial, honors the 16 million Americans who served in the armed forces, the more than 400,000 who died, and all who supported the war effort at home. An imposing circle of 56 granite pillars, each bearing a bronze wreath, represents the United States and its territories of 1941–45. Four bronze eagles, a bronze garland, and two 43-foot-tall arches inscribed with "Atlantic" and "Pacific," representing victory on both fronts, surround the large circular plaza. The roar of the water comes from the Rainbow Pool, here since the 1920s and renovated to form the memorial's centerpiece. There are also two fountains and two waterfalls. The Field of Stars, a wall of more than 4,000 gold stars, commemorates more than 400,000 Americans who lost their lives in the war. Bas-relief panels depict women in the military, medics, the bond drive, and V-J Day, all telling the story of how World War II affected Americans daily. ✉ *17th St. SW and Home Front Dr. SW, between Independence Ave. SW and Constitution Ave. NW, The Mall* ☎ *202/426–6841* 🌐 *www.nps.gov/nwwm* 🎟 *Free* [M] *Smithsonian.*

🍴 Restaurants

The dining experiences at the museums along the National Mall have significantly improved throughout the years. The National Museum of African American History and Culture, the National Gallery of Art, and the National Museum of the American Indian are leading the charge for dining experiences at the Mall. For a quick bite, stop at one of the many food trucks sprinkled around the Mall or head over to L'Enfant Plaza for fast food. If you are on the northeastern end of the Mall, walking north to the Penn Quarter may be closer. You will find a wide selection of restaurants, from fast casual to Michelin-starred eateries.

★ Dolcezza at the Hirshhorn

$ | **CONTEMPORARY** | Popular D.C. coffee and gelato chain Dolcezza set up shop at the Hirshhorn Museum a few years ago, making it the only locally owned café in a Smithsonian museum. On a hot summer day, cool down with a heaping cone of their beloved pistachio gelato or recharge with a strong espresso. **Known for:** stunning design; small-batch gelatos; specialty coffees. [$] *Average main: $10* ✉ *Independence Ave. SW and 7th St. SW, The Mall* ☎ *202/333–4646* 🌐 *www.hirshhorn.si.edu/dolcezza-at-hirshhorn* [M] *L'Enfant Plaza.*

Garden Café

$ | **AMERICAN** | After marveling at the masterpieces in the National Gallery West Building, sit down in a lovely open courtyard, complete with a fountain. The Garden Café features a selection of sandwiches, pastries, and snacks, and it is also an excellent spot for a coffee with its perfectly crafted lattes. **Known for:** high-end coffee beverages; a lovely setting; fast casual sandwiches. [$] *Average main: $12* ✉ *National Gallery of Art, West Building, 6th and Constitution Ave. NW, The Mall* ✣ *Enter at 6th St.* ☎ *202/842–6716, 202/712–7453 reservations* 🌐 *www.nga.gov/visit/cafes/garden-cafe.html* ⏲ *No dinner* [M] *Archives–Navy Memorial–Penn Quarter.*

★ Mitsitam Native Foods Cafe

$$ | **AMERICAN** | The food stations here offer both traditional and contemporary Native American dishes from throughout the western hemisphere. The culinary team offers seasonal menus from five regional cuisines, expanding the museum experience with insight into indigenous culinary history, cooking techniques, ingredients, and flavors. **Known for:** seasonal cuisine from different indigenous cultures; fry bread and corn totopos; bison burger. [$] *Average main: $17* ✉ *National Museum of the American Indian, 4th St. SW and Independence Ave. SW, The Mall* ☎ *202/868–7774* 🌐 *www.mitsitamcafe.com* ⏲ *No dinner* [M] *Federal Center SW.*

★ Pavilion Café

$ | **CAFÉ** | At the edge of the National Gallery of Art's Sculpture Garden, you can sidle up to the counter and feast your eyes on the menu items before deciding what you'll order at this casual, sit-down eatery. From pastries to anything-but-ordinary salads to hot and cold sandwiches with Southwestern or East Asian flavors, you'll have an array of choices. **Known**

for: summer barbecue during Jazz in the Garden; boozy beverages during winter; pastries made fresh in-house. $ *Average main: $13* ⊠ *National Gallery Sculpture Garden, Constitution Ave. NW and 7th St., The Mall* ✦ *At far end of National Gallery of Art Sculpture Garden* ☎ *202/289–3361* ⊕ *www.nga.gov/visit/cafes/pavilion-cafe.html* ☾ *No dinner* Ⓜ *Archives–Navy Memorial–Penn Quarter or L'Enfant Plaza.*

Rice Bar

$ | **KOREAN** | If you need to take a break from a museum without straying too far, check out Rice Bar, a fast-casual Korean restaurant located a block away from the Air and Space museum. The restaurant specializes in bibimbap, a Korean rice bowl dish usually topped with savory marinated beef, *gochujang* (chili pepper paste), and sautéed vegetables. **Known for:** plenty of vegetarian options; savory bulgogi bowls; fast service. $ *Average main: $13* ⊠ *600 Maryland Ave SW, The Mall* ☎ *292/554–2041* ⊕ *www.ricebardc.com* ☾ *Closed weekends* Ⓜ *L'Enfant Plaza.*

★ Sweet Home Café

$ | **AMERICAN** | Sweet Home Café, located at the National Museum of African American History and Culture, continues to be on the top of the list of best museum restaurants in Washington, D.C. since opening in 2016. It offers traditional and authentic dishes that rotate based on the seasons. **Known for:** regional food stations; local ingredients; rotating seasonal menus. $ *Average main: $14* ⊠ *National Museum of African American History, 1400 Constitution Ave. NW, The Mall* ☎ *202/633–6174* ⊕ *www.nmaahc.si.edu* ☾ *No dinner* Ⓜ *Smithsonian or Federal Triangle.*

🛏 Hotels

Most hotels within walking distance of the National Mall are found in nearby neighborhoods such as Penn Quarter, Downtown D.C., and the newly developed Southwest Wharf area. Nevertheless, there are a handful of properties located alongside the Mall. From a family-friendly Holiday Inn to a freshly renovated Waldorf Astoria, there is something for every taste.

Hilton Washington DC National Mall

$ | **HOTEL** | **FAMILY** | A stay at this LEED-certified hotel puts you close to the National Mall, with spectacular river and monument views from certain rooms—all of which have floor-to-ceiling windows. **Pros:** short walk to Smithsonian; nice pool and fitness center; pet-friendly. **Cons:** must use valet parking; area is sleepy at night; few nearby restaurants. $ *Rooms from: $199* ⊠ *480 L'Enfant Plaza SW, The Mall* ☎ *202/484–1000, 202/869–1952* ⊕ *www.hilton.com* ⇱ *372 rooms* ⦿ *Free Breakfast* Ⓜ *L'Enfant Plaza.*

Holiday Inn Washington Capitol-National Mall

$ | **HOTEL** | **FAMILY** | One block from the National Air and Space Museum, this family-friendly hotel is in an excellent location for those bound for the Smithsonian museums. **Pros:** rooftop pool and large deck area; kids eat for free; close to the best museums in town. **Cons:** limited dining options nearby; not much going on in the neighborhood at night; self-parking is available but expensive. $ *Rooms from: $159* ⊠ *550 C St. SW, The Mall* ☎ *202/479–4000* ⊕ *www.hicapitoldc.com* ⇱ *536 rooms* ⦿ *No Meals* Ⓜ *L'Enfant Plaza.*

3

The National Mall

Waldorf Astoria Washington, DC

$$$$ | **HOTEL** | The recently renovated and rebranded Waldorf Astoria makes for a great choice if searching for a luxury property near the National Mall. **Pros:** great fine dining options; one block away from the Mall; gorgeous views from clock tower. **Cons:** not much to do after-hours; valet parking only; expensive. $ *Rooms from: $500* ⊠ *1100 Pennsylvania Ave. NW, The Mall* ☎ *202/695–1100* ⊕ *www.hilton.com/en/hotels/dcawa-wa-waldorf-astoria-washington-dc* ⤳ *263 rooms* Ⓜ *Federal Triangle.*

🎭 Performing Arts

CONCERTS

Armed Forces Concert Series

MUSIC | FAMILY | In a Washington tradition, bands from the four branches of the armed services perform from June through August on weekday evenings on the U.S. Capitol West Front steps. Concerts usually include marches, patriotic numbers, and some classical music. Setup begins at 4 pm, with the concerts starting at 8 pm, but look out for scheduling changes or notices on individual bands' social media accounts. Food is permitted, but glass bottles and alcohol are not allowed. ⊠ *U.S. Capitol, Capitol Hill* ⊕ *www.aoc.gov/what-we-do/programs-ceremonies/concerts* 🎫 *Free* Ⓜ *Capitol S.*

★ National Gallery of Art Concert Series

CONCERTS | FAMILY | On Fridays from 5 to 8:30 pm from mid-May through the end of August, jazz groups from all over the country perform to packed crowds at the Pavilion Café in the Sculpture Garden. Listeners dip their feet in the fountain, sip sangria, and let the week wash away. Make sure to arrive early to snag a spot. ⊠ *6th St. and Constitution Ave. NW, The Mall* ☎ *202/842–6941* ⊕ *www.nga.gov*

🎫 *Free* Ⓜ *Archives–Navy Memorial–Penn Quarter.*

★ Smithsonian Institution Concert Series

CONCERTS | Throughout the year, the Smithsonian Associates sponsor programs that offer everything from big brass to Cajun zydeco bands; all events require tickets, and locations vary. The Smithsonian's annual summer Folklife Festival, held on the Mall, highlights several different cultures' cuisine, crafts, and day-to-day life. ⊠ *1000 Jefferson Dr. SW, The Mall* ☎ *202/357–2700, 202/633–1000 recording, 202/357–3030 Smithsonian Associates* ⊕ *www.si.edu* Ⓜ *Smithsonian.*

FILM

National Gallery of Art Film Series

FILM | Free classic, international, and art films—from Steven Spielberg's first feature-length film, *Duel,* to Béla Tarr's *Macbeth,* filmed inside a Budapest castle—as well as classic video art, are usually shown in this museum's large auditorium each weekend. Sometimes films complement the exhibitions. For more information, pick up a film calendar at the museum or visit their website. Guests must register in advance. ⊠ *National Gallery of Art, East Bldg., Constitution Ave. between 3rd and 4th Sts. NW, The Mall* ☎ *202/842–6799* ⊕ *www.nga. gov* Ⓜ *Archives–Navy Memorial–Penn Quarter.*

🛍 Shopping

Museum Store in the United States Holocaust Memorial Museum

SOUVENIRS | This unique museum store offers a slew of books, including memoirs, to further your knowledge of the Holocaust and the plight of other persecuted peoples throughout history. It's also a great place to buy mezuzah scrolls, menorahs, kiddush cups, seder plates, and other Jewish heritage items, as well as secular souvenirs. ✉ *100 Raoul Wallenberg Pl. SW, The Mall* ☎ *202/488–0400* ⊕ *www.ushmm.org/museum-shop* Ⓜ *Smithsonian.*

National Air and Space Museum Store

SOUVENIRS | FAMILY | One of the world's most visited museums has a newly renovated gift shop. You can find plenty of toys and games, plenty of souvenirs, including T-shirts and totes, and an extensive selection of *Star Wars* and *Star Trek* licensed products for sci-fi fans. The store showcases a wide assortment of kites and books; you can also find flight suits for both the young and young at heart. Space pens that work upside down and freeze-dried "astronaut" ice cream are best sellers. ✉ *Independence Ave. and 6th St. SW, The Mall* ☎ *202/633–4510* ⊕ *airandspace.si.edu* Ⓜ *L'Enfant Plaza or Smithsonian.*

★ National Archives Store and Gift Shop

CRAFTS | In a town full of museum shops, this store at the National Archives Museum stands out, with exclusive memorabilia, reproductions, apparel, books, gifts, and plenty of Founding Fathers' gear that let you own a piece of history. Authentic-looking copies of the Constitution and other historical documents are printed in Pennsylvania. The popular "red tape" paperweights are crafted in the United States with real red tape that once bound government documents: hence the phrase "cut through the red tape." Other popular products feature Rosie the Riveter and Stars and Stripes bags; Teddy in Hat items for young children; and apparel featuring Franklin, Hamilton, and other Founding Fathers. Throughout the store, interactive games associated with special exhibits provide entertaining insight on U.S. and even personal history: enter your last name into the computer to see how many Americans share your name and where in the country they live. ✉ *Constitution Ave. NW between 7th and 9th Sts., Washington* ☎ *202/357–5271* ⊕ *www.nationalarchivesstore.org* Ⓜ *Archives–Navy Memorial–Penn Quarter.*

★ National Gallery of Art West Building Shop

SOUVENIRS | This expansive shop, one of four in the National Gallery, offers a vast series of books, paper goods, apparel, fine jewelry, and knickknacks that all relate to or reflect the museum's art collection. Prices range from little over a dollar for a pencil to well over $100 for designer jewelry. Some items were created by the museum; the rest are specially curated and sourced by museum buyers. Grab a Monet umbrella on a rainy day or some Andy Warhol pop-art crayons to pair with your favorite artist-themed coloring book. Here you can find whatever you need—and many things you didn't even realize you wanted. ✉ *National Gallery of Art, West Bldg., 4th St. and Constitution Ave. NW, The Mall* ☎ *800/697–9350* ⊕ *shop.nga.gov* Ⓜ *Archives–Navy Memorial–Penn Quarter or L'Enfant Plaza.*

Store of the National Museum of African American History and Culture

SOUVENIRS | After traversing the many floors of the museum, shop here for a mug, a T-shirt, or a model of the museum building to commemorate your trip. Some of the merchandise is traditional and/or handmade, including sweetgrass baskets, jewelry, scarves, and even food items. You can also find the award-winning Sweet Home Café Cookbook featuring recipes of the Sweet Home Café at the shop. ✉ *National Museum of African American History and Culture, 1400 Constitution Ave. NW, The Mall* ☎ *844/750–3012* ⊕ *nmaahc.si.edu* Ⓜ *Smithsonian.*

USDA Farmers' Market

MARKET | Blueberry popcorn, anyone? On Fridays from May through October, 9 am to 2 pm, you can pick up fresh fruits, vegetables, bread, and other baked goods (and that flavored popcorn) across from the Smithsonian Metro station. Appropriately, the market is in the parking lot of the U.S. Department of Agriculture building. ⊠ *12th St. and Independence Ave. SW, The Mall* ☎ *202/708–0082* ⊕ *www. usda.gov/farmersmarket* Ⓜ *Smithsonian.*

Chapter 4

DOWNTOWN

WITH CHINATOWN AND PENN QUARTER

Updated by
Jessica van Dop DeJesus

👁 Sights	🍴 Restaurants	🛏 Hotels	🛍 Shopping	🍸 Nightlife
★★★★☆	★★★★☆	★★★★☆	★★★☆☆	★★★★☆

NEIGHBORHOOD SNAPSHOT

GREAT EXPERIENCES DOWNTOWN

CityCenterDC: This high-end, open-air shopping district also has some good restaurants including the acclaimed Fig & Olive.

International Spy Museum: Indulge your inner James Bond with a look at 007's Aston Martin, along with more serious toys used by real spies.

Dining: Penn Quarter is one of the city's best areas for dining, where José Andrés opened his first restaurant, Jaleo.

National Portrait Gallery and Smithsonian American Art Museum: These masterful museums have something for everyone.

Theater District: Performances ranging from Shakespeare to contemporary dramas and musicals are mounted in Penn Quarter's theaters.

GETTING HERE

The Federal Triangle or Archives–Navy Memorial–Penn Quarter Metro stops serve the government buildings along Pennsylvania Avenue. Gallery Place–Chinatown gives direct access to the Capital One Arena, Chinatown, and the nearby museums. Judiciary Square has its own stop, and Metro Center is the best choice for The National Theatre and Penn Quarter. Bus routes crisscross the area as well. Street parking on nights and weekends is limited.

PLANNING YOUR TIME

Downtown is densely packed with major attractions. Art lovers might focus on the **National Portrait Gallery** and **Smithsonian American Art Museum;** history buffs will enjoy the **National Building Museum;** families with kids may prefer the **International Spy Museum.** Come back at night to enjoy the many restaurants.

SAFETY

Downtown's blocks of government and office buildings still become a bit of a ghost town when the working day is done, but a revitalized Penn Quarter remains energized late into the evenings, especially when there are events at the Capital One Arena.

Downtown, Penn Quarter, and Chinatown are a tale of three cities. Washington, D.C.'s Downtown is staid, compact, and home to some beautiful hotels, though pretty quiet at night. Chinatown and the Penn Quarter jump at night with many shops, bars, and restaurants.

The Capital One Arena sits in the middle, and the nights are supercharged when the Capitals, Mystics, or Wizards are in town. The Capital One Arena is also where many world-class performers host their concerts. There are plenty of museums and theaters for the culture aficionados, such as the National Portrait Gallery and the Warner Theatre.

👁 Sights

The Downtown D.C. area is a one-stop shop for arts, culture, and great restaurants. From the historic Ford's Theatre to the National Building Museum, there are plenty of offerings throughout the neighborhood. The area is also easy to navigate—whether by foot, bicycle, or public transportation.

American Veterans Disabled for Life Memorial
MILITARY SIGHT | Located on a 2.4-acre tract adjacent to the National Mall and within full view of the U.S. Capitol, this memorial illustrates the journey of veterans with disabilities, from injury and healing to rediscovery of purpose. The plaza, with a star-shaped fountain and low triangular reflecting pool, features bronze sculptures, glass panels, and granite walls engraved with quotations from 18 veterans describing their experiences. With its single ceremonial flame, the fountain is the focal point, a powerful icon expressing water's healing, cleansing properties and the enlightenment, power, and eternal nature of fire. The needs of those with disabilities are front and center in the memorial's design. The low fountain can easily be surveyed by someone in a wheelchair, numerous benches in front of text panels, and hidden metal bars placed strategically to help visitors who need assistance to sit or stand. Designed by Michael Vergason Landscape Architects, of Alexandria, Virginia, the memorial is a fitting reminder of the cost of human conflict. ✉ 150 Washington Ave. SW, Downtown ⊕ www.avdlm.org ⌨ Free Ⓜ Federal Center SW.

Capital One Arena
SPORTS VENUE | One of the country's top-grossing sports and entertainment venues, the 20,000-seat Capital One Arena averages more than 200 events each year and has helped to turn the surrounding area into the most vibrant part of Downtown, where you'll find several of the city's best restaurants. Many restaurants nearby offer pre-theater menus and happy hour offerings before a big event. Sporting events include hockey featuring

Kids love the International Spy Museum, where they can adopt a cover identity and try out being a spy in an interactive mission.

the Stanley Cup champion, Washington Capitals; basketball with the Washington Wizards, Washington Mystics, and Georgetown Hoyas; and figure-skating events. Artists like Bruce Springsteen, Jennifer Lopez, Beyoncé, Mariah Carey, Paul McCartney, U2, and Lady Gaga have performed there. Outside, street musicians of all kinds and styles add to the experience. The Metro station is directly below the arena. ✉ *601 F St. NW, between 6th and 7th Sts., Chinatown* ☎ *202/628–3200* ⊕ *www.capitalonearena.com* Ⓜ *Gallery Pl.–Chinatown.*

★ **Ford's Theatre**

PERFORMANCE VENUE | FAMILY | April 14, 1865, shocked the nation: during a performance of *Our American Cousin,* John Wilkes Booth entered the Presidential Box at Ford's Theatre and shot Abraham Lincoln in the back of the head; the president died later that night. This blocklong, Lincoln-centered, cultural campus encompasses four sites. In the Museum, you'll explore Lincoln's presidency and Civil War milestones and learn about

Booth and those who joined his conspiracy to topple the government. Artifacts include Lincoln's clothing and weapons used by Booth. The Theatre, which stages performances throughout the year, is restored to look as it did when Lincoln attended, including the Presidential Box draped with flags as it was on the night he was shot. In the restored Petersen House, you can see the room where Lincoln died and the parlor where his wife, Mary Todd Lincoln, waited in anguish through the night.

The centerpiece of the Aftermaths Exhibits at the Center for Education and Leadership is a jaw-dropping, three-story tower of 6,800 books written about Lincoln. Visitors take an immersive step back in time, entering a 19th-century street scene where they find a reproduction of Lincoln's funeral train car and see its route to Springfield, Illinois. Visitors also learn about the chase for John Wilkes Booth and his co-conspirators' trial, and they interact with an "escape map" to the tobacco barn where Booth was captured. Exhibits also explore the fate of Lincoln's family after his death, explain the milestones of Reconstruction, and describe Lincoln's legacy and enduring impact on U.S. and world leaders. A visit ends with a multiscreen video wall that shows how Lincoln's ideas resonate today.

Visits to Ford's Theatre require a free, timed-entry ticket. Same-day tickets are available at the theater box office beginning at 8:30 am on a first-come, first-served basis. You can also reserve tickets in advance at ⊕ *www.fords.org* with a $3 fee per ticket. ⊠ *511 10th St. NW, Downtown* ☎ *202/347–4833* ⊕ *www.fords.org* ⊠ *Free; ticket reservations $3* ⩘ *Reserve tickets in advance* Ⓜ *Metro Center or Gallery Pl.–Chinatown.*

★ **International Spy Museum**
OTHER MUSEUM | FAMILY | Fun for kids of all ages, the museum displays the world's largest collection of spy artifacts. *The Secret History of History* takes you behind the headlines, from Moses' use of spies in Canaan and Abraham Lincoln's employment of the Pinkerton National Detective Agency as a full-scale secret service in the Civil War to the birth of WWII's OSS. Check out the spy gadgets, weapons, vehicles, and disguises, and then see if you have what it takes to be a spy in *School for Spies. Exquisitely Evil: 50 Years of Bond Villains* brings you face-to-face with 007's archenemies. *Operation Spy,* a one-hour immersive experience, works like a live-action game, dropping you in the middle of a foreign intelligence mission. Each step—which includes decrypting secret audio files, a car chase, and interrogating a suspect agent—is taken from actual intelligence operations. Advance tickets (purchased at the museum or on its website) are highly recommended. All tickets are date- and time-specific. Tickets are most likely available on Tuesday, Wednesday, and Thursday or daily after 2 pm. ⊠ *700 L'Enfant Plaza, Downtown* ☎ *202/393–7798* ⊕ *www.spymuseum.org* ⊠ *Permanent exhibition $21; combo Museum and Operation $30 (when purchased online)* Ⓜ *L'Enfant Plaza.*

National Building Museum
OTHER MUSEUM | FAMILY | Architecture, design, landscaping, and urban planning are the themes of this museum, the nation's premier cultural organization devoted to the built environment. The open interior of the mammoth redbrick building is one of the city's great spaces and has been the site of many presidential inaugural balls. The eight central Corinthian columns are among the largest in the world, rising to a height of 75 feet. Although they resemble Siena marble, each comprises 70,000 bricks covered with plaster and painted. The long-term exhibition *House and Home* features a kaleidoscopic array of photographs, objects, models, and films that takes visitors on a tour of houses both surprising and familiar, through past and present, exploring American domestic life and residential architecture. The museum also offers a series of temporary hands-on exhibitions focusing on construction. Although geared towards children, people of all ages enjoy the experience. ⊠ *401 F St. NW, between 4th and 5th Sts., Downtown* ☎ *202/272–2448* ⊕ *www.nbm.org* ⊠ *$10 adults, $7 children 3–17. Entrance to Great Hall, shop, and café free* ☉ *Closed Tues. and Wed.* ⩘ *Advance tickets recommended* Ⓜ *Judiciary Sq. or Gallery Pl.–Chinatown.*

★ **National Geographic Museum**
OTHER MUSEUM | FAMILY | Founded in 1888, the National Geographic Society is best known for its magazine, and entering this welcoming, 13,000-square-foot exhibition space feels like stepping into its pages. The compact museum offers family-friendly interactive exhibitions delving into the historical, cultural, and scientific research that distinguishes *National Geographic* magazine. There are items from the permanent collections—cultural,

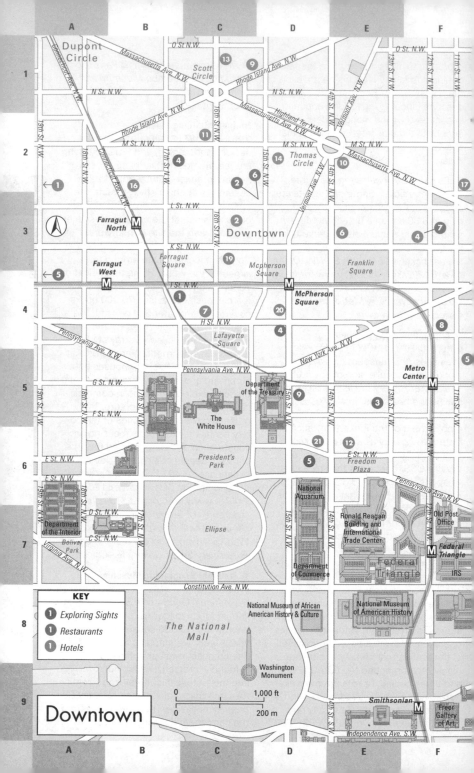

Sights ▼

1 American Veterans Disabled for Life Memorial **I9**
2 Ford's Theatre **G6**
3 International Spy Museum **G9**
4 National Geographic Museum **B2**
5 WWI Memorial/ Pershing Park **D6**

Restaurants ▼

1 Bombay Club **C4**
2 Dauphine's **C3**
3 District Taco **E5**
4 Joe's Seafood, Prime Steak & Stone Crab **D4**
5 Kaz Sushi Bistro **A4**
6 Little Chicken **C3**
7 Michele's **F3**
8 Modena **F4**
9 Old Ebbitt Grill **D5**
10 Stellina Pizzeria **I3**

Hotels ▼

1 AC Hotel Washington DC **A2**
2 Capital Hilton **C3**
3 Conrad Washington DC **G4**
4 Eaton DC **F3**
5 Grand Hyatt Washington **I5**
6 Hamilton Hotel **E3**
7 The Hay-Adams **C4**
8 Henley Park Hotel **G3**
9 Holiday Inn Central White House **C1**
10 Hotel Zena **E2**
11 The Jefferson **C2**
12 JW Marriott Washington, DC **E6**
13 Kimpton Hotel Banneker **C1**
14 The Madison Washington DC, A Hilton Hotel **D2**
15 Marriott Marquis Washington, D.C. **G3**
16 The Mayflower Hotel, Autograph Collection **B2**
17 Morrison-Clark Historic Inn **F2**
18 Renaissance Washington, D.C. Downtown Hotel **G4**
19 The St. Regis Washington, D.C. **C3**
20 Sofitel Washington, D.C. Lafayette Square **D4**
21 The Willard InterContinental **D6**

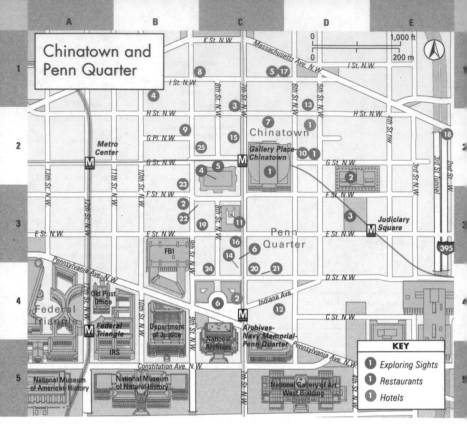

Chinatown and Penn Quarter

KEY

1 *Exploring Sights*

1 *Restaurants*

1 *Hotels*

Sights ▼

1 Capital One Arena C2
2 National Building
  Museum D2
3 National Law
  Enforcement
  Officers Memorial D3
4 National Portrait
  Gallery C2
5 Smithsonian American
  Art Museum C2
6 United States Navy
  Memorial C4

Restaurants ▼

1 Bantam King............. D2
2 Café Riggs B3
3 Cava...................... C2
4 Centrolina............... B1
5 Chaia C1
6 China Chilcano C3
7 Chinatown Garden....... C2
8 City Tap House C1
9 Cranes B2
10 Daikaya D2
11 Dirty Habit C3
12 Fiola C4
13 Full Kee D1
14 Hill Country
   Barbecue Market........ C4
15 HipCityVeg.............. C2
16 Jaleo C3
17 Karma Modern
   Indian D1
18 L'Ardente................. E2
19 minibar by José
   Andrés C3

20 Oyamel Cocina
   Mexicana................. C4
21 Rasika.................... C4
22 Shake Shack C3
23 The Smith B3
24 Teaism Penn Quarter.... C4
25 Zaytinya................. C2

Hotels ▼

1 Fairfield Inn & Suites
  Washington, DC/
  Downtown.............. D2
2 Kimpton Hotel Monaco
  Washington DC C3

historical, and scientific—and traveling exhibitions. It also has a virtual-reality theater experience. Nat Geo Nights—presentations by explorers with interactive activities, music, and food and drink specials—are held on the third Thursday of every month. The M Street Lobby photography exhibit, as well as the outdoor photo display around the perimeter of the museum, are free. ✉ *1145 17th St. NW, Downtown* ☎ *800/647–5463* ⊕ *www.nationalgeographic.org/society/ visit-our-museum* ⌨ *$20; M Street Photographic Gallery free* Ⓜ *Farragut N.*

National Law Enforcement Officers Memorial

OTHER MUSEUM | These 3-foot-high walls bear the names of more than 21,000 American police officers killed in the line of duty since 1791. On the third line of Panel 13W are the names of six officers killed by William Bonney, better known as Billy the Kid. J.D. Tippit, the Dallas policeman killed by Lee Harvey Oswald, is honored on the ninth line of Panel 63E. Other names include the 72 officers who died due to the events of 9/11. Directories here allow you to look up officers by name, date of death, state, and department. Call to arrange for a free tour. A National Law Enforcement Museum is in the works; until then, a small visitor center (✉ *400 7th St.*) has a computer for looking up names, a display on the history of law enforcement, and a small gift shop. ✉ *400 block of E St. NW, Penn Quarter* ☎ *202/737–3400* ⊕ *www.lawmemorial.org* ⌨ *Free* Ⓜ *Judiciary Sq.*

★ National Portrait Gallery

ART GALLERY | **FAMILY** | The intersection of art, biography, and history is illustrated here through images of people who have shaped U.S. history. There are prints, paintings, photos, and sculptures of subjects from George Washington to Madonna.

This museum shares the National Historic Landmark building Old Patent Office with the Smithsonian American

Art Museum. Built between 1836 and 1863 and praised by Walt Whitman as the "noblest of Washington buildings," it is deemed one of the country's best examples of Greek Revival architecture.

America's Presidents gallery, offering insights into the leaders—from George Washington until the present—is one of the most popular exhibitions. In this gallery, you'll see the only complete collection of presidential portraits outside the White House. Highlights include Gilbert Stuart's 1796 "Landsdowne" portrait of George Washington, Alexander Gardner's "cracked-plate" image of Abraham Lincoln from Lincoln's last formal portrait session before his assassination in 1865, a sculpture of Andrew Jackson on a horse, and political cartoonist Pat Oliphant's sculpture of George H.W. Bush playing horseshoes.

From portraits of World War II generals Eisenhower and Patton to Andy Warhol's *Time* magazine cover of Michael Jackson, the third-floor gallery, Twentieth-Century Americans, offers a vibrant tour of the people who shaped the country and culture of today. If seeing former first lady Michelle Obama is on your list, get to the gallery early, as this is a sought-after portrait.

There are free docent-led tours Saturdays and Sundays at noon and 2:30 pm. Check the website to confirm the times. At the Lunder Conservation Center on the third and fourth floors, you can watch conservators at work. ✉ *8th and F Sts. NW, Downtown* ☎ *202/633–8300* ⊕ *www.npg.si.edu* ⌨ *Free* Ⓜ *Gallery Pl.–Chinatown.*

Smithsonian American Art Museum

ART MUSEUM | From Childe Hassam's *The South Ledges, Appledore* to Nelson Shanks's *The Four Justices*, the Smithsonian American Art Museum features one of the world's largest collections of American art that spans more than four centuries. Over the past few decades,

Visitation has doubled at the National Portrait Gallery since Kehinde Wiley's portrait of President Barack Obama was unveiled in 2018. Amy Sherald's portrait of First Lady Michelle Obama is equally popular.

the museum has broadened its collection to include modern and contemporary art, too. Among the artists represented are Benny Andrews, José Campechi, Robert Indiana, Roy Lichtenstein, Isamu Noguchi, Robert Rauschenberg, Mickalene Thomas, and Charlie Willeto. The museum shares a National Historic Landmark building with the National Portrait Gallery.

On the first floor, you'll discover an enormous tinfoil altarpiece by James Hampton and more than 60 sculptures and paintings by Emery Blagdon that represent his thought-provoking and constantly changing *Healing Machine.* You can also experience American works from the 1930s, many created as part of New Deal programs. Highlights here include Marvin Beerbohm's *Automotive Industry,* Lily Furedi's *Subway,* and Edward Hopper's *Ryder's House.* Also on the first floor is the *Direct Carving* exhibit, which showcases artists who work directly on a piece of stone or wood.

Art from the Colonial period to the dawn of modernism is displayed throughout the galleries on the second floor. Discover masterpieces by Mary Cassatt, Frederick Carl Frieseke, Thomas Moran, Harriett Whitney Frishmuth, George Catlin, Albert Bierstadt, Winslow Homer, and John Singer Sargent, to name just a few.

The museum's third floor features modern and contemporary paintings and sculpture and the Watch This! gallery, where you can see a selection of works from the museum's media art and film collection. Highlights include Nam June Paik's billboard-size piece with 215 monitors showing video images from the Seoul Olympics, Korean folk rituals, and modern dance.

At any given time, many of the museum's holdings are in storage, but you can view more than 3,000 artworks in its Luce Foundation Center, a visible storage space on the third and fourth floors, where visitors can also watch the museum's conservators at work. Free docent-led tours of the museum are available every day at 12:30 and 2. ✉ *8th and G Sts. NW, Downtown* ☎ *202/633–7970*

🌐 *www.americanart.si.edu* 🎟 *Free* [M] *Gallery Pl.–Chinatown.*

United States Navy Memorial

MILITARY SIGHT | Although Pierre L'Enfant included a Navy Memorial in his plans for Washington, D.C., the memorial did not come to life until 1987. The main attraction here is a 100-foot-diameter granite map of the world, known as the Granite Sea. Fountains, benches, and six ship masts surround the map. The *Lone Sailor,* a 7-foot-tall statue, stands on the map in the Pacific Ocean between the United States and Japan. The Naval Heritage Center, next to the memorial in the Market Square East Building, displays videos and exhibits of uniforms, medals, and other aspects of navy life. If you've served in the navy, you can enter your service record into the log. Bronze relief panels on the Pennsylvania Avenue side of the memorial depict 26 scenes commemorating events in the nation's naval history and honoring naval communities. ✉ *701 Pennsylvania Ave. NW, Downtown* ☎ *202/737–2300* 🌐 *www.navymemorial.org* 🎟 *Free* [M] *Archives–Navy Memorial–Penn Quarter.*

WWI Memorial/Pershing Park

MILITARY SIGHT | In late 2014, Congress re-designated this quiet, sunken garden to honor General John J. "Black Jack" Pershing, the first—a century ago—to hold the title General of the Armies. An official unit of the National Park System, the memorial currently includes engravings on the stone walls recounting pivotal campaigns from World War I, when Pershing commanded the American Expeditionary Force and conducted other military exploits. Steps and small tables surround a fountain and duck pond, making for a pleasant midday respite. The park had a $46-million renovation of the memorial in 2021. ✉ *15th St. and Pennsylvania Ave., Downtown* 🌐 *www.nps.gov/articles/pershing-park.htm* [M] *McPherson Sq.*

🍴 Restaurants

Downtown D.C. has seen a growth in restaurant options in the past decade. Although the closings during the pandemic hit the neighborhood hard, new and exciting places have opened, offering various global cuisines and price points. From Michelin-starred restaurants to locally born fast-casual chains, there are plenty of options to satisfy a diverse palate. Long-standing neighborhood favorites were able to weather the restaurant crisis, adding new chefs and dishes to their menus.

★ Bantam King

$ | RAMEN | From the owners of Daikaya, Bantam King is another fun option for ramen in the Penn Quarter neighborhood. Chicken broth serves as the base of their flavorful ramen with noodles sourced from Sapporo, Japan. **Known for:** lively dining room; rich ramen bowls; fried chicken. [$] *Average main: $15* ✉ *501 G St. NW, Penn Quarter* ☎ *202/733–2612* 🌐 *bantamking.com* [M] *Chinatown.*

Bombay Club

$$ | INDIAN | One block from the White House, the beautiful Bombay Club serves classic and modern Indian fare in a refined setting. On the menu are unusual seafood specialties and a variety of vegetarian dishes, but the real standouts are the aromatic curries. **Known for:** great Indian curries; British colonial club vibe; upscale Sunday buffet brunch. [$] *Average main: $26* ✉ *815 Connecticut Ave. NW, Downtown* ☎ *202/659–3727* 🌐 *www.bombayclubdc.com* 🕒 *Closed Sun. No lunch Sat.* [M] *Farragut W.*

★ Café Riggs

$$ | BRASSERIE | FAMILY | This spacious restaurant is on the ground floor of the 130-year-old Riggs Bank Building, now known as the Riggs Hotel. The café boasts large Corinthian columns, original stone floors, a sky-high ceiling, and Palladian windows. **Known for:** raw bar; picturesque bar; luxury feel. [$] *Average* main: $26 ✉ 900 F St., Penn Quarter ⚓ Near Gallery Pl., heart of Penn Quarter ☎ 202/788–2800 ⊕ www.caferiggs.com Ⓜ Gallery Pl. Red and Yellow.

★ Cava

$ | **MEDITERRANEAN** | For those looking for a quick Mediterranean-inspired bite, Cava is a great option. Start with a base of grains, salads, or pita and top with a selection of proteins and savory dips and spreads such as hummus, tzatziki, spicy feta, and harissa. **Known for:** lunch on the go; affordable Mediterranean dishes; crazy feta sauce. Ⓢ Average main: $12 ✉ 707 H St. NW, Chinatown ⊕ cava.com Ⓜ Chinatown.

Centrolina

$$$ | **ITALIAN** | This bright, airy Italian osteria has an adjoining market and a daily changing menu that is all about locally sourced meats and produce and sustainable fish. Authentic and innovative with pasta and sauces made in-house, and the specials change regularly. **Known for:** innovative pasta dishes; daily changing menu; fun option in CityCenterDC development. Ⓢ Average main: $32 ✉ 974 Palmer Alley NW, Chinatown ⚓ Near convention center ☎ 202/898–2426 ⊕ centrolinadc.com ⊗ Closed Sun. Ⓜ Gallery Pl.–Chinatown.

★ Chaia

$ | **MEXICAN FUSION** | Chaia started its vegetarian taco fast-casual restaurant in Georgetown and has expanded its popular concept to Downtown D.C. Guests can choose from veggie tacos featuring braised mushrooms, kale and potato, roasted eggplant, and sweet potato hash. **Known for:** vegan options; vegetarian tacos; nice decor. Ⓢ Average main: $13 ✉ 615 I St. NW, Chinatown ☎ 202/290–1019 ⊕ www.chaiatacos.com ⊗ Closed Sun. Ⓜ Chinatown.

China Chilcano

$$ | **PERUVIAN** | The José Andrés formula is pleasantly familiar to D.C. diners who have visited his ever-growing empire of small-plate restaurants since Jaleo first opened in 1993. This hybrid of Peruvian and Chinese-Japanese styles, inspired by a 19th-century wave of migration to South America, is a popular spot amongst locals. **Known for:** part of chef José Andrés's empire; Peruvian-inspired shareable small plates; pisco fruit cocktails. Ⓢ Average main: $20 ✉ 418 7th St. NW, Penn Quarter ☎ 202/783–0941 ⊕ chinachilcano.com ⊗ No lunch weekdays Ⓜ Gallery Pl.–Chinatown.

Chinatown Garden

$$ | **CHINESE** | **FAMILY** | Sadly, D.C.'s Chinatown has lost many Chinese restaurants due to gentrification. Thankfully, China Garden still stands, offering the classics of American-Chinese cuisine such as General Tso's chicken, beef and broccoli, and fried rice. **Known for:** affordable Chinese food; vegeterian options; pagoda facade that you can't miss. Ⓢ Average main: $20 ✉ 618 H St. NW, Chinatown ☎ 202/737–8887 ⊕ chinatowngardendc.com Ⓜ Chinatown.

★ City Tap House

$$ | **AMERICAN** | **FAMILY** | This upscale gastropub chain just a block from the convention center offers more than 40 beers on tap and loads of bottles. The high ceilings, reclaimed wood walls, and copper bar give the large spot a warm, rustic feel. **Known for:** standard American pub fare; great selection of beers; communal tables and big-screen TVs. Ⓢ Average main: $22 ✉ 901 9th St. NW, Penn Quarter ☎ 202/733–5333 ⊕ pennquarter.citytap.com Ⓜ Gallery Pl.–Chinatown.

Cranes

$$$$ | **JAPANESE FUSION** | Cranes, a Michelin-starred restaurant at Penn Quarter is the brainchild of chef/owner Pepe Moncayo who creates a kaiseki experience (small, delicate plates) combining Japanese techniques and the flavors of his native Spain. In the evenings, you can experience an intricate omakase menu where the chef surprises you with a series of delicately crafted small

courses featuring ingredients such as soft shell crab, oysters, and tender duck breast. **Known for:** affordable lunch for a Michelin-starred restaurant; Japanese fusion menu; sake collection. [$] *Average main: $45* ✉ *724 9th St. NW, Petworth* ☎ *202/525–4900* 🌐 *cranes-dc.com* 🕓 *Closed Sun.* [M] *Chinatown.*

Daikaya

$ | **RAMEN** | This intimate, no-reservations, Sapporo-style ramen shop is one of the city's best bets for the tasty Japanese noodle soup. It offers five excellent types of ramen, with the vegan version a welcome option. **Known for:** expect a wait; loud, local-friendly vibe; fancier izakaya upstairs. [$] *Average main: $16* ✉ *705 6th St. NW, Chinatown* ☎ *202/589–1600* 🌐 *www.daikaya.com* [M] *Gallery Pl.–Chinatown.*

Dauphine's

$$$ | **FRENCH FUSION** | Dauphine's, a restaurant inspired by the playful spirit and iconic cuisine of New Orleans, is a new, exciting addition to the D.C. dining scene. The menu pays homage to the diverse cultural influences and rich culinary traditions of New Orleans. **Known for:** excellent service; wine expert available; great happy hour. [$] *Average main: $33* ✉ *1100 15th St. NW, Downtown* ☎ *202/258–3785* 🌐 *www.dauphinesdc.com* [M] *Farragut North.*

Dirty Habit

$$$ | **FUSION** | Inside trendy Hotel Monaco, Dirty Habit woos diners with a towering skylit space that until 1901 was the general post office. Homing in on globally inspired shared plates, the chef conjures up such satisfying dishes as poached hen dumplings and smoked Chilean sea bass. **Known for:** alfresco dining (and drinking) in the courtyard; popular happy hour; small plates in a historic space. [$] *Average main: $30* ✉ *Hotel Monaco, 555 8th St. NW, Penn Quarter* ☎ *202/783–6060* 🌐 *www.dirtyhabitdc.com* [M] *Gallery Pl.–Chinatown.*

District Taco

$ | **MEXICAN** | **FAMILY** | The line out the door at lunchtime is a dead giveaway that D.C.'ers have taken to this fast-casual, Yucatán-style Mexican restaurant that got its start as a food truck in 2009. While you can customize the toppings of your tacos or burritos, ordering them the Mexican way (with cilantro and onion) is a sure bet. **Known for:** food truck origins; all-day breakfast tacos; extensive salsa bar. [$] *Average main: $10* ✉ *1309 F St. NW, Downtown* ☎ *202/347–7359* 🌐 *www.districttaco.com* [M] *Metro Center.*

Fiola

$$$$ | **MODERN ITALIAN** | For those looking for an upscale Italian dining experience, Fiola is an option for you. Its dapper servers know their menu inside and out, and there's a sommelier to help with the wine choices. **Known for:** upscale and innovative Italian dishes; date-night crowd; encyclopedic beverage list. [$] *Average main: $47* ✉ *601 Pennsylvania Ave. NW, Penn Quarter* ✣ *Enter at 678 Indiana Ave.* ☎ *202/628–2888* 🌐 *www.fioladc.com* [M] *Archives–Navy Memorial–Penn Quarter.*

Full Kee

$ | **CHINESE** | The selection of authentic Chinese restaurants continues to dwindle in the neighborhood, but Full Kee remains a local's favorite. Overlook its unassuming exterior and interior and sample its addictive shrimp or scallops in garlic sauce or try the wide assortment of Cantonese-style roasted meats. **Known for:** rare good spot for Chinese food in Chinatown; Cantonese-style roasted meats; no-frills decor. [$] *Average main: $16* ✉ *509 H St. NW, Chinatown* ☎ *202/371–2233* 🌐 *fullkeerestaurant.com* [M] *Gallery Pl.–Chinatown.*

Hill Country Barbecue Market

$$ | **BARBECUE** | **FAMILY** | Few who stop by this bustling hive of smoky brisket and gooey ribs can deny it does Texas meat right. This is evident in the pay-by-the-pound ethos that lets you sample

one slice of lean beef and one scoop of gooey white shoepeg corn pudding alongside a succulent turkey breast. **Known for:** Texas-style brisket—with the rub; cafeteria-style, pay-by-the pound ordering; country western karaoke night every Wednesday. $ *Average main: $18 ⊠ 410 7th St. NW, Penn Quarter* ☎ *202/556–2050* ⊕ *www.hillcountrywdc. com* Ⓜ *Archives–Navy Memorial–Penn Quarter.*

HipCityVeg
$ | **VEGETARIAN** | Crispy Chick'n, juicy burgers, creamy shakes, and legendary sweet potato fries—HipCityVeg makes it easy for people to eat plant-based by presenting it in a way they already know and love. Created by Latina plant-based powerhouse Nicole Marquis, HipCityVeg is a 100% plant-based, fast-casual restaurant serving American Classics. **Known for:** vegan Philly cheesesteak; vegan milkshakes; rare vegan fast food option. $ *Average main: $10 ⊠ 712 7th St NW, Chinatown* ☎ *202/621–8057* ⊕ *hipcityveg.com* Ⓜ *Chinatown.*

Jaleo
$$$ | **SPANISH** | Make a meal of the long list of tapas at celebrity chef José Andrés's lively Spanish bistro, although the five types of handcrafted paella are the stars of the ample entrée menu. Tapas highlights include the *gambas al ajillo* (sautéed garlic shrimp), tender piquillo peppers stuffed with goat cheese, and the grilled homemade chorizo, which also comes draped in creamy mashed potatoes. **Known for:** José Andrés's original tapas eatery; sangria by the pitcher; different paella options. $ *Average main: $32 ⊠ 480 7th St. NW, Penn Quarter* ☎ *202/628–7949* ⊕ *www. jaleo.com* Ⓜ *Gallery Pl.–Chinatown.*

Joe's Seafood, Prime Steak & Stone Crab
$$$$ | **STEAKHOUSE** | Just a couple of blocks from the White House, this enormous space (a century-old bank building), with a towering second-floor terrace, centers on a vast black-granite bar adorned with marble columns and leather stools. Affiliated with the legendary Joe's Stone Crab in Miami, the D.C. Joe's distinguishes itself with steaks. **Known for:** primarily prime steaks but also fresh seafood; everything big: place, portions, prices; fun happy hour. $ *Average main: $52 ⊠ 750 15th St. NW, Downtown* ✛ *On 15th St., a block from Treasury Bldg.* ☎ *202/489–0140* ⊕ *joes. net/dc* Ⓜ *Metro Center.*

Karma Modern Indian
$$$$ | **INDIAN** | A mix of old and new, Karma Modern Indian offers a fresh perspective on Indian cuisine. The dining room is bright, stylish, and colorful, which pairs well with its beautifully plated dishes and cocktails. **Known for:** menu includes plenty of vegetarian options; modern and sleek dining room; yummy cocktails with Indian spices. $ *Average main: $38 ⊠ 611 I St. NW, Chinatown* ☎ *202/898–0393* ⊕ *karmamodernindian. com* ☽ *Closed Mon.* Ⓜ *Chinatown.*

Kaz Sushi Bistro
$$ | **JAPANESE** | Traditional Japanese cooking is combined with often inspired improvisations ("freestyle Japanese cuisine," in the words of chef-owner Kaz Okochi) at this serene location. For a first-rate experience, sit at the sushi bar and ask for whatever is best—you're in good hands. **Known for:** one of D.C.'s original sushi spots; unique Japanese dishes and small plates. $ *Average main: $26 ⊠ 1915 I St. NW, Downtown* ☎ *202/530–5500* ⊕ *www.kazsushibistro. com* ☽ *Closed Sun. and Mon.* Ⓜ *Farragut W.*

★ L'Ardente
$$$$ | **ITALIAN** | L'Ardente serves traditional Italian flavors in a glamorous setting (think Missoni curtains) in the heart of the city. The buzzy restaurant, known for its 40-layer lasagna and tiramisu flambé, is a place to be seen by politicians and celebrities, including former president Barack Obama. **Known for:** 40-layer lasagna; lively dining room; elaborate

cocktails. $ *Average main: $40* ✉ *200 Massachusetts Ave. NW, Downtown* ☎ *202/448-0450* ⊕ *lardente.com* Ⓜ *Judiciary Sq.*

Little Chicken

$ | AMERICAN | Nestled in a hidden alley between L and M streets (Midtown Center), Little Chicken is a fun spot serving all things fried chicken. Start with a locally brewed beer or a glass of champagne if you're feeling fancy. **Known for:** cocktails by the pitcher; crispy chicken sandwiches; fun, young vibe in a business area. $ *Average main: $12* ✉ *1100 15th St. NW, Downtown* ☎ *202/989-0292* ⊕ *justlittlechicken.com* Ⓜ *Farragut N.*

★ Michele's

$$$$ | AMERICAN | Located in the Eaton DC hotel, Michele's is home to a gorgeous bar and lounge producing exceptional craft cocktails and a chef's counter where guests can experience a unique raw bar tasting menu. Created by Michelin-starred chef Matt Baker, Michele's is named after his mother and draws inspiration from the American South, especially New Orleans and Texas, where the chef spent most of his formative years. **Known for:** elevated Southern cuisine; decadent raw bar; prix-fixe menu. $ *Average main: $85* ✉ *1201 K St., Downtown* ☎ *202/758-0895* ⊕ *michelesdc.com* ☞ *Prix-fixe menu for dinner only* Ⓜ *McPherson Sq.*

★ minibar by José Andrés

$$$$ | CONTEMPORARY | For those looking for a high-end gastronomic experience, head to minibar, a two-Michelin-starred restaurant owned by Spanish chef José Andrés. Here, his team showcases his molecular-gastronomy techniques with the 20 or so courses on the tasting menu that vary regularly (no à la carte orders allowed). **Known for:** hard-to-get reservations required; chocolate-covered foie gras; experimental cocktails. $ *Average main: $350* ✉ *855 E St. NW, Penn Quarter* ☎ *202/393–0812* ⊕ *www. minibarbyjoseandres.com/minibar* 🕑 *Closed Sun. and Mon.*

★ Modena

$$$ | ITALIAN | Modena, the Italian restaurant by DC restaurateur Ashok Bajaj, takes power dining to the next level with deliciously beautiful dishes inspired by the Italian region and beyond. Start your meal with a perfectly executed negroni and a starter from the antipasti trolley that stops at each table so diners can choose their favorite starters, from braised artichokes to panzanella salad. **Known for:** local ingredients; sidewalk patio for alfresco dining; wood-fired pizza. $ *Average main: $30* ✉ *1100 New York Ave. NW, Washington* ✛ *Actual entrance is at 12th and H Sts.* ☎ *202/216–9550* ⊕ *www.modenadc.com* Ⓜ *McPherson Sq.*

Old Ebbitt Grill

$$$ | AMERICAN | Visitors and employees from surrounding offices flock here to drink at the several bars, which seem to go on for miles, and enjoy well-prepared buffalo wings, hamburgers, and hearty sandwiches (the Reuben is a must). Old Ebbitt also has one of Washington's best-known raw bars, a 160-year-old institution (it claims Teddy Roosevelt may have "bagged animal heads" at the main bar). **Known for:** one of D.C.'s oldest bars; standard bar menu, including great oysters; an institution that shouldn't be missed. $ *Average main: $32* ✉ *675 15th St. NW, Downtown* ☎ *202/347–4800* ⊕ *www.ebbitt.com* Ⓜ *Metro Center.*

Oyamel Cocina Mexicana

$$ | MEXICAN | The specialty at chef José Andrés's Mexican stunner are *antojitos,* literally translated as "little cravings." But the high ceilings, gracious service, and gorgeous Frida Kahlo–inspired interior are anything but small, and even the smallest of dishes is larger than life when doused with chocolate mole poblano sauce or piquant lime-cilantro dressing. Standouts include homemade margaritas topped with a clever salt foam, the

D.C. Food Trucks 🍴

The nation's capital celebrates celebrity chefs and pricey bistros, but it also loves affordable and accessible dining, as evidenced by its many food trucks. The mobile-food rush reached its peak several years ago when local brick-and-mortar restaurateurs attempted to fight the trucks' appeal by passing an ordinance to keep them from staying too long in one place. That battle continues, but visitors keen to try the best D.C. trucks can always take advantage of social media. Check out the trucks' pages on Twitter and Instagram to track their locations—and in many cases, check out menus to see whether chicken vindaloo or red-velvet cupcakes are on the docket at these favorite spots.

Here are some examples:

Arepa Zone (🌐 *www.twitter.com/arepazone*) is a celebration of Venezuelan cuisine; arepas, *tequeños* (cheese sticks), and *cachapas* (taco-like sweet corn pancakes) all feature heavily.

PhoWheels (🌐 *www.twitter.com/phowheels*) makes pho so delicious you'll want a cup even on a hot D.C. day (go for the eye-round steak). Soup can be difficult to eat when sitting on a curb or park bench, but luckily PhoWheels also offers amazing *bánh mì* sandwiches and Vietnamese-style tacos.

seared Chesapeake perch with serrano and cilantro, and grasshopper tacos—yes, those are bugs basted in tequila and chili sauce, and they're delightful. **Known for:** street-inspired Mexican small plates; grasshopper tacos; affordable lunch deals. [$] *Average main: $23* ✉ *401 7th St. NW, Penn Quarter* ☎ *202/628–1005* 🌐 *www.oyamel.com* [M] *Archives–Navy Memorial–Penn Quarter.*

★ Rasika

$$ | INDIAN | Adventurous wine lists, stellar service, and inventive presentations that don't scrimp on the spice—this Indian kitchen is a local legend. A warm, romantic atmosphere means couples snatch up reservations weeks in advance. **Known for:** upscale Indian with unique dishes; plenty of options for vegetarians; tables that book up weeks in advance. [$] *Average main: $25* ✉ *633 D St. NW, Penn Quarter* ☎ *202/637–1222* 🌐 *www.rasikarestaurant.com* 🕒 *Closed Sun. No lunch Sat.* [M] *Archives–Navy Memorial–Penn Quarter.*

★ Shake Shack

$ | AMERICAN | FAMILY | Yes, it's a chain made most famous in New York City, but if you're craving a burger, you can get your fix at the D.C. Chinatown outpost. Juicy burgers with a special sauce, classic fries (get them with cheese), and tasty shakes make it worth the short wait—especially if you're looking for a delicious, reasonably priced lunch between visits to Downtown attractions. **Known for:** classic Shack Burger (and that sauce!); vanilla milk shakes; long lines that go fast. [$] *Average main: $9* ✉ *800 F St. NW, Penn Quarter* ☎ *202/800–9930* 🌐 *www.shakeshack.com/location/f-street-dc* [M] *Gallery Pl.–Chinatown.*

The Smith

$$ | AMERICAN | FAMILY | Bright, loud, raucous, and fun, with a brightly lit bar and long, communal tables, this branch of the New York City original makes it hard not to meet people. An "American" brasserie, it's an ample space with an even bigger menu. **Known for:** great bar scene; eclectic international menu; all-day breakfast. $ *Average main: $26 ⊠ 901 F St. NW, Downtown* ☎ *202/868–4900* ⊕ *thesmithrestaurant.com* Ⓜ *Gallery Pl.– Chinatown or Metro Center.*

Stellina Pizzeria

$$ | **ITALIAN** | For those craving authentic Italian pizza, head to Stellina Pizzeria. The latest outpost of this locally owned company is the work of native Italians Antonio Matarazzo and chef Matteo Venini. **Known for:** wood-fired pizzas; happy hour specials; long list of Italian wines. $ *Average main: $22 ⊠ 508 K St. NW, Downtown* ☎ *202/499–2094* ⊕ *stellinapizzeria.com/mt-vernon* ◷ *Closed Mon.* Ⓜ *Chinatown.*

Teaism Penn Quarter

$ | **ASIAN** | **FAMILY** | This informal teahouse stocks more than 50 imported teas (black, white, and green) and also serves light and delicious Japanese, Indian, and Thai food. You can mix small dishes—like udon noodle salad and grilled avocado—to create meals or snacks. **Known for:** impressive selection of teas; lunch dishes spanning several Asian cuisines; chocolate salty oat cookies. $ *Average main: $16 ⊠ 400 8th St. NW, Downtown* ☎ *202/638–6010* ⊕ *www.teaism.com* Ⓜ *Archives–Navy Memorial–Penn Quarter.*

★ Zaytinya

$$ | **MIDDLE EASTERN** | This sophisticated urban dining room with soaring ceilings is a local favorite for meeting friends or dining with a group (and popular enough that reservations can still be difficult to get). Here chef José Andrés devotes practically the entire menu to Turkish, Greek, and Lebanese small plates, known as meze. **Known for:** variety of meze; roasted lamb shoulder to share; vegetarian-friendly options. $ *Average main: $26 ⊠ 701 9th St. NW, Penn Quarter* ☎ *202/638–0800* ⊕ *www.zaytinya.com* Ⓜ *Gallery Pl.–Chinatown.*

🛏 Hotels

For those who have not stayed in Washington for a decade or so, throw away your expectations. Cutting-edge hotels, like Hotel Zena and Eaton Workshop closer to Downtown, have joined the traditional luxury names like St. Regis and The Jefferson, with the trustworthy Marriotts and Hiltons still visible and growing.

4

Downtown

★ AC Hotel Washington DC

$$$ | **HOTEL** | The AC Hotel by Marriott is minimalist and elegant, with a European flair (the brand started in Spain). **Pros:** in the heart of Downtown; great lobby bar; close to many restaurants. **Cons:** can get noisy; $45 for valet parking; far from monuments. $ *Rooms from: $350 ⊠ 1112 19th St. NW, Downtown* ⊹ *Just 2 blocks to Metro Red and Blue lines* ☎ *202/303–0190* ⊕ *www.marriott.com* ⇆ *219 rooms* ⏉ *No Meals* Ⓜ *Farragut N.*

Capital Hilton

$$$$ | **HOTEL** | The choice of many celebrities and dignitaries since it opened in 1943, the Hilton has modern perks like a health club and spa and is well located for shopping and eating out. **Pros:** nice guest rooms; desirable location; great gym, however, there's a daily fee unless you're a silver, gold, or diamond Hilton Honors member. **Cons:** expensive valet parking; reports of street noise; fee for Wi-Fi. $ *Rooms from: $457 ⊠ 1001 16th St. NW, Downtown* ☎ *202/393–1000* ⊕ *www.capital.hilton.com* ⇆ *544 rooms* ⏉ *No Meals* Ⓜ *Farragut N.*

★ Conrad Washington DC

$$$$ | **HOTEL** | The Conrad, a modern hotel at CityCentreDC near the convention center, features an enormous, light-filled atrium and verdant outdoor terraces. **Pros:** part of Hilton's luxury collection; large rooms with floor-to-ceiling windows; rooftop terraces and 24-hour gym. **Cons:** pricey; some might prefer a more intimate setting. $ *Rooms from: $667 ⊠ 950 New York Ave. NW, Downtown* ⊹ *CityCentreDC* ☎ *202/844–5900*

Did You Know?

The National Building Museum was originally built to house the United States Pension Bureau. A renovation of its Great Hall—with its soaring, 75-foot-tall Corinthian columns—was completed in 2020.

🌐 *conradwashingtondc.com* 🛏 *360 rooms* 🍴 *No Meals* [M] *Red, Blue, Yellow.*

Eaton DC

$$ | HOTEL | Eaton is a politically progressive hotel that offers retro-cool and comfortable rooms and digital content on hot-button issues, including climate change and immigration. **Pros:** communal space designed for discussions and festivals; beautiful rooftop bar; wellness center and bar on-site. **Cons:** hotel's political themes may not be for everyone; valet parking only (costs extra); smallish rooms. [$] *Rooms from: $246* ✉ *1201 K St. NW, Downtown* ☎ *202/289–7600* 🌐 *eatonworkshop.com* 🛏 *209 rooms* 🍴 *No Meals* [M] *Metro Center or McPherson Sq.*

Fairfield Inn & Suites Washington, DC/ Downtown

$$ | HOTEL | Bold, contemporary design provides a soothing retreat in a busy part of town, near many top attractions like the Capital One Arena, the National Portrait Gallery, and the Mall. **Pros:** complimentary hot breakfast buffet; lots of restaurants, entertainment, and attractions nearby; authentic Irish pub on-site. **Cons:** some complaints about street noise; small gym; not much nightlife nearby. [$] *Rooms from: $220* ✉ *500 H St. NW, Chinatown* ☎ *202/289–5959* 🌐 *www.marriott.com* 🛏 *198 rooms* 🍴 *Free Breakfast* [M] *Gallery Pl.–Chinatown.*

Grand Hyatt Washington

$$$ | HOTEL | A city within the city is what greets you as you step inside the Hyatt's doors and gaze upward to the balconies overlooking the blue lagoon and the many conveniences within the atrium. **Pros:** great location for sightseeing and shopping; often has weekend deals; nice gym and indoor pool. **Cons:** often filled with conventioneers; chain-hotel feel; expensive valet parking. [$] *Rooms from: $304* ✉ *1000 H St. NW, Downtown* ☎ *202/582–1234, 800/233–1234* 🌐 *www.hyatt.com* 🛏 *897 rooms* 🍴 *No Meals* [M] *Metro Center.*

Hamilton Hotel

$ | HOTEL | A short walk from the White House and the Mall, this appealing art deco hotel, on the National Register of Historic Places (it celebrated its centennial in 2022), is a good choice for visitors doing the sights, as well as business guests. **Pros:** central location near the White House; well-equipped fitness center; two restaurants and deluxe microbar. **Cons:** some street noise; small rooms; expensive valet parking. [$] *Rooms from: $202* ✉ *1001 14th St. NW, Downtown* ☎ *202/682–0111* 🌐 *www.hamiltonhoteldc.com* 🛏 *318 rooms* 🍴 *No Meals* [M] *McPherson Sq.*

★ The Hay-Adams

$$$ | HOTEL | Given the elegant charm and refined style, with guest rooms decorated in a class above the rest, it's no wonder this impressive Washington landmark continues to earn international accolades for its guest experience. **Pros:** impeccable service; basically next door to the White House; complimentary bikes, helmets, locks, and cycling maps. **Cons:** expensive parking; no pool; small bathrooms for this price point. [$] *Rooms from: $370* ✉ *800 16th St. NW, Downtown* ☎ *202/638–6600, 800/424–5054* 🌐 *www.hayadams.com* 💳 *No credit cards* 🛏 *145 rooms* 🍴 *No Meals* [M] *McPherson Sq. or Farragut N.*

Henley Park Hotel

$ | HOTEL | A Tudor-style building adorned with gargoyles, this National Historic Trust property has the cozy feel of an English country house, and the atmosphere extends to charming rooms that were once the choice of senators and notables from Washington society. **Pros:** centrally located; historic building; welcoming staff. **Cons:** some rooms are small with very tiny bathrooms; rooms can be noisy and not all have views; expensive valet parking. [$] *Rooms from: $190* ✉ *926 Massachusetts Ave. NW, Penn Quarter* ☎ *202/638–5200, 800/222–8474* 🌐 *www.henleypark.com* 🛏 *96 rooms*

🍽 *No Meals* Ⓜ *Mt. Vernon Sq. 7th St.–Convention Center.*

Holiday Inn Central White House

$ | **HOTEL** | **FAMILY** | Family-friendly and centrally located, The Holiday Inn Central White House has all the amenities to keep families (and business travelers) happy. **Pros:** central location; laundry facilities in-house; rooftop pool. **Cons:** single travelers may find it too family focused; bland chain hotel decor; 15-minute walk to metro. Ⓢ *Rooms from: $195* ⊠ *1501 Rhode Island NW, Downtown* ☎ *202/483-2000* ⊕ *ihg.com/holidayinn/hotels/us/en/washington/wasct/hoteldetail* 🔗 *100 rooms* Ⓜ *McPherson Square.*

★ Hotel Zena

$$ | **HOTEL** | From the two giant glamazon murals on the exterior to the dozen high heels encased in the front desk, Hotel Zena is all about women's empowerment. **Pros:** within walking distance of the White House and other attractions; happening rooftop pool and bar; hip hotel with women-focused art. **Cons:** expensive parking, valet only; lobby can get pretty loud on the weekends; during high season the room rate can skyrocket. Ⓢ *Rooms from: $212* ⊠ *1155 14th St. NW, Downtown* ☎ *202/737-1200* ⊕ *viceroyhotelsandresorts.com/zena* 🔗 *193 rooms* Ⓜ *McPherson Square.*

★ The Jefferson

$$$$ | **HOTEL** | Every inch of this 1923, Beaux-Arts landmark exudes refined elegance, from the intimate seating areas that take the place of a traditional check-in counter to the delicate blooms and glass atrium at the entryway to The Greenhouse, the fine-dining restaurant. **Pros:** exquisite historic hotel in a great location; impeccable service; Quill is about the best hotel bar in the city. **Cons:** expensive; some rooms have views of other buildings; not family-friendly. Ⓢ *Rooms from: $500* ⊠ *1200 16th St. NW, Downtown* ☎ *202/448-2300* ⊕ *www.jeffersondc.com* 🔗 *99 rooms* 🍽 *No Meals* Ⓜ *Farragut N.*

JW Marriott Washington, DC

$$$$ | **HOTEL** | From the location near the White House to the views from the top floors, it's hard to forget you are in the nation's capital when you stay in one of the beautifully furnished rooms here. **Pros:** in the heart of town; lovely rooms with a luxurious, traditional feel; good views from top floors. **Cons:** very busy; chain hotel feel; pricey in-house restaurants. Ⓢ *Rooms from: $449* ⊠ *1331 Pennsylvania Ave. NW, Downtown* ☎ *202/393–2000, 800/393–2503* ⊕ *www.jwmarriottdc.com* 🔗 *755 rooms* 🍽 *No Meals* Ⓜ *Metro Center.*

Kimpton Hotel Banneker

$ | **HOTEL** | The Banneker, named after Benjamin Banneker, one of the country's major Black innovators, is one of the latest additions to the local hotel scene. **Pros:** close to 14th Street corridor; amazing rooftop bar; thoughtful decor. **Cons:** the location is not as central; lower-level rooms have outside noise; 10-plus-minute walk from Metro. Ⓢ *Rooms from: $160* ⊠ *1315 16th St. NW, Downtown* ☎ *202/234–6399* ⊕ *thebanneker.com* 🔗 *144 rooms* Ⓜ *Farraut North.*

★ Kimpton Hotel Monaco Washington DC

$$$ | **HOTEL** | Elegance and whimsy are in perfect harmony at this popular boutique Kimpton hotel—Washington's first all-marble building—in the heart of the Penn Quarter. **Pros:** all the Kimpton extras like a nightly wine hour; amazing design throughout; historic charm. **Cons:** noisy part of town; no pool; expensive valet parking. Ⓢ *Rooms from: $325* ⊠ *700 F St. NW, Penn Quarter* ☎ *202/628–7177, 800/649–1202* ⊕ *www.monaco-dc.com* 🔗 *183 rooms* 🍽 *No Meals* Ⓜ *Gallery Pl.–Chinatown.*

The Madison Washington DC, A Hilton Hotel

$$ | **HOTEL** | The signatures of presidents, prime ministers, sultans, and kings fill the guest register at this classic Washington address, noted for polite service and stylish comfort and now rebranded as a Hilton. **Pros:** central location; pretty guest

rooms with plush furnishings and linens; staff goes the extra mile. **Cons:** 20-minute walk from the Mall; many rooms are a bit dark with no views; not enough plugs in the room for electronic devices. $ *Rooms from: $293* ✉ *1177 15th St. NW, Downtown* ☎ *202/862–1600* ⊕ *www.hilton.com* ⇄ *356 rooms* ⓘⓞⓘ *No Meals* Ⓜ *McPherson Sq.*

Marriott Marquis Washington, D.C.

$$$ | HOTEL | This eco-friendly hotel, directly adjacent to the Washington Convention Center, spans an entire city block and is capped with an enormous atrium skylight accentuating the dramatic lobby sculpture. **Pros:** location near Metro; nicely designed building; within walking distance of great restaurants. **Cons:** rooms overlooking atrium have less privacy and can be noisy; expensive fee for in-room Wi-Fi; big and impersonal. $ *Rooms from: $379* ✉ *901 Massachusetts Ave. NW, Downtown* ☎ *202/824–9200* ⊕ *www.marriott.com* ⇄ *1,175 rooms* ⓘⓞⓘ *No Meals* Ⓜ *Mt. Vernon Sq. 7th St.–Convention Center.*

★ The Mayflower Hotel, Autograph Collection

$$$ | HOTEL | FAMILY | With its magnificent block-long lobby filled with antique crystal chandeliers, layers of gold trim, and gilded columns, there's little wonder that this luxurious landmark has hosted presidential balls since its opening in 1925, as well as historic news conferences and even, for a short time, the Chinese Embassy. **Pros:** near dozens of restaurants; a few steps from Metro; the setting of plenty of political history and scandal. **Cons:** rooms vary greatly in size; expensive parking and pet fees; charge for in-room Wi-Fi unless you're a Marriott rewards member. $ *Rooms from: $369* ✉ *1127 Connecticut Ave. NW, Downtown* ☎ *202/347–3000, 800/228–7697* ⊕ *www. marriott.com* ⇄ *512 rooms* ⓘⓞⓘ *No Meals* Ⓜ *Farragut N.*

★ Morrison-Clark Historic Inn

$$ | HOTEL | A fascinating history makes these beautiful 1864 Victorian town houses attractive, as well as comfortable and well-located choices. **Pros:** charming alternative to cookie-cutter hotels; historic feel throughout; near convention center. **Cons:** some street noise; room size and style vary considerably; some bathrooms are pretty small. $ *Rooms from: $225* ✉ *1011 L St. NW, Downtown* ☎ *202/898–1200, 800/332–7898* ⊕ *www. morrisonclark.com* ⇄ *114 rooms* ⓘⓞⓘ *No Meals* Ⓜ *Metro Center.*

Renaissance Washington, D.C. Downtown Hotel

$$ | HOTEL | Large rooms with views and fine linens, extensive business services, and such amenities as a lavish fitness center and spa elevate this chain hotel into the luxury realm. **Pros:** convenient to Convention Center and Metro; nice lobby and rooftop terrace; great fitness center and spa. **Cons:** convention crowds; chain-hotel feel; expensive parking. $ *Rooms from: $264* ✉ *999 9th St. NW, Chinatown* ☎ *202/898–9000, 800/228–9898* ⊕ *www.marriott.com* ⇄ *807 rooms* ⓘⓞⓘ *No Meals* Ⓜ *Gallery Pl.–Chinatown.*

The St. Regis Washington, D.C.

$$$$ | HOTEL | Just two blocks from the White House, this gorgeous 1926 Italian Renaissance–style landmark attracts a business and diplomatic crowd. **Pros:** close to White House; historic property; exceptional service. **Cons:** most rooms don't have great views; very expensive; some rooms are noisy. $ *Rooms from: $590* ✉ *923 16th St. NW, Downtown* ☎ *202/638–2626* ⊕ *www.stregiswashingtondc.com* ⇄ *172 rooms* ⓘⓞⓘ *No Meals* Ⓜ *Farragut N or McPherson Sq.*

★ Sofitel Washington, D.C. Lafayette Square

$$$$ | HOTEL | Only a minute's walk from the White House, the French luxury chain could not have landed a better location, and its caring, multilingual staff offers a warm welcome and great service.

Pros: prestigious location; highly rated restaurant; lovely rooms. **Cons:** lobby on the small side; expensive parking; many rooms have internal views. $ *Rooms from: $749* ✉ *806 15th St. NW, Downtown* ☎ *202/730–8800* ⊕ *www.sofitel. com* ▤ *No credit cards* ⇄ *237 rooms* ⦿*No Meals* Ⓜ *McPherson Sq.*

★ The Willard InterContinental

$$$$ | HOTEL | FAMILY | Favored by American presidents and other newsmakers, this Washington landmark, only two blocks from the White House, offers superb service, a wealth of amenities, and guest rooms filled with period detail and Federal-style furniture. **Pros:** great on-site dining, high tea, and happy hour; impeccable service; exudes a real sense of history. **Cons:** expensive valet parking; no pool; street-facing rooms can be noisy. $ *Rooms from: $454* ✉ *1401 Pennsylvania Ave. NW, Downtown* ☎ *202/628–9100, 800/827–1747* ⊕ *www. washington.intercontinental.com* ⇄ *335 rooms* ⦿*No Meals* Ⓜ *Metro Center.*

Ⓨ Nightlife

You'll find plenty of bars and lounges in the Downtown area, which has been wonderfully revitalized. Development around Chinatown and the Capital One Arena has turned this into a lively neighborhood, especially when there's a sports or musical event at the arena. A few blocks south, the formerly quiet Penn Quarter is seeing larger evening crowds, thanks to the opening of several terrific new restaurants, cafés, bars, and a world-class theater scene. Many of the hotels in the area have also converted their rooftops to social media–perfect bars with views and cocktail programs ready to be pictured. Conveniently, especially if you plan to imbibe, you can quickly get Downtown on the Metro, exiting at the Archives–Navy Memorial–Penn Quarter station (Green and Yellow lines) or the Gallery Place–Chinatown stop (Green, Yellow, and Red lines).

BARS AND LOUNGES

Allegory

COCKTAIL LOUNGES | Allegory, an acclaimed Washington, D.C. speakeasy, is the first bar that blends art, literature, social justice, craft cocktails, and hospitality. You arrive at the bar through a secret passage of the Eaton DC's bar library. There you will find expertly concocted cocktails with a side of history centered on social justice. Usually, a DJ is spinning lively music. ✉ *1201 K St. NW, Downtown* ☎ *202/289–7600* ⊕ *allegory-dc.com* ⊘ *Closed Sun.* Ⓜ *Metro Center.*

Barmini

BARS | Only a small plaque on a bland concrete wall in a nondescript block of Penn Quarter identifies one of Washington's most sophisticated experiences. Step inside to see José Andrés's cocktail lab for his acclaimed chain of restaurants that looks the part, with white-on-white furnishings and mixologists in lab attire often seen pouring smoking libations out of beakers. A metal notebook features a menu of more than 100 alcohol-centered liquid experiments grouped by spirit. Make it a show with drinks such as the tequila-based Cedar and Agave, in which a glass and block of ice are infused with the smell of burning wood, table-side, or the Floral Cloud, a fruity gin-based beverage delivered in a hibiscus haze. Soak up the chemical reactions with snacks such as savory mini waffles. ✉ *501 9th St. NW, Penn Quarter* ☎ *202/393–4451* ⊕ *www. minibarbyjoseandres.com/barmini* ⊘ *Closed Sun. and Mon.* ☞ *Reservations required* Ⓜ *Archives–Navy Memorial– Penn Quarter.*

The Dignitary

BARS | Inside the shell of an art deco–inspired edifice that once housed a labor union is one of the newest and most comfortably elegant bars in D.C., the corner spot of the Marriott Marquis. Deeper inside the hotel, you'll find a bustling lobby bar and a large, noisy sports bar with 48 beers on tap. But The Dignitary attracts a more refined crowd with its focus on more than 50 types of bourbons and ryes poured by a crew of bartenders as experienced as they are friendly. This Dignitary also features an outdoor patio in the warmer months. ⊠ *901 Massachusetts Ave. NW, Downtown* ☎ *202/824–9681* ⊕ *www.marriott.com* Ⓜ *Mt. Vernon Sq. 7th St.–Convention Center.*

The Hamilton
LIVE MUSIC | From the street, it looks like a swanky Downtown D.C. restaurant with a high-ceilinged power bar to match. The magic happens, however, with live shows in The Hamilton's cavernous basement space. Care in equal parts has focused on acoustics, comfort, and tiered seating, which makes it hard to find a bad seat. There is secondary space above the bar–restaurant where the venue regularly hosts more intimate acts and "Free Late Night Music in the Loft." Check their website for the concert schedule. ⊠ *600 14th St. NW, Downtown* ☎ *202/787–1000* ⊕ *live.thehamiltondc.com* Ⓜ *Metro Center.*

Quill
PIANO BARS | The drinks are stiff and complex at this sophisticated bar tucked inside the Jefferson Hotel, and the mood is a quiet celebration of all things civilized. The dimly lit, two-room, wood-paneled art deco space provides an intimate atmosphere made even more welcoming by the friendly and expert service of the bartenders. The drinks come with a price tag, but it's worth it, given the attention to detail and service. ⊠ *The Jefferson, 1200 16th St. NW, Downtown* ☎ *202/448–2300* ⊕ *www.jeffersondc.com/dining/quill* Ⓜ *Farragut N.*

★ Silver Lyan
COCKTAIL LOUNGES | Take a break from the city and step down to Silver Lyan, the award-winning cocktail bar in the basement of the Riggs Hotel. The former bank vault kept many of the brass fixtures, creating a dark and mysterious setting. If you are a martini lover, order the martini that comes with a beautifully plated flight of olives, oysters, and pickled onions. ⊠ *900 F St NW, Penn Quarter* ☎ *202/638–1800* ⊕ *riggsdc.com/bars-restaurants/silver-lyan* ☾ *Closed Mon.* Ⓜ *Chinatown.*

Summit Lounge
COCKTAIL LOUNGES | With stunning 180-views of Washington, D.C., Summit Bar at the Conrad Hotel is the ideal place for a drink. On a warm summer night, have a frozé at the bar and chat with the lovely staff. If you're craving a snack, you can order bites from Estuary, the hotel's restaurant. ⊠ *950 New York Ave. NW, Downtown* ☎ *202/844–5900* ⊕ *conradwashingtondc.com/dine/rooftop* Ⓜ *Chinatown.*

COMEDY CLUBS
DC Improv
COMEDY CLUBS | The city's main spot for comedy offers a steady menu of well-known and promising stand-up headliners—recent acts have included Judah Friedlander—and a bevy of funny amateurs. Tickets vary depending on the act. Typically, there's a two-item minimum from a full food and drink menu. ⊠ *1140 Connecticut Ave. NW, Downtown* ☎ *202/296–7008* ⊕ *www.dcimprov.com* Ⓜ *Farragut N.*

DANCE CLUBS
The Park at Fourteenth
DANCE CLUBS | A high-end crowd includes visiting basketball players and R&B stars, who dance on four levels. The bouncers strictly enforce the fancy dress code. Splurge with VIP bottle service. You can arrange in advance to get a table or brave the long lines that develop later in the night. This is definitely a place to see and be seen. If you're not a night owl, check out their brunch service—it's just as festive. ⊠ *920 14th St. NW, Downtown* ☎ *202/737–7275* ⊕ *www.park14.com* ☾ *Closed Mon.–Wed.* Ⓜ *McPherson Sq.*

🎭 Performing Arts

Several of Washington's most prestigious performance centers can be found in Downtown D.C. Woolly Mammoth Theater, the Shakespeare Theatre's Sidney Harmon Hall, and other venues are surrounded by a bustling nightlife, where visitors have their choice of cuisines and after-performance conversation.

FILM

★ Landmark's E Street Cinema

FILM | Specializing in independent, foreign, and documentary films, this theater is beloved by D.C. movie enthusiasts both for its selection and its state-of-the-art facilities. *The Washington Post* has often declared it D.C.'s best movie theater, its concession stand is fabulous, and it is one of the city's few movie theaters that serve alcohol. ✉ *555 11th St. NW, Downtown* ☎ *202/452–7672* ⊕ *www. landmarktheatres.com* Ⓜ *Metro Center.*

MAJOR VENUES

Capital One Arena

CONCERTS | In addition to being the home of the NHL Stanley Cup champion Washington Capitals and Washington Wizards and Mystics basketball teams, this 19,000-seat arena also hosts D.C.'s biggest concerts and other major events. Drivers need to park in one of the many underground garages close by, but there are several convenient Metro lines, too. During warmer months, be sure to check out the frequent street concerts at the intersections surrounding the arena. ✉ *601 F St. NW, Chinatown* ☎ *202/661–5000* ⊕ *capitalonearena.viewlift.com* Ⓜ *Gallery Pl.–Chinatown.*

THEATER AND PERFORMANCE ART

Ford's Theatre

THEATER | FAMILY | Looking much as it did before President Lincoln was shot at a performance of *Our American Cousin,* Ford's hosts musicals and dramas with historical connections, and it stages *A Christmas Carol* every year. The historic theater is now maintained by the National Park Service. Tours of the venue and accompanying museum are free, but timed-entry tickets are required. Tickets to shows can range from $20 to $70. ✉ *511 10th St. NW, Downtown* ☎ *202/426–6925* ⊕ *www.fords.org* Ⓜ *Metro Center.*

The National Theatre

THEATER | FAMILY | Though rebuilt several times, The National Theatre has operated in the same location since 1835. It now hosts touring Broadway shows, from classics like *Porgy and Bess* and *Chicago* to contemporary shows like *The Tina Turner Musical.* Ticket prices vary with each show. ✉ *1321 Pennsylvania Ave. NW, Downtown* ☎ *800/447–7400* ⊕ *thenationaldc.org* Ⓜ *Metro Center.*

★ Shakespeare Theatre

THEATER | This acclaimed troupe crafts fantastically staged and acted performances of works by Shakespeare and other significant playwrights, offering traditional renditions but also some with a modern twist. Complementing the stage in the Lansburgh Theatre is Sidney Harman Hall, which provides a state-of-the-art, midsize venue for an outstanding variety of performances—from Shakespeare's *Much Ado About Nothing* to Racine's tragic *Phèdre*—by visiting companies like South Africa's Baxter Theatre, which staged a production of *Mies Julie.* ✉ *450 7th St. NW, Downtown* ☎ *202/547–1122* ⊕ *shakespearetheatre. org* Ⓜ *Gallery Pl.–Chinatown or Archives–Navy Memorial–Penn Quarter.*

Sixth & I Historic Synagogue

MUSIC | Known for its author readings and its comedy, with guests ranging from comedian Tina Fey to Nancy Pelosi, the Sixth & I Historic Synagogue has been named one of the most vibrant congregations in the nation. The intimate space, founded in 1852, hosts religious events as well. Tickets to performances are open to all. ✉ *600 I St. NW, Chinatown* ☎ *202/408–3100* ⊕ *www.sixthandi.org* Ⓜ *Gallery Pl.–Chinatown.*

Warner Theatre

MUSIC | One of Washington's grand theaters, the Warner hosts Broadway road shows, dance recitals, high-profile pop-music acts, and comedians in a majestic art deco performance space with wonderful acoustics. ⊠ *513 13th St. NW, Downtown* ☎ *202/783–4000* ⊕ *warnertheatredc.com* Ⓜ *Metro Center.*

★ Woolly Mammoth

THEATER | Unusual cutting-edge shows with solid acting have earned this company top reviews and 35 Helen Hayes Awards. The theater performs works for a decidedly urban audience that challenge the status quo. Its modern, 265-seat theater in bustling Downtown D.C accentuates the troupe's talent. The Woollies also create a unique lobby experience for each show, created to share the experience on social. ⊠ *641 D St. NW, Downtown* ☎ *202/393–3939* ⊕ *www. woollymammoth.net* Ⓜ *Gallery Pl.–Chinatown or Archives–Navy Memorial–Penn Quarter.*

🛍 Shopping

Downtown D.C. is spread out and sprinkled with federal buildings and museums. Shopping options run the gamut from the upscale CityCenterDC complex and Gallery Place shopping center to small art galleries and bookstores. Gallery Place houses familiar chain stores like Urban Outfitters, Bed Bath & Beyond, and Ann Taylor Loft; it also has a movie theater and a bowling alley. Other big names in the Downtown area include Macy's and chain stores like H&M, Target, and Banana Republic.

With its many offices, Downtown tends to shut down around 5 pm, except for the department stores and larger chain stores. A jolly happy-hour crowd springs up after work, and families and fans fill the streets during weekend sporting events at the Capital One Arena. Penn Quarter has some of the best restaurants

in town peppered among its galleries and specialty stores.

The worthwhile shops are not concentrated in one area, however. The Gallery Place–Chinatown Metro stop provides the most central starting point—you can walk south to the galleries and design shops or west toward the Metro Center and Farragut North. But this trek is only for the ambitious. Although Gallery Place is a nightlife hot spot, the Metro Center and the Farragut area are largely silent after working hours.

CLOTHING

J. Press

MIXED CLOTHING | Like its flagship store (founded in Connecticut in 1902 as a custom shop for Yale University), this Washington outlet keeps with the Ivy League traditions. Harris tweed and classic navy blazers are the best sellers. ⊠ *1801 L St. NW, Downtown* ☎ *202/857–0120* ⊕ *www.jpressonline.com* ⊙ *Closed Sun.* Ⓜ *Farragut N.*

Peruvian Connection

WOMEN'S CLOTHING | Shop for luxurious sweaters, scarves, and outerwear made from Peruvian alpaca. The investment pieces are made by skilled artisans from Peru. ⊠ *950 F St. NW, Penn Quarter* ☎ *202/737–4405* ⊕ *peruvianconnection. com* Ⓜ *Metro Center.*

CRAFTS AND GIFTS

★ Downtown Holiday Market

CRAFTS | FAMILY | This yearly holiday outdoor market is located in Penn Quarter, transforming two city blocks on F Street into a one-stop shop, open-air winter wonderland. The market features local businesses and entrepreneurs across the region, finding unique, festive treasures in the heart of the District starting mid-November and usually going through a few days before Christmas. The outdoor shopping village's expansive footprint allows for wide aisles for shopping, browsing, and also indulging in food stalls by local restaurants. ⊠ *F St. NW* and 9th St. NW, Petworth ⊕ downtown-holidaymarket.com ☞ Seasonal event: from mid-November to end of December M Chinatown.

★ Fahrney's Pens

CRAFTS | What began in 1929 as a repair shop and a pen bar—a place to fill your fountain pen before setting out for work—is now a wonderland for anyone who loves a good writing instrument. You'll find pens in silver, gold, and lacquer by the world's leading manufacturers. If you want to improve your handwriting, the store offers classes in calligraphy and cursive. And yes, the store still offers repair services for all writing instruments—in this digital age Fahrneys' endures. ⊠ 1317 F St. NW, Downtown ☎ 202/628–9525 ⊕ www.fahrneyspens.com ⊙ Closed weekends M Metro Center.

JEWELRY

★ Capitol Coin & Stamp Co

ANTIQUES & COLLECTIBLES | Are you searching for a William Howard Taft candy dish? How about a William McKinley 1896 campaign button? It's all here, whether you need it or not. Capitol Coin is a charming political memorabilia and coin shop (they don't sell stamps, despite the name), just a hop and skip from the White House. In the basement of a building next to the Secret Service, it's not easy to find, but for political junkies, it's worth the effort. It's been in operation at various locations for more than 40 years. The priciest political artifact is a medallion of George Washington's presidency that goes for about $2,000, but most offerings are relatively modest. For mementos, Capitol Coin beats the airport gift shops by a long shot. ⊠ 1616 H St. NW, Suite B-1, Downtown ⊹ Enter at 1616 and take elevator to basement ☎ 202/296–0400 ⊕ www.capitolcoin.com ⊙ Closed Wed. M Farragut W.

★ Tiny Jewel Box

JEWELRY & WATCHES | Despite its name, this venerable D.C. favorite contains six floors of precious and semiprecious wares, including unique gifts, home accessories, vintage pieces, and works by such well-known designers as David Yurman, Penny Preville, and Alex Sepkus. The Federal Collection on the sixth floor features handmade boxes and paperweights with decoupages of vintage prints of Washington commissioned by the Tiny Jewel Box. Even if you're not buying, come in and look around. ⊠ 1147 Connecticut Ave. NW, Downtown ☎ 202/393–2747 ⊕ www.tinyjewelbox.com ⊙ Closed Sun. M Farragut N.

SHOPPING MALLS

CityCenterDC

SHOPPING CENTER | CityCenterDC is an upscale gathering of high-end boutiques, restaurants, residential and office buildings, a park, and an open-air plaza, bordered by New York Avenue and 9th, 11th, and H Streets NW. It's all too easy to spend several thousand dollars in just a few minutes here, with leather goods from Longchamp, Louis Vuitton, and Salvatore Ferragamo; designer fashions and accessories from Burberry, Canali, CH Carolina Herrera, Kate Spade, Loro Piana, Paul Stuart, Zadig&Voltaire; outdoor clothing and sporting goods from Arc'teryx; Tumi luggage; and David Yurman jewelry. For a break from shopping or browsing, grab an indulgent treat from Dolcezza and relax in the plaza with its benches, tables, and fountains. ⊠ 825 10th St. NW, Dupont Circle ☎ 202/347–6337 ⊕ www.citycenterdc.com M Metro Center or Gallery Pl.–Chinatown.

🏃 Activities

SPAS

Celadon

SPAS | Locally owned Celadon Spa is a one-stop shop for beauty and self-care. From haircuts to microdermabrasion facials to full body massage, this full-service spa has a wide array of services for both men and women. ⊠ 1180 F St. NW, Downtown ⊙ Closed Sun. ☞ Appointment recommended M Metro Center.

CAPITOL HILL AND NORTHEAST

Updated by
Barbara Noe Kennedy

⊙ Sights	🍴 Restaurants	🛏 Hotels	🛍 Shopping	🍸 Nightlife
★★★★☆	★★★☆☆	★★★☆☆	★★★☆☆	★★★★☆

NEIGHBORHOOD SNAPSHOT

TOP EXPERIENCES

■ **The Capitol:** See where democracy is put into action. Start your tour at the visitor center, then walk among marble American heroes and gape at the soaring Rotunda.

■ **The Markets:** Eastern Market is the more traditional market, offering fresh produce, baked goods, and locally made crafts. Union Market is an upscale version, featuring fresh seafood and chic coffee shops, while nearby La Cosecha is the Latin American contemporary market. All are beloved weekend destinations.

■ **The Library of Congress and Supreme Court:** Flanking the Capitol, both are architectural wonders offering a must-see window into the nation's history and the workings of government.

■ **Union Station:** More than a train station, it's a stunning gem of neoclassical architecture, where the vaulted ceiling soars almost 100 feet above the massive marble floor. Shops and restaurants also await.

■ **Strolling and Dining:** The area has three lively commercial corridors: Pennsylvania Avenue, H Street, and Barracks Row (8th Street), one of the city's oldest neighborhoods and a vital bulwark in wars past. All feature a wide array of bars, restaurants, and shops.

■ **United States Botanic Garden:** Sniff the heavenly cacao tree, explore the jungle, gawk at the orchids, or stroll the paths of the National Garden.

GETTING HERE

From the Red Line's Union Station, you can walk to most destinations on Capitol Hill. A streetcar runs from behind the station along the full length of H Street—a good option for accessing the street's spirited nightlife. From the Blue, Orange, and Silver lines, the Capitol South stop is close to the Capitol and Library of Congress, and the Eastern Market stop leads to the market and Barracks Row. Bus Nos. 32 and 36 cut across Capitol Hill along Pennsylvania and Independence Avenues; and the Circulator bus connects Congress Heights with Union Station.

PLANNING YOUR TIME

With so much to see—and unpredictable security lines—touring Capitol Hill can be a time-consuming affair, so plan accordingly. **Capitol** tours conducted through the **Visitor Center** run for 90 minutes. Tours of the **Botanic Garden** run 45 minutes, and those at the **Library of Congress** an hour.

If you want to see **Congress** in session, contact your legislator (or, if you are visiting from abroad, your country's embassy) in advance, and bear in mind that the House and the Senate are usually not in session in August.

Supreme Court cases are usually heard from October through April, Monday through Wednesday, two weeks out of each month.

SAFETY

Although crime is rare around Capitol Hill, it does occur, particularly in fast-changing neighborhoods like the H Street Corridor. You can limit the risk with commonsense steps like keeping to well-populated areas, traveling with companions after dark, and hiding your valuables. In short, stay alert—D.C. is relatively safe, but it's still a city.

The people who live and work on "the Hill" do so in the shadow of the edifice that lends the neighborhood its name: the gleaming white U.S. Capitol.

But beyond the area's grand buildings lies a vibrant and diverse group of neighborhoods with charming residential blocks lined with Victorian row houses and a fine assortment of restaurants, shops, and bars, where senators, members of Congress, and lobbyists come to unwind or to continue their deal making. This area includes the Eastern Market, the Atlas District (also known as the H Street Corridor), 8th Street (also known as Barracks Row), Union Station, and Union Market.

◉ Sights

Belmont-Paul Women's Equality National Monument

MONUMENT | Standing strong on Capitol Hill for more than 200 years, this house witnessed the construction of the U.S. Capitol and Supreme Court, and its early occupants participated in the formation of Congress. In 1929, the National Woman's Party (NWP), founded by Alice Paul, an outspoken suffragist and feminist, purchased the house, and it soon evolved into a center for feminist education and social change. For more than 60 years, the trailblazing NWP utilized its strategic location, steps from the U.S. Capitol and its congressional offices, to lobby for women's political, social, and economic equality. Today an expansive collection of artifacts from the suffrage and equal rights campaigns brings the story of the women's rights movement to life. The innovative tactics and strategies these women devised became the blueprint for women's progress throughout the 20th

century. In 2016, President Obama designated the home as a national monument.

⚠ **The monument is closed for renovations through mid- to late 2023.** ✉ *144 Constitution Ave. NE, Capitol Hill* ⊹ *Entrance on 2nd St., next to Hart Senate Office Bldg.* ☎ *202/543–2240* ⊕ *www.nps.gov/bepa* 🎫 *Free* 🕐 *Closed for renovation until mid- to late 2023* Ⓜ *Union Station (Red Line) is the closest station to the north. To the south, Capitol South (Blue, Orange, Silver) is the next closest.*

Folger Shakespeare Library

LIBRARY | This Elizabethan monument, a white-marble art deco building decorated with sculpted bas-relief scenes from the Bard's plays, was designed by architect Paul Philippe Cret and dedicated in 1932. Inside, the design is Tudor England with oak paneling, high plaster ceilings, and ornamental floor tiles. Henry Clay Folger, the library's founder, personally selected the inscriptions by and about Shakespeare that are found throughout the property. Rare items and interactive displays fill two stunning exhibition halls spanning the length of the building, including a gallery displaying all 82 of the library's Shakespeare First Folios. Terra-cotta floor tiles feature titles of Shakespeare's plays and the masks of comedy and tragedy. A First Folio of Shakespeare is always on view and may be thumbed through here digitally.

Visitors are greeted at the entrance to the Elizabethan theater with a marble statue of Puck from *A Midsummer Night's Dream*. With its overhead canopy representing the sky, wooden balconies,

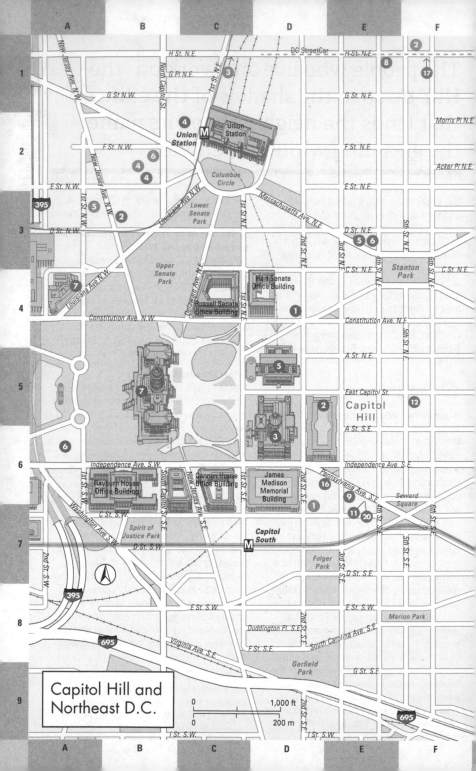

Capitol Hill and Northeast D.C.

Sights ▼

1 Belmont-Paul Women's
   Equality National Monument..... **D4**
2 Folger Shakespeare Library...... **D5**
3 Library of Congress................ **D6**
4 Smithsonian National
   Postal Museum **C2**
5 Supreme Court
   of the United States **D5**
6 United States Botanic Garden ... **A6**
7 United States Capitol.............. **B5**
8 United States
   National Arboretum **J1**

Restaurants ▼

1 Ambar Capitol Hill **G8**
2 Art and Soul **B3**
3 Belga Café............................ **G8**
4 Bistro Bis **B2**
5 Bistro Cacao **E3**
6 Café Berlin........................... **E3**
7 Charlie Palmer Steak.............. **A4**
8 Ethiopic Restaurant **E1**
9 Good Stuff Eatery.................. **E6**
10 Granville Moore's................... **I1**
11 Hawk 'n' Dove...................... **E6**
12 Jimmy T's Place.................... **F5**
13 The Market Lunch **G6**
14 Pineapple and Pears **G9**
15 Rose's Luxury **G9**
16 Sonoma Restaurant
   and Wine Bar **E6**
17 St. Anselm **F1**
18 Sticky Rice........................... **I1**
19 Ted's Bulletin **G8**
20 Tune Inn.............................. **E6**

Hotels ▼

1 Capitol Hill Hotel **D7**
2 City House Hostel
   Washington, D.C. **F1**
3 Hilton Garden Inn...................**C1**
4 Hilton Washington, D.C.
   Capitol Hill **B2**
5 Hyatt Regency Washington
   on Capitol Hill...................... **A3**
6 Phoenix Park Hotel **B2**

and oak columns, the theater is a reproduction of a 16th-century inn-yard playhouse. This is the site for performances of Shakespearean plays, chamber music, readings, lectures, and family programs; check the website for a calendar of events. Understandably, the collection of works by and about Shakespeare and his times is second to none, and the historic Reading Room is devoted to scholarly research. A manicured Elizabethan garden at the building's east end is open to the public, and the gift shop contains many collectibles featuring the Bard and English theater.

The library is closed for renovation, with plans to reopen in late fall 2023. Performances and other events will take place at other venues in Washington, D.C. ⊠ *201 E. Capitol St. SE, Capitol Hill* ☏ *202/544-7077 box office, 202/544-4600* ⊕ *www.folger.edu* ⊠ *Free* Ⓜ *Capitol S.*

★ Library of Congress
LIBRARY | Founded in 1800, the largest library in the world has more than 173 million items on approximately 838 miles of bookshelves. Only 51 million of its holdings are books—the library also has 3.6 million recordings, 14 million photographs, 5.5 million maps, 8.1 million pieces of sheet music, and 70 million manuscripts. Also here is the Congressional Research Service, which, as the name implies, works on special projects for senators and representatives.

Opened in 1897, the copper-domed Thomas Jefferson Building is the oldest of the three buildings that make up the library. The dome, topped with the gilt "Flame of Knowledge," is ornate and decorative, with busts of Dante, Goethe, and Nathaniel Hawthorne perched above its entryway. The *Court of Neptune,* Roland Hinton Perry's fountain at the front steps, rivals some of Rome's best fountains.

The Jefferson Building opens into the Great Hall, richly adorned with mosaics, paintings, and curving marble stairways. The octagonal Main Reading Room, its central desk surrounded by mahogany readers' tables under a 160-foot-high domed ceiling, inspires researchers and readers alike. Computer terminals have replaced card catalogs, but books are still retrieved and dispersed the same way: readers (16 years or older) open a free reader identification card issued by the library, hand request slips to librarians and wait for their materials to be delivered. Researchers aren't allowed in the stacks, and only members of Congress and other special borrowers can check books out. Items from the library's collection—which includes one of only three perfect Gutenberg Bibles in the world—are on display in the Jefferson Building's second-floor Southwest Gallery and Pavilion. Free timed-entry passes are required for entry.

■**TIP→ The Library puts on some amazing exhibits from its vast collection, including musical instruments, early maps, and baseball cards!** ⊠ *Jefferson Bldg., 10 1st St. SE, Capitol Hill* ☏ *202/707-9779* ⊕ *www. loc.gov* ⊠ *Free* ☾ *Closed Sun. and Mon.* Ⓜ *Capitol S.*

Smithsonian National Postal Museum
HISTORY MUSEUM | **FAMILY** | The National Museum of Natural History has the Hope Diamond, but the National Postal Museum has the envelope wrapping used to mail the gem to the Smithsonian—part of a collection that consists of nearly 6 million postal and philatelic objects. Exhibits, underscoring the important part the mail has played in America's development, include horse-drawn mail coaches, a railroad mail car, airmail planes, and a collection of philatelic rarities. Learn about stamp collecting, and tour *Systems at Work,* an exhibit that demonstrates how mail has gone from the mailbox to its destination for the past 200 years and features a high-definition

Continued on page 129

ON THE HILL, UNDER THE DOME: EXPERIENCING THE CAPITOL

United States Capitol

The top of the dome at the US Capitol.

State of the Union address at a session of Congress

In Washington, the Capitol literally stands above it all: by law, no other building in the city can reach the height of the dome's peak.

Beneath its magnificent dome, the day-to-day business of American democracy takes place: senators and representatives debate, coax, and cajole, and ultimately determine the law of the land.

For many visitors, the Capitol is the most exhilarating experience Washington has to offer. It wins them over with a three-pronged appeal:

■ It's the city's most impressive work of architecture.

■ It has on display documents, art, and artifacts from 400 years of American history.

■ Its legislative chambers are open to the public. You can actually see your lawmakers at work, shaping the history of tomorrow.

THE CAPITOL THROUGH THE CENTURIES

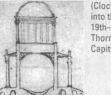

(Clockwise from top left) Moving into the new Capitol circa 1800; 19th–century print by R. Brandard; Thornton sketch circa 1797; the Capitol before the dome.

1792 - 1807
A Man with a Plan

William Thornton, a physician and amateur architect from the West Indies, wins the competition to design the Capitol. His plan, with its central rotunda and dome, draws inspiration from Rome's Pantheon. On September 18, 1793, George Washington lays the Capitol's cornerstone. In November 1800, Congress moves from Philadelphia to take up residence in the first completed section, the boxlike area between the central rotunda and today's north wing. In 1807, the House wing is completed, just to the south of the rotunda; a covered wooden walkway joins the two wings.

1814 - 1826
Washington Burns

In 1814, British troops march on Washington and set fire to the Capitol, the White House, and other government buildings. The wooden walkway is destroyed and the two wings gutted, but the walls remain standing after a violent rainstorm douses the flames. Fearful that Congress might leave Washington, residents fund a temporary "Brick Capitol" on the spot where the Supreme Court is today. By 1826, reconstruction is completed under the guidance of architects Benjamin Henry Latrobe and Charles Bulfinch; a low dome is made of wood sheathed in copper.

1850s - 1880s
Domed if You Do

North and south wings are added through the 1850s and '60s to accommodate the growing government of a growing country. To maintain scale with the enlarged building, work begins in 1885 on a taller, cast-iron dome. President Lincoln would be criticized for continuing the expensive project during the Civil War, but he calls the construction "a sign we intend the Union shall go on."

(Clockwise from top left) The crowd for the First Inauguration of Abraham Lincoln in 1861; today the Capitol is a tourist mecca with its own visitor center; *Freedom* statue.

1960s – Today

Expanding the Capitol

The east front is extended 33½ feet, creating 100 additional offices. In 1983 preservationists fight to keep the west front, the last remaining section of the Capitol's original facade, from being extended; in a compromise the facade's crumbling sandstone blocks are replaced with stronger limestone. In 2000 the ground is broken on the subterranean Capitol Visitor Center, to be located beneath the grounds to the building's east side. The extensive facility, three-fourths the size of the Capitol itself, was finally completed on December 2, 2008 to the tune of $621 million.

Freedom atop the Capitol Dome

The twin-shelled Capitol dome, a marvel of 19th-century engineering, rises 285 feet above the ground and weighs 4,500 tons. It can expand and contract as much as 4 inches in a day, depending on the outside temperature.

The allegorical figure on top of the dome is *Freedom*. Sculpted in 1857 by Thomas Crawford, *Freedom* was cast with help from Philip Reid, a slave. Crawford had first planned for the 19½-foot-tall bronze statue to wear the cloth liberty cap of a freed Roman slave, but Southern lawmakers, led by Jefferson Davis, objected. An "American" headdress composed of a star-encircled helmet

surmounted with an eagle's head and feathers was substituted. A light just below the statue burns whenever Congress is in session.

Before the visitor center opened, the best way to see the details on the *Freedom* statue atop the Capitol dome was with a good set of binoculars. Now, you can see the original plaster model of this classical female figure up close. Her right hand rests on a sheathed sword, while her left carries a victory wreath and a shield of the United States with 13 stripes. She also wears a brooch with "U.S." on her chest.

THE CAPITOL VISITOR CENTER

The enormous and sunlit Capitol Visitor Center (CVC) is the start for all Capitol tours, and brings a new depth to the Capitol experience with orientation theaters, an interactive museum, and live video feeds from the House and Senate. It also provides weary travelers with welcome creature comforts, including a 530-seat restaurant.

DESIGN

At 580,000 square feet, the visitor center is approximately three-quarters the size of the 775,000-square-foot Capitol. The center's belowground location preserves the historic landscape and views designed by Frederick Law Olmsted in 1874. Inside, skylights provide natural light and views of the majestic Capitol dome. The center opened in December 2008, three years late and $356 million over budget.

EMANCIPATION HALL

The center's largest space is a gorgeous sunlit atrium called Emancipation Hall in honor of the slaves who helped to build the Capitol in the 1800s. The plaster model of the *Freedom* statue, which tops the Capitol's dome, anchors the hall. Part of the Capitol's National Statuary Hall collection is also on display here.

MUSEUM

Other attractions include exhibits about the Capitol, historical artifacts, and documents. A marble wall displays historic speeches and decisions by Congress, like President John F. Kennedy's famous 1961 "Man on the Moon" speech and a letter Thomas Jefferson wrote to Congress in 1803 urging the funding of the Lewis and Clark Expedition.

KIDS AT THE CVC

The Capitol Visitor Center is a great place for families with children who may be too young or too wiggly for a tour of the Capitol. In the Exhibition Hall, the 11-foot tall touchable model of the Capitol, touch screen computers, and architectural replicas welcome hands-on exploration.

Challenge younger kids to find statues of a person carrying a spear, a helmet, a book, and a baby.

Tweens can look for statues of the person who invented television, a king, a physician, and a representative who said, "I cannot vote for war."

PLANNING YOUR CAPITOL DAY

LOGISTICS

To tour the Capitol, you can book free, advance passes at ⊕ *www.visitthecapitol.gov* or through your representative's or senator's offices. In addition, a limited number of same-day passes are available at the Public Walk-Up line on the lower level of the visitor center. Tours run every 15 minutes; the first tour begins at 8:50 and the last at 3:20, Monday through Saturday. The center is closed on Sunday.

Plan on two to four hours to tour the Capitol and see the visitor center. You should arrive at least 30 minutes before your scheduled tour to allow time to pass through security. Tours, which include a viewing of the orientation film *Out of Many, One,* last about one hour.

If you can't get a pass to tour the Capitol, the Capitol Visitor Center is still worth a visit. You can also take one of the free guided tours that do not require reservations.

To get passes to the chambers of the House and Senate, contact your representative's or senator's office. Many will also arrange for a staff member to give you a tour of the Capitol or set you up with a time for a Capitol Guide Service tour. When they're in session, some members even have time set aside to meet with constituents. You can link to the e-mail of your representative at ⊕ *www.house.gov* and of your senators at ⊕ *www.senate.gov.*

SECURITY

Expect at least a 30-minute wait going through security when you enter the Capitol Visitor Center. Bags can be no larger than 14 inches wide, 13 inches high, and 4 inches deep. View the list of prohibited items on ⊕ *www. visitthecapitol.gov.* (There are no facilities for storing prohibited belongings.) For more information, call ☎ *202/226–8000, 202/224–4049 TTY.*

BEAN SOUP AND MORE

A favorite with legislators, the Senate bean soup has been served every day for more than 100 years in the exclusive Senate Dining Room. It's available to the general public in the restaurant of the CVC (⊙ Open 7:30 AM–4 PM) on a rotating basis. You can also try making your own with the recipe on the Senate's Web site (⊕ www.senate.gov).

GETTING HERE— WITHOUT GETTING VOTED IN

The Union Station, Capitol South and Federal Center, SW Metro stops are all within walking distance of the Capitol. Follow the people wearing business suits—chances are they're headed your way. Street parking is extremely limited, but Union Station to the north of the Capitol has a public garage and there is some metered street parking along the Mall to the west of the Capitol.

RENOVATION

A complete renovation of the Capitol Dome was completed in late 2016, just before the presidential inauguration in January 2017.

TOURING THE CAPITOL

National Statuary Hall

Your 30- to 40-minute tour conducted by the Capitol Guide Service includes stops at the Rotunda, followed by the National Statuary Hall, the Hall of Columns, the old Supreme Court Chamber, the crypt (where there are exhibits on the history of the Capitol), and the gift shop. Note that you *don't* see the Senate or House chambers on the tour. (Turn the page to learn about visiting the chambers.) The highlights of the tour are the first two stops. . . .

THE ROTUNDA

You start off here, under the Capitol's dome. Look up and you'll see *Apotheosis of Washington,* a fresco painted in 1865 by Constantino Brumidi. The figures in the inner circle represent the 13 original states; those in the outer ring symbolize arts, sciences, and industry. Further down, around the Rotunda's rim, a frieze depicts 400 years of American history. The work was started by Brumidi in 1877 and continued by another Italian, Filippo Costaggini. American Allyn Cox added the final touches in 1953.

NATIONAL STATUARY HALL

South of the Rotunda is Statuary Hall, which was once the chamber of the House of Representatives. When the House moved out, Congress invited each state to send statues of two great deceased residents for placement in the hall. Because the weight of the statues threatened to make the floor cave in, and to keep the room from being cluttered, more than half of the sculptures have ended up in other spots in the Capitol. Ask your guide for help finding your state's statues.

ARTIST OF THE CAPITOL

Constantino Brumidi (1805-80) devoted his last 25 years to frescoing the Capitol; his work dominates the Rotunda and the Western Corridor. While painting the section depicting William Penn's treaty with the Indians for the Rotunda's frieze *(pictured above)*, a 74-year-old Brumidi slipped from the 58-foot scaffold, hanging on until help arrived. He would continue work for another four months, before succumbing to kidney failure.

TRY THIS

Because of Statuary Hall's perfectly elliptical ceiling, a whisper uttered along the wall can be heard at the point directly opposite on the other side of the room. Try it when you're there—if it's not noisy, the trick should work.

ONE BIG HAWAIIAN

With a solid granite base weighing six tons, Hawaii's Kamehameha I in Statuary Hall is among the heaviest objects in the collection. On Kamehameha Day (June 11, a state holiday in Hawai'i), the statue is draped with leis.

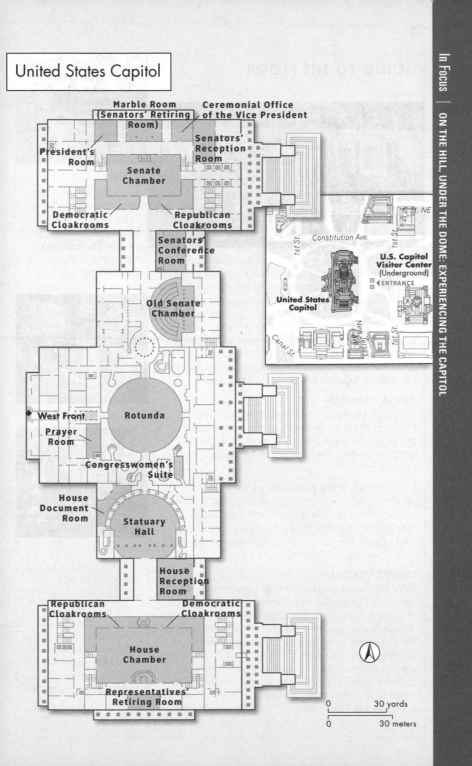

United States Capitol

Marble Room
(Senators' Retiring Room)

Ceremonial Office
of the Vice President

President's Room

Senators' Reception Room

Senate Chamber

Democratic Cloakrooms

Republican Cloakrooms

Senators' Conference Room

Old Senate Chamber

West Front

Rotunda

Prayer Room

Congresswomen's Suite

House Document Room

Statuary Hall

House Reception Room

Republican Cloakrooms

Democratic Cloakrooms

House Chamber

Representatives' Retiring Room

Constitution Ave.

C St. NE

1st St.

1st St.

U.S. Capitol Visitor Center (Underground)

ENTRANCE

United States Capitol

New Jersey Ave.

1st St.

Canal St.

0   30 yards
0   30 meters

GOING TO THE FLOOR

A tour of the Capitol is impressive, but the best part of a visit for many people is witnessing the legislators in action. Free gallery passes into the House and Senate chambers have to be obtained from your representative's or senator's office. They aren't hard to come by, but getting them takes some planning ahead. Once you have a pass, it's good for any time the chambers are open to public, for as long as the current Congress is sitting. Senate chambers are closed when the Senate is not in session, but the House is open.

Judiciary Committee

HOUSE CHAMBER

The larger of two chambers may look familiar: it's here that the president delivers the annual State of the Union. When you visit, you sit in the same balcony from which the First Family and guests watch the address.

Look carefully at the panels above the platform where the Speaker of the House sits. They're blue (rather than green like the rest of the panels in the room), and when the House conducts a vote, they light up with the names of the representatives and their votes in green and red.

House session

SENATE CHAMBER

With 100 members elected to six-year terms, the Senate is the smaller and ostensibly more dignified of Congress's two houses. Desks of the senators are arranged in an arc, with Republicans and Democrats divided by the center aisle. The vice president of the United States is officially the "president of the Senate," charged with presiding over the Senate's procedures. Usually, though, the senior member of the majority party oversees day-to-day operations, and is addressed as "Mr. President" or "Madam President."

SWEET SPOT IN THE SENATE
In the sixth desk from the right in the back row of the Senate chamber, a drawer has been filled with candy since 1968. Whoever occupies the desk maintains the stash.

Visiting Government Buildings 👁

You can visit many of Washington's government offices, but you have to do some advance planning in many cases. Here's a rundown of how far ahead you should make arrangements.

No Advance Planning Required

Two of the most impressive places in Washington don't require reservations. The **Library of Congress** and the **U.S. Supreme Court** are architectural and political treasures.

With its murals, paintings, sculptures and statues, and, of course, millions of books and manuscripts, the Library of Congress is truly spectacular. Even if you're not a bookworm, the free docent-led tour is one of the best things going in the city. Revolving exhibits prevent the experience from ever getting stale. The Supreme Court normally welcomes visitors to amble through its public spaces, which include the courtroom itself, though it's presently closed; check the website for updates. Court sessions, however, are open to the public on a first-come-first-served basis.

Capitol Visitor Center

One of the most visited attractions, the **Capitol Visitor Center** is the starting point for tours of the Capitol and where you'll discover a plethora of historical treasures, including a table used by Abraham Lincoln during his 1865 inaugural address. The underground complex is a destination in itself, with the model of the statue of *Freedom*, a 530-seat dining room that serves the famous Senate bean soup, and exhibits on the Capitol. A 13-minute orientation film lends some footing. The visitor center is open to visitors with tour reservations until 4:30 pm, Monday through Friday. Allow extra time to go through security.

To visit the Capitol, you can reserve advance tickets online at ⊕ *www.visitthecapitol.gov*, contact your representative or senator, or gamble for a limited number of same-day passes available on the website.

film highlighting amazing technologies. The William H. Gross Stamp Gallery, the largest of its kind in the world, has an additional 20,000 objects never before on public display, showing how closely stamps have intertwined with American history. The museum is next to Union Station in the old Washington City Post Office, designed by Daniel Burnham and completed in 1914. ✉ *2 Massachusetts Ave. NE, Capitol Hill* ☎ *202/633–5555* ⊕ *www.postalmuseum.si.edu* 🎟 *Free* Ⓜ *Union Station.*

★ Supreme Court of the United States

GOVERNMENT BUILDING | It wasn't until 1935 that the Supreme Court got its own building: a white-marble temple with twin rows of Corinthian columns designed by Cass Gilbert. Before then, the justices had been moved around to various rooms in the Capitol; for a while they even met in a tavern. William Howard Taft, the only man to serve as both president and chief justice, was instrumental in getting the court a home of its own, though he died before the building was completed. Today, you can sit in the gallery and see the court in action.

The court convenes on the first Monday in October and hears cases until April (though court typically is in session through June). There are usually two

The Supreme Court officially began meeting in this Corinthian-column-lined building in 1935.

arguments a day, beginning at 10 in the morning, Monday through Wednesday, in two-week intervals. For the most contentious cases, viewers have been known to queue up days before. Oral arguments typically conclude in April, and for the remainder of the term, the court releases orders and opinions.

The court displays its calendar of cases a month in advance on its website. You can't bring your overcoat or electronics such as cameras and cell phones into the courtroom, but you can store them in a locker. Entry to visit the resolving exhibits inside is suspended at the time of publication. ⊠ *1 1st St. NE, Capitol Hill* ☎ *202/479–3000* ⊕ *www.supremecourt. gov* ⊠ *Free* ⊗ *Closed weekends* Ⓜ *Union Station or Capitol S.*

★ United States Botanic Garden
GARDEN | FAMILY | Established by Congress in 1820, this is the oldest continually operating public garden in the United States. The conservatory sits at the foot of Capitol Hill and offers an escape from the stone-and-marble federal office

buildings surrounding it. Inside are exotic rain-forest species, desert flora, a room full of orchids, and plants from all parts of the world. Walkways suspended 24 feet above the ground in the Tropics house provide a fascinating view of the plants. Established in 2006, the National Garden is an outdoor gardening laboratory featuring a Rose Garden, Pollinator Garden, First Ladies' Water Garden, and Regional Garden of Mid-Atlantic plants. Across Independence Avenue, Bartholdi Fountain and Gardens is a peaceful spot with shaded benches around the historic 30-foot fountain by the sculpture of the Statue of Liberty. ⊠ *1st St. at 100 Maryland Ave. SW, Capitol Hill* ☎ *202/225–8333* ⊕ *www.usbg.gov* ⊠ *Free* Ⓜ *Federal Center SW.*

★ United States Capitol
GOVERNMENT BUILDING | Beneath the Capitol's magnificent dome, the day-to-day business of American democracy takes place: senators and representatives debate, coax, cajole, and ultimately determine the law of the land. For

Inside Congress: How Laws Are Made 👁

Amid the grand halls of the Capitol building, members of Congress and their aides are busy crafting the laws of our land. It's not a pretty process; as congressional commentators have quipped, laws are like sausages—it's best not to know how they're made. But for iron stomachs, here's a brief tour through Washington's sausage factory.

The Idea Stage

Most laws begin as proposals that any of Congress's 535 members may offer in the form of bills. Many are trivial, such as renaming post-office branches. Others are vital, like funding the federal government. Once introduced, all proposals move to a relevant congressional committee.

Congressional Committees and Committee Hearings

Although thousands of proposals are introduced each year, almost all die in committee. Congress never has enough time to entertain each bill, so committee leaders prioritize. Some bills are dismissed for ideological reasons.

For example, liberal proposals to enact tougher gun controls have a smaller chance moving through committees headed by conservative Republicans.

Others simply lack urgency. Efforts to rein in fuel costs, for instance, are popular when gas prices are high. Lobbying and special-interest money are other major factors influencing the content and even success or failure of individual bills.

For bills that advance, merits and drawbacks are debated in committee hearings. These hearings are usually open to the public; check under the "committee" headings for schedules. Committee members then vote on whether to move bills to the chamber floor.

Passing the House, Senate, and White House

A bill approved by committee still faces three formidable tests before becoming a law: it must pass the full House, the full Senate, and usually the White House.

Each legislative chamber has different rules for approving bills. In the House, proposals that clear a committee and have the blessing of House leaders need only a simple majority. In the Senate, legislation can be delayed by filibustering—a time-honored process of talking nonstop on the Senate floor—until at least 60 senators vote to end the delay. If the House and Senate pass different versions of the same proposal, then those differences are reconciled in a joint conference committee before returning to the respective floors for another round of voting.

A bill passed by both the House and Senate then proceeds to the White House. The president can either sign it—in which case it becomes law—or veto it, in which case it returns to Congress. Lawmakers can override a veto, but two-thirds of each chamber must support the override to transform a vetoed bill into law. When President Donald Trump vetoed a defense spending bill just before leaving office in 2021, for example, the House and Senate both mustered the required two-thirds votes, thereby overriding the presidential veto. The bill became a law.

many visitors, the Capitol is the most exhilarating experience Washington has to offer. It wins them over with a three-pronged appeal: it's the city's most impressive work of architecture; it has on display documents, art, and artifacts from 400 years of American history; and its legislative chambers are open to the public, allowing you to actually see your lawmakers at work.

Before heading to the Capitol, pay a little attention to the grounds, landscaped in the late 19th century by Frederick Law Olmsted, famed for New York City's Central Park. On these 274 acres are both the city's tamest squirrels and the highest concentration of TV news correspondents, jockeying for a good position in front of the Capitol for their "stand-ups." A few hundred feet northeast of the Capitol are two cast-iron car shelters, left from the days when horse-drawn trolleys served the Hill. Olmsted's six red-granite lamps directly east of the Capitol are worth a look, too. A small, hexagonal brick structure with shaded benches, a fountain, and a small grotto, called the Summerhouse, is a wonderful place to escape the summer heat.

The design of the building was the result of a competition held in 1792; the winner was William Thornton, a physician and amateur architect from the West Indies. With its central rotunda and dome, Thornton's Capitol is reminiscent of Rome's Pantheon. This similarity must have delighted the nation's founders, who sought inspiration from the principles of the Republic of Rome.

The cornerstone was laid by George Washington in a Masonic ceremony on September 18, 1793, and, in November 1800, both the Senate and the House of Representatives moved down from Philadelphia to occupy the first completed section: the boxlike portion between the central rotunda and today's north wing. (Efforts to find the cornerstone Washington laid have been unsuccessful;

a 1991 search was conducted using a metal detector to locate the engraved plate—it was not found. The location may be under the southeast corner of what is today National Statuary Hall.) By 1807, the House wing had been completed, just to the south of what's now the domed center, and a covered wooden walkway joined the two wings.

The "Congress House" grew slowly and suffered a grave setback on August 24, 1814, when British troops led by Sir Alexander Cockburn marched on Washington and set fire to the Capitol, the White House, and numerous other government buildings. (Cockburn reportedly stood on the House speaker's chair and asked his men, "Shall this harbor of Yankee democracy be burned?" The question was rhetorical; the building was torched.) The wooden walkway was destroyed, and the two wings gutted, but the exterior structure was left standing thanks to Architect Benjamin Henry Latrobe's use of fireproof building materials. Congress debated moving the Capitol to another location, but in 1815 it authorized President Madison to borrow from local banks to rebuild, on their existing sites, the Capitol, White House, and cabinet quarters. Latrobe supervised the rebuilding of the original Capitol, adding American touches such as the corncob-and-tobacco-leaf capitals to columns in the east entrance of the Senate wing. He was followed by Boston-born Charles Bulfinch and, in 1826, the Capitol, its low wooden dome sheathed in copper, was finished.

North and south wings were added in the 1850s and 1860s to accommodate a growing government trying to keep pace with a growing country. The elongated edifice extended farther north and south than Thornton had planned, and, in 1855, to keep the scale correct, work began on a taller, cast-iron dome. President Lincoln was criticized for continuing this expensive project while the country was in the throes of the Civil War, but he called the construction "a sign we intend the Union shall go on." This twin-shell dome, a marvel of 19th-century engineering, rises 288 feet above the ground and weighs 4,500 tons. It expands and contracts up to 4½ inches a day, depending on the outside temperature. The allegorical figure atop the dome, often mistaken·for Pocahontas, is called *Freedom*. Sculptor Thomas Crawford had first planned for the 19½-foot-tall bronze statue to wear the cloth liberty cap of a freed Roman slave, but Southern lawmakers, led by Jefferson Davis (who was Secretary of War and in charge of the Capitol construction), objected. An "American" headdress composed of a star-encircled helmet surmounted with an eagle's head and feathers was substituted. A light just below the statue burns whenever Congress is in session at night.

The Capitol has continued to grow. Between 1959 and 1962, the east front was extended 32 feet, creating 90 new rooms. Preservationists have fought to keep the west front from being extended because it's the last remaining section of the Capitol's original facade. A compromise was reached in 1983, when it was agreed that the facade's crumbling sandstone blocks would simply be replaced with stronger limestone.

Free gallery passes to watch the House or Senate in session can be obtained only from your representative's or senator's office; both chambers are open to the public when either body is in session. In addition, the House Gallery is open 9 am to 4:15 pm weekdays when the House is not in session. International visitors may request gallery passes from the House or Senate appointment desks on the upper level of the visitor center. Your representative's or senator's office may also arrange for a staff member to give you a tour of the Capitol or set you up with a time for a Capitol Guide Service Tour. When they're in session, some members even have time set aside to meet with

constituents. You can link to the home page of your representative or senators at ⊕ *www.house.gov* and ⊕ *www.senate.gov*.

Free reservations are required to visit the Capitol. They can be made through either the Capitol Visitor Center website or through the office of your representative or senators. Only those with tour reservations may enter the Capitol Visitor Center; allow time to go through security. Bags can be no larger than 18 inches wide, 14 inches high, and 8½ inches deep, and other possessions you can bring into the building are strictly limited. (The full list of prohibited items is posted at ⊕ *www.visitthecapitol.gov*.) There are no facilities for leaving personal belongings, but you can check your coat. If you're planning a visit, check the status of tours and access; security measures may change. Note that only those with tour reservations may enter the Capitol Visitor Center. ⊠ *E. Capitol Circle, at 1st St. and E. Capitol St. NE, Capitol Hill* ✛ *East end of The Mall* ☎ *202/226–8000* ⊕ *www.visitthecapitol.gov* ⧉ *Free* ☉ *Closed weekends* Ⓜ *Capitol S or Union Station.*

★ **United States National Arboretum**

GARDEN | During azalea season (mid-April through May), this 451-acre oasis operated by the U.S. Department of Agriculture is a blaze of color. In early summer, clematis, peonies, rhododendrons, and roses bloom. At any time of year, the 22 original Corinthian columns from the U.S. Capitol, re-erected here in 1990, are striking. All 50 states are represented by a state tree in the Grove of State Trees. Since 2014, a pair of American bald eagles have made a home near the azaleas, and the nest can be seen via an unobstructed viewing scope. The arboretum has guided hikes throughout the year, including a Forest Bathing Walk, and dogs are allowed on the grounds as long as they're on a leash at all times. Check the website for schedules and to register. Don't miss

The United States Botanic Garden, founded in 1820, is the oldest in North America.

the Bonsai and Penjing Museum. ✉ *3501 New York Ave. NE, Northeast* ☎ *202/245–2726* 🌐 *www.usna.usda.gov* 🎟 *Free.*

🍴 Restaurants

"The Hill," as locals know it, was once an enclave of congressional boardinghouses in the shadow of the Capitol building but is now D.C.'s largest historic district, with an eclectic mix of restaurants. Around the Capitol South Metro station, government offices end and neighborhood dining begins. Here, along tree-lined streets, some of the city's most acclaimed restaurants have joined the local bars and eateries that have long catered to lunch and happy-hour crowds during the week.

Neighborhood establishments and all-American pubs line historic Barracks Row, with Eastern Market anchoring the homey House side of the Hill; the Senate end is given a more hustle-and-bustle vibe with the chain dining and upscale boîtes of Union Station. The Atlas District, also known as the H Street Corridor, has an ever-changing mix of interesting restaurants, and a few blocks north is Union Market, where dozens of local food and beverage purveyors sell everything from arepas to Zinfandels.

Ambar Capitol Hill

$$$ | EASTERN EUROPEAN | Ambar, a handsome, noisy, two-story restaurant–bar at the heart of Barracks Row, is your spot for Balkan comfort food. The Belgrade-inspired menu is full of hearty novelties like lamb lasagna, almond-crusted chicken with apple-wasabi slaw, drunken mussels with capers and lemon, savory pies, a host of rich sausages, and all flavor of kebabs. **Known for:** reservations highly recommended; all-you-can-eat small plates; attentive and enthusiastic servers. [$] *Average main: $30* ✉ *523 8th St. SE, Eastern Market* ☎ *202/813–3039* 🌐 *www.ambarrestaurant.com* [M] *Eastern Market.*

Art and Soul

$$$$ | SOUTHERN | The decor may be somewhat generic, but the food is anything but. Located within the Yotel near the Capitol, Art and Soul serves up simple, honest dishes using the freshest local ingredients—with flavorful and artsy twists. **Known for:** friendly service; dog-friendly outdoor patio (complete with menu for Fido); chef's brunch tasting menu. $ *Average main: $36* ✉ *Yotel hotel, 415 New Jersey Ave. NW, Capitol Hill* ☎ *202/393–7777* ⊕ *www.artand-souldc.com* Ⓜ *Union Station.*

Belga Café

$$$ | **BELGIAN** | Belgium culture aficionados can go traditional with mussels and the crispiest of French fries or dabble in what the chef calls Eurofusion at this sleek café done up with dark wood and exposed brick. Classic dishes such as mussels marinières with white wine, shallots, and garlic help capture that Belgian charm. **Known for:** fun wine and beer dinners; extensive beer menu; waffle-centric brunch menu. $ *Average main: $35* ✉ *514 8th St. SE, Eastern Market* ☎ *202/544–0100* ⊕ *www.belgacafe.com* Ⓜ *Eastern Market.*

Bistro Bis

$$$ | **FRENCH** | The zinc bar, cherrywood interior, and white tablecloths create great expectations at Bistro Bis, where the seasonal menu offers modern takes on French bistro fare. Thanks to its prime location, acclaimed menu, deep wine list, and classic cocktails, it's a popular spot for Washington power brokers and insiders. **Known for:** excellent steak frites and steak tartare; sophisticated ambience that attracts a powerful clientele; an elegant apple tart. $ *Average main: $34* ✉ *Hotel George, 15 E St. NW, Capitol Hill* ☎ *202/661–2700* ⊕ *www.bistrobis.com* Ⓜ *Union Station.*

Bistro Cacao

$$$$ | **FRENCH** | French and romantic, adorned with velvet curtained walls in a 19th-century bordello sort of way, Bistro Cacao is the place to go for a special meal. An extensive menu has a modern innovative flair—think grilled Mediterranean sea bass with leek confit and filet mignon with red pearl onion sauce.

Known for: extensive wine list; lovely patio; steak frites. $ *Average main: $40* ✉ *316 Massachusetts Ave. NE, Capitol Hill* ☎ *202/546–4737* ⊕ *bistrocacao.com* ⊗ *Closed Wed. No lunch* Ⓜ *Union Station.*

Café Berlin

$$ | **GERMAN** | Occupying the ground level of three town houses, Café Berlin has been serving authentic German fare since 1985—traditional dishes like Wiener schnitzel and sauerbraten, but also seasonal dishes including fresh asparagus in spring and wild game in winter. The outdoor beer garden in the front yard whisks you away to a German biergarten, oblivious of the Massachusetts Avenue traffic rushing past. **Known for:** airy patio; European flair; authentic German cuisine. $ *Average main: $25* ✉ *325 Massachusetts Ave. NE, Capitol Hill* ☎ *202/543–7656* ⊕ *www.cafeberlin-dc.com* ⊗ *Closed Mon. and Tues.* Ⓜ *Union Station.*

Charlie Palmer Steak

$$$$ | **STEAKHOUSE** | It's hard not to feel like a master of the universe when ensconced in this coolly elegant dining room in the imposing shadow of the Capitol. A dramatic glass-enclosed wine cellar and quasi-Danish modern furniture form a backdrop to the contemporary cuisine. **Known for:** seafood isn't an afterthought; rooftop terrace overlooking the Capitol; outstanding cuts of beef. $ *Average main: $70* ✉ *101 Constitution Ave. NW, Capitol Hill* ☎ *202/547–8100* ⊕ *www.charliepalmer.com/charlie-palmer-steak-dc* ⊟ *No credit cards* ⊗ *Closed Sun. No lunch Sat.* Ⓜ *Union Station.*

Ethiopic Restaurant

$$ | **ETHIOPIAN** | **FAMILY** | The spongy rolls of sourdough *injera* bread (ubiquitous on Ethiopian plates) used in place of utensils can make traditional Ethiopian feel decidedly indelicate, but the bright surroundings and friendly service here make for a downright romantic experience. Venture off the well-beaten path of tender curry lamb to try the spicy chickpea dumplings

or fragrant simmered split peas, laden with garlic and served in a clay pot. **Known for:** minimalist yet friendly atmosphere; Ethiopian standards like beef tibs and injera; great Ethiopian coffee and beer options. $ *Average main: $23* ⊠ *401 H St. NE, Capitol Hill* ☎ *202/675–2066* ⊕ *www.ethiopicrestaurant.com* ☉ *Closed Mon. No lunch Tues.–Thurs.* Ⓜ *Union Station.*

★ Good Stuff Eatery

$ | **AMERICAN** | **FAMILY** | Fans of Bravo's *Top Chef* will first visit this brightly colored burgers-and-shakes joint hoping to spy charismatic celebrity chef Spike Mendelsohn, but they will return for the comfort-food favorites (and learn it's a family effort). The lines can be long, as it's a favorite lunch spot of congressional aides, but the Mendelsohns' inventive burgers are worth the wait (there also are creative salads and Southern-fried chicken sandwiches). **Known for:** fun burgers like the "Prez" (with bacon, onion marmalade, and Roquefort cheese); thick malted milkshakes; variety of dipping sauces for hand-cut skinny fries. $ *Average main: $9* ⊠ *303 Pennsylvania Ave. SE, Capitol Hill* ☎ *202/791–0168* ⊕ *www. goodstuffeatery.com* Ⓜ *Eastern Market.*

Granville Moore's

$$ | **BELGIAN** | This Belgian beer hall with a gourmet soul is worth a visit for both its intense beer list and mussels and frites, plus a few other unique salads, burgers, and soups. Snag a seat at the bar or at one of the cozy tables, and linger over unfiltered brews that range from Chimay to obscure options from the reserve and limited-stock beer selection. **Known for:** steamed mussels served in five unique sauces; wide-ranging Belgian beer list; crunchy frites and homemade dipping sauces. $ *Average main: $24* ⊠ *1238 H St. NE, Capitol Hill* ☎ *202/399–2546* ⊕ *www.granvillemoores.com* ☉ *No lunch. Closed Tues. and Wed. in summer* Ⓜ *Union Station.*

Hawk 'n' Dove

$$ | **AMERICAN** | It's not the dark labyrinth of fireplace-warmed warrens it once was, but this glistening, industrial-wood tavern still is the place to talk politics and mingle with Hill residents—everyone from dark-suited lobbyists to locals who have lived here for decades (and probably will admit they don't like the newer look). It serves a decent upscale menu ranging from game day food (corn dogs, beef sliders) to Neapolitan-style pizzas to kale-and-roasted-sweet-potato salad and chicken potpie. **Known for:** legendary history; vegetarian-friendly; excellent service. $ *Average main: $20* ⊠ *329 Pennsylvania Ave. SE, Capitol Hill* ☎ *202/547–0030* ⊕ *www.hawkndove-bardc.com* Ⓜ *Capitol South.*

Jimmy T's Place

$ | **AMERICAN** | Known for its boisterous owner and throngs of talkative regulars, this family-owned D.C. institution is tucked into the first floor of an old row house only five blocks from the Capitol. Enjoy favorites like light-and-fluffy waffles served with a solid slice of bacon and an egg. **Known for:** classic greasy-spoon atmosphere; breakfast combos like grits and scrapple; absolutely no substitutions and cash only. $ *Average main: $7* ⊠ *501 E. Capitol St. SE, Capitol Hill* ☎ *202/709–3557* ▭ *No credit cards* ☉ *Closed Mon. and Tues. No dinner* Ⓜ *Capitol S.*

The Market Lunch

$ | **AMERICAN** | **FAMILY** | Digging into a hefty pile of pancakes from this casual counter in Eastern Market makes for the perfect end to a stroll around the Capitol. Morning favorites include not only pancakes but also shrimp and grits; crab cakes, fried oysters, and fresh fish are popular at lunch. **Known for:** blueberry buckwheat pancakes; long lines and lots of kids; cash-only policy. $ *Average main: $14* ⊠ *225 7th St. SE, Eastern Market* ☎ *202/547–8444* ⊕ *www.marketlunchdc. com* ▭ *No credit cards* ☉ *Closed Mon. No dinner* Ⓜ *Eastern Market.*

★ Pineapple and Pearls

$$$$ | **CONTEMPORARY** | For his follow-up to the smash hit Rose's Luxury, chef Aaron Silverman opened this reservation-only dining room next door that offered only an expensive 12-course (give or take) tasting. But since Covid, he reimagined the whole thing, creating a festive, whimsical space offering four hefty courses (with two choices for each course). **Known for:** intense reservation process; whimsical and fun but delicious dishes; expensive four-course menu. [$] *Average main: $325* ✉ *715 8th St. SE, Eastern Market* ☎ *202/595–7375* 🌐 *www.pineappleandpearls.com* 🕒 *Closed Sun.–Tues.* [M] *Eastern Market.*

★ Rose's Luxury

$$$$ | **MODERN AMERICAN** | A darling of both diners and the media, Rose's Luxury lives up to the hype as one of the city's most welcoming and groundbreaking dining destinations. The dishes are as delightful as they are shocking, and cause visitors to wait in line for hours to visit the supremely stylish re-creation of a hipster's dream dinner party. **Known for:** innovative small plates; the sausage, lychee, and habanero salad; long waits for a table (with reservations only for big groups). [$] *Average main: $95* ✉ *717 8th St. SE, Eastern Market* ☎ *202/742–3570* 🌐 *www.rosesluxury.com* 🕒 *No lunch* [M] *Eastern Market.*

St. Anselm

$$$$ | **STEAKHOUSE** | Grilled meats are the specialty of this neighborhood Union Market tavern, with creative dishes including lamb leg steak and bone-in skate wing, along with the more traditional butcher's steak. Don't bypass the sides, including potato salad and broccoli—grilled, of course. **Known for:** offbeat decor; extensive wine menu; innovative dishes. [$] *Average main: $40* ✉ *1250 5th St. NE, Capitol Hill* ☎ *202/864–2199* 🌐 *stanselmdc.com* [M] *NoMa–Gallaudet U.*

Sonoma Restaurant and Wine Bar

$$ | **WINE BAR** | This chic, multilevel wine bar has pours aplenty (in both tasting portions and full glasses) along with well-thought-out charcuterie boards piled with prosciutto and fluffy, grill-charred focaccia. There's more-filling fare, too, like braised bone-in oxtail. **Known for:** hip and vast wine menu; happy hour catering to a congressional crowd; homemade charcuterie and thin-crust pizzas. [$] *Average main: $26* ✉ *223 Pennsylvania Ave. SE, Capitol Hill* ☎ *202/544–8088* 🌐 *www.sonomadc.com* 🕒 *Closed Sun. and Mon. No lunch Sat.* [M] *Capitol S.*

Sticky Rice

$$$ | **ASIAN FUSION** | Some of the city's best sushi is found at this unassuming Pan-Asian restaurant with a sense of humor on H Street. Innovative favorites include 2000 Leagues (tempura octopus with eel sauce) and Godzirra roll (crunchy prawns with spicy sauce). **Known for:** innovative cocktail menu; buckets of tater tots with special tater tot sauce; good vegetarian and gluten-free options. [$] *Average main: $30* ✉ *1224 H St. NE, Capitol Hill* ☎ *202/397–7655* 🌐 *stickyricedc.com* [M] *Union Station.*

Ted's Bulletin

$$ | **DINER** | **FAMILY** | One bite of the grilled cheese with tomato soup or the all-American burger will convince you that the kitchen's skills are no joke. There are plenty of other options at this popular neighborhood eatery, too, including creative salads, entrées such as filet mignon and salmon, crab cakes—and all-day breakfasts. **Known for:** creative approach to classic American dishes; milkshakes with clever names (with or without alcohol); homemade Pop-Tarts. [$] *Average main: $25* ✉ *505 8th St. SE, Eastern Market* ☎ *202/544–8337* 🌐 *www.tedsbulletin.com* [M] *Eastern Market.*

Tune Inn

$ | **DINER** | Part bar, part diner, part happy-hour haunt for Hill staffers, this Capitol Hill tradition is one of the neighborhood's last great dives. Opened in 1947, and still run by the same family, the space was upgraded after a fire in 2011 but retains its lodge-like decor, including a healthy display of taxidermied animals staring down from the walls. **Known for:** cheap beer and greasy grub; an utter absence of pretension; breakfast served all day. Ⓢ *Average main: $10* ✉ *331 Pennsylvania Ave. SE, Capitol Hill* ☎ *202/543–2725* ⊕ *www.facebook.com/pages/tune-inn-restaurant-bar/118011451549614* Ⓜ *Capitol S.*

🛏 Hotels

To be sure, politics and commerce, like oil and water, don't mix, but they sure make for a great neighborhood in which to spend a few nights. Fortunately, there's no lack of options when it comes to lodging on Capitol Hill. From modernist luxury suites to comfy boutique settings—there's even a hideaway hostel for the most thrifty travelers—the neighborhood offers plenty of choices to base your visit at the hub of some of Washington's best political, commercial, and cultural sights.

Capitol Hill Hotel
$$ | HOTEL | FAMILY | A great choice if you want to stay on the Hill and need some extra room to spread out: all Federalist-chic-style units are suites, with kitchenettes, large work desks, flat-screen TVs, and spacious closets. **Pros:** close to Metro and sights; access to on-site bikes; eco-friendly. **Cons:** expensive valet parking; hotel is spread out in two buildings, which can be inconvenient; extra fee to access certain amenities. Ⓢ *Rooms from: $270* ✉ *200 C St. SE, Capitol Hill* ☎ *202/543–6000* ⊕ *www.capitolhillhotel-dc.com* ⇌ *153 suites* ⦿ *Free Breakfast* Ⓜ *Capitol S.*

City House Hostel Washington, D.C.
$ | HOTEL | It looks like a hole-in-the-wall, but this hostel is a clean, comfortable oasis—in the heart of the bustling H Street Corridor and near public transit—that's perfect for backpackers and other cost-conscious travelers. **Pros:** smack in the center of a lively strip of bars, restaurants, and grocery stores; good chance to meet fellow travelers; by far the cheapest option close to the Capitol. **Cons:** H Street can be noisy; cramped accommodations; very few private rooms. Ⓢ *Rooms from: $25* ✉ *506 H St. NE, Capitol Hill* ☎ *202/370–6390* ⊕ *www.cityhousehostels.com/washington-dc-hostel* ⇌ *14 rooms* ⦿ *No Meals* Ⓜ *Union Station.*

Hilton Garden Inn
$$ | HOTEL | Just a block from a Metro stop, this hotel, though a bit off the beaten path in the NoMa neighborhood, is convenient for getting around the city. **Pros:** great views; indoor pool; business-friendly, including free Wi-Fi and printing. **Cons:** limited options at paid breakfast buffet; not in the center of town; no self-parking, and valet parking is pricey. Ⓢ *Rooms from: $290* ✉ *1225 1st St. NE, Capitol Hill* ☎ *202/408–4870* ⊕ *www.hiltongardeninn.com* ⇌ *204 rooms* ⦿ *No Meals* Ⓜ *NoMa–Gallaudet U.*

Hilton Washington, D.C. Capitol Hill
$ | HOTEL | Modernized guest rooms done in soft grays and golds, and a location near the Metro and sights make the Hilton Washington, D.C. Capitol Hill a reliable, comfortable place to stay. **Pros:** Capitol views from many rooms; pet-friendly; 24-hour fitness and business centers. **Cons:** some reports of mixed service; dearth of restaurants in the neighborhood; expensive valet parking. Ⓢ *Rooms from: $202* ✉ *525 New Jersey Ave. NW, Capitol Hill* ☎ *202/628–2100* ⊕ *www.hilton.com* ⇌ *267 rooms* ⦿ *No Meals* Ⓜ *Union Station.*

Hyatt Regency Washington on Capitol Hill
$$ | HOTEL | A favorite for political events, fund-raising dinners, and networking meetings, this standard-issue business hotel is a solid choice if you plan to spend

a lot of time on the Hill. **Pros:** beautiful sky-lit, heated indoor pool and outdoor sundeck; quick walk to Union Station; Old Town Trolley Tours stop at hotel. **Cons:** always very busy; expensive parking; anonymous feel. $ *Rooms from: $250* ✉ *400 New Jersey Ave. NW, Capitol Hill* ☎ *202/737–1234, 800/233–1234* 🌐 *www.hyatt.com* 🛏 *838 rooms* 🍴 *No Meals* [M] *Union Station.*

Phoenix Park Hotel

$$$ | HOTEL | If you prefer to be near the Hill but not in a convention hotel, this family-owned, European-style hotel—which offers small but beautifully appointed and comfortable guest rooms across the street from Union Station—may fit the bill. **Pros:** comfy beds with good linens; lively Dubliner Restaurant and Pub next door; free Wi-Fi. **Cons:** no swimming pool; small rooms; some rooms are noisy. $ *Rooms from: $320* ✉ *520 N. Capitol St. NW, Capitol Hill* ☎ *202/638–6900, 855/371–6824* 🌐 *www.phoenixparkhotel.com* 🛏 *149 rooms* 🍴 *No Meals* [M] *Union Station.*

🍸 Nightlife

BARS AND LOUNGES

Biergarten Haus

BEER GARDENS | Step off H Street and into a boisterous bit of Bavaria. There might be football on TV, but that's not enough to break the spell of a place so genuinely Germanic. With about a dozen German drafts on offer, along with other authentic specialties—Tito's Mule?—and five fully stocked bars (plus a full kitchen), there's something for everyone, including six different spaces. Get cozy inside, or head for the "pavilion," covered with heaters in winter and partially open in good weather; the tree-lined outdoor patio, sprinkled with fire pits and a heater in winter; four-seater cabins; an outdoor roof deck; and more. ✉ *1355 H St. NE, Capitol Hill* ☎ *202/388–4053* 🌐 *www.biergartenhaus.com.*

Dubliner

PUBS | A short walk from Union Station and Capitol Hill, this Washington institution in the Phoenix Park Hotel offers cozy paneled rooms, rich pints of Guinness, and other authentic fare. It's especially popular with locals and Hill staffers alike. While offering live Irish music seven nights a week, this charming spot never charges a cover, save for St. Patrick's Day. ✉ *4 F St. NW, Capitol Hill* ☎ *202/737–3773* 🌐 *www.dublinerdc.com* [M] *Union Station.*

Granville Moore's

PUBS | Beer and mussels: the appeal is that simple, and they're that satisfying. But the narrow, rustic bars on two floors are as popular with drinkers as diners. The Belgian-themed gastropub has one of the largest selections of beer, from pilsners to Flemish reds, in D.C. If you are hungry, offerings in this cozy spot go beyond mussels, and include steak frites and Flemish dip. Happy hour takes place daily between 5 pm and 7 pm. ✉ *1238 H St. NE, Capitol Hill* ☎ *202/399–2546* 🌐 *www.granvillemoores.com* 🕒 *Closed Tues., and Wed. in summer* [M] *Union Station.*

H Street Country Club

BARS | The only D.C. bar to offer indoor miniature golf, Skee-Ball, and giant Jenga has a friendly, laid-back vibe. Fish tacos and an impressive margarita list round out the fun mix at this popular nightspot. Big-screen sports line the walls downstairs, but you can usually catch a breath of fresh air on the roof deck. ✉ *1335 H St. NE, Capitol Hill* ☎ *202/399–4722* 🌐 *www.hstcountryclub.com* 🕒 *Closed Mon.–Wed.* [M] *Union Station.*

Little Miss Whiskey's Golden Dollar

BARS | A purple light at the door marks the spot of this eclectic, New Orleans–influenced watering hole–dance club at the center of H Street. The dark interior features old concert posters from cult favorites like Pantera and Iggy Pop. The bar downstairs offers an enormous list of bottled beers and a signature adult slushy—the "Awesomeness"—that packs a real punch. The upstairs bar hosts DJs every Friday and Saturday night, when the space heaves with dancers packed wall-to-wall. The bar's cheeky slogan—"a lousy bar for rotten people"—isn't quite right. The service here is great. ✉ *1104 H St. NE, Capitol Hill* ⊕ *www.littlemisswhiskeys.com* Ⓜ *Union Station.*

MUSIC CLUBS
Echostage
LIVE MUSIC | This sprawling complex of more than 30,000 square feet effectively re-creates the vibe of an otherwise bygone era in D.C.—one of mega-nightclubs in retrofitted warehouses in derelict neighborhoods. With unobstructed sight lines to the stage and a German-imported sound system, it's the place for club kids to dance to the biggest names in E.D.M., from Calvin Harris to David Guetta to Tiesto. Catch your breath at one of the two 60-foot bars lining either side of the dance floor. ■**TIP→ With no Metro stops nearby, driving or taking a cab/rideshare is required.** ✉ *2135 Queens Chapel Rd. NE, Northeast* ☎ *202/503–2330* ⊕ *www.echostage.com.*

Mr. Henry's
LIVE MUSIC | Capitol Hillers love this laid-back pub/restaurant, notably for its list of nightly specials including half-priced burgers on Mondays. But there's more than meets the eye at this eclectic indoor-outdoor dinner space; Mr. Henry's is also the last holdout of a once-thriving live-music scene on Capitol Hill. Probably the best known, local native Roberta Flack got her start in the upstairs performance space, where a dozen or so tables are scattered around the wood-paneled room. Live music is offered at least four nights a week; tickets can be purchased on the website. ✉ *601 Pennsylvania Ave. SE, Capitol Hill* ☎ *202/546–8412* ⊕ *www.mrhenrysdc.com* Ⓜ *Eastern Market.*

🎭 Performing Arts

The arts scene in Capitol Hill and Northeast D.C. has blossomed in recent years with the opening of several performance venues and the ever-changing mix of restaurants, bars, and stages along the H Street Corridor. Leading the charge is the Atlas Performing Arts Center, at the cutting edge of dance, music, and drama. For classical drama, you will discover great performances and an intimate atmosphere at the Folger Theatre near the Capitol (closed for a multiyear renovation).

DANCE
Dance Place
MODERN DANCE | This studio theater showcases an eclectic array of local, national, and international dance and performance art talent in an assortment of modern and ethnic shows. Performances take place most weekends, and drop-in dance classes are held daily. The company is a bit of a trek from Capitol Hill (about 3 miles north of the Capitol), but it's quite close to the Brookland–CUA Metro station on the Red Line, just three stops from Union Station. ✉ *3225 8th St. NE, Northeast* ☎ *202/269–1600* ⊕ *www.danceplace.org* Ⓜ *Brookland–CUA.*

MAJOR VENUES
Atlas Performing Arts Center
ARTS CENTERS | Known as the "People's Kennedy Center," this performance venue occupies a restored art deco movie theater in one of Washington's up-and-coming neighborhoods. The Atlas's four theaters and three dance studios house a diverse group of resident arts organizations, including the Mosaic Theater Company of D.C., the Joy of Motion Dance Center, Step Afrika!, and the Capital City Symphony. Street parking can be difficult, but you can take the DC Streetcar here from the Metro stop at Union Station. ✉ *1333 H St. NE, Capitol Hill* ☎ *202/399–7993* ⊕ *www.atlasarts.org* Ⓜ *Union Station.*

MUSIC
CHAMBER MUSIC
Coolidge Auditorium at the Library of Congress

CONCERTS | Since its first concert, in 1925, the 500-seat Coolidge has hosted most of the 20th and 21st centuries' greatest performers and composers, including Copland and Stravinsky. Today, the theater draws musicians from all genres, including classical, jazz, and gospel, and the hall continues to wow audiences with its near-perfect acoustics and sight lines. Concert tickets must be reserved in advance through the Library's website. ■ TIP→ **Because of the Library's security procedures, patrons are urged to arrive 30 minutes before the start of each event.** ✉ *Library of Congress, Jefferson Building, 101 Independence Ave. SE, Capitol Hill* ☎ *202/707–5000* ⊕ *www.loc. gov* Ⓜ *Capitol S.*

Folger Shakespeare Library

CONCERTS | The library's internationally acclaimed resident chamber music ensemble, the Folger Consort, regularly presents Medieval, Renaissance, and Baroque pieces performed on period instruments. The season runs from September to May. The library is closed for renovation until at least late fall 2023. ✉ *201 E. Capitol St. SE, Capitol Hill* ☎ *202/544–7077* ⊕ *www.folger.edu* Ⓜ *Union Station or Capitol S.*

CHORAL MUSIC
★ Basilica of the National Shrine of the Immaculate Conception

CONCERTS | The Choir of the National Shrine, a professional choir of 16 voices, performs every Sunday at the Shrine's Noon Mass, in addition to visiting choral and church groups that occasionally perform at one of the largest Catholic churches in the Americas. Every summer and periodically throughout the year, recitals featuring the massive pipe organ are offered. See the website for times and visiting performers. ✉ *400 Michigan Ave. NE, Northeast* ☎ *202/526–8300* ⊕ *www.nationalshrine. com* Ⓜ *Brookland–CUA.*

THEATER AND PERFORMANCE ART
Capital Fringe Festival

ARTS FESTIVALS | Since its founding in 2005, the Capital Fringe Festival has grown each year, and it currently offers no fewer than 50 productions (and more than 300 individual performers) over a several-week period in July. Local and national performers display the strange, the political, the surreal, and the avant-garde to eclectic crowds at all times of the day in venues throughout the city. With tickets around $15, this is an affordable theater experience. Tickets go on sale in June.

■ TIP→ **Don't forget your Fringe Button, a pin that grants the holder access to all festival events and benefits from local retailers.**

Be ready to party at the Festival Bar, in Georgetown, where performers, musicians, and patrons rock into the wee hours on festival days. ✉ *996 Maine Ave. SW, Suite 757, Capitol Hill* ⊕ *www. capitalfringe.org.*

★ Folger Theatre

THEATER | The theater at the Folger Shakespeare Library, an intimate 250-seat re-creation of the inn-yard theaters of Shakespeare's time, hosts three to four productions each year of Shakespearean or Shakespeare-influenced works. Although the stage is a throwback, the sharp acting and inspired direction consistently challenge and delight audiences. The theater is undergoing a multiyear renovation, but you can catch performances and other events at other venues in Washington, D.C. ✉ *Folger Shakespeare Library, 201 E. Capitol St. SE, Capitol Hill* ☎ *202/544–7077* ⊕ *www. folger.edu* Ⓜ *Union Station or Capitol S.*

Rorschach Theatre

THEATER | This company's intimate and passionate performances on stages throughout the city, including H Street's Atlas Performing Arts Center, highlight some of the most offbeat plays in Washington. The company offers lesser-known works by such playwrights as Fengar Gael, Kate Hamill, and Qui Nguyen. ⊠ *1333 H St. NE, Capitol Hill* ☎ *202/399–7993 Ext. 180* ⊕ *www.rorschachtheatre.com* Ⓜ *Union Station.*

👜 Shopping

Capitol Hill is surprisingly good territory for shopping. Eastern Market and the unique shops and boutiques clustered around the historic redbrick building are great for browsing. Inside Eastern Market are produce and meat counters, plus places to buy flowers and sweets.

■ **TIP→ The flea market, held outdoors on Sundays, presents nostalgia and local crafts by the crateful. There's also a farmers' market on Tuesdays and weekends.**

Along 7th Street, you can find a number of small shops selling such specialties as art books, handwoven rugs, and antiques. Cross Pennsylvania Avenue, and head south on 8th Street for historic Barracks Row, where shops, bars, and restaurants inhabit the charming row houses leading toward the Anacostia River. The other shopping lures near the Hill are Union Market and Union Station, D.C.'s gorgeous train station, these days actually a shopping mall that happens to also accommodate Amtrak and commuter trains.

Keep in mind that Union Station and Union Market are northeast of the Capitol, while Eastern Market is to the southeast. You can certainly walk between these sights, but be aware that, from Eastern Market, Union Station is roughly a mile away, and Union Market is another mile beyond that—trekking that might prove taxing after time already spent on your feet in the shops.

BOOKS
Capitol Hill Books

BOOKS | Pop into this three-story maze of used, new, and rare books, where the volumes are piled floor to ceiling, and no flat surface is left bare. (Even the bathroom is stacked high.) The knowledgeable staff will help you browse through a wonderful collection of out-of-print history titles, political and fiction writings, and mysteries. ⊠ *657 C St. SE, Eastern Market* ☎ *202/544–1621* ⊕ *www.capitolhillbooks-dc.com* Ⓜ *Eastern Market.*

★ East City Bookshop

BOOKS | A gathering spot for residents and visitors alike, East City stocks a wide selection of books, as well as art supplies, gifts, and toys. Check out the calendar of events, too—there's everything from story time for children to author-led book discussions to musical performances. ⊠ *645 Pennsylvania Ave. SE, Suite 100, Capitol Hill* ☎ *202/290–1636* ⊕ *www.eastcitybookshop.com* ⊗ *Closed Sun. and Mon.* Ⓜ *Eastern Market.*

Solid State Books

BOOKS | Opened by longtime D.C. booksellers in 2017, this modern, independent bookstore anchors retail on the H Street Corridor just steps from Union Station. It's bright, spacious, and features a great children's reading area behind the fully stocked bookcases. They also feature literary gifts, coffee, beer, and wine to augment a growing list of book clubs. ⊠ *600 H St. NE, Capitol Hill* ⊕ *A 10-minute walk from Union Station* ☎ *202/897–4201* ⊕ *www.solidstatebooksdc.com* Ⓜ *Union Station.*

CRAFTS AND GIFTS
Woven History/Silk Road

CRAFTS | Landmarks in this bohemian neighborhood, these connected stores sell gorgeous, handmade treasures from tribal communities from every country along the Silk Road. You'll find everything from colorful weavings, pillows, and embroidered quilts to exotic jewelry and bags, musical instruments, clothing, and gift items as well as antique furniture. Woven History has carpets in all sizes, specializing in traditionally woven, vege-table-dyed carpets. ⊠ *311–315 7th St. SE, Eastern Market* ☎ *202/543–1705* ⊕ *www. wovenhistory.com* Ⓜ *Eastern Market.*

FOOD
Hill's Kitchen

FOOD | If you're a cook or looking for a gift for someone who is, pop into this small shop across the street from the Eastern Market Metro. You'll find cookbooks, baking pans, aprons, towels and pot-holders, cookie cutters, barware, grilling tools, specialty foods, and much more. The shop is closed on Monday. ⊠ *713 D St. SE, Eastern Market* ☎ *202/543–1997* ⊕ *www.hillskitchen.com* Ⓜ *Eastern Market.*

MARKETS
★ Eastern Market

MARKET | For 150-plus years, this has been the hub of the Capitol Hill commu-nity. Vibrantly colored produce and flow-ers, freshly caught fish, fragrant cheeses, and tempting sweets are sold at the mar-ket by independent vendors. On week-ends year-round, local farmers sell fresh fruits and vegetables (Tuesdays, too), and artists and exhibitors sell handmade arts and crafts, jewelry, antiques, collectibles, and furniture from around the world. A flea market unfurls on Sundays. The city's oldest continuously operating public mar-ket continues to be a vibrant and lively gathering place, complete with entertain-ment, art showings, and a pottery studio for residents and visitors alike. ⊠ *225 7th St. SE, Eastern Market* ✛ *7th St. and North Carolina Ave. SE* ☎ *202/698–5253* ⊕ *www.easternmarket-dc.com* ⊗ *Indoor market closed Mon.* Ⓜ *Eastern Market.*

Radici Market

SOUVENIRS | The name means "roots" in Italian, and this little shop has quickly settled its roots into the Capitol Hill neighborhood. The charming owners have created a warm and inviting gath-ering spot and store with its brick walls,

Venetian glass light fixtures, terra-cotta tiles, beautiful food, and handmade Italian gift displays and tables both inside and out. This is a lovely spot for an afternoon pick-me-up of espresso and cannoli or an end-of-day glass of wine and *cicchetti Veneziani* (small bites). You'll also find everything you need for an Italian-themed picnic. Wine tastings are held on Thursday evening. ⊠ *303 7th St. SE, Eastern Market* ☎ *202/758–0086* ⊕ *www.radici-market.com* Ⓜ *Eastern Market.*

Union Market

OTHER SPECIALTY STORE | **FAMILY** | Arriving in 2012, massive Union Market is a feast for the senses that's a favorite destination for locals and out-of-town visitors alike. The space offers a smorgasbord of food and drink options, from sushi and piping hot empanadas to Bloody Marys and fish-and-chips. There are butchers and bakers and candles (though not candle-stick makers—yet), as well as cheese vendors, microbrewed coffee, and a shop selling spices you've never heard of. It's all made the market enormously popular, particularly on weekends, when parents descend to sip espresso while the youngsters bound around a generous outdoor seating area that features a host of lawn games.

Union Market is part of the new, buzz-ing Union Market District, filled with restaurants; a pop-up movie theater, the Angelika, which shows new releases and classic favorites; and La Cosecha, a contemporary Latin market two blocks away. ⊠ *1309 5th St. NE, Capitol Hill* ☎ *301/347–3998* ⊕ *www.unionmarketdc. com* Ⓜ *NoMA–Gallaudet U.*

Union Station

MALL | Resplendent with marble floors and vaulted ceilings, Union Station is a shopping mall as well as a train terminal. It also has restaurants and a food court with everything from sushi and smooth-ies to poke bowls. The east hall is filled with vendors of expensive domestic and

international wares who sell from open
stalls. From April through October, an
outdoor market is held Monday to Saturday with dozens of vendors selling fresh
produce, baked goods and quick snacks,
and arts and crafts. The Christmas
season brings lights, a train display, and
seasonal gift shops. ⊠ *50 Massachusetts
Ave. NE, Capitol Hill* ☎ *202/289–1908*
⊕ *www.unionstationdc.com* Ⓜ *Union
Station.*

TOYS
Labyrinth Games & Puzzles
TOYS | You won't find any video games
in this gem; rather, you'll discover an
outstanding selection of handmade
wooden puzzles and mazes, collectible
card and travel games, board games, and
brainteasers. A bonus to stopping in are
the dozens of activities and games for all
ages you can play. ⊠ *645 Pennsylvania
Ave. SE, Eastern Market* ☎ *202/544–1059*
⊕ *www.labyrinthgameshop.com* Ⓜ *Eastern Market.*

FOGGY BOTTOM

WITH THE WEST END AND THE WHITE HOUSE

6

Updated by
Jessica van Dop DeJesus

⊙ Sights	🍴 Restaurants	🛏 Hotels	🛍 Shopping	🍸 Nightlife
★★★★★	★★★☆☆	★★★★☆	★☆☆☆☆	★★☆☆☆

NEIGHBORHOOD SNAPSHOT

TOP EXPERIENCES

Department of State Diplomatic Reception Rooms: One of D.C.'s best-kept secrets, this suite of rooms is filled with museum-quality art and historical treasures inspired by the country's founding years. You must reserve well in advance.

John F. Kennedy Center for the Performing Arts: See popular live bands on the Millennium Stage, daily at 6 pm.

Thompson Boat Center: Take in Washington's marble monuments, lush Roosevelt Island, and the Virginia coastline with a kayak ride down the Potomac.

Touring the White House: The White House website has up-to-date information on White House tours.

GETTING HERE

The White House can be reached by the Red Line's Farragut N stop or the Silver, Blue, and Orange lines' McPherson Sq. and Farragut W stops. Foggy Bottom has its own Metro stop, also on the Silver, Blue, and Orange lines. A free shuttle runs from the station to the Kennedy Center. Many of the other attractions are a considerable distance from the nearest Metro stop. If you don't relish long walks or if time is limited, check the map to see if you need to make alternate travel arrangements to visit specific sights.

PLANNING YOUR TIME

Touring the area around the White House could easily take a day or even two. If you enjoy history, you may be most interested in the buildings in the Lafayette Square Historic District, **DAR Museum,** and **State Department.** Save the **Kennedy Center** for the evening. You'll find some notable restaurants here as well, including the West End's Blue Duck Tavern.

ART IN FOGGY BOTTOM

This is the main neighborhood in D.C. to explore the wide range of art created in America. Start with the **Renwick Gallery,** where the temporary installations are always worth the trip and has something for both the traditional and contemporary art lovers. If you want to explore more current history, head to the **Black Lives Matter Plaza,** a response to then-president Trump calling in the National Guard to disperse peaceful protestors for a cause that sparked worldwide protests.

The neighborhood comprising Foggy Bottom, the West End, and the White House includes some of D.C.'s most iconic attractions, the biggest being the White House itself, the home of every U.S. president but George Washington.

But there are also some excellent smaller museums, including the Octagon House, Renwick Gallery, Decatur House, and the Department of Interior Museum. You will find the Kennedy Center along the Potomac River and George Washington University's campus. The area has a strong residential character as well and is home to some of D.C.'s oldest houses.

◉ Sights

When you're in the Foggy Bottom area, there's a sight you cannot miss: The White House. You'll need to reserve far in advance (weeks, if not months) if you want to take a tour. If you miss out, stop by the nearby White House Visitor Center, which provides a good overview of the Executive Mansion's life and times. That said, the neighborhood also boasts a selection of smaller sights that are definitely worth your while, including the Museum of the Americas at the Organization of American States, Smithsonian's Renwick Gallery, and Decatur House. Although Foggy Bottom is not known for its nightlife, it does offer several iconic hotel bars and cozy lounges to catch up with friends. The neighborhood's culinary offerings have grown as well. From Indian fine dining to fried chicken sandwiches, there's something for everyone. One of the country's premier arts and performance centers, The Kennedy Center, is also part of this

neighborhood. Check their website for their unique programming.

American Red Cross

NOTABLE BUILDING | The national headquarters for the American Red Cross, a National Historic Landmark since 1965, is composed of three buildings. Guided tours show off the oldest, a Beaux Arts structure of blinding-white marble built in 1917 to commemorate women who cared for the wounded on both sides during the Civil War. Three stained glass windows designed by Louis Comfort Tiffany illustrate the values of the Red Cross: faith, hope, love, and charity. Other holdings you'll see on the 60-minute tour include an original N.C. Wyeth painting, sculptures, and artifacts that belonged to Clara Barton, the founder of the American Red Cross. Weather permitting, the tour includes a visit to the memorial garden. The management recommends booking your tour 2–3 weeks in advance. Reservations are required for the free tour, offered at 10 am and 2 pm on Wednesday and Friday; schedule via email at *tours@redcross.org*. ⊠ *430 17th St. NW, Foggy Bottom* ☎ *202/303–4233* ⊕ *www.redcross.org* ☞ *Free* ⊘ *No tours Thurs. and Sat.–Tues.* Ⓜ *Farragut W.*

Art Museum of the Americas

ART MUSEUM | Located on 18th Street, just steps from the National Mall, the Art Museum of the Americas (AMA) is still considered by many a hidden

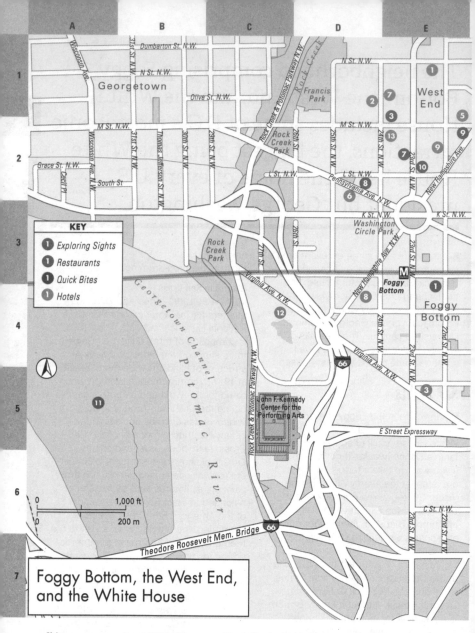

KEY

- 1 Exploring Sights
- 1 Restaurants
- 1 Quick Bites
- 1 Hotels

Foggy Bottom, the West End, and the White House

Sights ▼

1 American Red Cross ... **H6**
2 Art Museum of the Americas **G6**
3 Black Lives Matter Plaza **I3**
4 Corcoran School of the Arts + Design at GW.... **H5**
5 Daughters of the American Revolution (DAR) Museum.......... **H6**

6 Decatur House.......... **H4**
7 Federal Reserve Building **G3**
8 The George Washington University Museum and The Textile Museum.... **F4**
9 The Octagon Museum of the Architects Foundation.............. **G5**
10 Renwick Gallery of the Smithsonian American Art Museum............. **H4**

11 Theodore Roosevelt Island..................... **A5**
12 U.S. Department of the Interior Museum ... **G6**
13 U.S. Department of the Treasury.............. **I4**
14 The White House **I5**
15 White House Visitor Center **J5**

Restaurants ▼

1 Beefsteak................ **E3**
2 Bindaas.................. **F3**
3 Blue Duck Tavern....... **E1**
4 Call Your Mother Deli .. **F2**
5 Founding Farmers DC .. **F4**
6 Immigrant Food **H4**
7 Imperfecto.............. **E2**

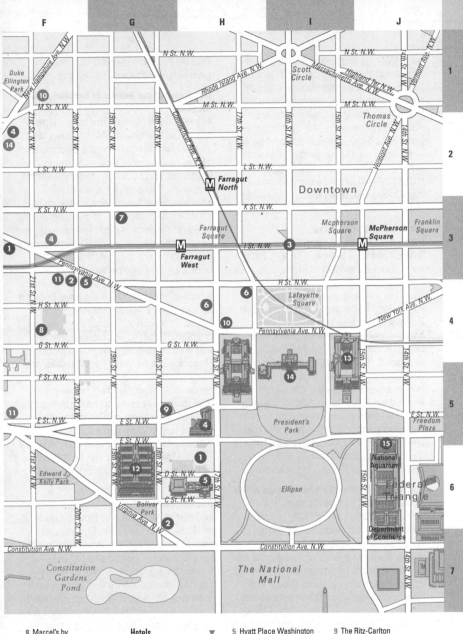

F G H I J

1

Duke Ellington Park

N St. N.W.

Rhode Island Ave. N.W.

Scott Circle

Massachusetts Ave. N.W.

Highland Ter. N.W.

Vermont Ave. N.W.

10 M St. N.W.

M St. N.W.

M St. N.W.

Thomas Circle

4

14

21st St. N.W.

20th St. N.W.

19th St. N.W.

18th St. N.W.

Connecticut Ave. N.W.

17th St. N.W.

16th St. N.W.

15th St. N.W.

14th St. N.W.

Vermont Ave. N.W.

2

L St. N.W.

L St. N.W.

Farragut North

K St. N.W.

Downtown

7

K St. N.W.

Mcpherson Square

McPherson Square

Franklin Square

1

4

Farragut Square

I St. N.W.

3

3

Pennsylvania Ave. N.W.

Farragut West

New York Ave. N.W.

11 2 5

H St. N.W.

6

H St. N.W.

Lafayette Square

21st St. N.W.

6

10

Pennsylvania Ave. N.W.

4

8

G St. N.W.

G St. N.W.

5

11

F St. N.W.

9

F St. N.W.

4

F St. N.W. Freedom Plaza

Edward J. Kelly Park

E St. N.W.

12

18th St. N.W.

1

15

National Aquarium

Federal Triangle

21st St. N.W.

20th St. N.W.

D St. N.W.

5

19th St. N.W.

Bolivar Park

C St. N.W.

6

Ellipse

14th St. N.W.

2

Virginia Ave. N.W.

Department of Commerce

Constitution Ave. N.W.

Constitution Ave. N.W.

7

Constitution Gardens Pond

The National Mall

14th St. N.W.

---

8 Marcel's by
Robert Wiedmaier **D2**

9 Rasika West End........ **E2**

10 RIS...................... **E2**

11 Western Market **F3**

Quick Bites ▼

1 Flower Child............. **F3**

Hotels ▼

1 Embassy Suites
Washington,
D.C. Georgetown........ **E1**

2 The Fairmont,
Washington, D.C.,
Georgetown **D1**

3 Hotel Hive **E5**

4 Hotel Lombardy......... **F3**

5 Hyatt Place Washington
DC/Georgetown/
West End **E1**

6 Melrose Georgetown
Hotel...................... **D2**

7 Park Hyatt
Washington.............. **E1**

8 Residence Inn Washington,
DC/Foggy Bottom **D4**

9 The Ritz-Carlton
Washington, D.C. **E2**

10 The St. Gregory Hotel
Dupont Circle **F1**

11 State Plaza Hotel **F5**

12 The Watergate
Hotel...................... **C4**

13 Westin Georgetown,
Washington D.C. **E2**

14 Yours Truly DC........... **F2**

gem. With its rotating exhibitions from prominent Latin American and Caribbean artists, there's always something new to experience at the museum. Take a break from the D.C. crowds and learn about the exhibitions, walk around the picturesque blue-tile corridor, and go for a walk along its serene garden. Admission is free. ⊠ *201 18th St. NW, Foggy Bottom* ☎ *220/370–0149* ⊕ *www.museum.oas. org* ✉ *Free* ☉ *Closed Mon., federal holidays, and Good Friday* Ⓜ *Farragut W.*

Black Lives Matter Plaza

OTHER ATTRACTION | After then-President Trump held up a Bible on June 1, 2020, for a photo op in front of historic St. John's Church, calling out the National Guard to waylay peaceful protestors for his safe passage, D.C. mayor Muriel Bowser had the words "Black Lives Matter" painted in yellow, 35-foot-long capital letters along a two-block-long section of 16th Street NW, in front of the church and within plain view of the White House several days after the incident. Since then, Black Lives Matter Plaza has become a community gathering spot featuring performances, yoga, and even weddings. In October 2021, it became a permanent installation. ⊠ *16th St. NW between H and K Sts., Foggy Bottom.*

Corcoran School of the Arts + Design at GW

COLLEGE | The Corcoran School, a prestigious art school since 1878, is now in partnership with George Washington University. Throughout the year, the school features events and performances by the students and other artists. The iconic, beautifully restored Beaux Arts Flagg Building, which started life as the historic Corcoran Gallery of Art in 1890, shuttered its doors in 2014. Don't miss the first-floor Luther W. Brady Art Gallery, which showcases temporary exhibits by renowned artists. Check the website for events like Friday @5, featuring live music and popular amongst young D.C. professionals. ⊠ *500 17th St. NW, Foggy Bottom* ☎ *202/994–1700* ⊕ *corcoran. gwu.edu* Ⓜ *Farragut W or Farragut N.*

Daughters of the American Revolution (DAR) Museum

ART MUSEUM | **FAMILY** | The Beaux Arts Memorial Continental Hall, built in 1929 as the headquarters for the Daughters of the Revolution (DAR), is home to Washington, D.C.'s only decorative arts museum. The enormous collection encompasses furniture, textiles, quilts, silver, china, porcelain, stoneware, earthenware, glass, and other items made and used in the daily lives of Americans from the Colonial era through the early 20th century. Thirty-one period rooms reflect more than two centuries of American interiors, including a 1690s New England hall, an 1860s Texas bedroom, and a 1920s Ohio parlor. Two galleries feature changing exhibitions of decorative arts, and a study gallery allows researchers close access to the collection. Docent tours of the period rooms are available on weekdays, depending on docent availability. You can also take a self-guided tour. The museum also hosts special events for children and adults; check the website for details. ⊠ *1776 D St. NW, Foggy Bottom* ☎ *202/628–1776* ⊕ *www. dar.org/museum* ✉ *Free* ☉ *Closed Sun.* Ⓜ *Farragut W.*

Decatur House

HISTORIC HOME | Decatur House was built in 1818–19 on Lafayette Square, just across from the White House, for naval hero Stephen Decatur and his wife, Susan. Designed by Benjamin Henry Latrobe, the country's first professional architect, it's one of Washington's oldest surviving homes. But Decatur didn't have long to enjoy it, since he died tragically 14 months later, after a duel with Commodore James Barron. Wealthy hotel and tavern owner John Gadsby purchased the distinguished Federal-style house as a retirement home in 1836. The large two-story dependency was used as quarters for numerous enslaved individuals in his household—Washington's only extant slave quarters. Tours—offered Monday at 10:30 am and 1 pm—feature these historic quarters and the house's first and second floors, much of which represent the taste of a later owner, Marie Beale, beloved for her salons with ambassadors and politicians. The White House Historical Society operates one of its three retail shops here, and you'll find an excellent selection of White House history–themed products, including the annual Christmas ornament. ⊠ *748 Jackson Pl. NW, Foggy Bottom* ☎ *202/218–4337* ⊕ *www.whitehousehistory.org/events/tour-the-historic-decatur-house* 🎫 *Free* ☉ *Closed for tours everyday but Mon.* Ⓜ *Farragut W.*

Federal Reserve Building

GOVERNMENT BUILDING | This imposing marble edifice, its bronze entryway topped by a massive eagle, was designed by Folger Shakespeare Library architect Paul Cret. Its appearance seems to say, "Your money's safe with us." Even so, there's no money here, as the Fed's mission is to set interest rates and keep the economy on track. The stately facade belies a friendlier interior, with a varied collection of art and several special art exhibitions every year. Tours of the building are available for groups of 10 or more, all aged 18 years or older; they must be booked at least two weeks in advance via email. ⊠ *20th St. and Constitution Ave. NW, Foggy Bottom* ☎ *202/452–3324* 📧 *SECY-VisitorServices@frb.gov* ⊕ *www.federalreserve.gov* 🎫 *Free* ☉ *Closed weekends* Ⓜ *Foggy Bottom–GWU.*

The George Washington University Museum and The Textile Museum

OTHER MUSEUM | Designed to celebrate the creative achievements of people in the capital city and around the world, this 46,000-square-foot LEED Gold–certified museum facility is on the campus of George Washington University. Rotating exhibits highlight global textiles and cultural traditions—from handmade rugs

and historical costumes to contemporary art and fashion—as well as displays on local D.C. history. The museum offers a dynamic range of free screenings, talks, and other public programs throughout the week in person and online. It's also home to a research library and two study centers, and you can find digital resources on textile creation and care on the website, along with highlights of the museum's collections. ⊠ *701 21st St. NW, Foggy Bottom* ☎ *202/994–5200* ⊕ *www.museum.gwu.edu* 🎫 *$8 suggested donation* ☉ *Closed Sun. and Mon.* Ⓜ *Foggy Bottom–GWU.*

The Octagon Museum of the Architects Foundation

HISTORIC HOME | FAMILY | Designed by Dr. William Thornton (original architect of the U.S. Capitol), the Octagon House was built by enslaved workers for John Tayloe III, a wealthy plantation owner, and completed in 1801. Thornton chose the unusual shape to conform to the acute angle formed by L'Enfant's intersection of New York Avenue and 18th Street. After the British burned the White House in 1814, Thornton convinced the Tayloes to allow James and Dolley Madison to stay in the Octagon. From September 1814 until March 1815, the Octagon became the temporary White House. In the second-floor study, the Treaty of Ghent, which ended the War of 1812, was ratified. The American Institute of Architects (AIA) established its national headquarters at the Octagon in 1898 and renovated the building as one of the country's first preservation projects. AIA stayed there for 70 years before moving into new modern headquarters directly behind. Self-guided tours take in historically furnished rooms; second-floor gallery spaces hold rotating exhibits on architecture, design, and history. ⊠ *1799 New York Ave. NW, Foggy Bottom* ☎ *202/626–7439* ⊕ *www.octagonmuseum.org* 🎫 *$10* ☉ *Closed Sun.–Wed.* Ⓜ *Farragut W or Farragut N.*

Directly across the street from the White House, the Renwick Gallery was the first purpose-built art museum in the United States. It's now a branch of the Smithsonian.

★ Renwick Gallery of the Smithsonian American Art Museum

ART MUSEUM | This luscious French Second Empire–style building rises across the street from the White House and the Eisenhower Executive Office Building. Even with such lofty neighbors, it is still the most appealing structure on the block. The Renwick Gallery, a branch museum of the Smithsonian American Art Museum, was the country's first purpose-built art museum, and it was known then as "the American Louvre." Designed by James Renwick Jr. in 1858 to hold the art collection of Washington merchant and banker William Wilson Corcoran. The National Historic Landmark building has been a branch of the Smithsonian American Art Museum dedicated to American crafts and decorative arts since 1972. The Renwick's exhibits are showcased in a captivating, interactive environment designed to illustrate the history of craft in America and its future. Exhibits highlight exciting contemporary artists using materials in innovative ways, redefining what craft is and taking it in bold new directions. ⊠ *Pennsylvania Ave. at 17th St. NW, Foggy Bottom* ☎ *202/633–7970* ⊕ *americanart.si.edu* ▨ *Free* Ⓜ *Farragut W and Farragut N.*

★ Theodore Roosevelt Island

WILDLIFE REFUGE | FAMILY | Designed as a living memorial to the environmentally minded 26th U.S. President, this wildlife sanctuary is off the George Washington Parkway near the Virginia side of the Potomac—close to Foggy Bottom, Georgetown, East Potomac Park, and the Kennedy Center. Hikers and bicyclists can reach the island by crossing the Theodore Roosevelt Memorial Bridge or walking for 15 minutes from the Rosslyn Metro. But bikes are not allowed on the island and must be docked near the footbridge. Take a ranger-led Island Safari to admire the many birds and other animals in the island's marsh and forests. ☎ *703/289–2500* ⊕ *www.nps.gov/this* ▨ *Free* Ⓜ *Rosslyn.*

U.S. Department of the Interior Museum

OTHER MUSEUM | The outside of the building is plain, but inside, a wealth of art, contained in two separate collections, reflects the department's work. The Office of the Secretary Art Collection, featuring heroic oil paintings of dam construction, gold panning, and cattle drives, is found throughout the building's hallways, offices, and meeting rooms. The Department of the Interior Museum Collection outlines the work of the Bureau of Land Management, the U.S. Geological Survey, the Bureau of Indian Affairs, the National Park Service, and other department branches. On Tuesday and Thursday at 2 pm, you can view 26 photographic murals by Ansel Adams and more than 40 dramatic murals painted by Maynard Dixon, John Steuart Curry, and other artists. Reservations are required for the Murals Tour; call at least two weeks in advance. The Indian Craft Shop across the hall from the museum sells Native American pottery, dolls, carvings, jewelry, baskets, and books. ⊠ *Stewart Lee Udall Department of the Interior Bldg., 1849 C St. NW, Foggy Bottom* ☎ *202/208–4743* ⊕ *www.doi.gov/interiormuseum* ⊠ *Free* ☉ *Closed weekends* ☞ *Visitors 18 and older must show a government-issued ID to enter the Stewart Lee Udall Department of the Interior Bldg.* Ⓜ *Farragut W.*

U.S. Department of the Treasury

GOVERNMENT BUILDING | Once used to store currency, this is one of the most impressive Greek Revival buildings in the United States. Robert Mills, the architect responsible for the Washington Monument and the Smithsonian American Art Museum, designed the colonnade on 15th Street. After the death of President Lincoln, the Andrew Johnson Suite was used as the executive office while Mrs. Lincoln moved out of the White House. One of the highlights is the Cash Room. Initially opened in 1869, it served as a bank, providing essential services to the public and supplying local banks with coins and currency. Renovated in 1985, visitors can tour the historic room. Tours of the Treasury Building are available only to U.S. citizens or legal residents, and you must make the reservation in advance through your congressional office. ⊠ *1500 Pennsylvania Ave. NW, Foggy Bottom* ☎ *202/622–2000 general info* ⊕ *home.treasury.gov/services/tours-and-library/tours-of-the-historic-treasury-building* ⊠ *Free* ☉ *Closed Sun.–Fri.* ☞ *Must reserve via your congressional office* Ⓜ *McPherson Sq. or Metro Center.*

The White House

GOVERNMENT BUILDING | Irish architect James Hoban designed America's most famous house in 1792. It was known officially as the Executive Mansion until 1902, when President Theodore Roosevelt renamed it the White House, long its informal name. The house has undergone many structural changes, including Harry Truman's addition of a second-story porch to the south portico. First Lady Jacqueline Kennedy undertook an extensive restoration in 1961 to preserve and showcase its historical and architectural significance. The self-guided tour includes rooms on the ground floor, but the State Floor has the highlights. The East Room is the White House's largest room, the site of ceremonies and press conferences; this is also where one of Abraham Lincoln's sons harnessed a pet goat to a chair and went for a ride. The portrait of George Washington that Dolley Madison saved from torch-carrying British soldiers in 1814 hangs in the room. Grover Cleveland, the only president to marry in the White House, wed in the Blue Room. The Red Room, decorated in early-19th-century American Empire style, has long been a first lady favorite. ⊠ *1600 Pennsylvania Ave. NW, Foggy Bottom* ☎ *202/208–1631 White House Visitor Center, 202/456–7041 24-hr info line* ⊕ *www.whitehouse.gov* ⊠ *Free* ☉ *Closed Sun. and Mon.* ☞ *Must reserve in advance* Ⓜ *Federal Triangle, Metro Center, or McPherson Sq.*

A statue of Andrew Jackson during the battle of New Orleans presides over Lafayette Square.

White House Visitor Center

VISITOR CENTER | FAMILY | The White House Visitor Center is a fantastic way to get an orientation before visiting the White House and an excellent alternative for those who could not get tickets. Displays, artifacts, photos, videos, and interactive exhibits recount the life and times of America's most famous house, providing behind-the-scenes insight into the workings of the White House. Afterward, go for a walk around the grounds of the President's park for the iconic views of the White House. ✉ *1450 Pennsylvania Ave. NW, Foggy Bottom* ☎ *202/208–1631* 🌐 *www.nps.gov* 🎟 *Free* 🕒 *Closed Sun. and Mon.* [M] *Metro Center or Federal Triangle.*

🍴 Restaurants

The history-steeped Foggy Bottom area boasts architectural landmarks like the Watergate Hotel. Around George Washington University, there's affordable, college-friendly fare with fast-casual restaurants and coffee shops. Nearby, the Kennedy Center draws a more mature crowd with tastes that have evolved past burgers and nachos. North of Foggy Bottom has become home to several fine dining establishments.

Beefsteak

$ | VEGETARIAN | Vegetarians and carnivores alike rejoice at Beefsteak, the vegetable-forward fast-casual restaurant by renowned chef and humanitarian José Andres. Located at the heart of Foggy Bottom, it offers colorful salads, veggie burgers, and hearty bowls. **Known for:** colorful vegetarian bowls; vegetable "burgers" with huge chunks of veggies; affordable vegetarian food. [$] *Average main: $10* ✉ *800 22nd St. NW, Foggy Bottom* ☎ *202/296–1439* 🌐 *www.beefsteakveggies.com/location/beefsteak-george-washington-university* 🕒 *Closed weekends* [M] *Foggy Bottom–GWU.*

Bindaas

$ | **INDIAN** | For a taste of Indian street food, head to Bindaas, a casual restaurant near George Washington University. Owned by the same restaurant group as Rasika, you will find high-quality Indian food in a more relaxed setting. **Known for:** casual setup; classic Indian dishes; wide selection of chaat (savory snacks). $ *Average main: $15* ⊠ *2000 Pennsylvania. NW, Foggy Bottom* ⊕ *www. bindaasdc.com* ☾ *Closed Mon.* Ⓜ *Foggy Bottom–GWU.*

Blue Duck Tavern

$$$$ | **MODERN AMERICAN** | With an open kitchen firmly committed to artistically crafted American cuisine, this high-end neighborhood tavern in the Park Hyatt Washington D.C. hotel uses the region's freshest seasonal ingredients to create rustic dishes such as wood oven–roasted bone marrow and roasted Rohan duck breast. The apple pie is probably the most iconic dish of this popular restaurant, so make sure to save room for dessert if it's on the menu. **Known for:** apple pie; wood oven–roasted bone marrow; creative breakfast and brunch menu. $ *Average main: $38* ⊠ *Park Hyatt Washington D.C., 1201 24th St. NW, Washington* ☎ *202/419–6755* ⊕ *www.blueduck-tavern.com* Ⓜ *Foggy Bottom–GWU.*

★ Call Your Mother Deli

$ | **BAKERY** | Craving bagels? One of the most popular bagel shops in D.C., Call Your Mother Deli, recently expanded to the West End neighborhood. **Known for:** bright and colorful design; loaded bagels; strong coffee. $ *Average main: $10* ⊠ *1143 New Hampshire Ave. NW, Foggy Bottom* ☎ *202/773–0871* ⊕ *www. callyourmotherdeli.com* Ⓜ *Foggy Bottom–GWU.*

Founding Farmers DC

$$ | **MODERN AMERICAN** | **FAMILY** | An ultramodern take on the old-school farmhouse, Founding Farmers has been a popular choice for both tourists and locals. The restaurant is known for its sustainable and local sourcing. **Known for:** kernel-speckled cornbread served piping hot in a cast-iron skillet; throwback sodas, such as the daily rickey and lemon-lime ginger; deviled eggs. $ *Average main: $18* ⊠ *1924 Pennsylvania Ave. NW, Foggy Bottom* ☎ *202/822–8783* ⊕ *www. wearefoundingfarmers.com* Ⓜ *Foggy Bottom–GWU.*

Immigrant Food

$$ | **INTERNATIONAL** | A global menu representing the different flavors brought to D.C. by immigrants is the theme behind this casual eatery near the White House. The menu takes you on a virtual trip around the world, serving dishes like West African gumbo bowl and Vietnamese Banh Mi with Caribbean spices. **Known for:** globally inspired fusion bowls; serves as an activist hub; popular brunch spot. $ *Average main: $20* ⊠ *1701 Pennsylvania Ave. NW, Foggy Bottom* ☎ *202/681–3848* ⊕ *immigrantfood.com* ☾ *Closed Mon.*

Imperfecto

$$$$ | **LATIN AMERICAN** | Although Imperfecto means imperfect in Spanish, there's nothing flawed about this Michelin-starred restaurant. The menu brings together Mediterranean and Latin American cultures with dishes such as moussaka and suckling pig with horchata (a popular Latin American rice-based drink). **Known for:** immaculately plated dishes; creative Chef's Table menu; sleek modern decor. $ *Average main: $150* ⊠ *1124 23rd St. NW, Foggy Bottom* ☎ *202/964–1012* ⊕ *www.imperfectodc. com* Ⓜ *Foggy Bottom–GWU.*

Marcel's by Robert Wiedmaier

$$$$ | **FRENCH** | Served in a warmly lit, elegant setting, the award-winning Belgian menu at Marcel's—the flagship restaurant of acclaimed chef Robert Wiedmaier—often includes multiple seafood choices (like perfectly seared diver scallops and Blue Bay mussels), succulent duck breast, and a selection of foie gras. Order the mixed-melon minestrone

with yogurt sorbet and cream for dessert. **Known for:** very upscale multicourse menus that change daily; flavorful Blue Bay mussels; affordable lounge happy hour. $ *Average main: $150* ✉ *2401 Pennsylvania Ave. NW, Washington* ☎ *202/296–1166* ⊕ *www.marcelsdc.com* ☾ *No lunch* Ⓜ *Foggy Bottom–GWU.*

★ Rasika West End

$$$$ | **INDIAN** | Rasika, an award-winning restaurant in West End, is one of the pioneers in Indian fine dining in Washington, D.C. With its sleek bar and modern dining room, Rasika is always buzzing with patrons. **Known for:** upscale Indian cuisine; modern dining room; chef-driven. $ *Average main: $65* ✉ *1190 New Hampshire Ave. NW, West End* ☎ *202/466–2500* ⊕ *www.rasikarestaurant.com* Ⓜ *Foggy Bottom–GWU.*

RIS

$$$ | **MODERN AMERICAN** | The brainchild of veteran chef Ris Lacoste, RIS serves elevated but comforting seasonal New American fare in an earthy-chic, light-filled space—the sort of place you'll find locals, the after-work crowd, and even a celebrity or two. You should definitely try the daily and seasonal specials, but you can always count on the mainstays, including onion soup, mussels, and RIS's "famous meatloaf." **Known for:** signature scallop margaritas and a gin mill featuring more than 75 varieties; a great "marquee menu" for pretheater diners, available 5 to 6:30 pm; daily specials featuring the chef's take on classic dishes and fresh-from-the-market produce. $ *Average main: $32* ✉ *2275 L St. NW, West End* ☎ *202/730–2500* ⊕ *risdc.com* Ⓜ *Foggy Bottom–GWU.*

★ Western Market

$ | **FUSION** | **FAMILY** | Are you looking for a place featuring local vendors and affordable eats? Check out Western Market, a new food hall close to George Washington University. **Known for:** diverse food options; great meet-up spot; popular with students. $ *Average main: $15* ✉ *2000 Pennsylvania Ave. NW, Suite 3500, Washington* ☎ *202/452–0924* ⊕ *westernmarketdc.com* Ⓜ *Foggy Bottom–GWU.*

☕ Coffee and Quick Bites

Flower Child

$ | **VEGETARIAN** | Yummy, made-from-scratch vegetarian, vegan, and paleo bowls, salads, and wraps are served in a cheery space. **Known for:** vegan, vegetarian, and gluten free–friendly; wine selection; cauliflower "risotto". $ *Average main: $9* ✉ *2112 Pennsylvania Ave NW, Foggy Bottom* ⊕ *www.iamaflowerchild.com* Ⓜ *Foggy Bottom–GWU.*

🛏 Hotels

With the Kennedy Center for the Performing Arts anchoring its southwestern side and the George Washington University campus to the north, this D.C. community is lively and energetic. You have a neighborhood mix of college students, bureaucrats, diplomats, and longtime Washingtonians. Its proximity to many attractions and institutions makes Foggy Bottom a prime destination for luxury and business-minded hotels.

Embassy Suites Washington, D.C. Georgetown

$$$ | **HOTEL** | **FAMILY** | All accommodations at this convenient hotel within walking distance of Georgetown and Dupont Circle have a living room and bedroom, making it an excellent choice for families. **Pros:** family-friendly; reception with complimentary drinks and apps every night; pool to keep the little ones—and sweaty tourists—happy. **Cons:** museums not in walking distance; four blocks from Metro; expensive parking (not valet). $ *Rooms from: $319* ✉ *1250 22nd St. NW, Foggy Bottom* ☎ *202/857–3388, 800/362–2779 customer support* ⊕ *www.embassysuites.com* ⇆ *318 rooms* ⭘❙ *Free Breakfast* Ⓜ *Foggy Bottom–GWU or Dupont Circle.*

★ The Fairmont, Washington, D.C., Georgetown

$$$ | HOTEL | FAMILY | Located between West End and Georgetown, one of Fairmont Hotel's key advantages is the convenient location. **Pros:** fitness fanatics will love the gym and 50-foot indoor pool; great no-charge pet program includes homemade treats for dogs; good family amenities. **Cons:** expensive parking; far from most major attractions; some rooms can be noisy. [$] *Rooms from: $296* ✉ *2401 M St. NW, Foggy Bottom* ☎ *202/429–2400, 866/540–4505* 🌐 *www.fairmont.com* 🛏 *413 rooms* 🍴 *No Meals* [M] *Foggy Bottom–GWU.*

★ Hotel Hive

$$ | HOTEL | Hip and trendy, D.C.'s first micro-hotel is designed for travelers who care more about exploring and socializing than spending much time in their room. **Pros:** great prices; on-site restaurant offers all-day dining; pet-friendly. **Cons:** occupancy limited to two people (usually with one bed); rooms on lower floors are noisy; very, very small rooms. [$] *Rooms from: $257* ✉ *2224 F St. NW, Foggy Bottom* ☎ *202/849–8499* 🌐 *www.hotelhive.com* 🛏 *83 rooms* 🍴 *No Meals.*

Hotel Lombardy

$$$ | HOTEL | This romantic property near the White House is an idyllic urban retreat—one where European antiques, Asian rugs, and original oil paintings lend a 1929 art deco building old-world charm and where guest rooms feature plush bedding, work desks, and steel-and-chrome bathrooms. **Pros:** homey rooms; beautiful lounge; complimentary Wi-Fi. **Cons:** old-fashioned decor; expensive valet parking; on busy street. [$] *Rooms from: $300* ✉ *2019 Pennsylvania Ave. NW, Foggy Bottom* ☎ *202/828–2600* 🌐 *www.hotellombardy.com* 🛏 *140 rooms* 🍴 *No Meals* [M] *Foggy Bottom–GWU.*

Hyatt Place Washington DC/Georgetown/West End

$$ | HOTEL | FAMILY | Families and business travelers will appreciate this modern hotel conveniently located in the West End neighborhood just a few blocks from the Foggy Bottom–GWU Metro and a short walk from Georgetown. **Pros:** complimentary daily breakfast buffet; fitness center and heated indoor pool; convenient location. **Cons:** decor is not very distinctive; expensive valet parking; relatively far from major sights. [$] *Rooms from: $279* ✉ *2121 M St. NW, Foggy Bottom* ☎ *202/838–2222* 🌐 *www.hyatt.com* 🛏 *168 rooms* 🍴 *Free Breakfast* [M] *Foggy Bottom–GWU.*

Melrose Georgetown Hotel

$ | HOTEL | Gracious, traditional rooms in a soothing palette of creams and grays with splashes of green, blue, and red all have oversized bathrooms. **Pros:** nice fitness center; closest Georgetown hotel to a Metro stop; walk to dining and shopping. **Cons:** street noise; no pool; expensive valet parking. [$] *Rooms from: $179* ✉ *2430 Pennsylvania Ave. NW, Georgetown* ☎ *202/955–6400, 800/635–7673* 🌐 *www.melrosehoteldc.com* 🛏 *240 rooms* 🍴 *No Meals* [M] *Foggy Bottom–GWU.*

★ Park Hyatt Washington

$$$$ | HOTEL | FAMILY | Understated elegance and refined service can be found at this soothing city getaway, where the guest rooms—designer Tony Chi's minimalist tribute to the American experience—feature walnut floors, hard-covered books, and folk-art accents. **Pros:** spacious and luxurious rooms; in-house restaurant serves fresh product-driven menu in contemporary, cozy setting; beautiful indoor saltwater pool. **Cons:** expensive valet parking; 10-minute walk to the Metro; many rooms lack good views. [$] *Rooms from: $516* ✉ *1201 24th St. NW, Foggy Bottom* ☎ *202/789–1234* 🌐 *www.hyatt.com* 🛏 *215 rooms* 🍴 *No Meals* [M] *Foggy Bottom–GWU.*

Residence Inn Washington, DC/Foggy Bottom

$$ | **HOTEL** | **FAMILY** | This all-suite hotel is close to the Kennedy Center, George Washington University, and Georgetown. **Pros:** near Metro; rooftop pool overlooks the Watergate Hotel; friendly and helpful staff. **Cons:** far from the museums; too quiet for some; small fitness room. [$] *Rooms from: $231* ✉ *801 New Hampshire Ave. NW, Foggy Bottom* ☎ *202/785–2000* 🌐 *www.marriott.com* 🛏 *103 suites* 🍴 *Free Breakfast* [M] *Foggy Bottom–GWU.*

★ The Ritz-Carlton Washington, D.C.

$$$$ | **HOTEL** | Luxury radiates from every polished marble surface at one of Washington's most upscale hotels, and personalized service makes you feel pampered. **Pros:** attentive service; convenient to several parts of town; attached to fabulous health club, spa, and pool. **Cons:** pricey room rates, especially during peak times; expensive valet parking; sleepy neighborhood. [$] *Rooms from: $665* ✉ *1150 22nd St. NW, Foggy Bottom* ☎ *202/835–0500, 800/241–3333* 🌐 *www.ritzcarlton.com* 🛏 *300 rooms* 🍴 *No Meals* [M] *Foggy Bottom–GWU.*

The St. Gregory Hotel Dupont Circle

$$ | **HOTEL** | This sophisticated and chic boutique hotel offers the ideal accommodations for business and leisure travelers, with ample-sized studios and suites. **Pros:** big rooms; great hotel bar; 24-hour fitness center. **Cons:** far from museums; expensive valet parking; area is quiet at night. [$] *Rooms from: $264* ✉ *2033 M St. NW* ☎ *202/530–3600* 🌐 *www.stgregoryhotelwdc.com* 🛏 *155 rooms* 🍴 *No Meals* [M] *Foggy Bottom–GWU or Farragut N.*

State Plaza Hotel

$ | **HOTEL** | This hotel is the perfect blend of elegance and comfort, just two blocks from the National Mall's west end and across the street from the State Department. **Pros:** free Internet access; walk to Metro and close to GWU; safe neighborhood at night. **Cons:** far from museums; expensive valet parking; small fitness center. [$] *Rooms from: $180* ✉ *2117 E St. NW, Foggy Bottom* ☎ *202/861–8200, 800/424–2859* 🌐 *www.stateplaza.com* 💳 *No credit cards* 🛏 *230 suites* 🍴 *No Meals* [M] *Foggy Bottom–GWU.*

★ The Watergate Hotel

$$$$ | **HOTEL** | Beautifully situated along the Potomac River, the legendary Watergate radiates sophistication and glamour, embracing its infamous past and celebrating its mid-century modern style. **Pros:** beautiful mosaic-tiled saltwater pool; fun, cheeky historical touches; gorgeously designed bars and restaurant with excellent menus. **Cons:** some rooms are small; elevators are a bit complicated to use; 1960s style is not for everyone. [$] *Rooms from: $584* ✉ *2650 Virginia Ave. NW, Foggy Bottom* ☎ *202/827–1600, 844/617–1972 reservations* 🌐 *www.thewatergatehotel.com* 🛏 *336 rooms* 🍴 *No Meals* [M] *Foggy Bottom–GWU.*

Westin Georgetown, Washington D.C.

$$$ | **HOTEL** | **FAMILY** | Although not truly in Georgetown (but nearby), this Westin location in a busy part of the West End makes it popular with business and leisure travelers. **Pros:** great fitness center; comfortable rooms; outdoor pool open seasonally. **Cons:** 10-minute walk to Metro; a bit out of the way for sightseeing; expensive parking. [$] *Rooms from: $389* ✉ *2350 M St. NW, Foggy Bottom* ☎ *202/429–0100* 🌐 *www.westingeorgetown.com* 🛏 *248 rooms* 🍴 *No Meals* [M] *Foggy Bottom–GWU.*

★ Yours Truly DC

$$ | **HOTEL** | With a hip open-plan lobby called "The Living Room," Yours Truly is a modern bohemian-style hotel in the West End neighborhood. **Pros:** fun lobby bar scene; modern room design; central location between three neighborhoods. **Cons:** lobby area can be loud in

the evenings; small standard rooms; far from the monuments. $ *Rooms from: $259* ✉ *1143 New Hampshire Ave. NW, West End* ☎ *202/775–0800* ⊕ *www. yourstrulydc.com* ↪ *355 Rooms* Ⓜ *Foggy Bottom–GWU.*

Nightlife

The area near the White House and Foggy Bottom has a quieter nightlife scene compared to its adjoining neighborhoods, Georgetown and Dupont Circle. Nevertheless, several bars and restaurants create the perfect space for a relaxed atmosphere for drinks and bar bites.

Casta's Rum Bar

BARS | Casta's Rum Bar sets the tone for a fun night out with its long, colorful corridors filled with murals depicting scenes of Cuba, the birthplace of co-owner Arian Castañeda. The bar also offers a full menu featuring savory empanadas and Cuban sandwiches. Free salsa dancing classes are offered every Wednesday for those wanting to improve their dancing skills. If you're more of a day drinker, head to their lively Sunday brunch parties. ✉ *1121 New Hampshire Ave. NW, West End* ☎ *202/660–1440* ⊕ *www.castasrumbar.com* Ⓜ *Foggy Bottom–GWU.*

🎭 Performing Arts

A wealth of venues offering concerts, film screenings, music, and dance surround the president's home and the adjacent Foggy Bottom neighborhood. Here you'll find the John F. Kennedy Center for Performing Arts and George Washington University's Lisner Auditorium—two great venues that present drama, dance, and music and offer a platform for some of the most famous American and international performers.

DANCE
The Washington Ballet

BALLET | The company's classical and contemporary dances are performed from September through June, with works by choreographers like George Balanchine, Paul Taylor, Marius Petipa, Sir Frederick Ashton, Annabelle Lopez Ochoa, and more. The main shows are mounted at the Kennedy Center, Harman Center for the Arts, Warner Theatre, and THEARC in Southeast D.C. Each December, the company also performs *The Nutcracker* at the Warner Theatre. ✉ *3515 Wisconsin Avenue NW, Washington* ☎ *202/362–3606* ⊕ *www.washingtonballet.org.*

MAJOR VENUES
DAR Constitution Hall

ARTS CENTERS | Acts ranging from the Bolshoi Ballet to U2 to B.B. King have performed at this 3,702-seat venue, one of Washington's grand old halls. It's well worth a visit for both the excellent performers it attracts and for its awesome architecture and acoustics. The design of the performance hall makes for an intimate concert space and great views from every angle of the venue. ✉ *1776 D St. NW, Foggy Bottom* ☎ *202/628–4780* ⊕ *www.dar.org/constitution-hall* ↪ *Check website for concert schedule* Ⓜ *Farragut W.*

★ John F. Kennedy Center for the Performing Arts

ARTS CENTERS | Overlooking the Potomac River, the gem of the Washington, D.C. performing arts scene is home to the National Symphony Orchestra and the Washington National Opera. The best out-of-town acts perform at one of three performance spaces—the Concert Hall, the Opera House, or the Eisenhower Theater. An eclectic range of performances is staged at the center's smaller venues, which showcase chamber groups, experimental works, cabaret-style performances, and the KC Jazz Club. But that's not all. On the Millennium Stage in the center's Grand Foyer, you can catch free performances almost any day at 6 pm. And the REACH, a major indoor-outdoor, state-of-the-art expansion designed by Steven Holl and completed in 2019, provides a dynamic, open-air, collaborative space and a pedestrian bridge that connects with the other presidential memorials on the National Mall.

■TIP➜ On performance days, a free shuttle bus runs between the Kennedy Center and the Foggy Bottom–GWU Metro stop. ✉ 2700 F St. NW, Foggy Bottom ☎ 202/416–8000 general, 800/444–1324 toll-free ⊕ www. kennedy-center.org ☞ Check website for programming schedule Ⓜ Foggy Bottom–GWU.

Lisner Auditorium
ARTS CENTERS | A nearly 1,500-seat theater on the campus of George Washington University attracts students and outsiders alike to its pop, classical, and choral music shows, modern dance performances, musical theater, and lectures by high-profile political and celebrity speakers. ✉ 730 21st St. NW, Foggy Bottom ☎ 202/994–6800 ⊕ lisner.gwu. edu ☞ Check website for event calendar Ⓜ Foggy Bottom–GWU.

MUSIC
Choral Arts Society of Washington
MUSIC | From fall to late spring, this 200-voice choir, founded in 1965 by Norman Scribner, performs a musical array, ranging from classical to tango to Broadway hits, at the Kennedy Center Concert Hall, Washington National Cathedral, and other venues. Three Christmas concerts are also scheduled each December, and there's a popular choral tribute to Martin Luther King Jr. during the winter season. ✉ Washington ☎ 202/244–3669 ⊕ www. choralarts.org.

Washington Performing Arts
MUSIC | One of the city's oldest arts organizations stages high-quality classical music, jazz, gospel, world music, modern dance, and performance art in major venues around the city. Past shows have featured the Alvin Ailey American Dance Theater, Yo-Yo Ma, the Chieftains, Herbie Hancock, and Savion Glover. ✉ Foggy Bottom ☎ 202/833–9800 ⊕ www. washingtonperformingarts.org ☞ Check website for event schedule.

OPERA
Washington National Opera
OPERA | Founded in 1956, the Washington National Opera presents a diverse repertory of grand operas plus world premieres, international tours, live recordings, radio broadcasts, and innovative education and community-engagement programs. The operas are performed across three main venues of the Kennedy Center in their original languages with English subtitles. In 2012, the WNO created the American Opera Initiative, which commissions young composers and librettists to write short chamber operas. In 2002, the WNO also started the Cafritz Young Artists of Washington National Opera, one of the nation's most competitive professional training programs, providing two years of intensive study to a carefully selected cadre of young singers and collaborative pianists. ✉ John F. Kennedy Center for the Performing Arts, 2700 F St. NW, Foggy Bottom ☎ 202/467–4600, 800/444–1324 ⊕ www.kennedy-center.org/wno ☞ Check website for event schedule Ⓜ Foggy Bottom–GWU.

ORCHESTRA
National Symphony Orchestra
MUSIC | Under the leadership of music director Gianandrea Noseda, the orchestra performs classic works by repertoire including classical and popular concerts, commissioned work, and genre-mixing collaborations at the Kennedy Center, Wolf Trap National Park in summer, and on the lawn of the U.S. Capitol (Memorial Day, Labor Day, and July 4) with some of the world's most renowned talent appearing as guest artists. ✉ John F. Kennedy Center for

Five Great Arts Experiences

■ **Arena Stage:** Housed in the audience-friendly Mead Center for American Theatre in the Southwest Waterfront, Arena Stage offers innovative new American plays as well as classic plays and musicals.

■ **John F. Kennedy Center for the Performing Arts:** The gem of the D.C. arts scene, this beautiful venue on the banks of the Potomac in Foggy Bottom is the one performance venue you might take with you if you were stranded on a desert island. The new REACH expansion adds ever more to its appeal.

■ **Shakespeare Theatre Company:** Among the top Shakespeare companies in the world, this troupe, which performs in a couple of venues in Penn Quarter, excels at both classical and contemporary interpretations and doesn't limit itself to the works of the Bard.

■ **Studio Theatre:** With its four intimate theaters and its hip urban locale, this 14th Street landmark provides the best in contemporary dramas and comedies.

■ **Woolly Mammoth Theatre Company:** This remarkable theater company headquartered in the heart of the Penn Quarter stages some of the most creative and entertaining new plays from the nation's best playwrights.

the Performing Arts, 2700 F St. NW, Foggy Bottom ☎ 202/467–4600 tickets and information, 800/444–1324 toll-free ⊕ www.kennedy-center.org/nso Ⓜ Foggy Bottom–GWU.

🛍 Shopping

In the area best known for the nation's most famous house, you can also shop for official White House Christmas ornaments and Easter eggs, jewelry inspired by Jackie Kennedy, and crafts made by living Native American artists and artisans. If you're looking for a tasty treat, grab the fixings for a picnic lunch at the FRESHFARM market held every Wednesday, April through mid-November, near Lafayette Square—the produce that's sold here is said to be as fresh as food grown in the White House garden. Otherwise, it's a good spot for people-watching and fine dining, but alas, there's very little shopping in this area.

CRAFTS AND GIFTS
★ **Indian Craft Shop**

CRAFTS | Jewelry, pottery, sand paintings, weavings, and baskets from more than 45 Native American tribes, including Navajo, Zuni, Cherokee, and Mohawk, are offered at this shop, located at the Department of the Interior. Items range from jewelry costing as little as $5 to collector-quality art pieces selling for more than $10,000. This shop has been open since 1938, and you will need an ID card to enter as it's inside a federal building. ✉ U.S. Department of the Interior, 1849 C St. NW, Room 1023, Foggy Bottom ☎ 202/208–4056 ⊕ www.indiancraftshop.com ⏱ Closed Sat.–Mon. (except 3rd Sat. of each month) and federal holidays Ⓜ Farragut W or Farragut N.

White House Historical Association Retail Shops

SOUVENIRS | The White House Historical Association operates two shops: The flagship store is in the White House Visitor Center, adjacent to the White House at

1450 Pennsylvania Avenue NW, and the smaller History Shop is in the historic Decatur House on Lafayette Square at 1610 H Street NW. Both shops sell the association's historic and official merchandise, all of it carefully crafted. Highlights include official White House Christmas ornaments (from 1981 to present day), jewelry inspired by First Ladies, ties with architectural motifs, and beautifully made porcelain. ✉ *White House Visitor Center Flagship Store, 1450 Pennsylvania Ave. NW, Foggy Bottom* ☎ *202/208–7031* ⊕ *shop.whitehousehistory.org* Ⓜ *Farragut W or Federal Triangle.*

MARKETS
FRESHFARM Foggy Bottom Market
MARKET | Pick up a crab cake, Belgian waffle, or small-batch craft spirit made by local vendors at this farmers' market on Wednesday from 3 to 7 in early April through November. Similar fare is available near Lafayette Square (✉ *810 Vermont Ave. NW)* on Thursday 11–2, April–mid-November. Other FRESHFARM markets are in the Capitol Riverfront (Sunday 9–1, May–September), Dupont Circle (Sunday 8:30–1:30, year-round), H Street NE (Saturday 9–12:30, April–mid-December), Penn Quarter (Thursday 3–7, June–mid-November), and elsewhere. All locations also sell local fruits and vegetables. ✉ *901 23rd St. NW, Foggy Bottom* ☎ *202/362–8889* ⊕ *www.freshfarmmarkets.org* Ⓜ *Foggy Bottom–GWU.*

🏃 Activities

BOATING
Thompson Boat Center
BOATING | The center rents nonmotorized watercraft, including canoes, kayaks, and stand-up paddleboards (from $16 per hour). Rowing sculls are also available (from $22 per hour), but you must be certified and validated for rental. Bikes are also available for rent ($11 per hour). The location provides a nice launching point into the Potomac, right in the center of the city and close to the monuments. In addition to its access to the river, Thompson is conveniently sited for getting onto the Rock Creek Trail and the C&O Towpath. Note: Thompson closes from Halloween through mid-April, based on the water's temperature. ✉ *2900 Virginia Ave. NW, Foggy Bottom* ☎ *202/333–9543* ⊕ *www.boatingindc.com* Ⓜ *Foggy Bottom–GWU.*

Chapter 7

GEORGETOWN

Updated by
Jessica van Dop DeJesus

👁 **Sights**
★★★☆☆

🍴 **Restaurants**
★★★★☆

🛏 **Hotels**
★★★★☆

🛍 **Shopping**
★★★★★

🍸 **Nightlife**
★★★★☆

NEIGHBORHOOD SNAPSHOT

TOP EXPERIENCES

C&O Canal: Walk or bike along the canal-side path, which offers picturesque views from the heart of Georgetown across Maryland.

Dumbarton Oaks: Stroll through the 10 acres of formal gardens—Washington's loveliest oasis, especially during cherry blossom season.

M Street: Indulge in some serious retail therapy (or just window-shopping). Finish at Georgetown University by the base of the famously steep staircase featured in the film *The Exorcist*—and climb it, if you dare.

Tudor Place: Step into Georgetown's past with a visit to the grand home of the Custis-Peter family. On view are antiques from George and Martha Washington's home at Mount Vernon and a 1919 Pierce-Arrow roadster.

Washington Harbour and Waterfront Park: Come on a warm evening to enjoy sunset drinks and fine dining while overlooking the Watergate, Kennedy Center, and Potomac River. Board a sightseeing cruise at the dock.

Wisconsin Ave.: M Street is known for its major retailers like Nike, Anthropologie, and Sephora, but Wisconsin Ave. is known for quirky, independently owned antiques shops, art galleries, and boutiques.

GETTING HERE

There's no Metro stop in Georgetown, so you have to take a bus or taxi or walk to this part of Washington, D.C. It's about a 20-minute walk from Dupont Circle or Foggy Bottom Metro stations. Perhaps the best transportation deal in Georgetown is the Circulator bus. For a dollar, you can ride daily from Union Station, Dupont Circle, or the Rosslyn Metro to the heart of Georgetown. On Saturdays, the Circulator runs until 3 am.

PLANNING YOUR TIME

Georgetown is known for its shopping, but you can also spend a pleasant day here enjoying the sights. Main attractions (**C&O Canal, Georgetown University, Tudor Place, Dumbarton Oaks, Oak Hill Cemetery, Georgetown Waterfront Park,** and **Dumbarton House**) are located throughout the neighborhood. The variety of shops, cafés, and restaurants will inspire you to stay a little longer to explore the area.

At first glance, Washington's oldest and wealthiest neighborhood may look genteel and staid, but don't be fooled: this is a lively part of town.

Georgetown is D.C.'s top high-end shopping destination, with everything from eclectic antiques and housewares to shoes and upscale jeans. At night, particularly on weekends, revelers along M Street and Wisconsin Avenue eat, drink, and make merry. Although the coveted brick homes north of M Street are the province of Washington's high society, the rest of the neighborhood offers ample entertainment for everyone.

◉ Sights

C&O Canal
SCENIC DRIVE | **FAMILY** | George Washington was one of the first to advance the idea of a canal linking the Potomac with the Ohio River across the Appalachians. Work started on the Chesapeake & Ohio Canal in 1828. When it opened in 1850, its 74 locks linked Georgetown with Cumberland, Maryland, 185 miles to the northwest (still short of its intended destination). Lumber, coal, iron, wheat, and flour moved up and down the canal, but it was never as successful as its planners had hoped, due to damaging floods and competition from the Baltimore & Ohio Railroad. Today the canal is part of the National Park System; walkers and cyclists follow the towpath once used by mules, while canoeists paddle the canal's calm waters. During the summer months, visitors can go on a boat tour of the canal at the Great Falls Tavern Visitor Center (a 30-minute drive from Georgetown), where tour guides share the canal's history and operate the canal locks and boat just as they would

have in the 1870s. Tours are free, but visitors must reserve one hour beforehand. ⊠ *1057 Thomas Jefferson St. NW, Georgetown* ☎ *301/767–3714 Great Falls Tavern Visitor's Center* ⊕ *www.nps.gov/choh* ✉ *The park is free to visit except the Great Falls Tavern area in Potomac, MD. Visit the website for updated fee information.*

Dumbarton House
HISTORIC HOME | Not to be confused with the Dumbarton Oaks museum, a beautiful garden and research center a few blocks away, this circa-1799 brick mansion was once the home of the first U.S. Register of the Treasury, Joseph Nourse. Today it's the headquarters for The Colonial Dames of America. Visitors can tour the antiques-filled Federalist home, which often hosts concerts, theatrical performances, and other community events. Docent-led tours are available on the weekend, and the house is open for self-guided tours from Friday to Sunday. Timed tickets are required. ⊠ *2715 Q St. NW, Georgetown* ☎ *202/337–2288* ⊕ *dumbartonhouse.org* ✉ *$10* ⏰ *Closed Mon.–Thurs.* Ⓜ *Dupont Circle.*

★ Dumbarton Oaks
GARDEN | Career diplomat Robert Woods Bliss and his wife, Mildred, bought the property in 1920 and tamed the sprawling grounds into 10 acres of splendid gardens designed by Beatrix Farrand. In 1940, the Blisses gave the estate to Harvard University as a study center, library, museum, and garden. The museum holds a small but world-renowned collection of Byzantine and pre-Columbian

A History of Georgetown

The area that would come to be known as George (after George II), then George Towne, and finally Georgetown, was part of Maryland when it was settled in the early 1700s by Scottish immigrants, many attracted by the region's tolerant religious climate.

Georgetown's position—at the farthest point up the Potomac accessible by ship—made it an ideal transit and inspection point for farmers who grew tobacco in Maryland's interior. In 1789, the state granted the town a charter, but two years later, Georgetown—along with Alexandria, its counterpart in Virginia—was included by George Washington in the Territory of Columbia, site of the new capital.

While Washington struggled, Georgetown thrived. Wealthy traders built their mansions on the hills overlooking the river; merchants and the working class lived in modest homes closer to the water's edge.

In 1810, a third of Georgetown's population was African American—both enslaved and free people. The Mt. Zion United Methodist Church on 29th Street is the oldest organized Black congregation in the city. When the church stood at 27th and P Streets, it was a stop on the Underground Railroad (the original building burned down in the mid-1800s).

Georgetown's rich history and success instilled in all its residents a feeling of pride that persists today. When Georgetowners thought the capital was dragging them down, they asked to return to Maryland, the way Alexandria returned to Virginia in 1845.

Tobacco's star eventually fell, and Georgetown became a milling center, using waterpower from the Potomac. When the Chesapeake & Ohio (C&O) Canal was completed in 1850, the city intensified its milling operations and became the eastern end of a waterway that stretched 184 miles west.

The C&O took up some of the slack when Georgetown's harbor began to fill with silt, and the port lost business to Alexandria and Baltimore. Still, the canal never became the success that George Washington had envisioned.

In the years that followed, Georgetown was a malodorous industrial district, a far cry from the fashionable spot it is today. Clustered near the water were a foundry, a fish market, paper and cotton mills, and a power station for the city's streetcar system.

When the New Deal and World War II brought a flood of newcomers to Washington, Georgetown's tree-shaded streets and handsome brick houses were rediscovered. Many of Georgetown's renters, including many of its Black residents, were pushed out in the process.

In modern times, some of Washington's most famous residents have called Georgetown home, including former *Washington Post* executive editor Ben Bradlee; political pundit George Stephanopoulos; Congresswoman Nancy Pelosi; Secretaries of State John Kerry, Henry Kissinger, and Madeleine Albright; Senator John Warner and his wife at the time, Elizabeth Taylor; and *New York Times* op-ed doyenne Maureen Dowd.

art, reflecting the enormous skill and creativity developed at roughly the same time in two very different parts of the world. The Byzantine collection includes beautiful examples of both religious and secular items executed in mosaic, metal, enamel, stone, textile, and ivory. Pre-Columbian works—artifacts and textiles from Mexico and Central and South America by peoples such as the Aztec, Maya, Inca, and Olmec—are arranged in an enclosed glass pavilion. Especially beautiful in the spring but worth visiting in any season, the gardens feature an orangery and a green terrace filled with iron furniture emblazoned with astrological motifs. ⊠ *1703 32nd St. NW, Georgetown* ☎ *202/339–6401, 202/339–6400 tours* ⊕ *www.doaks.org* ⊠ *Museum free; gardens from $7* ⊗ *Closed Mon.* ⋌ *Tickets must be purchased in advance* Ⓜ *Dupont Circle.*

Georgetown University

COLLEGE | The country's oldest Catholic university (founded in 1789) does not offer architectural tours, but visitors can download a self-guided campus tour from the university's website. The 100-acre campus features a mix of architectural styles, with the most striking building being Healy Hall, a Victorian Gothic masterpiece whose construction nearly bankrupted the institution. Architects oriented its front toward the city, not the Potomac River, to signal its educational stature. Old North, modeled after Princeton's main hall, has hosted more than a dozen U.S. presidents. Also worth a peek is the turn-of-the-century Riggs Library, which boasts impressive cast-iron railings. At the southern end of campus, between M and Prospect Streets, a set of 75 super-steep steps were immortalized in the 1973 film *The Exorcist*. Less sinister beings—Georgetown's many joggers—can be seen running up and down the stairs when the sun rises. ⊠ *3700 O St. NW, Georgetown* ☎ *202/687–0100* ⊕ *www.georgetown. edu* Ⓜ *Foggy Bottom–GWU.*

Oak Hill Cemetery

CEMETERY | Considered a best-kept secret of Washington, D.C.'s attractions, Oak Hill Cemetery functions as a public outdoor museum. Tucked away on R Street, away from the hustle and bustle of lower Georgetown, the cemetery is an idyllic space for nature and history lovers alike. Fans of George Saunders's best-selling novel *Lincoln in the Bardo* trek to this hillside corner of Georgetown near Rock Creek. Notable sights include a Gothic Revival chapel designed by James Renwick and the Carroll Family mausoleum, which, during the Civil War, briefly interred Abraham Lincoln's son Willie, who died in childhood from typhoid fever. In addition to visiting the places where notable figures reside, visitors will discover cenotaphs, sculptures, monuments, and inscriptions. Stop by the office for a free self-guided map. ⊠ *3001 R St. NW, Georgetown* ☎ *202/337–2835* ⊕ *www.oakhillcemeterydc.org* ⊠ *Free* Ⓜ *Dupont Circle.*

Old Stone House

HISTORIC HOME | **FAMILY** | Washington's oldest surviving building, this fieldstone house in the heart of Georgetown, was built in 1765 by a cabinetmaker named Christopher Layman. A succession of occupants used the house as a residence and business place until 1953 when the National Park Service purchased it. Over the next seven years, it underwent an extensive restoration that has preserved the building's Revolutionary War–era architecture and design. The furnishings of several of the rooms reflect the times, with the simple, sturdy artifacts—plain tables, spinning wheels, and so forth—of 18th-century middle-class life. You can take a self-guided tour of the house and its lovely English-style gardens. ⊠ *3051 M St. NW, Georgetown* ☎ *202/895–6070* ⊕ *www.nps.gov/olst* ⊠ *Free* ⊗ *Closed Tues.–Thurs.* Ⓜ *Foggy Bottom–GWU.*

Georgetown

KEY

- **1** Exploring Sights
- **1** Restaurants
- **1** Quick Bites
- **1** Hotels

Dumbarton Oaks Park

Rock Creek Park

Montrose Park

Rock Creek

Massachusetts Ave. N.W.

Rock Creek & Potomac Pkwy. N.W.

T St. N.W.
36th St. N.W.
35th St. N.W.
34th St. N.W.
37th St. N.W.
S St. N.W.
R St. N.W.
Reservoir Rd. N.W.

Wisconsin Ave. N.W.

32nd St. N.W.
31st St. N.W.
Avon Ln.

R St. N.W.

Dent Pl. N.W.
Cambridge Pl.

Dent Pl. N.W.
35th St. N.W.
34th St. N.W.
33rd St. N.W.
Volta Pl. N.W.
Q St. N.W.

P St. N.W.

O St. N.W.
30th St. N.W.
29th St. N.W.
28th St. N.W.

P St. N.W.
O St. N.W.
Dumbarton St. N.W.
31st St. N.W.

37th St. N.W.
36th St. N.W.
35th St. N.W.
33rd St. N.W.
Potomac St. N.W.
N St. N.W.
Prospect St. N.W.
M St. N.W.

Georgetown

Olive St. N.W.

M St. N.W.
Wisconsin Ave. N.W.
31st St. N.W.
Thomas Jefferson St. N.W.
30th St. N.W.
29th St. N.W.

Grace St. N.W.
Cecil Pl.
South St.

Georgetown Waterfront Park

Whitehurst Fwy.

Potomac River

Francis Scott Key Bridge

District of Columbia

Virginia

Thompson's Boat House Park

Rock Creek Park

Rock Creek & Potomac Parkway N.W.
27th St.
Virginia Ave.

66

66

0   1,000 ft
0   200 m

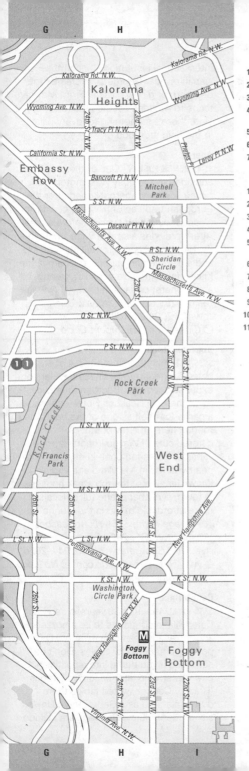

Sights ▼

1 C&O Canal................ **F9**
2 Dumbarton House **F4**
3 Dumbarton Oaks........ **D3**
4 Georgetown
   University................ **A5**
5 Oak Hill Cemetery........ **F3**
6 Old Stone House......... **E6**
7 Tudor Place............. **D4**

Restaurants ▼

1 Apéro.................... **G5**
2 Bourbon Steak........... **F7**
3 Cafe Milano **D6**
4 Chez Billy Sud............ **E7**
5 Das Ethiopian
   Cuisine **F6**
6 Fiola Mare **E8**
7 Guapo's **E8**
8 Kafe Leopold **C6**
9 Lutèce............,........ **C5**
10 Oki Bowl **C4**
11 1789 Restaurant......... **A6**

Quick Bites ▼

1 Baked & Wired........... **E7**
2 Café Georgetown....... **D6**
3 Dog Tag Bakery......... **D7**
4 Moby Dick
   House of Kabob......... **D7**

Hotels ▼

1 The Avery................ **G5**
2 Four Seasons Hotel,
   Washington, D.C. **F7**
3 The Graham
   Georgetown.............. **E6**
4 The Ritz-Carlton
   Georgetown,
   Washington, D.C. **D7**
5 Rosewood
   Washington, D.C. **D7**

Tudor Place

HISTORIC HOME | Stop at Q Street between 31st and 32nd Streets, and look through the trees to the north, to the top of a sloping lawn, to see the neoclassical Tudor Place, designed by Capitol architect Dr. William Thornton for one of Martha Washington's granddaughters. Completed in 1816, the house remained in the family for six generations, hosting countless politicians, dignitaries, and military leaders. On the house tour, you can see the most extensive collection of George and Martha Washington items on public display outside Mount Vernon, Francis Scott Key's law desk, and spurs belonging to soldiers executed for serving as spies during the Civil War. You can only visit the house by guided tour (given hourly; the last tour at 3 pm), but before and afterward, until 4 pm, you can wander freely with a map through the formal garden full of roses and boxwoods, many of which are more than a century old. Admission to the garden grounds is free, but reserved tickets are required. ✉ *1644 31st St. NW, Georgetown* ☎ *202/965–0400* 🌐 *www.tudorplace.org* 🎫 *Free* 🕒 *Closed Mon. and Tues.* [M] *Dupont Circle.*

🍴 Restaurants

Georgetown's picturesque Victorian streetscapes make it D.C.'s most famous neighborhood, with five-star restaurants in historic row houses and casual cafés between large national chain stores.

At its beginnings in the mid-1700s, Georgetown was a Maryland tobacco port. Today the neighborhood is one of D.C.'s premier shopping districts and a tourist and architectural attraction. Although you can find some chain restaurants in the area, there are plenty of independently owned restaurants catering to college students' budgets, middle-income travelers, and D.C.'s well-heeled elite.The mix of universities, international institutions, and embassies in or near Georgetown creates the demand for global cuisine. From Mexican tacos to Austrian pastries to French cuisine, there's something for every palate in the neighborhood.

Apéro

$$ | **FRENCH FUSION** | One of the latest additions to the busy Washington, D.C. dining scene is Apéro. Named after the European tradition of having a cocktail or glass of wine with snacks before a meal, Apéro provides a sizable wine list (owner Elli Benchimol is a sommelier), cocktails, and a never-ending supply of champagne. **Known for:** extensive wine list; trendy atmosphere; caviar selection. [$] *Average main: $25* ✉ *2622 P St. NW, Georgetown* ☎ *202/525–1682* 🌐 *aperodc.com* 🕒 *Closed Mon.* [M] *Dupont Circle.*

Bourbon Steak

$$$$ | **STEAKHOUSE** | In a city full of steak houses catering to business travelers on expense accounts, Bourbon Steak, located at the Four Seasons Hotel, has made a name for itself as one of the best. The menu offers an array of steaks, from curated cuts of Waygu imported from Japan to grass-fed bone-in rib eyes from nearby farms in Maryland and Virginia. **Known for:** one of the top steak houses in town; lively bar scene full of locals; more affordable menu in the lounge. [$] *Average main: $75* ✉ *Four Seasons Washington, DC, 2800 Pennsylvania Ave. NW, Georgetown* ☎ *202/944–2026* 🌐 *www.bourbonsteakdc.com* 🕒 *No lunch weekends* [M] *Foggy Bottom–GWU.*

Cafe Milano

$$$$ | **ITALIAN** | With 30 years in service, Cafe Milano continues to be a buzzed-about place in many Washington, D.C. political and celebrity circles. Don't be surprised if you bump into a politician or a waiter who later becomes famous (Bradley Cooper waited tables there during his time as a Georgetown University student). **Known for:** regulars include

Healy Hall, one of the most historic and prominent buildings of Georgetown University, houses the Riggs Library and is a National Historic Landmark.

local socialites, lobbyists, and diplomats; a patio for people-watching; the front wall of windows opens onto the street in nice weather. $ *Average main: $42* ✉ *3251 Prospect St. NW, Georgetown* ☎ *202/333–6183* ⊕ *www.cafemilano.net.*

★ Chez Billy Sud

$$$ | FRENCH | A favorite for an elegant working lunch, this cozy gem spotlights southern French cooking and serves lunch, dinner, and weekend brunch. On the menu, you will find classic French fare such as duck confit, steak and fries, and mussels. **Known for:** chicken liver mousse appetizer; elegant atmosphere; fine selection of French wines. $ *Average main: $30* ✉ *1039 31st St. NW, Georgetown* ☎ *202/965–2606* ⊕ *www.chezbillysud.com* ☾ *Closed Mon.*

★ Das Ethiopian Cuisine

$$ | ETHIOPIAN | The highest concentration of the Ethiopian diaspora lives in the Washington, D.C. metro area, which means there is no shortage of Ethiopian restaurants. DAS, a long-standing restaurant on M Street, provides an upscale dining experience with one of the District's most popular global cuisines. **Known for:** Ethiopian fine dining; spicy sauces; patio dining in nice weather. $ *Average main: $23* ✉ *1201 28th St. NW, Georgetown* ☎ *202/333–4710* ⊕ *www.dasethiopian.com* ☾ *Closed Mon. No lunch Tues. and Wed.* Ⓜ *Foggy Bottom–GWU.*

Fiola Mare

$$$$ | ITALIAN | The harborside setting for Fabio Trabocchi's ode to Italian-style seafood is one of the most sought-after spots in town. Dine alfresco, watch the water taxis float by, or sip an Aperol spritz on a banquette by the open kitchen and raw bar. **Known for:** lobster ravioli; well-priced, three-course, prix-fixe lunch; mouthwatering Italian desserts. $ *Average main: $60* ✉ *3050 K St. NW, Georgetown* ☎ *202/525–1402* ⊕ *www.fiolamaredc.com* ☾ *No lunch Mon.* Ⓜ *Foggy Bottom–GWU.*

Guapo's

$$ | MEXICAN | Craving Tex-Mex cuisine and a view? Guapo's, a locally owned Mexican restaurant with various locations throughout the Washington, D.C., area, has one of its outposts in the heart of the Washington Harbor. **Known for:** large margaritas; views of Washington Harbor; lively atmosphere. $ *Average main: $22* ⌧ *3050 K St. NW, Georgetown* ☎ *202/844–5777* ⊕ *guaposrestaurant. com* Ⓜ *Foggy Bottom–GWU.*

★ Kafe Leopold

$$ | AUSTRIAN | A slice of Europe in Georgetown, Kafe Leopold has an all-day coffee-and-drinks bar, olive-and-onion tarts, crispy schnitzel paired with arugula, and a decadent assortment of pastries. Tucked away in Cady's Alley, the restaurant sits on a quiet side street with design shops and restaurants. **Known for:** hearty Austrian fare; arty crowd great for people-watching; great weekend brunch and daily breakfast served until 4 pm. $ *Average main: $22* ⌧ *3315 Cady's Alley NW, Georgetown* ☎ *202/965–6005* ⊕ *www.kafeleopolds.com.*

Lutèce

$$$ | FRENCH FUSION | Lutèce finds its inspiration from Parisian "neo-bistros," French restaurants where chefs use a creative license with twists on traditional fare. The menu at Lutèce features French staples like duck and steak with unique pairings such as steak tartare with fermented chili. **Known for:** innovative wine list; creative French dishes; cozy dining room. $ *Average main: $35* ⌧ *1022 Hamlin St. NE, 1522 Wisconsin Ave., Georgetown* ☎ *292/333–8830* ⊕ *lutecedc.com* ◷ *Closed Tues. and Wed.* Ⓜ *Dupont Circle.*

Oki Bowl

$ | ASIAN FUSION | A delicious meal in a picture-ready place for under $20 is hard to come by in Washington, D.C., especially in Georgetown. Nevertheless, these gems still exist, like Oki Bowl, a lively ramen bar on Wisconsin Avenue. **Known for:** eclectic dining room; unique ramen flavors; sake selection. $ *Average main: $15* ⌧ *1608 Wisconsin Ave. NW, Georgetown* ☎ *202/944–8661* ⊕ *instagram.com/okibowlatgeorgetown* Ⓜ *Foggy Bottom–GWU.*

1789 Restaurant

$$$$ | AMERICAN | If you're looking for a classic Washington, D.C., fine-dining restaurant in an intimate setting, 1789 makes a perfect choice. Named after the year Archbishop John Carroll, the founding father of Georgetown University, purchased the building, 1789 has its share of history paired with its classic dishes such as seared scallops and beef tenderloin. **Known for:** rack of lamb; upscale, historic setting; several prix-fixe options. $ *Average main: $49* ⌧ *1226 36th St. NW, Georgetown* ☎ *202/965–1789* ⊕ *www.1789restaurant.com.*

☕ Coffee and Quick Bites

★ Baked & Wired

$ | BAKERY | FAMILY | Skip the chain bakeries and head to Baked & Wired for their legendary cupcakes (the red velvet is a must), savory scones, and chocolate chip cookies. Any D.C. native will tell you this is one of their favorite spots! **Known for:** chocolate chip cookies; coffee list; red velvet cupcakes. $ *Average main: $5* ⌧ *1052 Thomas Jefferson St., Georgetown* ☎ *703/663–8727* ⊕ *bakedandwired. com* Ⓜ *Foggy Bottom–GWU.*

Café Georgetown

$ | BAKERY | Inside a picturesque blue Georgetown row house, you will find Café Georgetown, a chic, European-inspired café serving pastries such as carrot cake and baklava. The café has an extended coffee and tea menu, but what guests come for is the exquisite latte art. **Known for:** baklava; beautiful patio; latte art. $ *Average main: $7* ⌧ *3141 N St. NW, Georgetown* ⊕ *cafegeorgetown. com* Ⓜ *Foggy Bottom–GWU.*

Dog Tag Bakery

$ | **BAKERY** | **FAMILY** | Eat tasty pastries and sandwiches with a purpose—the sales of this bakery support veteran and military spouses' entrepreneurship programs. This quaint bakery offers a variety of sweet and savory pastries, sandwiches, and coffee. **Known for:** proceeds help the veteran community; cozy decor; delicious cookies and pastries. [$] *Average main: $8* ✉ *3206 Grace St. NW, Georgetown* ☎ *202/407–9609* 🌐 *dogtaginc.org* 🕒 *Closed Wed.* [M] *Foggy Bottom–GWU.*

Moby Dick House of Kabob

$ | **MIDDLE EASTERN** | **FAMILY** | This casual spot with Persian fare and a focus on high-quality ingredients will steal your heart. Whether you're craving kebabs, falafel, baklava, or gyros, you cannot go wrong (although we do strongly recommend the baklava and the salmon kebabs). **Known for:** baklava and salmon kebabs; authentic Persian cuisine; fresh-baked pita with every order. [$] *Average main: $10* ✉ *1070 31st St., Georgetown* ☎ *202/333–4400* 🌐 *www.mobyskabob.com/stores/moby-dick-georgetown* [M] *Foggy Bottom–GWU.*

🛏 Hotels

Even to other native Washingtonians, this high-end neighborhood—home to Washington's elite—is a tourist destination. Historic homes on quiet streets with plenty of trees and a canal make this area ideal for strolling. M Street and Wisconsin Avenue restaurants and shops make it the hottest spot in town for those with money to burn. Georgetown University students keep this area bustling into the early hours.

★ The Avery

$$ | **B&B/INN** | Located along a row of quintessential Georgetown townhomes, The Avery is an intimate guesthouse that makes you feel as if you're staying with very stylish relatives. **Pros:** affordable prices for Georgetown; uniquely decorated rooms; located on a quiet street. **Cons:** 15-minute walk from main Georgetown activities; small property; no big hotel ammenities. [$] *Rooms from: $259* ✉ *2616 P St. NW, Georgetown* ☎ *202/990–3444* 🌐 *averygeorgetown.com* 🛏 *15 rooms* 🍴 *Free Breakfast* [M] *Dupont Circle.*

Four Seasons Hotel, Washington, D.C.

$$$$ | **HOTEL** | **FAMILY** | A favorite among celebrities, executives, and diplomats, the Four Seasons is one of the District's most sought-after luxury hotels. **Pros:** impeccable service; excellent fitness center and spa; gorgeous saltwater lap pool. **Cons:** pricey; challenging street parking; far from Metro. [$] *Rooms from: $795* ✉ *2800 Pennsylvania Ave. NW, Georgetown* ☎ *202/342–0444, 800/332–3442* 🌐 *www.fourseasons.com/washington* 🛏 *222 rooms* 🍴 *No Meals* [M] *Foggy Bottom–GWU.*

The Graham Georgetown

$$$ | **HOTEL** | Named after Alexander Graham Bell, the inventor who once lived in Georgetown, this upscale boutique hotel is on a residential street just steps from M Street's shops and eateries. **Pros:** quiet and spacious accommodations; popular rooftop bar; free Wi-Fi. **Cons:** expensive parking; no pool; small fitness room. [$] *Rooms from: $309* ✉ *1075 Thomas Jefferson St. NW, Georgetown* ☎ *202/337–0900* 🌐 *www.thegrahamgeorgetown.com* 🛏 *57 rooms* 🍴 *No Meals* [M] *Foggy Bottom–GWU.*

The Ritz-Carlton Georgetown, Washington, D.C.

$$$$ | **HOTEL** | **FAMILY** | Once an incinerator dating from the 1920s, this building still topped with a smokestack might seem the most unlikely of places for a luxury hotel, but settle into one of the large and chicly designed guest rooms. **Pros:** excellent new spa and fitness center; soaking tubs in all room categories; personalized service. **Cons:** far from the Metro; pricey; expensive parking. [$] *Rooms from: $779* ✉ *3100 South St. NW, Georgetown*

Hot Hotel Bars and Lounges

Some of the most iconic examples of power bars, where inside-the-Beltway decision makers talk shop and rub elbows, are housed in many of this town's historic hotels. So, grab a snifter of single malt and begin your people-watching at these classic D.C. hotel bars.

Quill at **The Jefferson** is a hidden gem in Downtown with live piano music, an outdoor terrace, and cocktail menus that change monthly. Ask for a basic drink, and the bartenders will add their creative touches to your handcrafted cocktail, all while providing great service. Plus, the nibbles of olives and nuts are simply divine.

The **Off the Record** bar at Downtown's **Hay-Adams Hotel** advertises itself as the place to be seen and not heard. And while it's just steps from the White House, that couldn't be more true. It's tucked away in the historic hotel's basement, and you really never know who you might run into here.

Although they don't boast the same old-world, dark-wood-and-red-leather charm of the bars at the historic hotels, the **Dirty Habit**, at the decidedly more modern **Hotel Monaco**, and **P.O.V.**, on the roof of the **W Washington, D.C.** (both Downtown), hold their own as stops on the see-and-be-seen hotel bar scene.

☎ *202/912–4200* 🌐 *www.ritzcarlton.com* 🛏 *86 rooms, 27 suites, 5 luxury suites* 🍴 *No Meals* [M] *Foggy Bottom–GWU.*

★ Rosewood Washington, D.C.
$$$$ | **HOTEL** | Highlights at the Rosewood include the rooftop infinity pool and bar—with views of the Washington Monument, Kennedy Center, and the Potomac—and the personalized attention each guest receives, even before check-in. **Pros:** easy walking distance to both M Street shops and Washington Harbour; stunning decor and art; D.C.'s only luxury hotel with a rooftop pool. **Cons:** expensive; far from Metro and Mall; expensive valet parking. [$] *Rooms from: $700* ✉ *1050 31st St. NW, Georgetown* ☎ *202/617–2400* 🌐 *www.rosewoodhotels.com/en/washington-dc* 🛏 *55 rooms* 🍴 *No Meals* [M] *Foggy Bottom–GWU.*

Nightlife

Due to its proximity to the university, weekends (and even weeknights) are a happening affair in Georgetown. A number of bars serve as restaurants by day until the college and intern crowds take over at night. Although most venues here tend to attract a younger set, the neighborhood still offers many options for patrons over 30, such as the legendary Blues Alley. There's little parking here, and no easy Metro access, so if you're not staying nearby your best bet is a taxi. In late spring and summer, head to the Washington Harbour for drinks and a riverside stroll.

BARS AND LOUNGES

The Berliner
BEER GARDENS | If day drinking is more of your thing, The Berliner is the place for you. With a unique beer garden set in a loft, the bar offers a lengthy beer menu of German beers. Additionally, it features locally made brews from D.C., Virginia, and Maryland. With communal seating, you may be able to make a new friend while indulging in German pretzels and wurst. Most guests will probably take a selfie with the popular mural of JFK alongside the building stating "Ich bin ein

Berliner" ("I am a Berliner"), an ode to his 1963 speech in Berlin. ✉ *3401 Water St. NW, Georgetown* ☎ *202/621–7000* ⊕ *theberlinerdc.com* ☽ *Closed Mon. and Tues.* Ⓜ *Rosslyn.*

El Centro
DANCE CLUBS | During the weekends, the long-standing Mexican restaurant El Centro becomes a dance club after service, attracting young professionals and students from the area. Sip on margaritas while dancing to the beat of Latin American tunes. ✉ *1218 Wisconsin Ave. NW, Georgetown* ☎ *202/333–4100* ⊕ *eatelcentro.com/georgetown* ☞ *Dancing is on Fri. and Sat. only* Ⓜ *Foggy Bottom–GWU.*

Fitzgerald's
COCKTAIL LOUNGES | Sexy, elegant, and slightly hidden, Fitzgerald's is the epitome of a Washington, D.C., cocktail bar. Plush emerald-green furniture and leather couches contrast with the brass fixtures and the 1960s paintings of football players. Aside from getting a martini, the bar offers classic bar fare, such as burgers. ✉ *1232 36th St. NW, Georgetown* ☎ *202/342–0009* ⊕ *fitzgeraldsdc.com* ☽ *Closed Sun.–Tues.* Ⓜ *Rosslyn.*

The Sovereign
BARS | With two bars serving 50 beers on tap and another 350 in bottles, The Sovereign's devotion is not in doubt. The staff knows the menu inside and out, so they can recommend the ideal beer for your taste. If you're hungry, too, the menu focuses on tasty Belgian fare like mussels with herbed mayonnaise. ✉ *1206 Wisconsin Ave. NW, Georgetown* ✛ *Entrance is off alley next to Abercrombie & Fitch* ☎ *202/774–5875* ⊕ *www.thesovereigndc.com* Ⓜ *Foggy Bottom–GWU.*

The Tombs
PUBS | Visitors to Georgetown University looking for a pint or some pub grub head down the stairs below 1789 restaurant to this traditional, half-century-old, collegiate watering hole adorned with rowing paraphernalia and steeped in charming Georgetown boosterism. One block from the main gate, it's the closest bar to campus, so it gets crowded with students at night. ✉ *1226 36th St. NW, Georgetown* ☎ *202/337–6668* ⊕ *www.tombs.com.*

Tony and Joe's
BARS | Right on Georgetown's waterfront, this seafood restaurant has a large outdoor patio where you can enjoy a drink alfresco on a spring or summer evening. The cocktails are a little pricey, but you can't beat the view of the Potomac River and Kennedy Center at night. ✉ *3000 K St. NW, Georgetown* ☎ *202/944–4545* ⊕ *www.tonyandjoes.com.*

MUSIC CLUBS
★ Blues Alley
LIVE MUSIC | Head here for a classy evening in an intimate setting, complete with great blues, jazz, and R&B from well-known performers such as Mose Allison and Wynton Marsalis and outstanding New Orleans cuisine such as jambalaya and fried catfish. Expect to pay a cover charge and a minimum of food or drink. Go to their website for a list of performances and to purchase tickets online. ■ **TIP→ You can come for just the show, but those who enjoy a meal get better seats.** ✉ *1073 Wisconsin Ave. NW, near M St., Georgetown* ☎ *202/337–4141* ⊕ *www.bluesalley.com* Ⓜ *Foggy Bottom–GWU.*

🎭 Performing Arts

Georgetown entertainment goes far beyond barhopping on a Saturday night. Smaller drama groups stage productions in several of Georgetown's larger churches; check local publications for the latest offerings.

GALLERIES
Georgetown University Art Galleries
ARTS CENTERS | The Georgetown University Art Galleries are composed of two distinct exhibition venues: the Maria & Alberto de la Cruz Art Gallery and the

Lucille M. & Richard F.X. Spagnuolo Art Gallery. During the academic year, the galleries present exhibitions featuring works by highly acclaimed professional artists, studio art faculty, and graduating art majors and host various innovative, interdisciplinary public programs. ⊠ *1221 36th St. NW, Suites 101 and 102, Georgetown* ⊕ *delacruzgallery.georgetown. domains* ⊠ *Free* ⊙ *Closed Mon.–Wed.*

MUSIC
Dumbarton Concerts
CONCERTS | A fixture in Georgetown since 1772 (in its current location since 1850), Dumbarton United Methodist Church sponsors a concert series that has featured the Harlem Quartet, the Smithsonian Jazz Masterworks, the St. Petersburg String Quartet, plus a multigenerational community of emerging artists. It's also home to Inner City-Inner Child, Inc. Founded in 1979 as a chamber music concert series, Dumbarton Concerts/Inner City-Inner Child, Inc. is a music, arts, and education organization that is doing extraordinary work in Washington, D.C. Mission: Dumbarton Concerts/Inner City-Inner Child presents programs that promote diversity, community, accessibility, and a love of music and learning throughout greater Washington, D.C. The Dumbarton Concerts music series showcases established and emerging artists for multigenerational and international audiences and creates a community for patrons and music lovers. Inner City-Inner Child improves academic achievement, and uplifts and inspires children ages 0 to 5 in D.C.'s most economically disadvantaged communities using the transformative power of the arts.

■TIP➜ **Before or after a performance, stroll through the nearby Dumbarton Oaks estate and park.** ⊠ *Dumbarton United Methodist Church, 3133 Dumbarton Ave. NW, Georgetown* ☎ *202/965–2000* ⊕ *dumbartonconcerts.org* Ⓜ *Foggy Bottom–GWU.*

🛍 Shopping

Although Georgetown, the capital's center for famous residents, is not on a Metro line, and street parking is tough to find, people still flock here to shop.

National chains and designer shops now stand side by side with the specialty shops that first gave the district its allure, but the historic neighborhood is still charming and its street scene lively. Most stores lie east and west on M Street and to the north on Wisconsin Avenue. The intersection of M and Wisconsin is the nexus for chain stores and big-name designer shops. The farther you venture in any direction from this intersection, the more eclectic and exciting the shops become. Some big-name stores are worth a look for their architecture alone; several shops blend traditional Georgetown town house exteriors with airy, modern showroom interiors. Art lovers will enjoy the several galleries and antiques shops, especially on Wisconsin Avenue. Vintage fashion connoisseurs will appreciate the designer consignment shops where you can find rare pieces.

Shopping in Georgetown can be expensive, but you don't have to add exorbitant parking lot fees. The D.C. Circulator is your best bet for getting into and out of Georgetown, especially if it's hot or you're laden with many purchases. This $1 bus runs along M Street and up Wisconsin Avenue, the major shopping strips.

The nearest Metro station, Foggy Bottom–GWU, is a 10- to 15-minute walk from the shops.

ANTIQUES AND COLLECTIBLES
Cote Jardin Antiques
ANTIQUES & COLLECTIBLES | From ornate mirrors to unique furniture pieces, Cote Jardin has a wide selection of antiques. Located in a town house on O Street, the display will give you inspiration for your

home decor. ✉ *3218 O St. NW, George-town* ☎ *202/333–3067* ⊕ *cotejardinan-tiques.com* ⊗ *Closed Sun. and Mon.*

Marston Luce

ANTIQUES & COLLECTIBLES | House and garden accessories are in the mix here, but the emphasis is on 18th- and 19th-century French and Swedish painted furniture, sourced by the owner on yearly buying trips to Europe. Find unique art, mirrors, and sculptures here. ✉ *1651 Wisconsin Ave. NW, Georgetown* ☎ *202/333–6800* ⊕ *www.marstonluce.com* ⊗ *Closed Sun.* Ⓜ *Foggy Bottom–GWU.*

★ Opportunity Shop of the Christ Child Society

ANTIQUES & COLLECTIBLES | This gem of a consignment–thrift store has been a Georgetown landmark since 1954, with volunteers who have been with the store for more than 40 years. You'll find gorgeous fine jewelry, antiques, crystal, silver, and porcelain. Prices are moderate, and profits go to a good cause—the Christ Child Society provides for the needs of local children. ✉ *1427 Wisconsin Ave. NW, Georgetown* ☎ *202/333–6635* ⊕ *www.christchildddc.org* ⊗ *Closed Mon. and Tues.* Ⓜ *Foggy Bottom–GWU.*

ART GALLERIES

Addison Ripley

ART GALLERIES | Stunning, large-scale contemporary work by national and local artists, including painters Manon Cleary and Wolf Kahn and photographer Frank Hallam Day, is exhibited at this well-respected gallery, which is closed both Sunday and Monday. You can also schedule an appointment. ✉ *1670 Wisconsin Ave. NW, Georgetown* ☎ *202/338–5180* ⊕ *www.addisonripleyfineart.com* ⊗ *Closed Sun. and Mon.* Ⓜ *Foggy Bottom–GWU.*

Maurine Littleton Gallery

ART GALLERIES | This gallery is devoted to glass, metal, and ceramics. It's worth a look to see the work by some of the world's finest contemporary artists. The intimate, bright space is owned and managed by the daughter of Harvey K. Littleton, founder of the American Studio Glass movement. The gallery is open by appointment only. ✉ *1667 Wisconsin Ave. NW, Georgetown* ☎ *202/494–2666* ⊕ *www.littletongallery.com* ⊗ *By appointment only* Ⓜ *Foggy Bottom–GWU.*

Susan Calloway Fine Arts

ART GALLERIES | Stunning art draws people into this two-floor gallery, where a mix of vintage, contemporary, and classical paintings are hung salon-style. You'll find large abstract oils and a lovely selection of landscapes, but don't miss the box full of small original paintings in the back, most priced under $100. ✉ *1643 Wisconsin Ave., Georgetown* ☎ *202/965–4601* ⊕ *www.callowayart.com* ⊗ *Closed Sun. and Mon.* Ⓜ *Foggy Bottom–GWU or Dupont Circle.*

BOOKS

Bridge Street Books

BOOKS | This charming independent store focuses on politics, history, philosophy, poetry, literature, music, film, and Judaica. First opened in 1980, it's a long-standing independent store in the neighborhood. ✉ *2814 Pennsylvania Ave., NW, Georgetown* ☎ *202/965–5200* ⊕ *www.bridgestreetbooks.com* Ⓜ *Foggy Bottom–GWU.*

The Lantern

BOOKS | Founded by local Bryn Mawr College alumnae, The Lantern is a shop for used and rare books run by volunteers. The profits of the sales go to the college to support students' summer internships. Inside you can find an eclectic collection of books and rare magazines. ✉ *3241 P St. NW, Georgetown* ☎ *202/333–3222* ⊕ *lanternbookshop.org* ⊗ *Closed Mon.–Wed.* Ⓜ *Foggy Bottom–GWU.*

HEALTH AND BEAUTY
GLOSSLAB

OTHER HEALTH & BEAUTY | The popular New York City nail salon GLOSSLAB opened an outpost in Georgetown. Their sleek and modern nail studios are a great place to stop in for a quick, efficient, and clean mani-pedi before shopping, exploring the sights, or grabbing a bite. ✉ *1533 Wisconsin Ave. NW, Georgetown* ☎ *877/839–1854* ⊕ *glosslab.com/location/georgetown* Ⓜ *Foggy Bottom–GWU.*

HOME FURNISHINGS
★ A Mano

CRAFTS | The name is Italian for "by hand," and it lives up to this moniker, stocking colorful hand-painted ceramics, hand-dyed tablecloths, blown-glass stemware, hand-embroidered bed linens, and other home and garden accessories by American, English, Italian, and French artisans. Some of the jewelry pieces are simply stunning, and the kids' gifts are adorable. You can also get certain items monogrammed on-site. ✉ *1677 Wisconsin Ave. NW, Georgetown* ☎ *202/298–7200* ⊕ *www.amano.bz.*

Random Harvest

ANTIQUES & COLLECTIBLES | Whether you're looking for something that's decorative or functional (or a combination of both), you'll find it here. Random Harvest sells new and antique treasures for the home, including pillows, mirrors, glassware, barware, and lamps. There's also a nice selection of American and European vintage furniture. ✉ *1313 Wisconsin Ave. NW, Georgetown* ☎ *202/333–5569* ⊕ *www.randomharvesthome.com* ☽ *Closed Tues.* Ⓜ *Foggy Bottom–GWU.*

JEWELRY
★ Ann Hand

JEWELRY & WATCHES | Catering to Washington's influential and prestigious, this jewelry and gift shop specializing in patriotic pins may seem intimidating, but prices begin at $35. Hand's signature pin, the Liberty Eagle, is $200. Photos on the walls above brightly lit display cases show the city's most prominent figures wearing their designs, making this a worthwhile visit while shopping in Georgetown. ✉ *3236 Prospect St. NW, Georgetown* ☎ *202/333–2979* ⊕ *www.annhand.com* ☽ *Closed weekends.*

★ Jewelers' Werk Galerie

ART GALLERIES | If you're looking for statement jewelry or just want to admire wearable art, add Jewelers' Werk Galerie to your list. Owner Ellen Reiben personally curates an eclectic collection made by artists from around the globe. ✉ *3319 Cady's Alley NW, Georgetown* ☎ *202/337–3319* ⊕ *jewelerswerk.com* ☽ *Closed Sun.* Ⓜ *Foggy Bottom–GWU.*

SHOES
Georgetown Running Company

SHOES | One thing you will notice in Georgetown is the abundance of runners. If you feel inspired to run, check out Georgetown Running Company, a store dedicated to the sport. Their staff are all runners and offer free gait analysis to determine the best running shoe for you. ✉ *3401 M St. NW, Georgetown* ☎ *202/337–8626* ⊕ *fleetfeet.com/s/georgetownrunning* Ⓜ *Rosslyn.*

SHOPPING MALLS
Georgetown Park

MALL | FAMILY | There's a good mix of retailers at this mall in the center of Georgetown, including Anthropologie & Co. (which has floors devoted to housewares and bridal), H&M, J. Crew, and T.J. Maxx. Stop at the Georgetown Visitor Center inside the main entrance to learn about what's happening in the neighborhood. You can even try your hand at bocce or bowling at Pinstripes, a bistro and entertainment spot with a wonderful patio. Grab macaroons at locally owned Olivia Macaroons. ✉ *3222 M St. NW, Georgetown* ☎ *202/965–1280* ⊕ *www.georgetownpark.com* Ⓜ *Foggy Bottom–GWU.*

WOMEN'S CLOTHING
Ella-Rue

SECOND-HAND | Although it's a small shop, you'll find a wonderful selection of high-end consignment clothing, shoes, and handbags here. In addition to consignment, they also offer ready-to-wear pieces. On any given day, you might discover pieces by designers like Carolina Herrera, Gucci, Stella McCartney, or Zac Posen. The staff is especially helpful and works hard to help you find the perfect ensemble for your next special event or important meeting. ✉ *3231 P St. NW, Georgetown* ☎ *202/333–1598* ⊕ *www. ella-rue.com.*

★ The Phoenix

CRAFTS | All under one roof (with 30 solar panels) in a delightful shop owned and operated by the Hays family since 1955, you can find contemporary clothing in natural fibers by global designers such as Eileen Fisher, OSKA, White+Warren, Michael Stars, and Lilla P. There's also a stunning selection of jewelry from Germany, Turkey, Israel, and Italy; gorgeous leather handbags by Annabel Ingall; floral arrangements from a sustainable farm in Virginia; and fine- and folk-art pieces from Mexico. ✉ *1514 Wisconsin Ave. NW, Georgetown* ☎ *202/338–4404* ⊕ *www. thephoenixdc.com* ⊙ *Closed Mon.* Ⓜ *Foggy Bottom–GWU.*

★ Reddz Trading

SECOND-HAND | You can't miss the bright red storefront of this consignment shop, which sells clothing, accessories, jewelry, and shoes. Unlike traditional consignment stores, Reddz buys its merchandise for cash or trade so inventory is added regularly. It's not uncommon to find pieces with the price tags still attached. ✉ *1413 Wisconsin Ave. NW, Georgetown* ☎ *202/506–2789* ⊕ *www.reddztrading. com.*

relish

WOMEN'S CLOTHING | In fashionable Cady's Alley, this dramatic space holds a women's collection handpicked seasonally by the owner. Modern, elegant, and practical selections include European classics and well-tailored modern designers, such as Marc Jacobs, Pierre Hardy, Thom Browne, Uma Wang, and Dries Van Noten. ✉ *3312 Cady's Alley NW, Georgetown* ☎ *202/333–5343* ⊕ *www. relishdc.com* ⊙ *Closed Mon.* Ⓜ *Foggy Bottom–GWU.*

🏃 Activities

BIKING

The numerous trails in the District and its surrounding areas are well-maintained and clearly marked, including those along the C&O Canal segment in Georgetown. Washington's large parks are also popular with cyclists, especially Rock Creek Park, which is close to the neighborhood. Plus, with bike lanes on all major roads and the Capital Bikeshare scheme (and other rental outlets), it's also a great way to get around town.

Big Wheel Bikes

BIKING | FAMILY | This 45-year-old company near the C&O Canal Towpath rents multispeed and other types of bikes hourly or for the day. Rates begin at $35 per day for an adult bike with a three-hour minimum. Tandem bikes, kids' bikes, and bikes with baby carriers are also available. Other locations are in Bethesda, near the Capital Crescent Trail, and Old Town Alexandria, if you want to ride the Mount Vernon Trail. ✉ *1034 33rd St. NW, Georgetown* ☎ *202/337–0254* ⊕ *www. bigwheelbikes.com.*

Capital Crescent Trail

BIKING | Suited for bicyclists, walkers, rollerbladers, and strollers, this paved trail stretches along the old Georgetown Branch, a B&O Railroad line that was completed in 1910 and in operation until 1985. The 7½-mile route's first leg runs from Georgetown near Key Bridge to central Bethesda at Bethesda and Woodmont Avenues. At Bethesda and Woodmont, the trail heads through a well-lighted tunnel near the heart of Bethesda's lively business area and continues into Silver Spring. The 3½-mile stretch from Bethesda to Silver Spring is gravel, though the all-volunteer Coalition for the Capital Crescent Trail spearheads efforts to pave it. As this section is officially named, the Georgetown Branch Trail connects with the Rock Creek Trail, which goes to Rockville in the north and Memorial Bridge past the Washington Monument in the south. On weekends when the weather's nice, all sections of the trails are crowded. ⊠ *Georgetown* ✥ *From the intersection of Wisconsin Ave. and M St., go down Wisconsin Ave. to its end under Whitehurst Freeway at the bottom of the hill, and turn right onto Water St. The CCT begins at the end of Water St.* ☎ *202/234–4874 Coalition for the Capital Crescent Trail* ⊕ *www.cctrail. org.*

BOATING
Potomac Tiki Club

BOAT TOURS | You can also catch a view of Georgetown from the water—with a drink in hand. Potomac Tiki Club offers private, small-boat tours that take you along the Washington Harbor. Most of the tours are private, and they average around $45 per person, depending on the number of people on board. The service is also BYOB—guests can bring wine, beer, and soft drinks. These tours are quite popular, so we recommend booking ahead. ⊠ *3100 K St. NW, Georgetown* ☎ *202/952–7010* ⊕ *seasuitecruises.com/ locations/potomac-paddle-club-george- town* ⊠ *Starts at $45* ☞ *Must reserve in advance* Ⓜ *Foggy Bottom–GWU.*

SPAS
Bluemercury

SPAS | Hard-to-find skin-care lines—La Mer and Trish McEvoy, among others— are what set this homegrown, now national, chain apart. The retail space up front sells soaps, lotions, perfumes, cosmetics, and skin- and hair-care prod- ucts. Behind the glass door is the "skin gym," where you can treat yourself to facials, waxing, and oxygen treatments. You'll also find branches in Dupont Circle, Downtown, and Union Station. ⊠ *3059 M St. NW, Georgetown* ☎ *202/965–1300* ⊕ *www.bluemercury.com* Ⓜ *Foggy Bottom–GWU.*

Take Care

SPAS | Locally owned Take Care is a holis- tic spa and retailer of natural skin-care, beauty, and wellness brands. Beyond spa treatments and retail, they also host wellness classes and workshops. ⊠ *1338 Wisconsin Ave. NW, Georgetown* ☎ *202/717–2600* ⊕ *takecareshopdc.com* Ⓜ *Foggy Bottom–GWU.*

Chapter 8

DUPONT CIRCLE AND KALORAMA

8

Updated by
Claire Handscombe

👁 **Sights**
★★★☆☆

🍴 **Restaurants**
★★★★★

🛏 **Hotels**
★★★★☆

🛍 **Shopping**
★★★★☆

🍸 **Nightlife**
★★★★☆

NEIGHBORHOOD SNAPSHOT

A GOOD WALK: KALORAMA

To see the embassies and luxurious homes that make up the Kalorama neighborhood, begin your walk at the corner of S and 23rd Streets.

Head north up 23rd, keeping an eye out for the emergency call boxes now turned into public art.

At the corner of Kalorama Road, head west, but don't miss the Tudor-style mansion at ✉ *2221 Kalorama Rd.*, now home to the French ambassador.

Turn right on Kalorama Circle, where you can look down at Rock Creek Park and into Adams Morgan. Kalorama means "beautiful view" in Greek, and this is the sight that inspired the name.

From here you can retrace your steps, or take Kalorama Circle back to Kalorama Road, turn right, and make a left on Wyoming to bring you back to 23rd.

TOP EXPERIENCES

Dupont Circle: Grab a cup of coffee and a newspaper, and soak up the always-buzzing scene around the fountain.

National Geographic Society: See *National Geographic* magazine come to life in rotating exhibits at the society's Explorers Hall.

Phillips Collection: Admire masterpieces such as Renoir's *Luncheon of the Boating Party* and Degas's *Dancers at the Barre* at the country's first museum of modern art.

Woodrow Wilson House: Glimpse the life of the 28th American president, who lived here during his retirement, surrounded by all the modern luxuries of the early 1900s.

GETTING HERE

Dupont Circle has its own stop on the Metro's Red Line. Exit on Q Street for the Phillips Collection, Anderson House, and Kalorama attractions. On-street parking in residential areas is becoming increasingly difficult to find, especially on weekend evenings.

SAFETY

Dupont Circle is one of the safer areas in Washington, but muggings still occur here from time to time. Avoid dark, empty areas between bars late at night; stay sober; and avoid crowds on sidewalks, where you might encounter pickpockets.

PLANNING YOUR TIME

The Dupont Circle neighborhood charms whatever the time or season. By day, there is the Phillips Collection's impressive impressionist art, the historic Woodrow Wilson House, and Kramers for browsing books. Evenings, the neighborhood's restaurants, bars, nightclubs, and its own adult game room keep things hopping. Locals prize the FRESHFARM market, open Sunday mornings year-round.

Dupont Circle, named for Civil War hero Admiral Samuel F. Dupont, is the grand hub of D.C., literally. This traffic circle is essentially the intersection of the main thoroughfares of Connecticut, New Hampshire, and Massachusetts Avenues. More important though, the area around the circle is a vibrant center for urban and cultural life in the district.

Along with wealthy tenants and basement-dwelling young adults, several museums and art galleries call this upscale neighborhood home. Offbeat shops, bookstores, coffeehouses, and varied restaurants help the area stay funky and diverse. Nearby, the Kalorama neighborhood's mansions welcome powerful movers and shakers from both political parties. Embassies enhance the elegance.

Add to the mix stores and clubs catering to the neighborhood's gay community, and this area becomes a big draw for nearly everyone. Perhaps that's why the fountain at the center of the Dupont traffic island is such a great spot for people-watching.

◉ Sights

When you think of sightseeing in Washington, D.C., the Dupont Circle neighborhood does not leap to mind immediately. This is an area made for strolling, people-watching, drinking, dancing, eating, and shopping. Nevertheless, there are definitely a few Dupont landmarks worth visiting. Unlike D.C.'s major museums and monuments, which are operated by the federal government, some of these sites charge an admission fee.

Anderson House
HISTORIC HOME | The palatial, Gilded Age Anderson House is the headquarters of the Society of the Cincinnati, the nation's oldest historical organization promoting knowledge and appreciation of America's independence. The society was founded by Revolutionary War veterans in 1783—George Washington was its first president general—and this has been its home since 1938. Guided tours of the first and second floors reveal the history of the society, the significance of the American Revolution, and the lives and collections of the home's first owners, Larz and Isabel Anderson. Built in 1905, the home was the Andersons' winter residence and retains much of its original contents—an eclectic mix of furniture, tapestries, paintings, sculpture, and Asian art. Larz, a U.S. diplomat from 1891 to 1913, and his wife, Isabel, an author and benefactress, assembled their collection as they traveled the world during diplomatic postings. Today, the house also features an exhibition gallery, open every day except Monday, and a research library that you can visit by appointment.

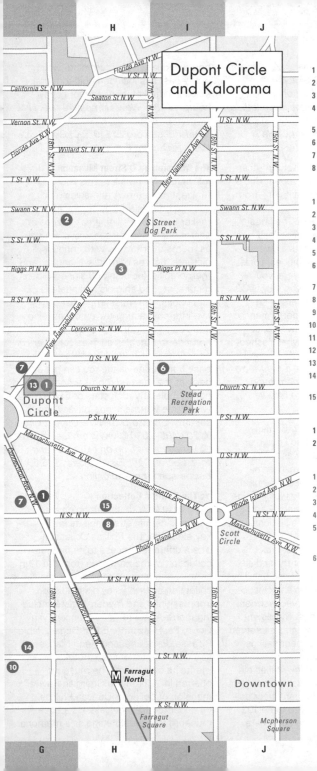

Sights ▼

1 Anderson House **E5**
2 Dupont Underground **F5**
3 Heurich House Museum **F6**
4 The Mansion on O Street
 Museum **E6**
5 The Phillips Collection **E4**
6 Spanish Steps **D3**
7 The Whittemore House **G5**
8 Woodrow Wilson House **C3**

Restaurants ▼

1 Annabelle **E4**
2 Anju **G3**
3 Bistrot du Coin **E3**
4 CHIKO **E5**
5 Dawson's Market **F3**
6 Hank's Oyster Bar
 Dupont Circle **I5**
7 HipCityVeg **G6**
8 Iron Gate **H7**
9 Kramers **F5**
10 Little Sesame **G9**
11 Mission Dupont **F4**
12 Obelisk **E5**
13 The Pembroke **G5**
14 Pisco y Nazca
 Ceviche Gastrobar **G8**
15 Tabard Inn Restaurant **H7**

Quick Bites ▼

1 Tatte Bakery & Café **G6**
2 Teaism Dupont Circle **E4**

Hotels ▼

1 The Dupont Circle Hotel **G5**
2 Hotel Madera **E6**
3 Lyle **H3**
4 The Mansion on O Street **E6**
5 Residence Inn
 Washington, D.C./
 Dupont Circle **E6**
6 The Ven Embassy Row **E5**

✉ *2118 Massachusetts Ave. NW, Dupont Circle* ☏ *202/785–2040* ✉ *library@ societyofthecincinnati.org (for appointments)* ⊕ *www.societyofthecincinnati.org* ▣ *Free* ⊘ *Closed Mon.; library visits by appointment only* Ⓜ *Dupont Circle.*

Dupont Underground

OTHER ATTRACTION | The former streetcar station, located alongside Dupont Circle, has consistently reinvented itself—from nuclear-era fallout shelter to a short-lived food court in the early '90s. The latest incarnation, a funky arts space, has survived since 2016. It hosts a diverse range of changing art exhibitions, social gatherings, and concerts. Here, you might catch an exhibit of works by D.C.'s up-and-coming photographers or an underground (literally) jazz performance. The space is only open for events, so check the website to see what's scheduled. ✉ *19 Dupont Circle NW, Dupont Circle* ✛ *Entrance looks like a red Metro sign that says "Dupont Underground"* ⊕ *www.dupontunderground.org.*

Heurich House Museum

HISTORIC HOME | This opulent, Romanesque Revival mansion, also known as the Brewmaster's Castle, was the home of Christian Heurich, a German immigrant who made his fortune in the beer business. Heurich's brewery was in Foggy Bottom, where the Kennedy Center stands today. The building, a National Register of Historic Places landmark, is considered one of the most intact Victorian houses in the country, and all the furnishings were owned and used by the Heurichs. The interior is an eclectic mix of plaster detailing, carved wooden doors, and painted ceilings. The downstairs Breakfast Room, which also served as Heurich's *bierstube* (or beer hall), is decorated like a Rathskeller with the German motto "A good drink makes old people young." Heurich must have taken the proverb seriously. He drank beer daily, had three wives, and lived to be 102. Head to the website to see up-to-date

hours and latest programming, which in the past has included guided tours, a holiday market, and outdoor happy hours. ✉ *1307 New Hampshire Ave. NW, Dupont Circle* ☏ *202/429–1894* ⊕ *www. heurichhouse.org* ▣ *$10* ⊘ *Closed Sun.– Wed.* Ⓜ *Dupont Circle.*

The Mansion on O Street Museum

HISTORIC HOME | FAMILY | This is D.C.'s funkiest museum. A reimagining of your grandma's attic by surreal filmmaker Federico Fellini, it has dozens of secret doors and passageways, as well as rooms overflowing with antiques, pictures, figures of medieval angels, and memorabilia, including 60 signed Gibson guitars, stuffed animals, chandeliers, and books. The museum, housed in five interconnecting town houses, also doubles as an inn, where rooms pay homage to notables such as John Lennon, Winston Churchill, and Rosa Parks, once a frequent visitor. You can get a peek at the themed rooms when they're not occupied by rock stars or CEOs, who value the mansion's privacy and security. ✉ *2020 O St. NW, Dupont Circle* ☏ *202/496–2020* ⊕ *www.omuseum.org* ▣ *Varies depending on exhibition and tour. Secret Door Experience is $26.50 per person if booked online.*

★ The Phillips Collection

ART GALLERY | With its setting on a quiet residential street and its low-key elegance, the Phillips Collection offers unhurried access to its first-rate collection of masterpieces from the 19th century and later. At the heart of the collection are works by distinguished impressionist and modern artists, including Pierre-Auguste Renoir, Vincent van Gogh, Paul Cézanne, Edgar Degas, Pablo Picasso, Paul Klee, and Henri Matisse. A stunning quartet of Mark Rothko works merits its own room. The museum opened in 1921 in the Georgian Revival mansion of collector Duncan Phillips, who wanted to showcase his art in a museum that would stand as a memorial

The many fountains in Dupont Circle make it a nice place for a walk.

to his father and brother. In the intervening years, the museum expanded, and now includes much more gallery space, a café, a gift shop, and an auditorium. ✉ 1600 21st St. NW, Dupont Circle ☎ 202/387-2151 ⊕ www.phillipscollection.org ✉ $16 ⊘ Closed Mon. Ⓜ Dupont Circle.

Spanish Steps
HISTORIC SIGHT | Named for the Spanish Steps in Rome, D.C.'s Spanish Steps aren't quite as grand as their European counterparts, but they do provide a tranquil reprieve from the hustle and bustle of the city. Located next to Embassy Row, the steps offer a view of the Dupont Circle neighborhood. A lion-head fountain at the top is a good place to relax with a book or make a wish in the fountain with pennies. The steps are near the Woodrow Wilson House. ✉ 1725 22nd St. NW, Dupont Circle Ⓜ Dupont Circle.

The Whittemore House
HISTORIC HOME | You don't have to be a Democrat to enjoy this historic building, which became the headquarters for the Women's National Democratic Club in 1927. The exquisitely decorated mansion, built in the 1890s and designed by D.C. architect Harvey Page for opera singer Sarah Adams Whittemore, has housed senators and cabinet members over the years. Now it's best known for its library, where Eleanor Roosevelt did her radio broadcasts, and its full-length portraits of first ladies, painted in a whimsical style by folk artist April Newhouse. ✉ 1526 New Hampshire Ave. NW, Dupont Circle ☎ 202/232-7363 ⊕ democraticwoman.org/museum-gallery Ⓜ Dupont Circle (Q St. exit).

Woodrow Wilson House
HISTORIC HOME | President Wilson and his second wife, Edith Bolling Wilson, retired in 1921 to this Georgian Revival house designed by Washington architect Waddy B. Wood. It was on this quiet street that Wilson lived out the last few years of his life. It is the only presidential museum in the nation's capital. Wilson died in 1924—Edith survived him by 37 years—and

bequeathed the house and its contents to the National Trust for Historic Preservation. Tours of the home can be general or themed or even virtual, and they provide a wonderful glimpse into the lives of this couple and the dignitaries who visited them here. Items on display include his cane collection, a Gobelin tapestry, a mosaic from Pope Benedict XV, the pen used by Wilson to sign the declaration that launched the United States into World War I, and the shell casing from the first shot fired by U.S. forces in the war. The house also contains memorabilia related to the history of the short-lived but influential League of Nations, including the colorful flag Wilson hoped would be adopted by that organization. ✉ 2340 S St. NW, Dupont Circle ☎ 202/387–4062 ⊕ www.woodrowwilsonhouse.org 🖾 $15 ☉ Closed Sun. and federal holidays ☞ Guided tours typically Sat. noon–3 Ⓜ Dupont Circle.

🍴 Restaurants

Diners who want to spend $200 per person for an exquisite meal as well as those looking for something memorable yet more affordable will be happy in this neighborhood. Connecticut Avenue alone offers blocks and blocks of interesting restaurants. Throughout the neighborhood, happy hours—often with creative small bites—abound, even at many upscale venues. Greek, Italian, French, Asian, Russian, Latin American, and Middle Eastern cuisines are represented, as is distinctive American regional cooking.

Anju
$$$ | KOREAN | Anju, the reinvention of chef Danny Lee's Mandu, serves unique takes on Korean classics with mainstays such as succulent seared *galbi* (short rib) with Bibb lettuce and perilla leaves, as well as—in an homage to its old name —*mandu* (dumplings). Many of Anju's recipes come from Lee's mom, chef Yesoon Lee, who you can sometimes spot on-site, and, since opening in 2019,

it has dominated the best restaurant lists of local publications and bloggers. **Known for:** modern Korean food; creative tasting menu; creative cocktails. $ *Average main: $30* ✉ *1805 18th St. NW, Dupont Circle* ☎ *202/845–8935* ⊕ *www.anjurestaurant.com* ☉ *No lunch weekdays.*

Annabelle
$$$ | AMERICAN | The latest creation by famed D.C. restaurateur Ashok Bajaj is located where the legendary Restaurant Nora used to sit. This modern American eatery focuses on locally sourced ingredients, handmade pasta, and whimsical desserts. **Known for:** extensive wine list; beautiful decor; led by former White House chef Frank Ruta. $ *Average main: $30* ✉ *2132 Florida Ave. NW, Dupont Circle* ☎ *202/916–5675* ⊕ *www.annabelledc.com* ☉ *Closed Sun. and Mon. (temporarily).*

Bistrot du Coin
$$$ | FRENCH | A well-established local favorite, this cozy bistro has a monumental zinc bar and a menu of moderately priced French classics, including onion soup, duck breast, cassoulet, and steaks garnished with a pile of crisp fries. Enjoy your meal with a glass of the house Beaujolais, a Côtes du Rhône, or an Alsatian white. **Known for:** many varieties of mussels; a big party every July 14, Bastille Day; fun local hangout. $ *Average main: $30* ✉ *1738 Connecticut Ave. NW, Dupont Circle* ☎ *202/234–6969* ⊕ *www.bistrotducoin.com* Ⓜ *Dupont Circle.*

CHIKO
$ | ASIAN FUSION | CHIKO (a hybrid of Chinese and Korean, as is the food) Dupont Circle is the second outpost of this revered restaurant, featured in many of the city's "Best of" lists. Although the model is fast-casual, there's nothing fast or casual about the quality of food presented at the restaurant. **Known for:** award-winning D.C. dining; upscale fast casual; modern Korean food. $ *Average main: $15* ✉ *2029 P St. NW, Dupont*

Circle ☎ 202/331–3040 🌐 www.chikodc.com.

Dawson's Market

$ | **AMERICAN** | Tucked away on picturesque S Street NW, Dawson's Market (formerly Glen's) is a hybrid grocery store and coffee shop–café. With a focus on locally sourced ingredients, the café offers delicious sandwiches, freshly made pizzas, and hearty soups. **Known for:** local ingredients; tasty sandwiches; market space. [$] *Average main: $12 ✉ 2001 S St. NW, Dupont Circle ☎ 202/588–5698 🌐 dawsonsmarket.com.*

★ Hank's Oyster Bar Dupont Circle

$$$ | **SEAFOOD** | At this chic take on the shellfish shacks of New England, daily offerings include a half-dozen varieties of oysters on the half shell and lobster rolls, fried shrimp, oyster po'boys, and other fish dishes. For those who prefer turf to surf, the molasses-braised beef short ribs and roasted chicken entrées are excellent choices. **Known for:** a bittersweet chocolate chunk at the end of the meal; half-price oyster bar happy hours; great cocktails. [$] *Average main: $32 ✉ 1624 Q St. NW, Dupont Circle ☎ 202/462–4265 🌐 www.hanksdc.com ⏲ Dinner and weekend brunch only; closed Mon. [M] Dupont Circle.*

HipCityVeg

$ | **VEGETARIAN** | Vegans and carnivores alike will rejoice over HipCityVeg's creative, plant-based, fast-casual menu. The Philadelphia-born company serves a popular vegan cheesesteak, accompanied by sweet potato fries, of course. **Known for:** vegan Philly cheesesteak; vegan milkshakes; one of the few plant-based fast-food spots in the city. [$] *Average main: $13 ✉ 1300 Connecticut Ave. NW, Dupont Circle ☎ 202/318–6010 🌐 www.hipcityveg.com.*

Iron Gate

$$ | **MEDITERRANEAN** | In the former carriageway and stable house of a Dupont Circle town house, Iron Gate's romantic setting complements its upscale Mediterranean fare, served either à la carte or via a tasting menu with optional wine pairings. The menu changes but always includes a seasonal variation on the house focaccia, buratta and feta dip, and staples like the mixed grill and whole fish for two. **Known for:** five-course and multicourse "family" table tasting menus; patio adorned with fairy lights and wisteria vines; eclectic cocktails. [$] *Average main: $25 ✉ 1734 N St. NW, Dupont Circle ☎ 202/524–5202 🌐 www.irongaterestaurantdc.com ⏲ No lunch Mon. [M] Dupont Circle.*

Kramers

$$ | **CAFÉ** | **FAMILY** | From early morning until well into the evening, you'll find chatty diners at this bookstore café. Breakfast fare is popular, with crab cake benedict one of the top choices. **Known for:** crave-worthy desserts; full bar; popular patio. [$] *Average main: $22 ✉ 1517 Connecticut Ave. NW, Dupont Circle ☎ 202/387–3825 🌐 kramers.com [M] Dupont Circle.*

Little Sesame

$ | **ISRAELI** | For those craving the flavors of Israel, Little Sesame is the place. This fast-casual spot in the Golden Triangle serves bowls of creamy hummus topped with colorful veggies and savory proteins. **Known for:** hummus bowls; vanilla tahini soft serve; Israeli cuisine. [$] *Average main: $12 ✉ 1828 L St. NW, Dupont Circle ☎ 202/975–1971 🌐 www.eatlittlesesame.com.*

Mission Dupont

$$ | **MEXICAN** | Mission Dupont serves tacos, burritos, nachos, and other Tex-Mex fare in a casual setting. It's a popular hangout for young professionals, graduate students, and interns, who particularly enjoy the legendary happy hour. **Known for:** fairly priced cocktails; casual atmosphere; close to the Metro. [$] *Average main: $20 ✉ 1606 20th St. NW, Dupont Circle ☎ 202/525–2010 🌐 www.missiondupont.com.*

Obelisk

$$$$ | ITALIAN | Despite its tiny dining room, this Italian stalwart, under the helm of veteran chef Esther Lee, has maintained a pull on special-occasion diners since the late 1980s, offering only a pricey, five-course, prix-fixe dinner that changes nightly. A sample menu—with its mouthwatering delicacies—is posted on the website to give diners an idea of what to expect. **Known for:** standout burrata; attentive service; accommodating many dietary restrictions (except for vegan and celiac) with advance notice. [$] *Average main: $113* ✉ *2029 P St. NW, Dupont Circle* ☎ *202/872–1180* 🌐 *www.obeliskdc.com* 🕓 *Closed Sun.–Wed. No lunch* [M] *Dupont Circle.*

The Pembroke

$$$ | AMERICAN | The Pembroke at the Dupont Circle Hotel is one of the most beautifully designed D.C. hotel restaurants, and it's not unusual to see an influencer posing in the newly renovated space. A wraparound porch allows for tons of natural light, and a coral leather booth is the perfect place to be seen while eating a colorful salad, hearty steak, or delicate seafood dish from the American-focused menu. **Known for:** Instagram-worthy setting; steak and seafood dishes; incredible key lime pie. [$] *Average main: $34* ✉ *1500 New Hampshire Ave. NW, Dupont Circle* ☎ *202/448–4302* 🌐 *www.theprembrokedc.com.*

★ Pisco y Nazca Ceviche Gastrobar

$$ | PERUVIAN | Visit South America without leaving the Golden Triangle at Pisco y Nazca, a modern Peruvian restaurant known for its authentic food. Start with a pisco sour—the bar makes the traditional version of Peru's national cocktail as well as creative, tropically flavored varieties—and then choose from dishes that include colorful ceviche plates and *lomo saltado* (stir-fried beef). **Known for:** fun and affordable happy hour; traditional pisco sour and other cocktails; authentic Peruvian cuisine. [$] *Average main: $25* ✉ *1823 L St. NW, Dupont Circle* ☎ *202/559–3726* 🌐 *www.piscoynazca.com.*

Tabard Inn Restaurant

$$$ | AMERICAN | The inn is historical, with its fireplaces and antique furnishings, but the restaurant's culinary sensibilities are thoroughly modern. The menu changes seasonally but consistently offers excellent seafood and vegetarian options. **Known for:** D.C. landmark where movers and shakers sometimes breakfast; great brunch (complete with homemade doughnuts); attractive patio. [$] *Average main: $35* ✉ *Hotel Tabard Inn, 1739 N St. NW, Dupont Circle* ☎ *202/331–8528* 🌐 *www.tabardinn.com* [M] *Dupont Circle.*

Coffee and Quick Bites

Tatte Bakery & Café

$ | BAKERY | One of the newest additions to the trendy brunch scene beloved especially of young professionals in D.C., Tatte in Dupont Circle sits in the triangular point of a building, with windows on both sides—ideal for letting in the right light for the Instagram pictures you'll be inspired to take in this aesthetically pleasing café. From biscuit-and-egg sandwiches to quiche to the North African poached-egg dish, shakshuka, there's something here for every palate. **Known for:** great coffee; baked goods that look as good as they taste; gluten free, vegetarian, and vegan options. [$] *Average main: $12* ✉ *1301 Connecticut Ave NW, Dupont Circle* ☎ *202/919–8300* 🌐 *tattebakery.com.*

Teaism Dupont Circle

$ | ASIAN FUSION | The imposing exterior belies the spare yet serene two-story space offering breakfast specialties, healthy Japanese and Thai-style entrées that make for great comfort food and desserts. Don't sleep on the homemade cookies! **Known for:** large variety of teas; Japanese bento boxes; salty oat cookies. [$] *Average main: $14* ✉ *2009 R St. NW,*

Dupont Circle ✣ 2 blocks north of Dupont Circle Metro ☎ 202/667–3827 🌐 www.teaism.com [M] *Dupont Circle.*

Hotels

Around the Dupont traffic circle you'll find everything that makes D.C. what it is: embassies from all over the world with their ethnically diverse communities, vibrant Connecticut Avenue, and an assortment of theaters, museums, and galleries—seemingly on every block. This rich Washington neighborhood has something for everyone. And, of course, the Circle is also known for its fabulously eclectic gatherings of people. The posh Kalorama neighborhood, immediately to the northwest, includes gorgeous mansions.

★ The Dupont Circle Hotel

$$ | HOTEL | This newly renovated hotel has a stylish lobby; a sleek bar, The Doyle, where dapper bartenders serve craft cocktails; and modern, minimalist rooms done in neutral colors with splashes of orange or purple. **Pros:** right on Dupont Circle; free Wi-Fi; fitness center. **Cons:** traffic and noise on Dupont Circle; pretty busy on the weekends; limited storage space in some rooms. [$] *Rooms from: $228* ✉ *1500 New Hampshire Ave. NW, Dupont Circle* ☎ *202/483–6000* 🌐 *www.doylecollection.com/dupont* 🛏 *312 rooms* 🍴 *No Meals* [M] *Dupont Circle.*

Hotel Madera

$$$$ | HOTEL | FAMILY | Despite its tiny lobby, this sophisticated and art-focused Kimpton hotel, just south of vibrant Dupont Circle, provides the perfect respite after an evening of restaurant and club hopping along P Street and Connecticut Avenue. **Pros:** nightly cocktail hour; nice residential neighborhood convenient to Metro; spacious rooms. **Cons:** gym is relatively small; no pool; Wi-Fi for $14.99. [$] *Rooms from: $419* ✉ *1310 New Hampshire Ave. NW, Dupont Circle* ☎ *202/296–7600, 800/430–1202* 🌐 *www.hotelmadera.com* 🛏 *82 rooms* 🍴 *No Meals* [M] *Dupont Circle.*

Lyle

$$ | HOTEL | FAMILY | Tucked away on a quiet tree-lined street, this stylish Kimpton property makes for a comfortable and convenient base for exploring the city. **Pros:** very pet-friendly with dog park close by; rooms have either walk-in closets or kitchenettes; complimentary morning tea and coffee in the restaurant. **Cons:** rooms can be noisy; no business center. [$] *Rooms from: $225* ✉ *1731 New Hampshire Ave. NW, Dupont Circle* ☎ *202/964–6750* 🌐 *www.lyledc.com* 🛏 *198 rooms* 🍴 *No Meals* [M] *Dupont Circle.*

The Mansion on O Street

$$$$ | HOTEL | FAMILY | Rock 'n' roll palace meets thrift shop in this guesthouse, a funky D.C. landmark that draws celebrities and notables. **Pros:** also doubles as a museum that can be toured; fun ambience; nearly all the items are on sale. **Cons:** claustrophobic for those who like uncluttered decor; a few rooms are close to the catering kitchen; nonrefundable reservation deposit of one-night's lodging. [$] *Rooms from: $475* ✉ *2020 O St. NW, Dupont Circle* ☎ *202/496–2000* 🌐 *www.omansion.com* 🛏 *15 rooms* 🍴 *No Meals* [M] *Dupont Circle.*

Residence Inn Washington, D.C./Dupont Circle

$$ | HOTEL | FAMILY | This hotel is not posh, but it is ideal for families or business travelers staying for a few days, and all rooms have kitchen facilities, including a full-size refrigerator. **Pros:** free hot breakfast daily in very attractive dining area; two blocks from Metro; clean and comfortable. **Cons:** small gym and business center; no pool; corporate, uninspiring decor. [$] *Rooms from: $221* ✉ *2120 P St. NW, Dupont Circle* ☎ *202/466–6800, 800/331–3131* 🌐 *www.marriott.com* 🛏 *107 suites* 🍴 *Free Breakfast* [M] *Dupont Circle.*

The Ven Embassy Row

$ | **HOTEL** | Just steps from Dupont Circle, this modern boutique hotel now owned by Marriott has a stylish, playful lobby in subdued colors and rooms designed for a young, hip crowd. **Pros:** yoga classes offered on the rooftop in good weather; central location; business center. **Cons:** pricey valet parking; smallish baths and closets; rooftop pool area can get crowded. [$] *Rooms from: $200* ✉ *2015 Massachusetts Ave. NW, Dupont Circle* ☎ *202/265–1600* 🌐 *www.thevenembassyrow.com* 🛏 *231 rooms* 🍴 *No Meals* [M] *Dupont Circle.*

🍸 Nightlife

Bars and nightclubs dot Connecticut Ave, where, after 10 pm most nights, Café Citron brings out the bongos and pulses to a Latin rhythm. Close by, you'll find Dupont's gay scene (or what's left of it), concentrated mainly on 17th Street. A variety of gay-friendly, lively, and offbeat bars and restaurants stretch between P and R Streets, many with outdoor seating. JR's Bar & Grill and Cobalt are favorites. D.I.K. Bar is the place to be on Tuesday through Saturday for the always-popular karaoke nights. In October, the annual High Heel Drag Race proceeds down 17th Street; elaborately costumed drag queens and other revelers strut their stuff along the route from Church to R Streets and then race to the finish line.

BARS AND LOUNGES

The Admiral

PUBS | The Admiral, which is just steps from Dupont Circle, has one of the largest outdoor spaces in D.C., namely a 2,000-plus-square-foot patio. Although it serves pub food such as burgers, chicken wings, and quesadillas, it's an upgrade from the typical sports bar thanks to rich wood paneling and hip, Navy-themed, neon art. On the weekends, it serves as a late-night hangout with drinks and food served until last call. ✉ *1 Dupont Circle NW, Dupont Circle* ☎ *202/506–6696* 🌐 *www.theadmiraldc.com.*

Board Room

PUBS | "Put down your smart phone and interact!" is the motto at this pub, with 20-plus beers on tap, a full bar, and many board games to rent—from tried-and-true classics to vintage oddities. To enhance the fun, you can bring in your own food or have it delivered. Just don't bring in booze or other beverages; you are expected to buy them on the premises. Check before bringing a party of 10 or more; another thing worth checking is whether you can bring under 21s, who tend to be welcome at weekend lunchtimes. Reservations are accepted. ✉ *1737 Connecticut Ave. NW, Dupont Circle* ☎ *202/518–7666* 🌐 *www.boardroomdc.com* [M] *Dupont Circle.*

Hank's Oyster Bar

BARS | A small, sleek, and unpretentious nautical-themed bar offers a half-price raw bar after 10 pm every night of the week, here and at its locations on the Wharf and Old Town Alexandria. The bartenders are friendly, giving you tastes of different wines or drinks to try, along with recommendations on the daily catch and other food options, including one of the best lobster rolls around. ✉ *1624 Q St. NW, Dupont Circle* ☎ *202/462–4265* 🌐 *www.hanksoysterbar.com* [M] *Dupont Circle.*

JR's Bar & Grill

BARS | A popular institution on the 17th Street strip, this narrow, window-lined space packs in a mostly male, mostly professional, gay crowd. Various nights offer show-tune sing-alongs, trivia contests, and a "Sunday Funday" daylong happy hour. ✉ *1519 17th St. NW, Dupont Circle* ☎ *202/328–0090* 🌐 *www.jrsbar-dc.com* [M] *Dupont Circle.*

St. Arnold's Mussel Bar on Jefferson

BARS | This unassuming space in the basement of a Dupont town house is named after the patron saint of brewing, and it's certainly blessed with its choice of hard-to-find Belgian beers. The Belgian theme continues on the menu, and mussels are prepared in numerous ways, including with blue cheese and bacon, a Thai curry sauce, or with white wine and crushed chili. ⊠ *1827 Jefferson Pl. NW, Dupont Circle* ☎ *202/833–1321* ⊕ *www. starnoldsdc.com* Ⓜ *Dupont Circle.*

DANCE CLUBS
Cafe Citron
DANCE CLUBS | One of the longest-running Latin clubs in D.C., Cafe Citron maintains its relevance with the salsa-dancing set. After 10 pm Wednesday through Saturday, the café becomes a nightclub featuring DJs who play primarily Latin music, spiced with Euro dance and techno. The café also offers daily happy hours from 6 until 8, and dinner is served until 11 pm. Salsa classes run on Wednesdays, Fridays, and Saturdays at 7:30 pm. Work up an appetite and indulge in Latin American snacks such as Bolivian salteñas. ⊠ *1343 Connecticut Ave. NW, Dupont Circle* ☎ *202/422–3005* ⊕ *www. cafecitrondc.com* ⊘ *Closed Sun.–Tues.* Ⓜ *Dupont Circle.*

🎭 Performing Arts

Talented troupes perform in unique venues that are sprinkled throughout the Dupont Circle neighborhood, among them the Keegan Theatre on Church Street, which aims to present classic and modern plays and musicals at affordable ticket prices. Sunday chamber concerts also are performed at the Phillips Collection, providing an exquisite venue for both eyes and ears.

MAJOR VENUES
Edlavitch Jewish Community Center of Washington, DC
ARTS CENTERS | Film, music, theater, and more explore the Jewish experience. On offer here are documentary screenings, live music and theater, and family events around the Jewish holidays. You can also sign up for classes about language and faith as well as topics of interest to theater lovers. ⊠ *1529 16th St. NW, Dupont Circle* ☎ *202/777–3210* ⊕ *www.edcjcc. org* Ⓜ *Dupont Circle.*

MUSIC
Phillips Collection
MUSIC | Duncan Phillips's mansion is more than an art museum. On Sunday afternoon from October through May, chamber groups from around the world perform in the elegant Music Room. Plus, on the first Thursday of the month, from 5 to 8:30 pm, the museum offers Phillips After 5, treating visitors to musical performances, food and drink, gallery talks, films, and more. ⊠ *1600 21st St. NW, Dupont Circle* ☎ *202/387–2151* ⊕ *www.phillipscollection.org* Ⓜ *Dupont Circle.*

THEATER
The Keegan Theatre
THEATER | A hidden gem in Dupont Circle, this 120-seat theater offers a rich variety of classic and modern plays and musicals, with a focus on powerful storytelling in an intimate setting. ⊠ *1742 Church St. NW, Dupont Circle* ☎ *703/265–3767* ⊕ *keegantheatre.com* Ⓜ *Dupont Circle.*

Theater J
THEATER | One of the country's most distinguished Jewish performance venues offers an ambitious range of programming that includes work by noted playwrights, directors, designers, and actors. Past performances have included one-person shows featuring Sandra Bernhard and Judy Gold as well as edgier political pieces. ⊠ *1529 16th St. NW, Dupont Circle* ☎ *202/777–3210* ⊕ *www. theaterj.org* Ⓜ *Dupont Circle.*

🛍 Shopping

You might call Dupont Circle a younger, less staid version of Georgetown—almost as pricey, but with more apartment buildings than houses. Its many restaurants, offbeat shops, and specialty stores give it a cosmopolitan air. The street scene here is more urban than Georgetown's, with bike messengers and chess aficionados filling up the park. The Sunday farmers' market attracts shoppers with organic food, artisan cheeses, homemade soap, and hand-spun wool. Browsing is an adventure in this neighborhood. Several boutiques offer designer clothing for women, and Dupont shops also include exquisite jewelry from Turkey as well as inexpensive bling and well-designed products for home and baby.

ART GALLERIES
IA&A at Hillyer
ART GALLERIES | Around the corner from the Phillips Collection, this art space features works from local, regional, and international contemporary artists, and also regularly hosts artist talks and other events. With a mission to support emerging artists and to encourage artistic collaboration across the globe, Hillyer offers intellectually stimulating exhibits that provoke and intrigue. Special events take place on the first Friday and third Thursday of the month, with talks and tours available at other times, too. ⊠ *9 Hillyer Ct. NW, Dupont Circle* ☎ *202/338–0325* ⊕ *athillyer.org* Ⓜ *Dupont Circle.*

★ Studio Gallery
ART GALLERIES | Founded in 1956 by Jennie Lea Knight (whose work is in the collections of many D.C. museums), Studio exhibits contemporary work by local artists, some of whom have also received international acclaim. The spacious gallery occupies two floors in an elegant town house, and exhibitions change frequently. Don't miss the sculpture garden in back of the house. ⊠ *2108 R St. NW, Dupont Circle* ☎ *202/232–8734* ⊕ *www.studiogallerydc.com* ⊙ *Closed Sun.–Thurs.* Ⓜ *Dupont Circle.*

BOOKS
★ Kramers
BOOKS | One of Washington's most legendary independent bookstores has a choice selection of fiction and nonfiction. It also hosts author talks, trivia nights, and comedy shows throughout the year. Kramers features a bar and a restaurant, which are open from morning until night. ⊠ *1517 Connecticut Ave. NW, Dupont Circle* ☎ *202/387–1400* ⊕ *www.kramers. com* Ⓜ *Dupont Circle.*

Second Story Books
BOOKS | One of the largest used and rare book stores in the country, Second Story Books has grown along with its neighborhood, and its orderly and classy space houses rare books, signed first editions, maps, posters, manuscripts, CDs, prints, and DVDs. (There are often bargain books for sale, usually outside the store.) A knowledgeable staff is always on hand to help you shop. ⊠ *2000 P St. NW, Dupont Circle* ☎ *202/659–8884* ⊕ *www. secondstorybooks.com* Ⓜ *Dupont Circle.*

CLOTHING
★ Secondi
MIXED CLOTHING | One of the city's finest consignment stores carries a well-chosen selection of women's designer and casual clothing, accessories, and shoes. Its airy and well-curated second-story space offers Isabel Marant, Louis Vuitton, Donna Karan, Prada, Chanel, and Marchesa labels. ⊠ *1702 Connecticut Ave. NW, 2nd fl., Dupont Circle* ☎ *202/667–1122* ⊕ *www.secondi.com* Ⓜ *Dupont Circle.*

CRAFTS AND GIFTS
The Chocolate Moose
CRAFTS | This store is simple, sheer fun for adults and kids alike. Looking for clacking, windup teeth? You can find them here, along with unusual greeting cards, whimsical and colorful socks, and unique housewares and handicrafts. If playing with all those fun toys makes you hungry, you can pick up a select line of premium European chocolates. ⊠ *1743 L St., NW, Dupont Circle* ☎ *202/463–0992* ⊕ *www.chocolatemoosedc.com* ⊙ *Closed Sat.–Mon.* Ⓜ *Farragut N.*

Chapter 9

ADAMS MORGAN

Updated by
Claire Handscombe

👁 **Sights**
★☆☆☆☆

🍴 **Restaurants**
★★★★★

🛏 **Hotels**
★★☆☆☆

🛍 **Shopping**
★★★☆☆

🍸 **Nightlife**
★★★★★

NEIGHBORHOOD SNAPSHOT

TOP EXPERIENCES

Eat ethnic food: Take a culinary trip around the world in Adams Morgan. From Ethiopia to El Salvador to Japan to Turkey, there is a vast selection of nations represented within the restaurant scene.

Hang out like a local: Adams Morgan, with its quirky shops and international restaurants, seems like a world away from conservative Capitol Hill. Work up a sweat running up the hills of Meridian Hill Park to catch a glorious view of Washington, D.C. Afterward, cool down with artisan gelato at Pitango or browse the shelves at Lost City Books.

Move and connect: Meridian Hill Park brings the community together through different events. You can catch drumming circles, meditation, and yoga at the park.

Stay out all night: If you want to party on until the break of dawn, this is the place to do it. Don't miss the live blues music at Madam's Organ or the craft cocktails at Jack Rose Dining Saloon and The Green Zone.

GETTING HERE

Adams Morgan has two Metro stops that are a pleasant 10-minute walk away. From the Woodley Park–Zoo/Adams Morgan Metro station, take a short walk south on Connecticut, then turn left on Calvert Street, and cross over Rock Creek Park on the Duke Ellington Bridge. If you get off at the Dupont Circle Metro stop, walk east, turning left on 18th Street.

The heart of Adams Morgan is at the intersection of Columbia Road and 18th Street. Don't even dream about finding parking here on weekend evenings.

If you are taking the Metro, make sure to check the D.C. Metro website (⊕ *wmata.com*) to confirm weekend hours. You can also get there quickly by cab or rideshare.

Several buses such as the 90, 96, 42, 43 also take you to Adams Morgan.

PLANNING YOUR TIME

Start your day with a walk around the neighborhood. After the few sights, be sure to stop in at the Line Hotel's coffee shop or for cheesy *pupusas* (flatbreads) at El Tamarindo. Keep moving on to 18th Street for some window-shopping, cocktails, small plates, and live music. Dance the night away at the various clubs and bars, then grab some late-night pizza or empanadas.

NEIGHBORHOOD HISTORY

Adams Morgan may sound like a regular name, but there is always a reason for most things in D.C. After the neighborhood experienced a decline during and after the Second World War, racial issues created a tense environment. Between the 1950s and '60s, the neighborhood, originally called Lanier Heights, became Adams Morgan after the combination of the two schools in the area, the dominant white-attending John Quincy Adams and the predominantly black-attending, Thomas P. Morgan.

To the urban and hip, Adams Morgan is like a beacon in an otherwise stuffy landscape. D.C. may have a reputation for being staid and traditional, but drab suits, classical tastes, and bland food make no appearance here.

Adams Morgan takes its name from two elementary schools that came together in 1958 after desegregation. It remains an ethnically diverse neighborhood with a blend of cuisines, offbeat shops, and funky bars and clubs.

Adams Morgan and its neighboring Columbia Heights comprise the city's Latin Quarter. The area wakes up as the sun goes down, and young Washingtonians in their weekend best congregate along the sidewalks, crowding the doors of this week's hot bar or nightclub. Typical tourist attractions are sparse, but the scene on a Saturday night has its own appeal. If you're here on the second Saturday in September, sample the vibrant neighborhood culture at the Adams Morgan Day Festival, which happens to be D.C.'s largest neighborhood festival.

◉ Sights

Less touristy and more community-based, Adams Morgan is great for a day of light sightseeing followed by window-shopping and heavy eating. Known for its bustling food-and–live music scene, there's always a place to pop into and lose track of time.

Meridian Hill Park

CITY PARK | Landscape architect Horace Peaslee created Meridian Hill Park, a noncontiguous section of Rock Creek Park, after a 1917 study of the parks of Europe. As a result, it contains elements of gardens in France, Italy, and Switzerland. John Quincy Adams lived in a mansion here after his presidency, and the park later served as an encampment for Union soldiers during the Civil War. All 50 states are represented by a state tree or flower. Meridian Hill is unofficially known as **Malcolm X Park** in honor of the civil rights leader. Weekends bring a mix of pickup soccer games, yoga, joggers running the stairs, and a weekly (weather permitting) drum circle. A statue of **Joan of Arc** poised for battle on horseback stands above the terrace, and a statue of **Dante** is on a pedestal below. Cell-phone tours illuminate the history of the landmarks inside the park. ⊠ *Meridian Hill Park, 16th St. NW and W St. NW, Adams Morgan* ⊕ *www.nps.gov/mehi* Ⓜ *U St./ African-American Civil War Memorial/ Cardozo or Columbia Heights.*

◉ Restaurants

In Adams Morgan, find everything from greasy spoons and jumbo-slice pizza joints to exquisite fine-dining options. The next culinary frontier lies just east along Columbia Road, where immigrant communities dine, and young families flock to increasingly upscale bistros for refined takes on comfort-food favorites.

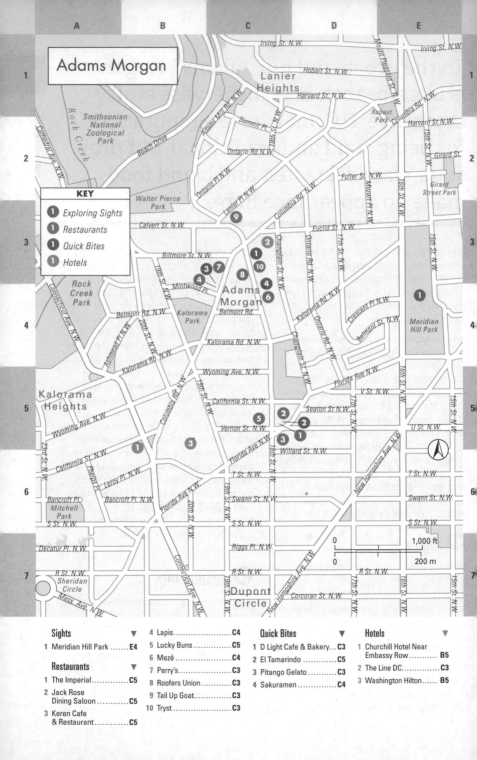

Adams Morgan

KEY
- ① Exploring Sights
- ① Restaurants
- ① Quick Bites
- ① Hotels

The Imperial

$$ | AMERICAN | This design-forward restaurant has a stunning, two-tier, see-and-be-seen rooftop, as well as plenty of other Instagrammable spots. It also offers colorful cocktails and an eclectic menu of Mid-Atlantic staples such as crab cakes and Virginia oysters—not to mention decadent seafood towers (and towering burgers) that are in keeping with its name. **Known for:** beautiful design; happening patio area; creative cocktail program. $ *Average main: $25* ✉ *2001 18th St. NW, Adams Morgan* ☎ *202/299–0334* ⊕ *www.imperialdc.com* ⊗ *Closed Mon. and Tues.*

★ Jack Rose Dining Saloon

$$$ | AMERICAN | With an extensive collection of whiskey bottles currently on the wall (your experience may vary), the food sometimes gets overshadowed here. But Southern-inspired dishes like smoked whiskey wings, lump crab cakes, pickled-corn hush puppies, and buttermilk biscuits make the menu much more than just something to accompany all the booze. **Known for:** small plates of modern Southern cuisine; fun rooftop tiki bar; immense selection of whiskeys. $ *Average main: $27* ✉ *2007 18th St. NW, Adams Morgan* ☎ *202/588–7388* ⊕ *www. jackrosediningsaloon.com* ⊗ *Closed Mon. and Tues.* Ⓜ *U St./African-American Civil War Memorial/Cardozo.*

Keren Cafe & Restaurant

$ | AFRICAN | The Washington, D.C., metro area is home to one of the largest Eritrean populations in the United States, and many in the community get their taste of home at this well-established restaurant. Try the *shiro,* an aromatic Eritrean chickpea stew served in a clay pot along with spongy *injera* bread. **Known for:** Eritrean food; American and Eritrean breakfast; late-night dining. $ *Average main: $16* ✉ *1780 Florida Ave. NW, Adams Morgan* ☎ *202/265–5764* ⊕ *www. orderkerencafeandrestaurant.com.*

★ Lapis

$$ | AFGHAN | The modern Afghan cuisine shines at this chic yet comfortable—and well-priced—Adams Morgan spot which also caters well to vegetarians and those on a gluten-free diet. Seven different varieties of kebabs (prepared via a secret recipe "known only to our mom and the NSA") are the stars of the menu, but you'll also want to try the dumplings. **Known for:** different types of kebabs prepared with top-secret family recipe; carefully crafted cocktails; excellent bottomless brunch. $ *Average main: $25* ✉ *1847 Columbia Rd. NW, Adams Morgan* ☎ *202/299–9630* ⊕ *www.lapisdc. com* Ⓜ *Dupont Circle.*

Lucky Buns

$ | BURGER | As the name suggests, Lucky Buns focuses on burgers and sandwiches. Indulge in a decadent double-patty burger or a spicy chicken sandwich, a favorite with D.C. food writers. **Known for:** juicy burgers; cocktails; outdoor dining on the patio. $ *Average main: $10* ✉ *2000 18th St. NW, Adams Morgan* ☎ *202/506–1713* ⊕ *luckybunsdc.com* Ⓜ *Woodley Park–Zoo/Adams Morgan.*

Mezè

$$ | TURKISH | A fixture in the neighborhood dining scene, this authentic Turkish restaurant and wine bar with a patio serves dishes such as *doner* kebabs, *manti,* and dolmas. If cocktails are more your thing, take advantage of the mojito bar, offering a wide selection of the drink in flavors like watermelon and blueberry. **Known for:** Turkish kebabs and dolmas; mojito bar; extensive wine selection. $ *Average main: $20* ✉ *2437 18th St. NW, Adams Morgan* ☎ *292/797–0017* ⊕ *www.mezedc.com* ⊗ *Closed Mon. No lunch except for weekend brunch* Ⓜ *Woodley Park–Zoo/Adams Morgan.*

★ Perry's

$ | JAPANESE FUSION | One of the best places for sushi in D.C., this upscale restaurant also has plenty to delight those who prefer other types of Japanese and

The stairs in Meridian Hill Park are popular with joggers: run up and down 10 times, and you've covered almost a mile.

Japanese-inspired food. The seaweed salad is delicious, as are the gyoza and hoisin buns. **Known for:** excellent-value happy hour; great rooftop with lovely sunset views; all-you-can-eat drag brunch. [$] *Average main: $13* ✉ *1811 Columbia Road NW, Adams Morgan* ☎ *202/234–6218* 🌐 *perrysam.com* 🕒 *No lunch Mon.–Sat.* [M] *Woodley Park–Zoo/ Adams Morgan.*

Roofers Union

$$ | CONTEMPORARY | The cavernous space that once hosted one of the capital's most notoriously crazy bars is now a symbol of the area's maturation, thanks to a slick makeover and classy comfort-food lineup. The hearty but well-designed fare includes a fried-chicken sandwich redolent of sriracha sauce that will rock a spice-lover's world. **Known for:** comfort food with great options; hip, youthful vibe; excellent rooftop deck and bar. [$] *Average main: $22* ✉ *2446 18th St. NW, Adams Morgan* ☎ *202/232–7663* 🌐 *www.roofersuniondc.com* 🕒 *Closed Mon. No lunch except for Sun. brunch* [M] *Woodley Park–Zoo/Adams Morgan.*

★ Tail Up Goat

$$ | CONTEMPORARY | The menu changes regularly in this classy restaurant, but the spicy pork-belly ragù is a sure thing (when available). Best to make reservations (which open two weeks in advance at 10 am) at this 66-seat restaurant that only seats groups of four or fewer. **Known for:** lots and lots of carbs; constantly changing menu; small groups only (four people or fewer). [$] *Average main: $25* ✉ *1827 Adams Mill Rd. NW, Adams Morgan* ✣ *Entrance on Lanier Pl. side of building* ☎ *202/986–9600* 🌐 *www.tailupgoat.com* 🕒 *Closed Mon. No lunch* [M] *Woodley Park–Zoo/Adams Morgan.*

Tryst

$ | AMERICAN | FAMILY | Bohemian and unpretentious, yet also a D.C. institution of sorts, this coffeehouse–bar serves fancy sandwiches and exotic coffee creations. Comfy chairs and couches fill the big open space, where you can sit for hours sipping a cup of tea—or a martini—while chatting or clacking away at your laptop. **Known for:** diverse coffees from around the world; all-day brunch menu; premium sandwiches and design-your-own salads. $ Average main: $11 ⊠ 2459 18th St. NW, Adams Morgan ☎ 202/232–5500 ⊕ www.trystdc.com Ⓜ Woodley Park–Zoo/Adams Morgan.

☕ Coffee and Quick Bites

D Light Cafe & Bakery

$ | CAFÉ | Open since 2021, this Ukrainian-owned café serves an eclectic breakfast and brunch menu of pastries, burgers, soups, shakshuka, and more. **Known for:** kind, attentive staff; very Instagrammable decor; strawberry-flavored pink dream latte. $ Average main: $9 ⊠ 2475 18th St NW, Adams Morgan Ⓜ Woodley Park–Zoo/Adams Morgan.

El Tamarindo

$ | LATIN AMERICAN | With almost 40 years in operation, El Tamarindo, an El Salvadorean and Mexican restaurant, has weathered the neighborhood's many changes. Guests come for their savory pupusas (a thick corn tortilla) with various fillings to satisfy every taste from a vegan to a carnivore. **Known for:** pupusas; late-night bites; lively brunch. $ Average main: $15 ⊠ 1785 Florida Ave. NW, Adams Morgan ☎ 202/328–3660 ⊕ eltamarindodc.com Ⓜ Dupont Circle.

Pitango Gelato

$ | ITALIAN | FAMILY | If you need a break and a quick hit of sugar in between sightseeing, Pitango is a great place to stop for a while, or just pick up a sorbet or gelato on the fly. It would be hard to pick a standout flavor among the stellar rotating cast, but their most popular is Fondante, a rich chocolate. **Known for:** Wi-Fi and lots of seating; ideal for remote work; many dairy-free alternatives; vegan sorbets. $ Average main: $6 ⊠ 1841 Columbia Road NW, Adams Morgan ☎ 202/615–2419 ⊕ pitangogelato.com.

Sakuramen

$ | RAMEN | This cozy gem strikes the perfect balance between keep-it-simple affordability and adventurous flair. Beyond the ramen bowls, other memorable fuel for a night on the town or a long winter's walk includes juicy marinated *bulgogi* beef buns and *gyoza*, crispy fresh Japanese dumplings. **Known for:** innovative ramen; casual basement vibe; beef buns and crispy dumplings. $ Average main: $16 ⊠ 2441 18th St. NW, Adams Morgan ☎ 202/656–5285 ⊕ www.sakuramen.net ⊘ Closed Mon. No lunch Tues.–Thurs.

🛏 Hotels

This thriving multiethnic community is the place to be for a fabulous assortment of aromas, languages, tastes, and late-night entertainments. A short walk from a nearby hotel or Metro stop rewards you with salsa, hip-hop, jazz, or the latest in experimental performance art. Its neighborhoods of 19th- and early-20th-century homes and row houses and its proximity to Rock Creek Park provide this bustling area with a tranquil shell.

Churchill Hotel Near Embassy Row

$ | HOTEL | One of the Historic Hotels of America, this Beaux Arts landmark built in 1906 has spacious guest rooms that are comfortable, elegant, and include small work and sitting areas; many also have excellent views. **Pros:** good-size rooms; relaxed and quiet; comfortable walking distance to Adams Morgan and northern Dupont Circle. **Cons:** older building; some rooms very small; no room service. $ Rooms from: $129 ⊠ 1914 Connecticut Ave. NW, Adams Morgan ☎ 202/797–2000, 800/424–2464 ⊕ www.thechurchillhotel.com ⇄ 173 rooms ⦿ No Meals Ⓜ Dupont Circle.

★ The Line DC

$$ | HOTEL | A former church, The Line Hotel DC was made for those who want to stay among the locals. **Pros:** uniquely designed rooms; excellent restaurant;

pets (dogs, cats, large, small) stay free. **Cons:** can be loud; lots of stairs to climb; rooms are on the small side. [$] *Rooms from: $240* ✉ *1770 Euclid St. NW, Adams Morgan* ☎ *202/588–0525* 🌐 *www.thelinehotel.com/dc* 🛏 *220 rooms* 🍴 *No Meals.*

Washington Hilton

$$$ | **HOTEL** | Yes, it's a fairly large hotel and can be busy at times, but this historic 1965 hotel, at the intersection of Dupont Circle, Adams Morgan, and U and 14th Streets, has a great location and is a perfect spot to unwind after a day of business or seeing the sights. **Pros:** great lobby; plenty of services; lots of restaurants and shops within walking distance. **Cons:** corporate feel; busy, noisy location; fee for Wi-Fi. [$] *Rooms from: $348* ✉ *1919 Connecticut Ave. NW, Adams Morgan* ☎ *800/445–8667* 🌐 *www.washington.hilton.com* 🛏 *1,117 rooms* 🍴 *No Meals* [M] *Dupont Circle.*

Nightlife

Adams Morgan is Washington's version (albeit much smaller) of New Orleans' French Quarter. The streets are often jammed with people of all ages and descriptions. Bars and restaurants of all types line the streets, making it easy to find one that will suit your tastes. Be prepared for crowds on the weekends and a much tamer vibe on weeknights. Getting here is easy, with four nearby Metro stops: Woodley Park–Zoo/Adams Morgan (Red Line), Dupont Circle (Red Line), Columbia Heights (Green and Yellow lines), and U Street/African-American Civil War Memorial/Cardozo (Green and Yellow lines). Taxis are easy to find except after last call, when the crowds pour out of bars.

BARS AND LOUNGES

Green Zone

BARS | Named after Baghdad's Green Zone, the theme of the bar is bringing people together, and Middle Eastern and other international DJs often perform there on weekends. Popular ever since it opened, it's now a fixture on the "best cocktails" lists compiled by D.C. publications and blogs. The creative drinks combine Middle Eastern spices such as saffron and za'atar with Western spirits like rum and whiskey. Pair your beverage with Lebanese olives, creamy hummus, and savory falafel. ✉ *2226 18th St. NW, Adams Morgan* 🌐 *www.thegreenzonedc.com.*

Madam's Organ

LIVE MUSIC | Neon lights behind the bar and walls covered in kitsch and works by local artists add to the gritty feel of this legendary trilevel place that's hard to miss and hard not to like. An eclectic clientele listens to the live music that's performed every night and soaks up rays on the roof deck by day. ✉ *2461 18th St. NW, Adams Morgan* ☎ *202/667–5370* 🌐 *www.madamsorgan.com* [M] *Woodley Park–Zoo/Adams Morgan.*

Performing Arts

Adams Morgan has long been the hub of the city's best avant-garde performances, primarily offered by the District of Columbia Arts Center. You can enjoy an incredible meal at one of many nearby ethnic restaurants, see a performance at the Gala Hispanic Theatre, and then head to one of the neighborhood's colorful bars after the show.

THEATER AND PERFORMANCE ART

District of Columbia Arts Center

ARTS CENTERS | Known by area artists as DCAC, this cross-genre space shows changing exhibits in its gallery and presents avant-garde performance art, improv, and experimental plays in its tiny, funky black-box theater. DCAC is the home of Washington's oldest experimental theater group, Theatre Du Jour. ✉ *2438 18th St. NW, Adams Morgan* ☎ *202/462–7833* 🌐 *www.dcartscenter.org* [M] *Woodley Park–Zoo/Adams Morgan.*

Gala Hispanic Theatre

THEATER | This company attracts outstanding Hispanic actors from around the world, performing works by such leading dramatists as Federico García Lorca and Mario Vargas Llosa. Plays are presented in English or in Spanish with projected subtitles. The company performs in the Tivoli Theatre in Columbia Heights, a hot spot for Latino culture and cuisine. ⊠ Tivoli Sq., 3333 14th St. NW and Park Rd., Columbia Heights, Adams Morgan ☎ 202/234–7174 ⊕ www.galatheatre.org Ⓜ Columbia Heights.

🛍 Shopping

Scattered among the dozens of Latin, Ethiopian, and international restaurants in this most bohemian of Washington neighborhoods is a score of eccentric shops. If quality is what you seek, Adams Morgan and nearby Woodley Park can be a minefield; tread cautiously. Still, this is good turf for the bargain hunter.

■ TIP➜ If bound for a specific shop, you may wish to call ahead to verify hours.

The evening hours bring scores of revelers to the row, so plan to go before dark unless you want to couple your shopping with a party pit stop.

How to get there is another question. Though the Woodley Park–Zoo/Adams Morgan Metro stop is relatively close to the 18th Street strip (where the interesting shops are), getting off here means that you will have to walk over the bridge on Calvert Street, or hop on the Circulator bus just outside the Metro entrance for one stop. Five minutes longer, the walk from the Dupont Circle Metro stop is more scenic; you cruise north on 18th Street through tree-lined streets of row houses and embassies. You can also easily catch Metrobuses No. 42 or L2 or a cab from Dupont to Adams Morgan.

BOOKS
Lost City Books

BOOKS | FAMILY | Since 1981, this multi-level used-book store has been selling "rare to medium rare" books with plenty of meaty titles in all genres, especially out-of-print literature. Formerly called Idle Time Books, Lost City Books retains all the charm that has kept it in business for more than four decades, with the addition of thoughtful curation and a well-organized selection of books, making it both easy and enjoyable to browse in a recently remodeled, warm and cozy space. ⊠ 2467 18th St. NW, Adams Morgan ☎ 202/232–4774 ⊕ lostcitybookstore.com Ⓜ Woodley Park–Zoo/Adams Morgan.

★ Urban Dwell

BOOKS | If you're looking to bring home a D.C.-themed souvenir or a gift for a loved one, stop by this classy, well-curated shop. There's a great selection of children's books and clothes as well as tasteful jewelry, games, books, and all kinds of knickknacks to add a special touch to your home. ⊠ 1837 Columbia Road NW, Adams Morgan ☎ 202/558–9087 ⊕ urbandwelldc.com.

CHOCOLATE
The Chocolate House

CHOCOLATE | FAMILY | For chocoholics with a gourmet palate, this is one-stop shopping. Offerings are both foreign (Michel Cluizel from France and Amedei from Italy) and domestic (Askinosie from Missouri and Amano from Utah). Selections from D.C.-area chocolatiers make for tasty souvenirs. ⊠ 1904 18th St. NW, Adams Morgan ☎ 202/903–0346 ⊕ www.thechocolatehousedc.com Ⓜ Dupont Circle.

CLOTHING
Le Bustiere Boutique

WOMEN'S CLOTHING | Tucked away on the second floor of a building on busy Columbia Road, this local- and woman-owned boutique offers high-end lingerie, swimwear, and sleepwear. The staff provides the kind of personal service that enables you to find just the right piece to suit your needs. ✉ *1744 Columbia Rd., Suite 2, Adams Morgan* ☎ *202/745–8080* ⊕ *lebustiere.com* Ⓜ *Woodley Park–Zoo/ Adams Morgan.*

Meeps

SECOND-HAND | Catering to fans of retro glamour and low prices, this week-ends-only shop near the bottom of the Adams Morgan strip stocks vintage clothes and costumes (from the '60s through the '90s) for women and men. ✉ *2104 18th St. NW, Adams Morgan* ☎ *202/265–6546* ⊕ *www.meepsdc.com* ⊙ *Closed weekdays* Ⓜ *Dupont Circle.*

Mercedes Bien Vintage

SECOND-HAND | The carefully selected vintage clothing and shoes sold here include everything from cocktail dresses to cowboy boots. You will also find jewel-ry and belts, all handpicked by the owner, Mercedes, who has been in the vintage business since the early '80s. This small shop offers exceptional, personal service and is only open on weekends. ✉ *2423 18th St. NW, Adams Morgan* ☎ *202/360– 8481* ⊙ *Closed weekdays* Ⓜ *Woodley Park–Zoo/Adams Morgan.*

SHOES

Fleet Feet Sports Shop

SHOES | The expert staff at this friendly shop will assess your feet and your train-ing schedule before recommending the perfect shoes, apparel, or accessories for running, swimming, soccer, or cycling. The shop also hosts running events, a great way to explore the city. ✉ *1841 Columbia Rd. NW, Adams Morgan* ☎ *202/387–3888* ⊕ *www.fleetfeetdc.com* Ⓜ *Woodley Park–Zoo/Adams Morgan.*

Chapter 10

U STREET CORRIDOR AND SHAW

WITH LOGAN CIRCLE AND COLUMBIA HEIGHTS

Updated by
Akilah Stroman

TRUE REFORMER BUILDING

◉ Sights	🍴 Restaurants	🛏 Hotels	🛍 Shopping	🍸 Nightlife
★★☆☆☆	★★★★★	★☆☆☆☆	★★★★☆	★★★★★

NEIGHBORHOOD SNAPSHOT

TOP EXPERIENCES

African American Civil War Memorial and Museum: Learn about the lives of slaves and freedmen, and discover whether your ancestors fought in Black Civil War regiments.

Ben's Chili Bowl: This D.C. institution has perfected its recipe over the last 50 years.

Street art: Keep your eyes open for colorful murals throughout the neighborhood. From the famous murals of Ben's Chili Bowl to Blagden Alley, there's plenty of street art to take in.

International food: From Ghana to El Salvador to Italy, you can take a culinary trip around the world in this neighborhood.

Live music: Music greats like Duke Ellington made this neighborhood famous back in the 1920s. Dance at El Techo, or rock out at the 9:30 Club or Black Cat.

GETTING HERE

The Green Line Metro stops at 13th and U. To get to the African American Civil War Memorial, exit onto 10th Street. There's limited street parking, but you are better off taking a cab or other ride service since the area is popular, though the area is also walkable.

The Shaw–Howard University metro station is at 8th and S.

Buses 90 and 92 travel from Woodley Park through Adams Morgan to 14th and U, while Buses 52, 53, and 54 travel north from several downtown Metro stops up 14th Street.

NEIGHBORHOOD HISTORY

Commonly known as the "Black Broadway" of Washington D.C., the U Street corridor has always been a haven for Black excellence. During the first half of the 1900s, this neighborhood was a place where Black people were free to own businesses when other neighborhoods where subjected to Jim Crow laws. This created a space where some of the most influential Black leaders and academics, such as famous Duke Ellington and graduates of Howard University.

PLANNING YOUR TIME

You can spend a good day eating your way through the many international restaurants in the area, admiring the colorful row houses, and taking pictures of the intricately designed murals. You can fill an evening with a traditional theater experience or a live music show. U Street is a nightlife destination for the city, with its many clubs and bars, while Shaw is a good bet for craft cocktail bars and unique dining.

Home-style Ethiopian food, offbeat boutiques, and live music are fueling the revival of the U Street, Logan Circle, and Shaw areas. This part of the District once survived on memories of its heyday as a center of Black culture and jazz music in the first half of the 20th century; now it's a vibrant, food-savvy restaurant and nightlife destination.

The area was especially vibrant from the 1920s to the 1950s, when it was home to jazz genius Duke Ellington, social activist Mary McLeod Bethune, and poets Langston Hughes and Georgia Douglas Johnson. In the 1950s, Supreme Court Justice Thurgood Marshall, then still a lawyer, organized the landmark *Brown v. Board of Education* case at the 12th Street YMCA. Now, murals and artwork speckled across the Shaw neighborhood reflect the art and artists that have added to the town's vibrancy, among a lively resurgence of culture, cuisine, and nightlife.

U Street has become a nightlife destination with music venues and theaters, but Shaw and Logan Circle have emerged as the new restaurants strips for fantastic and niche culinary experiences.

⊙ Sights

This area of the District is not one for sightseers, but there's one noteworthy museum you may wish to visit.

African American Civil War Memorial and Museum

HISTORY MUSEUM | This museum highlights and commemorates the contributions of the 209,145 members of the United States Colored Troops, who have long been ignored in the history of the Civil War. It also sets out to serve the educational needs of the local, national, and international community through learning and experiences within the interpretation on the history of the USCT. The museum is free to visitors. Give yourself an hour to explore the main exhibit, *Glorious March to Liberty, Civil War to Civil Rights.* Tours are available by appointment only. ⊠ *1925 Vermont Ave. NW, Logan Circle* ☎ *202/667–2667* ⊕ *www.afroamcivilwar. org* ⌕ *Free* Ⓜ *Shaw–Howard U.*

DC Alley Museum

OTHER ATTRACTION | If you love street art, take a stroll along the DC Alley Museum, funded by the DC Commission on the Arts and Humanities Public Art Building Communities Program. Local artists take turns creating art in the many garages surrounding Blagden Alley in Shaw. The murals take on local issues, social justice,

and women's rights. The museum is open-air, and you can go whenever you choose as there are no admission charges. You can find more details about the artists and the art on the website. ✉ *Blagden Alley, Shaw* ⊕ *www.dcalley-museum.com* Ⓜ *Convention Center*.

Mary McLeod Bethune Council House National Historic Site

HISTORIC HOME | The site of the first headquarters for the National Council of Negro Women, the Mary McLeod Bethune Council House celebrates the life and legacy of Bethune, who founded the council and also served as president of the National Association of Colored Women. It was the council's headquarters from 1943 to 1966, and Bethune herself lived here from 1943 to 1949. The archives of the history of African American women in the United States and Bethune's legacy are housed here as well. After a lengthy construction project to update the archival research areas and to stabilize the physical foundations, the site reopened to the public in 2018. ✉ *1318 Vermont Ave. NW, Shaw* ☎ *202/426–5961* ⊕ *www.nps.gov/mamc* ⊘ *Closed Sun.–Wed.* Ⓜ *Dupont Circle*.

🍴 Restaurants

U Street links Shaw, centered near Howard University's campus, to Adams Morgan, and is known for indie rock clubs, edgy bars, and trendy restaurants. Although the urban hipster vibe is being threatened by skyrocketing rents and the intrusion of chain stores, you'll still find more tattoos and sneakers than pinstripes and pearls here. Logan Circle is southwest from both of Shaw's Metro stations: U Street/African American Civil War Memorial/Cardozo and Shaw–Howard University (both on the Green and Yellow lines).

All-Purpose Pizzeria

$ | ITALIAN | You can get nearly any pizza you might want, from a classic Margherita style with the standard mozzarella, tomato, and oregano toppings to more elaborate pizzas like Enzo the Baker with smoked bacon, Calabrian chilis, and red onion. For lighter fare, try some of the hand-selected meats off the salumi menu or one of the *spuntini* ("little snacks") that include braised octopus and squash "hummus." There are no shortages of antipasti and salad offerings, either. **Known for:** seasonally inspired pizzas; delicious antipasti; pickup and delivery. $ *Average main: $16* ✉ *1250 9th St. NW, Shaw* ☎ *202/849–6174* ⊕ *allpurposedc.com* Ⓜ *Mt. Vernon Sq. 7th St.–Convention Center*.

★ Anafre

$$ | MEXICAN | At this celebrated restaurant, whose name means "clay oven," chef Antonio Solis infuses his creative dishes with the regional flavors of his native Mexico. The *queso fundido* (savory melted cheese) served in a banana leaf is one of the most requested starters. **Known for:** authentic Mexican food; lively space; extensive cocktail list. $ *Average main: $18* ✉ *3704 14th St. NW, Columbia Heights* ☎ *202/758–2127* ⊕ *www.anafredc.com*.

Appioo

$$ | AFRICAN | Washington, D.C. is a hub for the African diaspora, with many different countries represented in the city's culinary scene. Appioo, a well-established Ghanaian restaurant owned by chef Prince Matey, is set in the basement of a row house and has an intimate dining room decorated with intricate African wood sculptures. **Known for:** authentic Ghanian food; live music; intimate dining room. $ *Average main: $18* ✉ *1924 9th St. NW, Shaw* ☎ *202/588–7366* ⊕ *www.appiooafricanbargrill.com* Ⓜ *Shaw*.

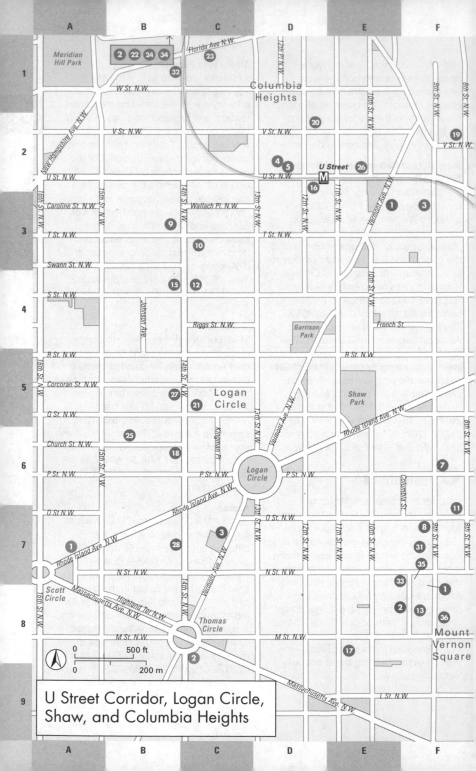

Sights ▼

1 African American
Civil War Memorial and
Museum **E3**
2 DC Alley Museum........ **E8**
3 Mary McLeod Bethune
Council House
National Historic Site....**C7**

Restaurants ▼

1 All-Purpose Pizzeria..... **F8**
2 Anafre.................... **B1**
3 Appioo **F3**
4 Ben's Chili Bowl......... **D2**
5 Ben's Next Door **D2**
6 Calabash Tea &
Tonic...................... **G3**
7 Chaplin's **F6**
8 Chercher Ethiopian
Restaurant................ **F7**
9 Colada Shop............. **B3**
10 Compass Rose **C3**
11 Convivial **F6**
12 Cork Wine Bar
& Market................. **C4**
13 The Dabney............... **F8**
14 DCity Smokehouse **I4**
15 Doi Moi................... **B4**
16 Dukem.................... **D2**
17 El Rinconcito Cafe **E8**
18 Estadio **B6**
19 Haikan.................... **F2**
20 Izakaya Seki............. **D2**
21 Le Diplomate **C5**
22 Los Hermanos........... **B1**
23 Maydan **C1**
24 Mezcalero **B1**
25 Milk Bar Flagship
@ Logan Circle.......... **B6**
26 Oohhs & Aahhs **E2**
27 Pearl Dive
Oyster Palace **B5**
28 the pig................... **B7**
29 The Red Hen..............**I4**
30 The Royal **H3**
31 San Lorenzo
Ristorante + Bar **F7**
32 Seven Reasons **B1**
33 Seylou Bakery
and Mill **F7**
34 Thip Khao................ **B1**
35 Tiger Fork **F7**
36 Unconventional
Diner **F8**

Hotels ▼

1 The Darcy................ **A7**
2 Hotel Zena................**C8**

★ Ben's Chili Bowl

$ | **AMERICAN** | **FAMILY** | A U Street fixture for decades, Ben's serves chili—on hot dogs, on Polish-style sausages, on burgers, and on its own—to Washingtonians and visitors alike. The shiny, red-vinyl stools give the impression that little has changed since the 1950s (the original location still doesn't accept credit cards), but don't be fooled: this favorite of former President Barack Obama has rocketed into the 21st century with an iPhone app, an upscale Southern cuisine restaurant next door, and menu additions like turkey burgers and meatless chili that nod to modern times. **Known for:** legendary half-smoke chili bowls; Southern-style breakfast; cheese fries and milkshakes. $ *Average main: $7* ⊠ *1213 U St. NW, U Street* ☎ *202/667–0058* ⊕ *www. benschilibowl.com* ▭ *No credit cards* Ⓜ *U St./African American Civil War Memorial/ Cardozo.*

Ben's Next Door

$ | **SOUTHERN** | A Black-owned establishment that brings you delicious food and even better drinks. Its location being so close to Maryland, some dishes are Maryland inspired and to die for. **Known for:** shrimp and grits; unlimited mimosas on weekends; Sunday brunches. $ *Average main: $15* ⊠ *1211 U St. NW* ☎ *202/667– 8880* ⊕ *bensnextdoor.com.*

Calabash Tea & Tonic

$ | **CAFÉ** | This award-winning teahouse, named Yelp's "Most Loved Business in D.C." in 2019, features more than 80 teas, tonics, and body products based on founder Dr. Sunyatta Amen's Jamaican Maroon and Native American great-grandmothers' time-tested formulas. After you're greeted at the counter, one of Calabash's skilled staff will craft a concoction based on your needs or desires. **Known for:** custom teas to cure ailments; vegan desserts and pastries; bohemian decor. $ *Average main: $7* ⊠ *1847 7th St. NW, Shaw* ☎ *202/525– 5386* ⊕ *www.calabashtea.com* Ⓜ *Shaw.*

Chaplin's

$ | **ASIAN** | Inspired by the 1930s star Charlie Chaplin, this is the first ramen house–cocktail bar in Shaw. Burmese chef Myo Htun transports you with his take on traditional *gyoza* (wonton wrappers stuffed with pork and cabbage), *shumai* (small stuffed dumplings), and any number of ramen combinations, while Ari and Micah Wilder offer carefully curated cocktails. **Known for:** delicious ramen and gyoza; homemade cocktails; 1930s film theme. $ *Average main: $14* ⊠ *1501 9th St. NW, Shaw* ☎ *202/644–8806* ⊕ *www. chaplinsdc.com* Ⓜ *Mt. Vernon Sq. 7th St.–Convention Center.*

Chercher Ethiopian Restaurant

$ | **ETHIOPIAN** | In Shaw, a neighborhood known for its traditional Ethiopian food, this celebrated spot offers both authentic flavor and great prices. Named for the West Hararghe zone of Ethiopia, the restaurant celebrates the traditional cuisine that is eaten mostly utensil-free, using a special spongy bread, *injera*, to scoop up food that's laid out on a large platter. **Known for:** authentic and delicious injera; plenty of vegan options; great value. $ *Average main: $14* ⊠ *1334 9th St. NW, Shaw* ☎ *202/299–9703* ⊕ *www. chercherrestaurant.com.*

★ Colada Shop

$ | **CUBAN** | Escape to Cuba via a *cafesito* at this spot, which has a two-floor patio and is situated just off lively 14th Street. If you'd like something more potent than a coffee, there are plenty of cocktails, from piña coladas to guava frosé. **Known for:** Cuban-style coffee; stylish decor; Latin pastries. $ *Average main: $12* ⊠ *1405 T St. NW, U Street* ☎ *202/931–4947* ⊕ *www.coladashop.com.*

Compass Rose

$$ | **FUSION** | Take a trip around the world at Compass Rose, a restaurant celebrating global cuisine. Inspired by her travels, owner Rose Previte features many of her favorite dishes, from ceviches to kebabs to the signature *khachapuri* (Georgian

cheese-filled bread). **Known for:** eclectic decor; creative menu; extensive wine list. [$] *Average main: $20* ✉ *1346 T St. NW, U Street* ☎ *202/506–4765* 🌐 *www.compassrosedc.com* 🕓 *Closed Mon. and Tues.*

Convivial
$$ | **FRENCH** | This cozy French restaurant serves classics such as ratatouille, steak frites, and coq au vin. The extensive wine list focuses on French varieties, guaranteeing perfect pairings. **Known for:** French plates meant for sharing; lots of local regulars; lively patio. [$] *Average main: $25* ✉ *801 O St. NW, Logan Circle* ☎ *202/525–2870* 🌐 *www.convivialdc.com* 🕓 *No lunch* [M] *Mt. Vernon Sq. 7th St.–Convention Center.*

★ Cork Wine Bar & Market
$$ | **WINE BAR** | This rustic, dimly lit wine bar brings chic cuisine to the city's hippest neighborhood. The wine list features rare varietals—with a dozen still under $11 per glass—but even teetotalers will be enchanted by the menu's classic dishes. **Known for:** more than 50 wines by the glass; relaxing patio; favorite small plates to share. [$] *Average main: $24* ✉ *1805 14th St. NW, U Street* ☎ *202/265–2675* 🌐 *www.corkdc.com* 🕓 *Closed Mon.* [M] *U St./African American Civil War Memorial/Cardozo.*

★ The Dabney
$$ | **AMERICAN** | While many of D.C.'s standout restaurants earn their accolades for takes on cuisine from far-flung corners of the globe, at the Dabney, Virginia-born chef Jeremiah Langhorne draws rave reviews for his commitment to Mid-Atlantic cuisine. Larger plates might include whole lacquered quail stuffed with cornbread or a family-style serving of chicken and dumplings, but small plates predominate, and waiters will help you balance out your meal. **Known for:** creative cocktails; low-key farmhouse vibe; handcrafted desserts. [$] *Average main: $21* ✉ *122 Blagden Alley NW, Shaw* ☎ *202/450–1015* 🌐 *www.thedabney.com* 🕓 *Closed Sun. and Mon.* [M] *Mt. Vernon Sq. 7th St.–Convention Center.*

DCity Smokehouse
$ | **BARBECUE** | **FAMILY** | DCity Smokehouse continues to be a beloved neighborhood barbecue spot. Located in residential Bloomingdale, the restaurant serves a variety of meats smoked in-house. **Known for:** barbecue; neighborhood staple; affordable eats. [$] *Average main: $15* ✉ *203 Florida Ave. NW, Bloomingdale* ☎ *202/733–1919* 🌐 *www.dcitysmokehouse.com.*

Doi Moi
$$ | **ASIAN** | The rise of foodie culture can leave adventurous diners feeling like they've turned over every culinary stone, but this pilgrimage into the Southeast Asian unknown will wow even the most jaded eater. Doi Moi (Vietnamese for "new changes") puts a new spin on several traditional Southeast Asian cuisines: fried beef jerky with shark sriracha, wok-tossed mussels, and crispy fried snapper are leading lights. **Known for:** adventurous Asian cuisine spanning several regions; bright and modern interior; special vegetarian and gluten-free menus. [$] *Average main: $25* ✉ *1800 14th St. NW, U Street* ☎ *202/733–5131* 🌐 *www.doimoidc.com* 🕓 *No lunch* [M] *U St./African American Civil War Memorial/Cardozo.*

★ Dukem
$$ | **ETHIOPIAN** | For more than 20 years, Dukem has been a favorite of those seeking authentic Ethiopian food. Guests come for the injera, a spongy flatbread topped with tibs, a dish with cubed tender lamb or beef fried with onion, rosemary, jalapeño pepper served with injera, and salad and spicy awazie sauce. **Known for:** well-established restaurant; vegetarian- and vegan-friendly options; occasional live Ethiopian music on weekends. [$] *Average main: $18* ✉ *1114–1118 U St. NW, U Street* ☎ *202/667–8735* [M] *U St.*

El Rinconcito Cafe

$ | **LATIN AMERICAN** | A trip to D.C. is not complete without tasting *pupusas,* the El Salvadoran tortillas filled with chorizo, cheese, and chicharrón. El Rinconcito Cafe, a fixture in Shaw for El Salvadoran and Mexican cuisine, specializes in pupusas and also serves quesadillas, tacos, and enchiladas—all at affordable prices. **Known for:** pupusas; affordable meals; neighborhood spot for El Salvadoran food. [$] *Average main: $10* ✉ *1129 11th St. NW, Shaw* ☎ *202/789–4110* 🌐 *www.rinconcitocafe.com* [M] *Convention Center.*

★ Estadio

$$$ | **SPANISH** | The name of this polished palace means "stadium," and its gorgeously baroque interior, which surrounds a high-wire open kitchen, makes a perfect stage for energetic and flavorful uses of top-notch ingredients. The menu, developed during research jaunts throughout Spain, is a master class in tapas, with smoky grilled scallions punched up by garlicky romesco sauce and *tortilla española* smoother than any served in Barcelona. **Known for:** classic Spanish tapas with new flavors; boozy slushies; beautiful dining room. [$] *Average main: $28* ✉ *1520 14th St. NW, Logan Circle* ☎ *202/319–1404* 🌐 *www.estadio-dc.com* 🕒 *Closed Tues. No lunch Mon.–Thurs.* [M] *U St./African American Civil War Memorial/Cardozo.*

Haikan

$ | **JAPANESE** | Located on a lively block, Haikan is a recent addition from the popular Daikaya Group, famous for its ramen restaurants throughout the city. The restaurant serves different types of ramen, featuring pork-based, Sapporo-style dishes. **Known for:** Sapporo-style ramen; lively dining room; rotating selection of Japanese appetizers. [$] *Average main: $15* ✉ *805 V St. NW, Shaw* ☎ *202/299–1000* 🌐 *www.haikandc.com* 🕒 *Closed Mon. and Tues. except for takeout* [M] *Shaw.*

Izakaya Seki

$$ | **JAPANESE** | The only crowd-pleasing flourishes here are the freshness of the scallop carpaccio and the perfect sear on the grilled yellowtail jaw, and that's all adventurous foodies will need to make the most of a quiet evening at this family-owned, off-the-beaten-path spot marked by little more than a red Japanese lantern outside the door. Dare to try some beef tongue or cured squid off the sake accompaniments menu of smaller plates. **Known for:** authentic, non-Americanized Japanese cuisine; timed reservations for large groups; small, adventurous plates like beef tongue. [$] *Average main: $22* ✉ *1117 V St. NW, U Street* ☎ *202/588–5841* 🌐 *www.sekidc.com* 🕒 *Closed Mon. No lunch* [M] *U St./African American Civil War Memorial/Cardozo.*

★ Le Diplomate

$$$ | **BRASSERIE** | In this faithful re-creation of a convivial Parisian bistro, the attention to detail makes a night here into more than just a meal. This excellent spot prizes quality above all, from graceful martinis and hand-stuffed ricotta ravioli to succulent, textbook-worthy steak frites and roasted chicken. **Known for:** Parisian-bistro vibe; juicy steak frites; popular brunch menu. [$] *Average main: $30* ✉ *1610 14th St. NW, U Street* ☎ *202/332–3333* 🌐 *www.lediplomatedc.com* [M] *U Street/ Cardozo.*

Los Hermanos

$ | **LATIN AMERICAN** | The owners of Los Hermanos (meaning "brothers" in Spanish), which was initially a bodega, began offering home cooked–style Dominican food after customers began asking about the smells that were coming from the back of the store. A must-order is *mangú*, the national dish of the Dominican Republic made with mashed plantains and accompanied by salami, fried cheese, and egg. **Known for:** authentic Dominican food; affordable prices; casual neighborhood restaurant.

$ *Average main: $12* ⊠ *1428 Park Rd. NW, Columbia Heights* ☎ *202/483–8235* ⊕ *www.loshermanosfordc.com* Ⓜ *Columbia Heights.*

Maydan

$$$$ | **MIDDLE EASTERN** | Michelin-starred Maydan is an idyllic culinary journey to the Middle East with an intricate entrance, wood fire taking center stage, and a colorful bar. Maydan transformed their outdoor seating into a Middle-Eastern dining experience called "Tawle." Guests must order from the prix-fixe menu, which includes a variety of family-style dishes inspired by the Middle East, Northern Africa, and the Caucuses. **Known for:** Michelin starred; Middle Eastern wood-fired kebabs; craft cocktails. $ *Average main: $65* ⊠ *1346 Florida Ave. NW, U Street* ⊕ *www.maydandc.com* ☾ *Closed Mon. and Tues.* Ⓜ *U Street/ Cardozo.*

Mezcalero

$ | **MEXICAN** | Mezcalero, the more casual sister restaurant to Anafre by chef Antonio Solis, serves a variety of appetizers such as Mexican-style ceviche, guacamole, and grilled oysters. The authentic burritos are generously filled with carne asada, chorizo, or mixed vegetables, and, as the restaurant's name implies, mezcal plays a big role on the cocktail list. **Known for:** authentic Mexican food; great happy hour specials; mezcal cocktails. $ *Average main: $12* ⊠ *3714 14th St. NW, Columbia Heights* ☎ *202/803–2114* ⊕ *www.mezcalerodc.com* Ⓜ *Columbia Heights.*

Milk Bar Flagship @ Logan Circle

$ | **AMERICAN** | If you're a fan of sprinkles, pie, ice cream, and birthday cake, then this is the place for you to eat in or grab something to go. But don't expect run-of-the-mill pastries: founder Christina Tosi has created an empire of modernized American confections, including soft serve made with cereal-infused milk, cakes shrunken into truffles, and favorites like the Compost Cookie and Crack Pie. **Known for:** American desserts with a modern twist; signature birthday layer cake and cereal-milk soft serve; baking classes on-site. $ *Average main: $6* ⊠ *1525 15th St. NW, at Church St. NW, Logan Circle* ☎ *202/506–1357* ⊕ *milkbarstore.com* Ⓜ *Dupont Circle or Mt. Vernon Sq. 7th St.–Convention Center.*

Oohhs & Aahhs

$ | **SOUTHERN** | No-frills soul food is what you'll find at this friendly eat-in or take-out place, where the price is right, and the food is delicious. Ultrarich macaroni and cheese, succulent chicken and waffles, and teriyaki salmon just beg to be devoured, and collard greens are cooked with vinegar and sugar rather than the traditional salt pork. **Known for:** homestyle soul cooking; mac and cheese, collard greens, and hummingbird cake; late-night weekend hours. $ *Average main: $15* ⊠ *1005 U St. NW, U Street* ☎ *202/667–7142* ⊕ *www.oohhsnaahhs. com* Ⓜ *U St./African American Civil War Memorial/Cardozo.*

Pearl Dive Oyster Palace

$$ | **SEAFOOD** | Chef Jeff Black does serve three kinds of po'boys, but that's about as working-class as it gets at this dazzlingly decorated homage to the bivalve. East and West Coast oysters come raw, with perfect dipping sauces—at half-price all day on Monday and during happy hour every other day—or warm in five irresistible guises, from bacon wrapped to crusted in cornmeal and sprinkled with sweet-potato hash. **Known for:** upscale oysters (both raw and warm); steak options for non–oyster lovers; classy cocktails. $ *Average main: $24* ⊠ *1612 14th St. NW, U Street* ☎ *202/319–1612* ⊕ *www.pearldivedc.com* ☾ *No lunch Mon.–Thurs.* Ⓜ *U St./African American Civil War Memorial/Cardozo.*

the pig

$$ | **AMERICAN** | As the name implies, this restaurant celebrates pork—from patties to barbecue ribs to pulled-pork sandwiches, all made with meat sourced from a Maryland farm. Enjoy signature cocktails such as the Three Little Pigs—8 Weeks 'til the Slaughter (a Manhattan), the Pegroni (a Negroni), and the Swine Boulevard (a Boulevardier). **Known for:** pork-themed menu; craft cocktails; both small and large plates. $ *Average main: $20* ⊠ *1320 14th St. NW, Logan Circle* ☎ *202/290–2821* ⊕ *www.thepigdc.com* Ⓜ *Mt. Vernon Sq. 7th St.–Convention Center.*

★ The Red Hen

$$$ | **AMERICAN** | The cozy farmhouse-like setting helped make the Red Hen a must-try for Italian-influenced takes on American dishes. If the name and giant hen on the facade have you thinking poultry, you'd be right to follow your instincts and order the pan-roasted half chicken. **Known for:** savvy wine list; pan-roasted half chicken; delicious pasta options. $ *Average main: $28* ⊠ *1822 1st St. NW, U Street* ☎ *202/525–3021* ⊕ *www. theredhendc.com* ☽ *No lunch* Ⓜ *Shaw–Howard U.*

The Royal

$ | **LATIN AMERICAN** | The Royal is both a Michelin-recognized Bib Gourmand restaurant and a well-priced, local favorite for breakfast, lunch, dinner, or just for a matcha latte while working on your laptop at the bar. The second concept by owner Paul Carlson is a celebration of his family's international roots, with a strong emphasis on vegetarian and gluten-free options. **Known for:** Colombian-inspired food; small plates and homemade cocktails; neighborhood favorite. $ *Average main: $15* ⊠ *501 Florida Ave. NW, Shaw* ☎ *202/332–7777* ⊕ *www.theroyaldc.com* Ⓜ *Shaw–Howard U.*

San Lorenzo Ristorante + Bar

$$ | **ITALIAN** | Chef and owner Massimo Fabbri, previously of Tosca and Posto, opened the first restaurant of his own to highlight the tastes of Tuscany and pay homage to his roots. Named for the patron saint of chefs, this soothing restaurant reminds you of Italy itself with a cream and golden palette, wooden beams, distressed plaster, and Italian art. **Known for:** sophisticated yet casual style; classic Tuscan dishes like rosticciana and pappardelle with rabbit ragù; homemade pastas. $ *Average main: $25* ⊠ *1316 9th St. NW, Shaw* ☎ *202/588–8954* ⊕ *www. sanlorenzodc.com* Ⓜ *Mt. Vernon Sq. 7th St.–Convention Center.*

★ Seven Reasons

$$$ | **LATIN AMERICAN** | At Seven Reasons, one of D.C.'s most talked-about restaurants in the past two years, chef Enrique Limardo honors his native Venezuela with creative versions of *arepas* (stuffed cornmeal cakes) and *arroz bomba* (rice with seafood). The restaurant also takes you on a Latin American tour with offerings such as Argentinean-style steak or Peruvian-style ceviche. **Known for:** picturesque rooftop patio; high-end Latin American cuisine; open kitchen plan. $ *Average main: $35* ⊠ *2208 14th St. NW, U Street* ☎ *202/417–8563* ⊕ *www.sevenreasons-dc.com* ☽ *Closed Mon.* Ⓜ *U St.*

★ Seylou Bakery and Mill

$ | **AMERICAN** | Skip the chains and head to this beloved local coffee shop and whole-grain bakery offering fresh sourdough creations, whole wheat almond croissants, and seasonal veggie frittatas. Grab a specialty coffee, a yerba-maté or nettle tea, and a 100% whole-wheat chocolate croissant or buckwheat muffin on your way to tour the city. **Known for:** freshly made breads and whole wheat pastries; specialty coffees and teas; locally sourced ingredients. $ *Average main: $7* ⊠ *926 N St. NW, Suite A, Shaw* ☎ *202/842–1122* ⊕ *www.seylou.com* ☽ *Closed Mon.–Thurs.* Ⓜ *Mt. Vernon Sq. 7th St.–Convention Center.*

Thip Khao

$ | **LAO** | **FAMILY** | Chef-owner Seng Luang-grath learned to cook as a young girl in a refugee camp and later brought the cuisine of Laos and Thailand to northern Virginia and then D.C. The atmosphere at her Columbia Heights outpost might be casual, but the flavors of its food are complex. **Known for:** deep menu of authentic Laotian cuisine; minced-meat salads known as laab; bourbon and ginger cider drinks. $ *Average main: $16* ⊠ *3462 14th St. NW, Logan Circle* ☎ *202/387–5426* ⊕ *thipkhao.com* ⊘ *Closed Tues.* Ⓜ *Columbia Heights.*

Tiger Fork

$ | **CHINESE FUSION** | Come here if you're looking for edgier Hong Kong cuisine, perhaps pork ribs slathered in soy-and-ginger sauce, a tofu claypot, *cheung fun* with shrimp and flowering chives, or chili wontons. Finish your meal with a traditional street dessert: a bubble waffle topped with "fun stuff" (sprinkles, lychee, Pocky sticks, and dulce de leche). **Known for:** Asian street-style food; late-night menu; bubble waffles. $ *Average main: $16* ⊠ *922 N St. NW, Shaw* ✛ *Enter in rear, off Blagden Alley* ☎ *202/733–1152* ⊕ *www.tigerforkdc.com* Ⓜ *Mt. Vernon Sq. 7th St.–Convention Center.*

Unconventional Diner

$$ | **AMERICAN** | All the typical diner and Southern favorites on the menu here have an unusual twist, befitting the name of this restaurant. Start with the kale nachos or potpie poppers, then, if you're really hungry, dive into a plate of fried chicken or the "French Dip" pappardelle. **Known for:** modernized American diner food; potpie poppers (bite-size chicken potpies); good daily breakfast and week-end brunch. $ *Average main: $20* ⊠ *1207 9th St. NW, Shaw* ☎ *202/847–0122* ⊕ *unconventionaldiner.com* Ⓜ *Mt. Vernon Sq. 7th St.–Convention Center.*

🛏 Hotels

A stay in this hip neighborhood affords a cooler, more-local District experience. Hotels here are right in the mix of some of the city's most unique restaurants and bars, and the area is just a Metro or car ride away from the major sites and museums.

The Darcy

$$$ | **HOTEL** | **FAMILY** | One of the city's latest hotel triumphs, this stylish treasure just around the corner from the buzzy 14th Street Corridor aims to bring a sophisticated European touch to the cosmopolitan capital city. **Pros:** sophisticated style and lobby; central location; pet-friendly. **Cons:** no spa or pool; only expensive valet parking available; closest Metro is a 10-minute walk. $ *Rooms from: $300* ⊠ *1515 Rhode Island Ave. NW, Logan Circle* ☎ *202/232–7000* ⊕ *www.thedarcyhotel.com* ⇨ *226 rooms* ❑ *No Meals* Ⓜ *Dupont Circle.*

Hotel Zena

$ | **HOTEL** | Located in Thomas Circle, Hotel Zena (which stands out with a towering mural of two stunning women in warrior regalia) is an homage to women; guests are welcomed with a massive art installation of the late feminist icon, Ruth Bader Ginsburg, made of hand-painted tampons. **Pros:** centrally located; creative, woman-focused theme; rooftop pool and bar. **Cons:** open lobby restaurant with no private dining area; message many be too partisan for some; expensive parking. $ *Rooms from: $151* ⊠ *1155 14th St. NW, Logan Circle* ☎ *202/737–1200* ⊕ *www.viceroyhotelsandresorts.com/ zena* ⇨ *191 rooms* Ⓜ *Mt. Vernon Sq.*

🍸 Nightlife

Decades ago, the U Street corridor was famous as D.C.'s Black Broadway. After many dormant years, the neighborhood has come roaring back with a lively bar, club, and music scene that's expanding both north and south along 14th Street. The U Street corridor is easily accessible from the U Street/African American Civil War Memorial/Cardozo Metro stop, on the Green and Yellow lines. Taxis also are easy to find.

In the last couple of years, nearby Shaw has become the most revitalized downtown neighborhood in the capital. But any night out in Shaw almost by default includes spending time in the U Street corridor to the north and west—especially because some destinations, like the Howard Theatre and the 9:30 Club, straddle both increasingly diverse urban neighborhoods. Shaw is centered on 7th Street, with Howard University and Hospital to the north and the Washington Convention Center at the very southern edge.

BARS AND LOUNGES
All Souls
BARS | All Souls feels like the perfect dive, a great place to meet up with friends and chat away in a booth, fresh drink or craft beer in hand. The simple yet refined cocktails are described in loving detail, alongside interesting wines and craft brews, on signs at the bar. You can order snacks, but you can also bring food in or have it delivered, making this feel even more like a friendly, neighborhood hangout. ✉ 725 T St. NW, Shaw ☎ 202/733–5929 ⊕ allsoulsbar.com Ⓜ Shaw–Howard U.

Anxo Cidery
BARS | Take a trip to Spain at Anxo (an-cho) Cidery. Here you can sample a multitude of ciders, a drink tied to the culture of the Basque country, and explore the unusual combinations produced from apples: from bright or fruit-forward to structured or rustic. Try one of the many flights, a dessert ice cider, and even some obscure, rare ciders. The bar also serves beer, wine, and cocktails for those who want something more familiar, and there's a menu of pintxos (small bites) as well. ✉ 711

Kennedy St., Shaw ☎ 202/986–3795 ⊕ www.anxodc.com Ⓜ Shaw–Howard U.

Black Jack
BARS | A red-velvet, almost vaudeville-like interior around the bar offers a saucy experience upstairs from the highly rated Pearl Dive Oyster Palace. In the back, you'll find a bocce court surrounded by stadium-style seats so onlookers can recline, imbibe, and cheer simultaneously. Though the most exquisite cocktail confections can be pricey, there's also an impressive beer lineup and a worthwhile menu ranging from mussels to pizza. There's a happy hour every day; it runs all day on Sunday. ✉ 1612 14th St. NW, Logan Circle ☎ 202/319–1612 ⊕ www. blackjackdc.com ⊘ Closed Sun.–Tues. Ⓜ U St./African American Civil War Memorial/Cardozo.

Busboys and Poets
CAFÉS | Part eatery, part bookstore, and part event space, this popular local hangout draws a diverse crowd and hosts a wide range of entertainment, from poetry open mics to music to guest authors and activist speakers. The name is an homage to Langston Hughes, who worked as a busboy in D.C. before becoming a famous poet. This original location is open until 1 am on Friday and Saturday—there's another Downtown (✉ 1025 5th St. NW), as well as outposts in upper D.C., Maryland, and Virginia. ✉ 2021 14th St. NW, U Street ☎ 202/387–7638 ⊕ www.busboysandpoets.com Ⓜ U St./African American Civil War Memorial/Cardozo.

Calico
GATHERING PLACES | Tucked away in Blagden Alley in the heart of Shaw, this hipster's dream offers kitschy decor made modern and an ethereal garden backyard. Take a boozy adult juice box to the urban backyard, featuring a 3,000-square-foot patio with farmhouse tables, string lights, plants, and a vintage greenhouse. Formerly a boxing gym and art studio, the restaurant offers a

menu with elevated takes on cookout classics like crab cakes, short ribs, and hoagies. ⊠ *50 Blagden Alley NW, Shaw* ☎ *202/791–0134* ✆ *Closed Mon.* Ⓜ *Mt. Vernon Sq. 7th St.–Convention Center.*

Chi-Cha Lounge

COCKTAIL LOUNGES | Groups of young professionals relax on sofas and armchairs in this hip hangout modeled after an Ecuadorian hacienda, while Latin jazz mingles with pop music in the background and old movies run silently behind the bar. The place gets packed on weekends, so come early to get a coveted sofa along the back wall. Pair your cocktails with a Cocina Nikkei (Japanese Peruvian) menu, including ceviche and gyozas (Japanese dumplings). Or try a hookah filled with a range of flavored tobaccos, from apple to watermelon. A dress-to-impress dress code is strictly enforced. ⊠ *1624 U St. NW, U Street* ☎ *202/234–8400* ⊕ *www. chichaloungedc.com* Ⓜ *U St./African American Civil War Memorial/Cardozo.*

ChurchKey

BARS | There's an astounding selection of beers at ChurchKey—555 varieties from more than 30 countries, including 50 beers on tap and exclusive draft and cask ales. If you have trouble making a choice, bartenders will offer you 4-ounce tasters. The urban-vintage vibe balances unassuming and pretentious in pretty much equal measure, reflected in a menu that ranges from tater tots to Caesar salads to rotating flatbread options. ⊠ *1337 14th St. NW, Logan Circle* ☎ *202/567–2576* ⊕ *www.churchkeydc.com* Ⓜ *McPherson Sq.*

★ Cork Wine Bar

WINE BARS | On weekends, the crowds can spill onto 14th Street—but one of the best wine bars in D.C. is worth the wait. An outstanding wine list (mainly French and Italian) is matched with delectable small plates, perfect for sharing. ⊠ *1805 14th St. NW, U Street* ☎ *202/265–2675* ⊕ *www.corkdc.com* ✆ *Closed Mon.* Ⓜ *U St./African American Civil War Memorial/Cardozo.*

Dacha Beer Garden

BEER GARDENS | Set off by a three-story mural of Elizabeth Taylor, Dacha has become the go-to outdoor drinking venue in midtown D.C., with lines of people (and their dogs) waiting to get in most evenings any time of year whenever the weather isn't bitterly cold or inclement. (A windscreen wall and heaters help keep patrons toasty during the winter.) The beer garden serves drafts of craft beers from Germany, Belgium, and the United States as well as Bavarian-inspired nosh, while the adjoining café serves hot coffee and bagels and sandwiches during the day. ⊠ *1600 7th St. NW, Shaw* ☎ *202/350–9888* ⊕ *www.dachadc.com* Ⓜ *Shaw–Howard U.*

El Techo

CAFÉS | Sip margaritas under the palm trees at El Techo, a unique rooftop bar, where the scene is tropical thanks to a canopy of plants and whimsical flowers. The bar also offers an extensive menu of small bites and tacos, as well as heavier dishes such as carne asada and paella for two. A DJ spins upbeat Latin dance music, and there are plenty of seating areas for those who do not feel like dancing. The retractable roof allows for year-round fun. ⊠ *606 Florida Ave. NW, Shaw* ☎ *202/836–4270* ⊕ *www.eltecho-dc.com* Ⓜ *Shaw.*

La Jambe

WINE BARS | Named both for the legs of a wine and a leg of ham, this is the place to fill your metaphorical hollow leg with wine, cheese, and charcuterie. Choose from a variety of reds, whites, and everything in between (even a few French cider styles), or go for a flight of brandy and whisky. All of the cocktails and spirits here are either from France or the District. Happy hour runs from 5 to 7, Tuesday through Friday, and brunch is served from 11 to 3 on weekends. ⊠ *1550 7th St. NW, Shaw*

☎ *202/627–2988* ⊕ *www.lajambedc.com* ⊘ *Closed Mon. and Tues.* Ⓜ *Shaw–Howard U.*

Lulu's Winegarden

WINE BARS | The owner of The Royal and his wife transformed the former Vinoteca into Lulu's Winegarden. The drink menu focuses on wine, offering rare finds and keeping them at under $50 a bottle. Named after the owner's daughter, the bar–restaurant has three lush outdoor dining spaces: the 24-seat, ivy-lined front patio; the charming, plant-filled, 40-seat back courtyard; and the 16-seat, terra-cotta-hued "streatery" outfitted with tropical fauna and lounge seating. The menu offers savory dips like whipped feta and smoked whitefish paired with a bottle of wine from the long list. ☒ *1940 11th St. NW, U Street* ☎ *202/332–9463* ⊕ *www. vinotecadc.com* ⊘ *Closed Mon.* Ⓜ *U St./ African American Civil War Memorial/ Cardozo.*

Maxwell Park

WINE BARS | At Maxwell Park, dinner and dessert are both a glass of wine. The themed menu, which changes monthly, offers more than 50 wines by the glass. Try a sweet wine or aperitif for dessert, or mix things up with a cocktail, perhaps a seasonal gin and homemade tonic. If you don't know what you want, ask one of the trained sommeliers about the 500 labels on the bottle list, or have a 2.5-ounce tasting glass (just watch the prices because there are some rare wines here). Enjoy the outdoor patio, which is heated in winter, or cozy into the bar, open nightly at 5. ☒ *1336 9th St. NW, Shaw* ☎ *202/792–9522* ⊕ *maxwelldcwine.com* Ⓜ *Mt. Vernon Sq. 7th St.–Convention Center.*

★ Morris American Bar

BARS | Founded by *Top Chef* alum Spike Mendelsohn and D.C. nightlife entrepreneur Vinoda Basnayake, this Shaw bar serves spectacular cocktails. You'll feel like you're simultaneously at a 1950s-era diner, sitting on a backyard patio, and in a Wes Anderson film. The happy-hour menu features slightly cheaper cocktail options, wine, and beer, while the full menu offers cleverly crafted cocktails. Both menus change monthly, so make sure you return to see what's new, and if you're unsure of what to order, just ask a bartender. The bar menu includes cheese and charcuterie boards, dips, and salads. ☒ *1020 7th St. NW, Shaw* ☎ *833/366–7747* ⊕ *morrisbardc.com* ⊘ *Closed Mon.* Ⓜ *Mt. Vernon Sq. 7th St.–Convention Center.*

Nellie's Sports Bar

BARS | This popular sports bar with a gay following makes everyone feel welcome. Catch the games on multiple screens, or try your luck with "drag bingo" or trivia games. Spaces in this eclectic two-story venue range from roof deck to cozy pub room to a dining area serving all-American pub grub–meets–Venezuelan specialties, from empanadas to arepas. Every weekend brings a reservations-required brunch buffet with drag queens as servers. ☒ *900 U St. NW, U Street* ☎ *202/332–6355* ⊕ *www.nelliessportsbar.com* Ⓜ *U St./African American Civil War Memorial/Cardozo.*

Number Nine

BARS | The heart of Logan Circle nightlife is this predominantly male gay bar attracting guests of all ages. The downstairs lounge offers plush banquettes and street views, while big-screen viewing is offered upstairs at the 9½ video bar. The daily happy hour (5–9 pm) offers two-for-one drinks. At any time this is a great place for a cocktail and some good conversation in a bustling neighborhood that includes, a block away on 14th Street, Trade, which is another popular, no-frills gay bar from the same owners as Number Nine. ☒ *1435 P St. NW, Logan Circle* ☎ *202/986–0999* ⊕ *www.numberninedc.com* Ⓜ *Dupont Circle.*

The Passenger

BARS | If you're looking for Chartreuse on tap, a handwritten crafted cocktail list, and a laid-back vibe, this is the place for you. It has the feeling of a local dive bar but with the cocktail menu and bar bites of a funky D.C. bar. Be dazzled by the seemingly hundreds of bottles lining the bar, and enjoy the occasional band upstairs on weekends. ⊠ *1539 7th St. NW, Shaw* ☎ *202/853–3588* ⊕ *www. passengerdc.com* ⊗ *Closed Mon.* Ⓜ *Mt. Vernon Sq. 7th St.–Convention Center.*

The Saloon

BARS | This classic watering hole has no TVs, no light beer, and no martinis. What it does have are locals engaged in conversation—a stated goal of the owner—and some of the world's best beers, including the rare Urbock 23, an Austrian brew that is rated one of the tastiest and strongest in the world, with 9.6% alcohol content (limit one per customer). The Saloon also offers a broader bar menu, too. ⊠ *1205 U St. NW, U Street* ☎ *202/462–2640* ⊗ *Closed Sun. and Mon.* Ⓜ *U St./African American Civil War Memorial/Cardozo.*

Service Bar

BARS | At one of the city's most creative cocktail bars, the space is cozy, the vibe is casual, and the crowd is artsy. Interestingly named cocktails include the Griselda Blanco, which is served in a tiki glass and made with tequila, mezcal, coconut, lime, grapefruit, and cardamom bitters. Bring your appetite as the bar also serves food, including a popular fried-chicken sandwich—or skip the bun, and order a full fried-chicken dinner. ⊠ *926–928 U St. NW, U Street* ☎ *202/462–7232* ⊕ *www. servicebardc.com* ⊗ *Closed Mon.*

DANCE CLUBS
★ Flash

DANCE CLUBS | The decline of megaclubs in D.C. has coincided with a rise in more intimate and inviting venues for those serious about dancing. This photography-themed jewel near the Howard Theatre replaced a pawnshop—a telling sign of this changing neighborhood. An operational photo booth is an entry point

to the main upstairs dance floor, which envelops you in walls lined with 10,000 LED lights and a best-in-the-business Funktion One sound system. Pioneering underground DJs—Carl Craig, Chus & Ceballos—move their flocks of a couple hundred fans while intermittently flashing them from the rigged 24 parabolic reflectors behind them. ⊠ *645 Florida Ave. NW, Washington* ☎ *202/827–8791* ⊕ *www.flashdc.com* ⊗ *Closed Mon. and Tues.* Ⓜ *Shaw–Howard U.*

JAZZ AND BLUES
New Vegas Lounge

LIVE MUSIC | The New Vegas Lounge may be a vestige from a grittier, less affluent era, but the Logan Circle club is in its nearly fifth decade of offering live blues every weekend. Vegas Lounge is run by the wife and sons of its late founder, known as Dr. Blues. Friday- and Saturday-night performances by the house ensemble, the Out of Town Blues Band, attract an eclectic crowd, from veteran blues fans to newer residents who don't know from Muddy Waters—drawn to the club out of sheer curiosity, or because it's a refreshing cultural and historical diversion in the neighborhood. ⊠ *1415 P St. NW, Logan Circle* ☎ *202/483–3971* ⊕ *www.newvegasloungedc.com* ⊗ *Closed Sun.–Thurs.* Ⓜ *Dupont Circle.*

ROCK AND POP
★ Black Cat

LIVE MUSIC | Way before its stretch of 14th Street became the trendiest few blocks in town, the Black Cat was a destination for alternative music and quirky nostalgic dance parties. The venue is a host for midsize rock concerts and smaller, local acts focused on indie, alternative, and underground music, with favorites such as the Dandy Warhols, the Ravonettes, and Ex Hex. The Black Cat also regularly hosts artistic events, including comedy, edgy burlesque, and independent film nights. The postpunk crowd whiles away the time in the ground floor's Red Room, a side bar with pool tables, an eclectic jukebox, and no cover charge. The club is also home to Food for Thought, a legendary vegetarian café. ✉ *1811 14th St. NW, U Street* ☎ *202/667–4490* ⊕ *www. blackcatdc.com* Ⓜ *U St./African American Civil War Memorial/Cardozo.*

DC9

LIVE MUSIC | With live music most days of the week, this small two-story rock club with an upper deck hosts fledgling indie bands and the occasional nationally known act. There's a narrow bar on the ground floor, a sizable concert space on the second floor, and an enclosed roof deck on top. DJs take the controls for weekend-night dance parties. Concertgoers can enjoy snacks, sandwiches, and burgers every night and until 1 am on weekends. ✉ *1940 9th St. NW, U Street* ☎ *202/483–5000* ⊕ *www.dcnine.com* ◷ *Closed Mon. and Tues.* Ⓜ *U St./African American Civil War Memorial/Cardozo.*

★ 9:30 Club

LIVE MUSIC | The inimitable 9:30 Club is consistently ranked as one of the best concert venues in the country—as much a place in which bands aspire to play as it is a place that music fans love to patronize. The best indie and up-and-coming performers are the main attractions, though every now and then a bigger act such as Adele, Drake, Ed Sheeran, or Leon Bridges stop by to soak up the vibe of this large but cozy space wrapped by balconies on three sides. Once graced by legends such as Nirvana, Bob Dylan, and Johnny Cash, the venue is now a great spot for big labels looking for an intimate vibe. For its various music genres, from country to pop, this venue has become one of the most attended clubs of its size.

■ TIP➜ **There are no bad views here, and the excellent sound system means you can stand anywhere for a great show experience.** ✉ *815 V St. NW, U Street* ☎ *202/265–0930* ⊕ *www.930.com* Ⓜ *U St./African American Civil War Memorial/ Cardozo.*

🎭 Performing Arts

With unique plays and intimate venues, the U Street corridor, Shaw, and Logan Circle have plenty of cultural experiences to choose from.

In the 1930s and 1940s, U Street was known for its classy theaters and jazz clubs. Throughout its history, U Street, known as the "Black Broadway," has witnessed iconic musicians such as Duke Ellington and Ella Fitzgerald perform in historic venues like the Howard Theatre. After decades of decline following the 1968 riots, the neighborhood has been revitalized, gentrifying at lightning speed while retaining a diverse mix of multi-ethnic young professionals and older, working-class African Americans. U Street resident and Associate Justice of the Supreme Court Sonia Sotomayor has said, "U Street is the East Village." At night, the neighborhood's club, bar, and restaurant scene comes alive. During the day the street scene is more laid-back, with more locals than tourists occupying the distinctive shops.

MAJOR VENUES
★ The Howard Theatre

MUSIC | Opened in 1910, the Howard Theatre continues to be a draw in Washington, D.C. Initially a venue to highlight African American artists, the Howard Theatre now hosts diverse performances, from '80s hard rock by Sebastian Bach of Skid Row to old-school hip-hop by Slick Rick to Puerto Rican reggae by Cultura Profética. Listed on the National Register of Historic Places in 1974, it has also hosted many American musical icons, from Duke Ellington to Ella Fitzgerald, in its intimate space. The theater closed in 1970 and reopened in 2012 after an extensive remodel. ✉ *620 T St. NW, U Street* ☎ *202/803–2899* ⊕ *thehowardtheatre.com* Ⓜ *Shaw–Howard U.*

Lincoln Theatre

MUSIC | The Lincoln Theatre is a historical venue from 1922, back when Washington natives Duke Ellington and Pearl Baily were joined by the likes of Ella Fitzgerald, Billie Holiday, Nat King Cole, and Louis Armstrong. Today, the 1,200-seat theater presents modern musical artists, including Kendrick Lamar, Hozier, and Billy Idol, as well as comedic performers like Demetri Martin, Tig Notaro, and Ilana Glazer. ⌧ *1215 U St. NW, U Street* ☎ *202/328–6000* ⊕ *www.thelincolndc. com* Ⓜ *U St./African American Civil War Memorial/Cardozo.*

THEATER
The In Series
MUSIC | Cabaret, experimental chamber opera, and Spanish musical theater (also known as zarzuela) are among the hallmarks of this company founded in 1982. Performances are held at Source, GALA Hispanic Theater, and the Atlas Performing Arts Center. ⌧ *1835 14th St. NW, U Street* ☎ *202/204–7763* ⊕ *www.inseries. org* ⊗ *Closed weekends.*

★ Studio Theatre
THEATER | This multifaceted theater company, one of the city's busiest, produces an eclectic season of contemporary European and offbeat American plays in four spaces: the original Mead and Milton theaters, the newer 200-seat Metheny Theatre, and the experimental Stage 4. ⌧ *1501 14th St. NW, Dupont Circle* ☎ *202/332–3300* ⊕ *www.studiotheatre. org* Ⓜ *Dupont Circle.*

Washington Stage Guild
THEATER | This company performs neglected classics as well as contemporary literary plays in the Undercroft Theatre of Mount Vernon Place United Methodist Church. In recent years, they have produced lesser-known works by Oscar Wilde and George Bernard Shaw. Contemporary plays such as *Tryst* by Karoline Leach and David Marshall Grant's *Pen* are also offered. ⌧ *900 Massachusetts Ave. NW, Logan Circle* ☎ *240/582–0050* ⊕ *www.stageguild.org* Ⓜ *Dupont Circle.*

🛍 Shopping

ANTIQUES AND COLLECTIBLES
★ GoodWood
ANTIQUES & COLLECTIBLES | It's described by its owners as an American mercantile and dry goods store, but when you open the door, you'll feel as if you've been invited into a friend's warm and inviting loft. Displays throughout the store beautifully showcase 19th-century antique furniture. You'll also discover leather goods; vintage mirrors and other decorative home items; men's and women's grooming products and perfumes from around the world; Peruvian alpaca and wool scarves; Swedish clogs; and comfortable dresses, sweaters, and tops from American and international designers. ⌧ *1428 U St. NW, U Street* ☎ *202/986–3640* ⊕ *www. goodwooddc.com* Ⓜ *U St./African American Civil War Memorial/Cardozo.*

CLOTHING
Bonobos
MEN'S CLOTHING | This signature men's shop achieved its fame with comfortable, stylish pants. Shopping and shipping are made easy here: simply go into the guide shop, find your style and fit, and then have your finds shipped directly to you. You can make a one-hour appointment (with a complimentary beer), walk out without bags, and enjoy free shipping and returns. ⌧ *1924 8th St. NW, No. 123, Shaw* ☎ *202/868–1210* ⊕ *bonobos.com/ guideshop* Ⓜ *Shaw–Howard U.*

Current Boutique
MIXED CLOTHING | Don't be fooled by the new dresses in the front—this shop is a consignment shopper's dream. "Current" styles from brands such as Tory Burch, BCBG, Marc Jacobs, and Diane Von Furstenberg just might fit better when you buy them at a third of their original price. ⌧ *1809 14th St. NW, U Street* ☎ *202/588–7311* ⊕ *www.currentbou-tique.com* Ⓜ *U St./African American Civil War Memorial/Cardozo.*

Marine Layer

MIXED CLOTHING | This San Francisco–based retailer is known for its soft, eco-friendly, and durable T-shirts. The company's signature fabric, MicroModal, is made from beechwood pulp and woven into the product line for men and women. In addition to T-shirts, you'll find equally comfortable dresses, pants, outerwear, loungewear, sweaters, and hats. ✉ *1627 14th St. NW, Logan Circle* ☎ *202/864–6686* 🌐 *www.marinelayer.com* Ⓜ *U St./African American Civil War Memorial/Cardozo.*

GIFTS

Cherry Blossom Creativei

STATIONERY | Although you can find modern, upscale stationery brands and office products here, what you should come for are the company's unique neighborhood maps, which are as colorful and creative as they are decorative and beautiful—certainly suitable for framing. In addition to maps of trendy District neighborhoods, look for those of New York, San Francisco, Chicago, and Baltimore. ✉ *2128 8th St. NW, Shaw* ☎ *202/319–2979* 🌐 *www.cherryblossomworkshop.com* ⏲ *Closed Sun.–Fri.* Ⓜ *Shaw–Howard U.*

★ Grand Cata

WINE/SPIRITS | Best friends Julio Robledo and Pedro Rodriguez teamed up to open this wine and spirits store focusing on small Latin American producers. You can find a rare Uruguayan Tannat or a fine Mexican sparkling wine. Not a wine drinker? Grand Cata also offers a wide selection of spirits, mostly from small-batch producers in Mexico and Spain, as well as craft beers. Don't forget the snacks: the selection here includes those from Rodriguez's native Puerto Rico. Wine- and food-centered books, cocktail bar accessories, and other musings make unique gifts. Check the shop's calendar for details on free wine tastings. ✉ *1550 7th St. NW, Shaw* ☎ *202/525–5702* 🌐 *www.grandcata.com.*

Lee's Flower and Card Shop

FLORIST | Sisters Stacie and Kristie Lee own the beloved U Street flower and card shop initially opened by their paternal grandparents in 1945. Aside from preparing flower arrangements for the District's many social events, they also provide cards and small potted plants, making it an ideal spot to grab a green gift for a local friend. ✉ *1026 U St. NW, U Street* ☎ *202/265–4965* 🌐 *www.leesflowerandcard.com.*

Shinola

OTHER SPECIALTY STORE | Once a Studebaker showroom in the 1920s, this gorgeous shop is now one of Michigan-based Shinola's nationwide flagship stores. You'll find leather-band watches; supple leather bags, coats, and journals; elegant and classic silver, gold, and rose-gold jewelry designed by Pamela Love; home accessories; and yes, even bicycles. ✉ *1631 14th St. NW, U Street* ☎ *202/470–0200* 🌐 *www.shinola.com* Ⓜ *U St./African American Civil War Memorial/Cardozo.*

HOME FURNISHINGS

★ Miss Pixie's

FURNITURE | The well-chosen collectibles—handpicked by Miss Pixie herself—include gorgeous textiles, antique home furnishings, lamps, mirrors, glass- and silverware, and artwork. The reasonable prices will grab your attention, as will the location, in an old car-dealer showroom. ✉ *1626 14th St. NW, U Street* ☎ *202/232–8171* 🌐 *www.misspixies.com* Ⓜ *U St./African American Civil War Memorial/Cardozo or Dupont Circle.*

Zawadi

SOUVENIRS | The name means "gifts" in Swahili, but you may want to buy the beautiful African art, textiles, home accessories, and jewelry for yourself. ✉ *1524 U St. NW, Suite 1, U Street* ☎ *202/232–2214* 🌐 *www.zawadiarts.com* ⏲ *Closed Mon.–Wed.* Ⓜ *U St./African American Civil War Memorial/Cardozo.*

Chapter 11

UPPER
NORTHWEST

Updated by
Barbara Noe Kennedy

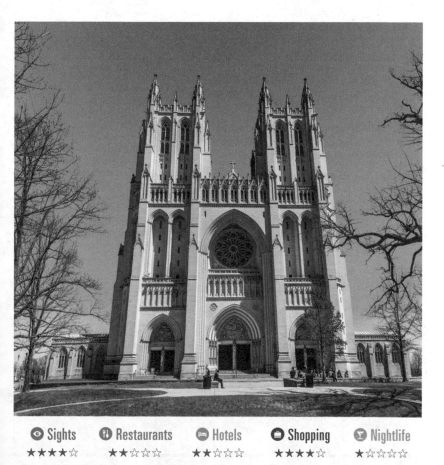

👁 **Sights**
★★★★☆

🍴 **Restaurants**
★★☆☆☆

🛏 **Hotels**
★★☆☆☆

🛍 **Shopping**
★★★★☆

🍸 **Nightlife**
★☆☆☆☆

NEIGHBORHOOD SNAPSHOT

TOP EXPERIENCES

House Museums: The Hillwood Estate, Museum & Gardens showcase cereal heiress Marjorie Merriweather Post's collection of Imperial Russian art and Fabergé eggs, as well as 25 gorgeous acres of formal French and Japanese gardens. Chagalls, Picassos, and Monets inside contrast with the architecture at the modernist Kreeger Museum.

Smithsonian's National Zoo: Visit the lions, elephants, and other members of the animal kingdom (including the giant pandas until they depart for China in December 2023) while you enjoy a stroll outdoors.

Shopping in Friendship Heights: Once the closest thing D.C. had to Rodeo Drive, this area is still a great shopping destination but isn't as high-end anymore; sure, there are still loads of big names, including Tiffany and Saks Fifth Avenue, but now those upscale retailers are sharing equal billing with T.J. Maxx and H&M.

U.S. Naval Observatory: View the heavens through one of the world's most powerful telescopes (on some Monday evenings with a reservation).

Washington National Cathedral: Look for the Darth Vader gargoyle on the soaring towers of this landmark, then relax among the rosebushes in the Bishop's Garden. Concerts are held here, too.

GETTING HERE

Connecticut Avenue attractions, such as the zoo, are accessible from the Red Line Metro stops between Woodley Park–Zoo/Adams Morgan and Van Ness–UDC. The Friendship Heights bus travels north from Georgetown along Wisconsin Avenue and takes you to the National Cathedral.

Parking can be tricky along Massachusetts Avenue. It is more practical for good walkers to hoof it up the street or take Bus N2, N3, N4, or N6 between Dupont Circle and Friendship Heights. For more-outlying sights, driving or cabbing it may be the best way to visit.

PLANNING YOUR TIME

The area has plenty of restaurants and some sights but limited nightlife compared to other parts of the city. You may want to plan your zoo trip around daily programs, such as the small-mammal feeding. Animals are most active in the early morning and late afternoon. Sights can be far apart, so leave time for travel and parking, if necessary.

NEIGHBORHOOD FACTS

On the border of D.C. and Maryland, the Upper Northwest is tree-filled residential neighborhood. Luxury shopping and stunning historical architecture dominate this area. Though in the area's early days, commercial business was not allowed in order to create a space where home and work were separate at a time when work was close by, if not within the same building of a person's residence.

The Upper Northwest corner of D.C. is predominantly residential and in many places practically suburban. There are several good reasons, however, to visit the leafy streets, including the National Zoo and National Cathedral.

If the weather is fine, spend an afternoon strolling through Hillwood Gardens or tromping through Rock Creek Park's many acres. You'll have to travel some distance to see multiple attractions in one day, but many sights are accessible on foot from local Metro stops.

⊙ Sights

Fort Reno Park
CITY PARK | At 429 feet above sea level, the highest point in Washington has been used in different eras as a Civil War fort, the site of telegraph and radio towers, and a reservoir. In 1864, outnumbered Union troops defended the capital from a formidable Confederate advance led by General Early, in the only battle to take place in the capital. Today, the park is enjoyed by soccer players, dog-park regulars, and picnickers. Most of the Civil War–era earthworks are gone, and two curious faux-medieval towers, built in 1929, mark the reservoir site, which is not accessible to the public. Nonetheless, the park has an appealing city view and plenty of room to run around. A popular, free outdoor concert series takes place every summer featuring many of the area's most esteemed indie-rock acts, from The Owners to Sleep-Marks to My Sonic Daydream. ⊠ *4800 Chesapeake St., NW, Upper Northwest* ☎ *202/895–6070 visitor information* ⊕ *www.fortreno.com* Ⓜ *Tenleytown–AU.*

Glover Archbold Park
NATURE SIGHT | Groves of beeches, tulip trees, and oaks flourish at this 183-acre park, part of the Rock Creek system, which begins just west of Georgetown and ends, nearly 2½ miles later, near Van Ness Street. Along the way, you'll experience a tree-shaded valley stream and possible bird sightings. And chances are, you'll have the trail mostly to yourself. ⊠ *Wisconsin Ave. at Van Ness St. NW, Upper Northwest* ⊕ *www. nps.gov/places/glover-archbold-park.htm* Ⓜ *Tenleytown–AU.*

Hillwood Estate, Museum, and Gardens
HISTORIC HOME | Cereal heiress Marjorie Merriweather Post was a celebrated philanthropist, businessperson, and socialite, who was also known for her passion for collecting art and creating some of the most beautiful homes of the 20th century. Of these, the 25-acre Hillwood Estate, which Post bought in 1955, is the only one now open to the public. The 36-room Georgian mansion, where she regularly hosted presidents, diplomats, and royalty, is sumptuously appointed, with a formal Louis XVI drawing room, private movie theater and ballroom, and magnificent libraries filled with portraits of the glamorous hostess and her family and acquaintances, as well as works from her rich art collection. She was especially fascinated with Russian art, and her collection of Russian icons, tapestries, gold and silver work, imperial

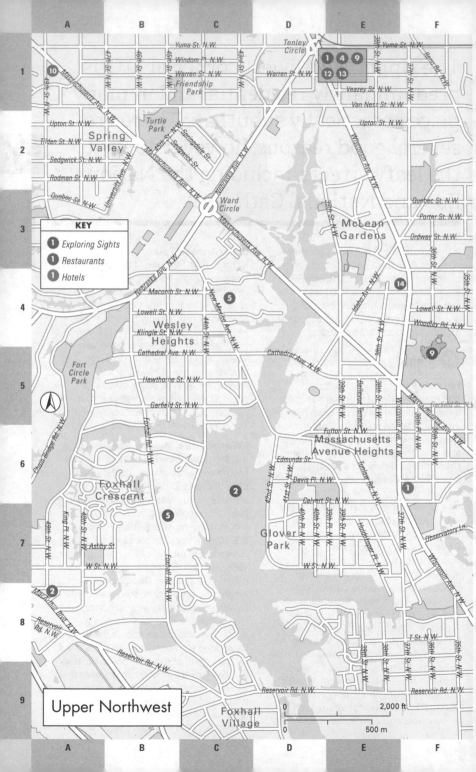

Upper Northwest

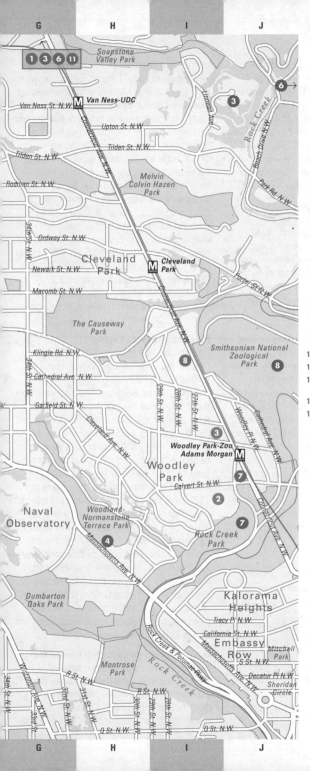

Sights ▼

1 Fort Reno Park **E1**
2 Glover Archbold Park **C6**
3 Hillwood Estate, Museum, and Gardens......................... **J1**
4 Kahlil Gibran Memorial Garden............................... **H7**
5 The Kreeger Museum............ **B7**
6 President Lincoln's Cottage **J1**
7 Rock Creek Park **J7**
8 Smithsonian's National Zoo **J5**
9 Washington National Cathedral **F5**

Restaurants ▼

1 The Avenue......................... **G1**
2 BlackSalt Fish Market & Restaurant **A8**
3 Bread Furst......................... **G1**
4 Cafe of India....................... **E1**
5 Chef Geoff **C4**
6 Comet Ping Pong **G1**
7 District Kitchen **J6**
8 Duke's Counter..................... **I5**
9 Le Chat Noir **E1**
10 Millie's............................... **A1**
11 Parthenon Restaurant............ **G1**
12 Pete's New Haven Style Apizza **E1**
13 Sushiko Chevy Chase **E1**
14 2 Amys **F4**

Hotels ▼

1 Glover Park Hotel Georgetown ... **F6**
2 Omni Shoreham Hotel.............. **I6**
3 Woodley Park Guest House **I6**

porcelain, and Fabergé eggs is considered to be the largest and most significant outside Russia. She devoted equal attention to her gardens; you can wander through 13 acres of them. Allow two to three hours to tour. ⊠ *4155 Linnean Ave. NW, Upper Northwest* ☎ *202/686–5807, 202/686–8500* ⊕ *www.hillwoodmuseum. org* ⊠ *$18 ($15 weekdays if purchased online)* ⊘ *Closed Mon.* Ⓜ *Van Ness–UDC.*

Kahlil Gibran Memorial Garden

CITY PARK | In a town known for political combat, this tiny urban park is a wonderful place to find some peace. The shady park combines Western and Arab symbols and is perfect for contemplation. From the Massachusetts Avenue entrance, a stone walk bridges a flower-bedecked swale. Farther on are limestone benches engraved with sayings from Gibran. They curve around a star-shaped fountain and a bronze bust of the namesake Lebanese-born poet, who emigrated to the United States at the turn of the 20th century and remains one of the best-selling poets of all time. His best-known work, *The Prophet*, has sold more than 11 million copies and has been translated into more than 100 languages. The garden is near the grounds of the United States Naval Observatory and across from the British Embassy. ⊠ *3100 block of Massachusetts Ave. NW, Upper Northwest* ☎ *202/895–6000* ⊠ *Free* Ⓜ *Woodley Park–Zoo/Adams Morgan or Dupont Circle.*

The Kreeger Museum

OTHER MUSEUM | The cool white domes and elegant lines of this postmodern landmark stand in stark contrast to the traditional feel of the rest of the Foxhall Road neighborhood. Designed in 1963 by iconic architects Philip Johnson and Richard Foster, the building was once the home of GEICO executive David Lloyd Kreeger and his wife, Carmen. Music is a central theme of the art and the space: the Kreegers wanted a light-filled residence that would also function as a gallery and recital hall. The art collection includes works by Degas, Cézanne, Monet, Picasso, and Munch; and outstanding examples of African and Asian art. Especially stunning are the outdoor sculptures by Henry Moore, Isamu Noguchi, and others, including John L. Dreyfuss—six of his large-scale pieces surround the museum's reflecting pool. The domed rooms also have wonderful acoustics, and serve as an excellent venue for the classical concerts that are regularly performed here. The museum is not reachable by Metro; you need to take a car or taxi to get here. ⊠ *2401 Foxhall Rd. NW, Upper Northwest* ☎ *202/337–3050* ⊕ *www.kreegermuseum.org* ⊠ *$10; Sculpture Garden free* ⊘ *Closed Sun. and Mon.* ♿ *All visitors require a time-entry pass, available on the website.*

President Lincoln's Cottage

HISTORIC HOME | In June 1862, President Lincoln moved from the White House to this Gothic Revival cottage on the grounds of the Soldiers' Home to escape the oppressive heat of Washington and to grieve for the loss of his son Willie. Lincoln and his wife, Mary, lived in the cottage until November of that year, and because they found it to be a welcome respite from wartime tensions, they returned again during the summers of 1863 and 1864. Lincoln ultimately spent a quarter of his presidency at this quiet retreat; he was here just one day before he was assassinated. One of the most significant historic sites of Lincoln's presidency, it was here that he developed his ideas for what would become the Emancipation Proclamation. Visitors may picnic on the cottage grounds, which have been landscaped to look as they did when Lincoln lived here.

■TIP→ As you go up the hill toward the Cottage, there's a panoramic view of the city, including the Capitol dome. The 251-acre Soldiers' Home sits atop the third-tallest point in D.C. ⊠ *140 Rock Creek Church Rd., at Upshur St. NW, Petworth*

☎ *202/829–0436* ⊕ *www.lincolncottage. org* ✉ *$15* Ⓜ *Georgia Ave.–Petworth.*

★ Rock Creek Park

CITY PARK | **FAMILY** | The 1,754 acres surrounding Rock Creek have provided a cool oasis for visitors and D.C. residents ever since Congress set them aside for recreational use in 1890. The bubbling, rocky stream draws nature lovers to the miles of paved walkways. Bicycle routes, jogging and hiking paths, and equestrian trails wind through the groves of dogwoods, beeches, oaks, and cedars, and picnic areas are scattered about. An asphalt bike path running through the park has a few challenging hills but is mostly flat, and it's possible to bike several miles without having to stop for cars (Beach Drive is closed entirely to cars on weekends). The most popular run in Rock Creek Park is along a trail that follows the creek from Georgetown to the National Zoo, about 4 miles round-trip. Rangers at the Nature Center and Planetarium introduce visitors to the park and keep track of daily events; guided nature walks leave from the center. The park is open only during daylight hours. ✉ *5200 Glover Rd. NW, Nature Center and Planetarium, Upper Northwest* ☎ *202/895–6070* ⊕ *www.nps.gov/rocr* Ⓜ *Friendship Heights, transfer to E4 bus to Glover Rd.*

★ Smithsonian's National Zoo

ZOO | **FAMILY** | The Smithsonian's National Zoo and Conservation Biology Institute features 1,800 animals representing 360 species, as close as you can get to their native surroundings. Arrive between 11 and 2 (weather permitting), and you can catch orangutans traversing the "O" line, a series of cables and towers near the Great Ape House that allow the primates to swing hand over hand about 50 feet above your head. The famous pandas are leaving at the end of 2023, but there are plenty of other animals that beguile. The multigenerational herd of elephants—part of the zoo's conservation campaign to save this endangered species from extinction—is a perennial favorite. Along the Claws and Paws Pathway, the binturongs (also known as bearcats) smell like buttered popcorn, and petite Pallas's cats hide in plain sight. The zoo was designed by famed landscape architect Frederick Law Olmsted, who also designed New York's Central Park. Try visiting early morning or late afternoon, since many animals sleep midday. Nighttime visits are especially fun during the Christmas holiday as the zoo sparkles with the annual ZooLights event. ✉ *3001 Connecticut Ave. NW, Upper Northwest* ☎ *202/633–2614* ⊕ *nationalzoo. si.edu* ✉ *Free* ☞ *Entry passes must be reserved on the website. Visitors who wish to drive to the zoo must obtain a paid parking pass, also available at the website.* Ⓜ *Cleveland Park or Woodley Park–Zoo/Adams Morgan.*

★ Washington National Cathedral

RELIGIOUS BUILDING | Construction of the world's sixth-largest cathedral began in 1907 with a rock from the village of Bethlehem and the structure has been the spiritual symbol of Washington ever since. It was finally completed in 1990. Like its 14th-century English Gothic counterparts, it has a nave, flying buttresses, transepts, and vaults, all built stone by stone. The stunning cathedral is Episcopalian, but it's the site of frequent interfaith services. State funerals for presidents Eisenhower, Reagan, Ford, and George H. W. Bush, as well as Senator John McCain, were held here, and the tomb of Woodrow Wilson—the only president buried in Washington, D.C.—is in the south nave. The Pilgrim Observation Gallery provides a wonderful view of the city, and the cathedral is blessed with the lovely Bishop's Garden, designed by Frederick Law Olmsted Jr., with fruit trees, towering oaks and yews, and roses interspersed with stonework from European ruins. A variety of tours is offered, including the popular "Gargoyle" tours. The cathedral is acclaimed for its *year-round concerts, national holiday commemorations, and other musical performances.* ✉ *3101 Wisconsin Ave., NW, Upper Northwest* ☎ *202/537–6200, 202/537–2228 box office* 🌐 *www.nationalcathedral.org* 🎟 *From $15* 🕒 *Grounds open dawn–dusk* ☞ *Admission is free for worship services; sightseeing requires a ticket* [M] *Cleveland Park or Tenleytown–AU, then take any 30 series bus.*

🍴 Restaurants

After the requisite cooing over the wallabies and other cuddly creatures at the National Zoo, consider wandering around this popular neighborhood, where you'll see plenty of locals eating, drinking, and playing. Many Hill staffers, journalists, and other inside-the-Beltway types live along this hilly stretch of Connecticut Avenue. Eateries and shops line the few blocks near each of the Red Line Metro stops. Eateries in Cleveland Park range from tiny takeout spots to upscale restaurants where you stand a good chance of spying your favorite Sunday-morning talk-show guests at a nearby table. International cuisines are abundant here, especially in Cleveland Park. Lined up along the stately stretch of modern row houses are diverse dining options ranging from Afghan to Ethiopian to Thai.

The Avenue

$$ | **AMERICAN** | **FAMILY** | This inviting, all-American bar and restaurant is right near the D.C./Maryland border; brick and wood make the space feel cozy and warm. Seafood, sandwiches, and hefty salads highlight the menu. **Known for:** large outdoor patio; food truck with crab delicacies; multilevel establishment. [$] *Average main: $21* ✉ *5540 Connecticut Ave., Northwest* ✥ *A 0.7-mile hike from Metro; if driving, street parking is usually available* ☎ *202/244–4567* 🌐 *www.theavenuedc.com* [M] *Friendship Heights.*

BlackSalt Fish Market & Restaurant

$$$$ | **SEAFOOD** | Just beyond Georgetown in the residential neighborhood of Palisades, BlackSalt is part fish market, part gossipy neighborhood hangout, part swanky restaurant. Fish offerings dominate, and vary from classics like New England clam chowder and fried Ipswich clams to more-offbeat fixings like Japanese-style seafood stew and chocolate peanut butter torte for dessert. **Known for:** fresh fish dishes; one of the best brunches in D.C.; brioche French toast. [$] *Average main: $45* ✉ *4883 MacArthur Blvd., Upper Northwest* ☎ *202/342–9101* 🌐 *www.blacksaltrestaurant.com.*

Bread Furst

$ | **BAKERY** | Owner-baker Mark Furstenberg has been honored with the James Beard Award for Outstanding Baker, so you know the bread here is amazing. But there are also delicious breakfast, brunch, and lunch menus that, while simple, rely on local farmers for fresh, seasonal ingredients. **Known for:** neighborhoodly ambience; bread, of course: from country levain to French baguettes to ryes to rich brioche, all baked fresh; pies made with Virginia peaches and Maryland apples. [$] *Average main: $15* ✉ *4434 Connecticut Ave., NW, Cleveland Park* ☎ *202/765–1200* 🌐 *breadfurst.com* ☞ *Parking is available in the rear* [M] *Van Ness–UDC.*

Cafe of India

$$ | **INDIAN** | **FAMILY** | The menu at this traditional Indian restaurant features a few surprises, including an inventive shrimp and coconut masala, a local favorite. The dining room has an elegant feel, with long drapes, white tablecloths, and fine crystal. **Known for:** crackling spinach, shrimp, and coconut masala; extensive Indian beer and wine list; authentic Indian cuisine. [$] *Average main: $18* ✉ *4909 Wisconsin Ave., Tenleytown* ☎ *202/244–1395* 🌐 *www.cafeofindiadc.com* [M] *Tenleytown.*

Chef Geoff

$$ | **AMERICAN** | A D.C. staple for 20-plus years, Chef Geoff's is family- and neighborhood-friendly—the type of place to come in as you are, weary feet and all. The contemporary American, chef-driven menu has something for everyone: pizzas, salads, elaborate main dishes, and an extensive bar menu. **Known for:** buzzy happy hours; a go-to for every craving; family friendly. $ *Average main: $20* ✉ *3201 New Mexico Ave. NW, Upper Northwest* ☎ *202/237–7800* ⊕ *www. chefgeoff.com* Ⓜ *Tenleytown–AU.*

Comet Ping Pong

$ | **PIZZA** | **FAMILY** | Pizza (and beer) in the front, Ping-Pong (and foosball) in the back make this pizza joint a neighborhood favorite for folks of all ages. While you can make your own pizza (including one with a gluten-free crust) from almost four dozen toppings, you'll be well served to opt for one of the kitchen's specialty pies. **Known for:** make-your-own pizzas with dozens of toppings; live music; sunrise pizza for brunch. $ *Average main: $16* ✉ *5037 Connecticut Ave. NW, Upper Northwest* ☎ *202/364–0404* ⊕ *www. cometpingpong.com* ☾ *No lunch Mon.– Fri.* Ⓜ *Cleveland Park.*

District Kitchen

$$ | **AMERICAN** | **FAMILY** | The exposed brick and warm woods may signal upscale saloon, but District Kitchen is much more, offering an eclectic, farm-to-table menu featuring the restaurant's signature dish, a large and tasty bowl of paella. Sure, there are burgers, steaks, and the like, but also ceviche, cheese plates, lamb ragù, and at least one or two tempting fish options. **Known for:** monster signature paella dish; good seafood; nice beer selection. $ *Average main: $22* ✉ *2606 Connecticut Ave. NW, Woodley Park* ☎ *202/238–9408* ⊕ *www. districtkitchen.com* ☾ *Closed Mon. No dinner Sun. No lunch except brunch on weekends* Ⓜ *Woodley Park–Adams Morgan/Zoo.*

Duke's Counter

$ | **BRITISH** | **FAMILY** | A shabby-chic bar–restaurant directly across the street from the National Zoo has been deemed by one local paper to have the best burger in D.C. If it's not the best, it's close: a big, tasty patty made from charbroiled Angus beef that's on a pub menu with other continental options, including mum's tuna melt and pastrami on weck—check the chalkboard for the latest seasonal fare. **Known for:** excellent burgers; wide-ranging menu of sandwiches and small plates; small and busy (so get there early or wait). $ *Average main: $15* ✉ *3000 Connecticut Ave., Northwest* ☎ *202/733–4808* ⊕ *www.dukescounter.com* Ⓜ *Woodley Park–Zoo/Adams Morgan.*

★ Le Chat Noir

$$$ | **FRENCH** | This unpretentious but intimate and stylish bistro recalls a Parisian café, with dark woods, white tablecloths, and cozy tables—not to mention the owner himself is from Paris. The main floor has two dining rooms, one of which has floor-to-ceiling windows that open to the street when weather permits. **Known for:** classic French bistro; great date spot; alfresco dining feel. $ *Average main: $30* ✉ *4907 Wisconsin Ave., Tenleytown* ☎ *202/244–2404* ⊕ *www.lechatnoirrestaurant.com* Ⓜ *Tenleytown.*

Millie's

$$ | **AMERICAN** | **FAMILY** | The menu at this classic neighborhood bar–restaurant concentrates on seafood, with both Cape Cod and Baja influences, bringing a coastal dining experience to the city with a winning formula. Look for cod, lobster rolls, fish tacos, and even panfried trout. **Known for:** inventive seafood; casual coastal atmosphere; takeout ice-cream counter. $ *Average main: $21* ✉ *4866 Massachusetts Ave. NW, Northwest* ☎ *202/733–5789* ⊕ *www.milliesdc.com* Ⓜ *Tenleytown–AU.*

★ Parthenon Restaurant
$$ | GREEK | You can never have enough Greek restaurants, and Parthenon is among the best in town. This is traditional Greek food, including great moussaka, pastitsio, salads, and grilled fish. **Known for:** traditional Greek cooking in a taverna setting; large portions; attached to Chevy Chase Lounge. *$ Average main: $25 ✉ 5510 Connecticut Ave. NW, Upper Northwest ☎ 202/966–7600 🌐 www.parthenon-restaurant.com Ⓜ Friendship Heights.*

★ Pete's New Haven Style Apizza
$ | PIZZA | FAMILY | Pete's is a locally owned, Friendship Heights landmark, serving "New Haven-style" (thin-crust, coal-fired) pizzas and offering an extensive toppings list. The spacious patio gives you enough room to spread out. **Known for:** white-clam pizza; chef-driven; locally owned. *$ Average main: $15 ✉ 4940 Wisconsin Ave., Friendship Heights ☎ 202/237–7383 🌐 petesapizza.com Ⓜ Friendship Heights.*

Sushiko Chevy Chase
$$ | JAPANESE | At the city's self-touted first raw-fish restaurant, the cuts are always ocean fresh, the cocktails fruity, and the presentations classic. Think blue crab topped with avocado and tuna crowned by jalapeño, while hot delicacies like melt-on-the-tongue fried tempura are always reliable. **Known for:** pioneer of the D.C. sushi scene; classic sushi presentations; cozy, romantic setting. *$ Average main: $24 ✉ 5455 Wisconsin Ave. NW, Chevy Chase ☎ 301/961–1644 🌐 www.sushikorestaurants.com ⏲ Closed Sun. No lunch ☞ No cash Ⓜ Friendship Heights.*

★ 2 Amys
$$ | PIZZA | FAMILY | Call it the Brando of D.C. pizzerias, because this Neapolitan sensation has played godfather to a number of throne-stealing wood ovens elsewhere in town since it opened more than a decade ago. Simple recipes allow the ingredients to shine through and make the "wine bar" menu of small Italian plates as exemplary as the pies. **Known for:** authentic Neapolitan wood-fired pizza with a chewy crust; homemade charcuterie at the wine bar; family-friendly (read: noisy) atmosphere. *$ Average main: $19 ✉ 3715 Macomb St. NW, Upper Northwest ☎ 202/885–5700 🌐 2amyspizza.com ⏲ No lunch Mon.–Fri.*

Hotels

Whether you travel north through Rock Creek Park on a scenic jaunt, head up Connecticut Avenue past the National Zoo, or take Wisconsin Avenue starting at the Washington National Cathedral, you see a diverse collection of prosperous neighborhoods with single-family homes, apartment high-rises, and shopping districts. These Upper Northwest communities won't have as many museums or as much history as the other parts of D.C., but they still have plenty of sights, movie theaters, and mini malls.

Glover Park Hotel Georgetown
$ | HOTEL | Perched atop a hill in a quiet residential neighborhood, the Glover Park Georgetown offers beautifully decorated rooms away from the city bustle. **Pros:** free private parking nearby; spacious rooms, some with views and kitchenettes; quiet residential neighborhood. **Cons:** distance from Metro and Downtown; uninspired restaurant; feels a little worn. *$ Rooms from: $200 ✉ 2505 Wisconsin Ave. NW, Upper Northwest ☎ 202/337–9700, 855/334–5197 reservations 🌐 www.gloverparkhotel.com 🛏 158 rooms 🍽 No Meals Ⓜ Woodley Park–Zoo/Adams Morgan.*

★ Omni Shoreham Hotel
$$ | HOTEL | FAMILY | Since its opening in 1930, this elegant landmark overlooking Rock Creek Park, a Historic Hotels of America member, has welcomed heads of state, U.S. politicians, and celebs like the Beatles, Judy Garland, and Bob Hope. **Pros:** historic property with

gorgeous grounds and good views from many rooms; great pool and sundeck; walking/jogging trails through Rock Creek Park. **Cons:** not near major sights; noisy at times; extremely large. $ *Rooms from: $210* ✉ *2500 Calvert St. NW, Woodley Park, Upper Northwest* 🕾 *202/234–0700, 888/444–6664 reservations* ⊕ *www. omnihotels.com* ⇌ *832 rooms* ❖ *No Meals* Ⓜ *Woodley Park–Zoo/Adams Morgan.*

★ Woodley Park Guest House

$$$ | **B&B/INN** | Experience the height of hospitality at this charming bed-and-breakfast on a quiet residential street near the zoo. **Pros:** close to Metro; excellent breakfast; friendly and welcoming hosts. **Cons:** some rooms are small; limited privacy; no television. $ *Rooms from: $325* ✉ *2647 Woodley Rd. NW, Woodley Park, Upper Northwest* 🕾 *202/667–0218* ⊕ *www.woodleyparkguesthouse.com* ⇌ *15 rooms* ❖ *Free Breakfast* Ⓜ *Woodley Park–Zoo/Adams Morgan.*

🎭 Performing Arts

Summer is when the performing arts come alive in Upper Northwest D.C. Highlights include the refurbished Avalon Theatre, which features outstanding documentaries and hard-to-find independent films.

FILM
Avalon Theatre

FILM | **FAMILY** | This classic movie house from 1923 is D.C.'s only nonprofit film center. The theater offers a wide array of studio films and independent and foreign films, plus monthly showcases of the best in French, Israeli, Czech, and Greek cinema. The theater also offers programming for families and children. ✉ *5612 Connecticut Ave. NW, Upper Northwest* 🕾 *202/966–6000 info line, 202/966–3464 box office* ⊕ *www.theavalon.org* Ⓜ *Friendship Heights.*

MUSIC
Apollo Orchestra

CONCERTS | Founded in 2010, this orchestra is made up of D.C.'s finest freelance classical musicians. Their main purpose is to provide free classical orchestra performances to local communities in D.C. Performing all over the city, this is one of the best classical music experiences in the area. ✉ *1 Chevy Chase Circle, Upper Northwest* ⊕ *www. apolloorchestra.com* 🎫 *Free* Ⓜ *Red Line: Friendship Heights.*

Washington National Cathedral

MUSIC | Concerts and recitals by visiting musicians augment the choral and church groups that frequently perform in this breathtaking cathedral. Recitals on the massive pipe organ are offered every Sunday afternoon, and the choir often sings evensong at 5:30 during the week. ✉ *3101 Wisconsin Ave. NW, Upper Northwest* ⊹ *From Cleveland Park or Tenleytown–AU Metro station, take any 30 series bus* 🕾 *202/537–6200, 202/537–2228 box office* ⊕ *www.nationalcathedral.org* Ⓜ *Tenleytown–AU.*

🛍 Shopping

The major thoroughfare, Wisconsin Avenue, runs northwest through the city from Georgetown toward Maryland. It crosses the border in the midst of the Friendship Heights shopping district, which is also near Chevy Chase. It's at this border where you'll find the Chevy Chase Pavilion with retailers, including H&M, J.Crew, Old Navy, and World Market. Other chains like Saks Fifth Avenue and Bloomingdale's can be found at The Shops at Wisconsin Place. This neighborhood also boasts stand-alone designer stores like Christian Dior, and Ralph Lauren. There are a few local gems in the surrounding area. Other neighborhoods in the District yield more interesting finds and offer more enjoyable shopping and sightseeing, but it's hard to beat

Friendship Heights/Upper Northwest for sheer convenience and selection.

BOOKS

★ Politics and Prose

BOOKS | After being bought by two former *Washington Post* reporters in 2011, this legendary independent continues the tradition of jam-packed author events and signings. In the downstairs coffee shop and wine bar, The Den, you can debate the issues of the day or read a book while enjoying a casual meal or snack. ⊠ *5015 Connecticut Ave. NW, Upper Northwest* ☎ *202/364–1919* ⊕ *www. politics-prose.com* Ⓜ *Van Ness–UDC.*

CLOTHING

Everett Hall

MEN'S CLOTHING | D.C.'s own Everett Hall designs men's suits that are richly classic in their material and cutting-edge in their design, color, and sensibility. Starting at around $1,500, the suits appeal to professionals who want something unique. ⊠ *Chevy Chase Pavilion, 5301 Wisconsin Ave. NW, Friendship Heights* ☎ *202/362–0191* ⊕ *www.everetthallboutique.com* Ⓜ *Friendship Heights.*

Tabandeh

JEWELRY & WATCHES | Located in the Shops at Wisconsin Place, this avant-garde women's collection includes an expertly selected cache of Rick Owens tops and Ann Demeulemeester clothing, along with accessories including stunning leather belts and handbags. The jewelry pieces in the store are dazzling— rings, necklaces, earrings, and pendants made with precious and semiprecious stones from designers like Samiar 13 and Erickson Beamon—and are sure to add panache to your wardrobe. ⊠ *5330-F Western Ave. NW, Upper Northwest* ☎ *202/244–0777* ⊕ *www.tabandehjewelry.com* ⊘ *Closed Sun.* Ⓜ *Friendship Heights.*

FOOD AND WINE

Calvert Woodley Fine Wines and Spirits

WINE/SPIRITS | In addition to the excellent selection of wine and hard liquor, 200 kinds of cheese and other picnic and cocktail-party fare are on hand. The international offerings have made this a favorite pantry for embassy parties. ⊠ *4339 Connecticut Ave. NW, Upper Northwest* ☎ *202/966–4400* ⊕ *www. calvertwoodley.com* Ⓜ *Van Ness–UDC.*

Rodman's Discount Foods and Drugstore

GENERAL STORE | The rare store that carries wine, cheese, and space heaters, Rodman's is a fascinating hybrid of Target and Dean & DeLuca. The appliances are downstairs, the imported peppers and chocolates upstairs. It opened in 1955. ⊠ *5100 Wisconsin Ave. NW, Upper Northwest* ☎ *202/363–3466* ⊕ *www. rodmans.com* Ⓜ *Friendship Heights.*

Chapter 12

D.C. WATERFRONT

Updated by
Claire Handscombe

👁 Sights	🍴 Restaurants	🛏 Hotels	🛍 Shopping	🍸 Nightlife
★★★★☆	★★★★★	★★★★★	★★★★☆	★★★★★

NEIGHBORHOOD SNAPSHOT

TOP EXPERIENCES

The Wharf: The newest spot on the District's Waterfront offers many dining options at all price points, live music, seasonal events, and waterfront recreation.

Pier at The Wharf: From bench swings and boardwalks to paddleboards and a kids' park, the piers at The Wharf are the best places to experience the Waterfront in D.C.

The Yards: The Yards offer miles of walking track along D.C.'s Waterfront, a grassy area for picnics and concerts, first-class restaurants, D.C.'s first winery, and a wading pool for the kids.

Music Venues: The Anthem is the District's newest music venue and great for a night out, with its 6,000-person-capacity industrial space packed with the newest performers. Also, check out Union Stage and Pearl Street Warehouse at The Wharf.

Dining: Waterfront restaurants are among the best and newest in the District, with tons of different cuisines, styles, and price options. Be sure to reserve: they're also popular.

GETTING HERE

By road, Metro, or via the Potomac River, the Waterfront has many options for transportation. Take the Green Line directly to the Navy Yard–Ballpark station to put you right by The Yards and Nationals Stadium. The Waterfront station will put you a 10- to 15-minute walk from The Wharf. The round-trip SW Neighborhood Shuttle also runs daily between The Wharf and L'Enfant Plaza/VRE station, the National Mall, and L'Enfant Retail on 10th Street SW. The Wharf also has water-taxi service from Transit Pier, connecting to stops in Georgetown, Maryland's National Harbor, and Old Town Alexandria in Virginia. Check out The Wharf's website for hours of operation. Parking at the Waterfront can be limited and expensive, so keep that in mind before going, and expect heavy traffic on weekends. The Green Line continues on to Anacostia, but you can also reach the area by bicycle, bus, or even boat.

PLANNING YOUR TIME

Allow extra time if exploring any of the museums. If you are in the mood for a concert, check out the many venues. All the restaurants here are popular and busy, so make reservations. Most of the shops in the Waterfront are open daily and great if you have time to kill before a meal. If you want a sportier day, pack accordingly for getting in the Potomac or pool.

NEIGHBORHOOD FACTS

Named as one of the best places to live in D.C., the Waterfront has the most modern feel out of the neighborhoods. Initially known as a more industrial neighborhood, controversial urban renewal projects have since created a modern environment with tradition still holding strong, such as the **Municipal Fish Market** being America's oldest operating fish market.

The District has finally expanded the Waterfront with the Navy Yard and The Wharf, the two newest areas along the water.

World-class parks, waterfront recreation, convenient shopping, one-of-a-kind dining, two sports stadiums, and premier events are all part of Capitol Riverfront, a 500-acre neighborhood along the Anacostia River in Southeast D.C. that encompasses the Navy's oldest onshore outpost.

The Naval Yard is where you'll find the National Museum of the U.S. Navy; its west side is flanked by a waterfront boardwalk that is part of the Anacostia Riverwalk Trail, which is popular with cyclists, runners, and walkers. Watersports opportunities are also abundant along the boardwalk thanks to a 52-slip marina where you can rent kayaks, canoes, and paddleboards.

◉ Sights

Some of the sights in this area are actually in the Navy Yard. To gain entrance, you'll need a government-issued photo ID (driver's license, passport card, or passport) if you are over 18.

Audi Field

SPORTS VENUE | Soccer is incredibly popular in the nation's capital, finding a major following among the international residents who miss the big matches of home, as well as families whose kids play the sport. In 2018, fans of Washington's Major League Soccer team, D.C. United, were wowed with the opening of Audi Field, an innovative, 20,000-seat stadium near the revitalized Southwest Waterfront and just a few blocks from Nationals Park. In addition to 31 luxury suites, the facility boasts 500,000 square feet of on-site retail, office, and residential space. The team's 2018 acquisition of the international superstar Wayne Rooney only fueled the excitement, and he has now returned as the manager. ⊠ 100 Potomac Ave. SW, Southwest ☎ 202/587–5000 ⊕ www.dcunited.com/audi-field Ⓜ Navy Yard–Ballpark.

Congressional Cemetery

CEMETERY | Established in 1807 "for all denominations of people," this cemetery is the final resting place for such notables as U.S. Capitol architect William Thornton, Marine Corps march composer John Philip Sousa, Civil War photographer Mathew Brady, FBI director J. Edgar Hoover, and many members of Congress. Air Force veteran and gay rights activist Leonard Matlovich is also buried here under a tombstone that reads "When I was in the military, they gave me a medal for killing two men, and a discharge for loving one." The cemetery is about a 20-minute walk from the Capitol. You can take a self-guided tour year-round during daylight hours; pick up a map at the gatehouse or download one from the cemetery website. On Saturdays and some Sundays from April through October, you can join a one-hour docent-led tour at 11 am. Check the website for all kinds of themed tours and other events, including film screenings during the summer. ⊠ 1801 E St. SE, Capitol Hill ☎ 202/543–0539 ⊕ www.congressional-cemetery.org ⌂ $5 for tours Ⓜ Stadium–Armory or Potomac Ave.

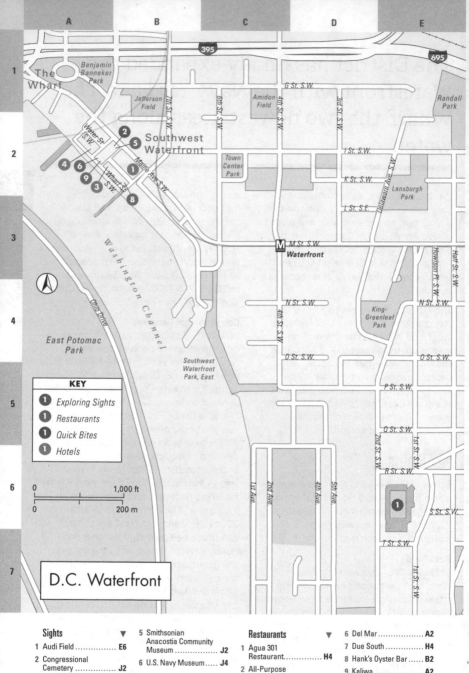

D.C. Waterfront

KEY

- **1** Exploring Sights
- **1** Restaurants
- **1** Quick Bites
- **1** Hotels

0 — 1,000 ft
0 — 200 m

Sights ▼

1 Audi Field **E6**
2 Congressional
Cemetery **J2**
3 Kenilworth Park and
Aquatic Gardens........ **J1**
4 Nationals Park **F4**
5 Smithsonian
Anacostia Community
Museum **J2**
6 U.S. Navy Museum..... **J4**

Restaurants ▼

1 Agua 301
Restaurant.............. **H4**
2 All-Purpose
Pizzeria.................. **G5**
3 Bluejacket.............. **H4**
4 Chloe.................... **H4**
5 Colada Shop............. **B2**
6 Del Mar.................. **A2**
7 Due South **H4**
8 Hank's Oyster Bar **B2**
9 Kaliwa.................... **A2**
10 La Famosa................ **I4**
11 Osteria Morini........... **H4**
12 Shilling Canning
Company................. **H4**

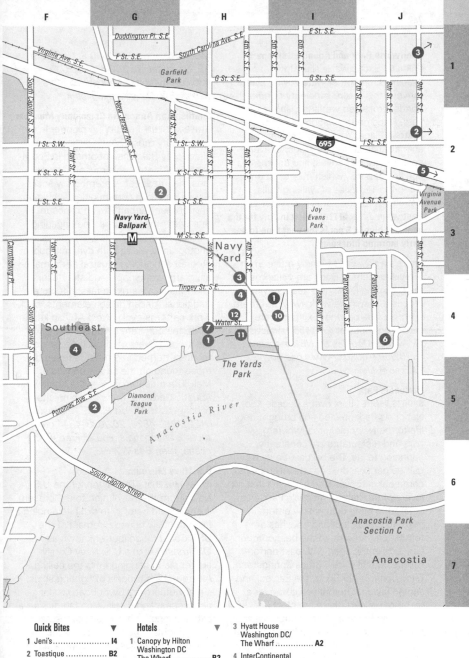

Kenilworth Park and Aquatic Gardens
GARDEN | Exotic water lilies, lotuses, hyacinths, and other water-loving plants thrive in this 8-acre sanctuary of quiet ponds, protected wetlands, and marshy flats, listed on the National Register of Historic Places. The gardens' wetland animals include turtles, frogs, beavers, spring azure butterflies, and dozens of species of birds, which may be seen along the 1½-miles of walking trails. Watch out for the Lotus and Water Lily Festival in July. ■TIP➜ Visit in July for the peak lily bloom; 9 am is the best time to see early morning blossoms.

There's a tiny, child-friendly museum in the visitor center. Dogs are welcome but must be on a leash. The nearest Metro stop is a 10-minute walk away, but there is ample free parking. Exit gates are locked promptly at 4. ✉ 1550 Anacostia Ave., at Douglas St. NE, Anacostia ☎ 202/692–6080 ⊕ www.nps.gov/keaq ⚇ Free Ⓜ Deanwood.

Nationals Park
SPORTS VENUE | Just over a decade ago, Nationals Park opened and brought new life to the Navy Yard area, where new bars and restaurants are constantly springing to life. The ballpark hosts 81 games per season, and while Nats fans come out in droves, the park isn't just for lovers of the game. Nationals Park was created to bring high-quality entertainment to the District and now has a reputation for some of the best outdoor concerts in the area, with past performances by Billy Joel, Bruce Springsteen, Elton John, Taylor Swift, the Eagles, and James Taylor. Whether you come for a game or concert, there are plenty of retail spaces and food-service venues like the Budweiser Terrace with its happy hour, a Ben's Chili Bowl, and Shake Shack. There are also activities and areas for children and families with the brand-new Kids Play Area and the state-of-the-art Nursing

Mothers Lounge. ✉ 1500 S. Capitol St. SE, Southeast ☎ 202/675–6287 ⊕ www. mlb.com/nationals/ballpark ⚇ Tours $25–$35 Ⓜ Navy Yard–Ballpark.

Smithsonian Anacostia Community Museum
OTHER MUSEUM | FAMILY | A pioneer in the community museum movement, in a historically Black neighborhood in Southeast Washington, this museum examines the impact of contemporary social issues on urban communities, including environment, urban life, and encounters with other cultures. The engaging exhibitions employ video, art, crafts, and photography, along with dynamic public programs including musical performances, crafts workshops, and storytellers. The museum's striking facade features traditional African design elements: brickwork patterns evoke West African kente cloth, the concrete cylinders reference the stone towers of Zimbabwe, and diamond-patterned adornments resemble those found on the adobe houses of Mali. The museum is near the Kenilworth Aquatic Gardens. There's free on-site parking. ✉ 1901 Fort Pl. SE, Anacostia ☎ 202/633–4820, 202/633–4844 group tours ⊕ anacostia.si.edu ⚇ Free Ⓜ Anacostia, then Bus W2/W3.

U.S. Navy Museum
OTHER MUSEUM | The history of the U.S. Navy, from the Revolution to the present, is chronicled here, with exhibits ranging from the fully rigged foremast of the USS Constitution (better known as Old Ironsides) to a U.S. Navy Corsair fighter plane hanging from the ceiling. All around are models of fighting ships, a real Vietnam-era Swift boat, working periscopes, and displays on famous naval battles along with portraits of the sailors who fought in them. In front of the museum is a collection of guns, cannons, and missiles. The Navy Art Collection, including many works by Navy artists, is also housed in the museum. Explore

The District has more than one botanical garden. Kenilworth Park and Aquatic Gardens focuses on wetland flora and fauna and is on the National Register of Historic Places.

the Cold War Gallery in Building 70 with exhibits that explore the Navy's response to the threat of Soviet military power and communist ideology.

⚠ **All visitors to the museum must have a valid photo ID and report to the Visitor Control Center (VCC) at the Washington Navy Yard's primary access gate at 11th and O Streets. The VCC is only open weekdays until 3:30 pm. If you're planning to visit the museum on the weekend, you must be pre-vetted. A Base Access Pass Registration must be filled out seven days before your visit. Call ☎ *202/433–3018* for access-related questions.** ✉ *Navy Yard, 805 Kidder Breese St. SE, Bldg. 76, Southeast* ✣ *Enter through visitor gate at 11th and O Sts. SE and show valid photo ID; you'll receive a pass and map of surroundings* ☎ *202/685–0589 museum, 202/433–4882 USS Barry* 🌐 *www.history.navy.mil* 🎟 *Free* [M] *Eastern Market or Navy Yard–Ballpark.*

🍴 Restaurants

Some great new restaurants have opened in The Wharf to supplement the area's other dining spots. Many of these eateries are particularly popular on game days.

Agua 301 Restaurant

$ | **MEXICAN** | You'll be impressed by the modern approaches to traditional Mexican food at this restaurant, which aims to be more than a simple neighborhood Tex-Mex joint. More-conventional tacos and empanadas stand beside an innovative Mexican-inflected take on paella, and lighter options include ceviche, soups, salads, and *bocaditos* (little bites to accompany your drinks). **Known for:** modern Mexican cuisine; great empanadas and tacos; extensive mezcal and tequila list. [$] *Average main: $15* ✉ *Yards Park, 301 Water St. SE, Southeast* ☎ *202/484–0301* 🌐 *www.agua301.com* [M] *Navy Yard–Ballpark.*

★ All-Purpose Pizzeria

$$ | **ITALIAN** | "Best pizza in D.C." is a hotly contested title, but All-Purpose Pizzeria down on the Capitol Riverfront is a strong contender. Its whole wheat dough is carefully made with high-quality ingredients, and you'll find a mix of classic and intriguing choices like chili-roasted corn, chili-lime aioli, or truffle honey. **Known for:** riverfront rooftop; Italian antipasti dishes; Italian-style cocktails. [$] *Average main: $20* ✉ *79 Potomac Ave. SE, D.C. Waterfront* ☎ *202/629–1894* 🌐 *allpurposedc.com* [M] *Navy Yard–Ballpark.*

Bluejacket

$$ | **CONTEMPORARY** | Most restaurants pair beer with food, but here you'll find the opposite: the refined but hearty new American fare is designed to complement the 10 brews on tap. If you're not sure whether an herbal saison or the spicy fruit of a Scotch ale would go best with a bone-in beef short rib in a Kansas City rub, don't be afraid to ask the gracious cast of servers. **Known for:** in-house brewery that produces excellent speciality beer; industrial vibe; fantastic Sunday brunch. [$] *Average main: $20* ✉ *300 Tingey St. SE, D.C. Waterfront* ☎ *202/524–2862* 🌐 *www.bluejacketdc.com* [M] *Navy Yard.*

★ Chloe

$$ | **INTERNATIONAL** | Successfully balancing casual with sophisticated and local with upscale, this is the perfect neighborhood restaurant, and its inclusion in the Michelin Guide is further proof. Chef Haidar Karoum, previously at Proof, Estadio, and Doi Moi, traces a delicious personal culinary journey at Chloe, with dishes from across the globe that are served with noteworthy flair. **Known for:** seasonal, internationally inspired small plates; superb desserts; sophisticated yet casual dining experience. [$] *Average main: $25* ✉ *1331 4th St. SE, D.C. Waterfront* ☎ *202/313–7007* 🌐 *restaurantchloe.com* 🕓 *No lunch weekdays* [M] *Navy Yard–Ballpark.*

★ Colada Shop

$ | **CUBAN** | There was great excitement in summer 2020, when the second Colada Shop opened, an extension of its very popular first branch in Northwest D.C. Its breakfast menu, in particular, is extensive and appealing, bringing a Cuban twist to familiar-sounding offerings and serving a wide variety of coffees, including café con leche and café bonbon, made with condensed milk. **Known for:** wide range of great coffee; Cuban twist on breakfast; great empanadas. [$] *Average main: $12* ✉ *10 Pearl St. SW, D.C. Waterfront* ☎ *202/932–2980* 🌐 *coladashop.com* [M] *Waterfront.*

Del Mar

$$$$ | **SPANISH** | The newest concept by celebrated chef Fabio Trabocchi celebrates coastal Spain with authentic seafood, tapas, paella, aged charcuterie, and fresh meats. Start your meal in this elegant yet fun restaurant with a seasonal gin and tonic made with house-mixed tonics and additions. **Known for:** traditional Spanish cuisine emphasizing seafood; large menu of mostly shareable plates; elegant dining experience. [$] *Average main: $36* ✉ *791 Wharf St. SW, D.C. Waterfront* ☎ *202/525–1402* 🌐 *www.delmardc.com* [M] *Waterfront.*

Due South

$$ | **AMERICAN** | If you are looking for good renditions of Southern cuisine with flavorful, modernist twists, you'll feel at home here. You can't go wrong with the blackened catfish, and definitely don't skip out on dessert, often served with handmade ice cream from the shop next door. **Known for:** buttermilk fried chicken; shrimp and grits; frosé. [$] *Average main: $24* ✉ *301 Water St. SE, Southeast* ☎ *202/479–4616* 🌐 *duesouthdc.com* [M] *Navy Yard–Ballpark.*

Hank's Oyster Bar

$$$ | **AMERICAN** | The decor and the "urban beach food," with such classics as fried oysters and delicious crab cakes, will transport you to New England; for those who don't like fish, there is tropical jerk chicken, molasses-braised short ribs, or Mediterranean couscous. One of several locations in the metro area created by chef Jamie Leeds, The Wharf location is the biggest Hank's yet and offers both indoor and outdoor seating for the full waterfront effect. **Known for:** New England seafood and decor; waterfront views for happy hour; seasonal seafood and cocktails. $ *Average main: $30* ✉ *701 Wharf St. SW, D.C. Waterfront* ☎ *202/817–3055* ⊕ *hanksoysterbar.com* Ⓜ *Waterfront.*

Kaliwa

$$$ | **ASIAN FUSION** | One of the more unique culinary experiences at The Wharf, Kaliwa offers an Asian-fusion style incorporating tastes from the Philippines, Korea, and Thailand, all cooked in an open kitchen that may make you feel like you're in an Asian street market. The menu includes everything from cold, sushi-type small plates to full-on spicy Thai-style curries. everything on the menu is a bit of a *kaliwa* (twist) on an old favorite. **Known for:** Asian-style street food; dishes drawing from three distinct Asian cuisines; fun drinks. $ *Average main: $28* ✉ *751 Wharf St. SW, D.C. Waterfront* ☎ *202/516–4739* ⊕ *www. kaliwadc.com* Ⓜ *Waterfront.*

★ La Famosa

$$ | **PUERTO RICAN** | Bright and cheerful, with a pleasant patio, this Puerto Rican restaurant is a recently added gem to the D.C. dining scene. The flavors are fresh and delightful; don't miss the octopus salad or the mahi sandwich, which comes with slaw and and sweet pepper aioli. **Known for:** contactless ordering; excellent cocktail selection; fresh Puerto Rican pastries. $ *Average main: $22* ✉ *1300 4th St. SW, D.C. Waterfront* ☎ *202/921–9882* ⊕ *eatlafamosa.com.*

★ Osteria Morini

$$$ | **ITALIAN** | The stylish design and superlative pastas of this take on cuisine from northern Italy's Emilia-Romagna region might seem like an unexpected match for the sports fans flocking to Nationals Park. But you can't ask for a better way to cap off a day at the ballpark than the wood-grilled meats here. **Known for:** prosciutto, mortadella, and wood-grilled meats; pleasant patio location close to the water; proximity to the baseball stadium. $ *Average main: $32* ✉ *301 Water St. SE, Southeast* ☎ *202/484–0660* ⊕ *osteriamorini.com* Ⓜ *Navy Yard–Ballpark.*

★ Shilling Canning Company

$$$ | **AMERICAN** | Shilling Canning takes pride in the quality of its fresh, locally sourced ingredients, and it shows. The Shilling family hails from Baltimore, where they were known for their positive values and respect for the community, as well as their excellent food products— chef Shilling and his team are clearly devoted to honoring the family legacy with a similar ethos. **Known for:** great customer service; a pleasant patio; upscale, locally sourced food. $ *Average main: $35* ✉ *360 Water St. SE, D.C. Waterfront* ☎ *202/554–7474* ⊕ *shillingcanning.com* Ⓜ *Navy Yard–Ballpark.*

☕ Coffee and Quick Bites

Jeni's

$ | **ICE CREAM** | **FAMILY** | The eponymous Jeni first opened a D.C. ice-cream shop in 2017, with branches proliferating since then and quickly gaining devoted fans. And for good reason! **Known for:** dairy-free and gluten-free options; wide range of unique, rotating flavors; delicious buttercrisp waffle cones. $ *Average* main: $6 ✉ 1300 4th St. SW, Suite 120, D.C. Waterfront ☎ 202/733–1477 ⊕ jenis. com Ⓜ Navy Yard.

Toastique

$ | **AMERICAN** | Aptly named, this little spot serves all things on toast, including an avocado smash (with marinated tomatoes and radishes, it's the hands-down favorite), the PB Crunch (with bananas, strawberries, and granola), and a tomato burrata (also with herbed ricotta, basil, and a balsamic glaze). But the restaurant is not created from bread alone; you'll also find a variety of juices, smoothies, and fruit bowls. **Known for:** gourmet toasts; cold-pressed juices; refreshing smoothies. Ⓢ Average main: $13 ✉ 764 Main Ave. SW, D.C. Waterfront ☎ 202/484–5200 ⊕ www.toastique.com Ⓜ Waterfront.

🛏 Hotels

The Waterfront is by far one of the most interesting areas in which to stay right now, with spectacular views, unique and sophisticated dining, and plenty of water and outdoor activities to keep you busy. There is also great nightlife here, with lots of bars and hip music venues. All the hotels are very new and chic, as well as conveniently located for the Waterfront and National Mall.

Canopy by Hilton Washington DC The Wharf

$$$ | **HOTEL** | **FAMILY** | At the forefront of the Wharf's revitalized hospitality scene, this new concept hotel by Hilton offers stylish rooms with rustic barn doors, a cool tan-and-beige palette, and plenty of extras. **Pros:** most rooms have water views; fun rooftop bar; convenient location. **Cons:** no pool; shared space with Hyatt House; can be loud at night. Ⓢ Rooms from: $296 ✉ 975 7th St. SW, D.C. Waterfront ☎ 202/488–2500 ⊕ www.hilton.com/en/hotels/dcacupy-canopy-washington-dc-the-wharf

↪ 175 rooms ℐ⊙ℐ Free Breakfast Ⓜ Waterfront.

Courtyard Washington Capitol Hill/Navy Yard

$$ | **HOTEL** | Just a block from a Metro station and within walking distance to Nationals Park, this is a smart choice for budget-savvy travelers. **Pros:** good value; popular bar; close to Metro. **Cons:** popular with groups, so some nights may be noisy; parking in nearby garage is expensive; restaurants in area can be busy. Ⓢ Rooms from: $228 ✉ 140 L St. SE, Navy Yard, D.C. Waterfront ☎ 202/479–0027 ⊕ www.marriott.com/en-us/hotels/wasny-courtyard-washington-capitol-hill-navy-yard ↪ 204 rooms ℐ⊙ℐ No Meals Ⓜ Navy Yard–Ballpark.

Hyatt House Washington DC/The Wharf

$$ | **HOTEL** | Just above the hubbub of The Wharf waterfront, the new Hyatt House offers a convenient location with some welcome amenities, including a pool and family-sized suites with kitchenettes. **Pros:** family-friendly setup; convenient location; outdoor pool. **Cons:** the area can be noisy; shared spaces with Canopy Hotel; restaurants can be very busy. Ⓢ Rooms from: $251 ✉ 725 Wharf St. SW, D.C. Waterfront ☎ 202/554–1234 ⊕ www.hyatt.com/en-US/hotel/washington-dc/hyatt-house-washington-dc-the-wharf/wasxs ↪ 237 rooms ℐ⊙ℐ Free Breakfast Ⓜ Waterfront.

InterContinental Washington D.C.–The Wharf

$$$ | **HOTEL** | Styling itself as an urban resort, D.C.'s new InterContinental offers spacious, modern rooms and a dazzling, soaring, wood-and-stone, open-atrium lobby with floor-to-ceiling windows looking out over the river. Rooms, nearly 70% of which have some waterfront views, are comfortable and spacious, with fast Wi-Fi, Nespresso coffeemakers, and digital controls for everything. **Pros:** fantastic rooms with great views; central

location; unique spa and pool. **Cons:** area can be loud at night; restaurants in area can be very busy; no meals included. $ *Rooms from: $393* ⊠ *801 Wharf St. SW, D.C. Waterfront* ☎ *202/800–0844* ⊕ *wharfintercontinentaldc.com* ⥂ *284 rooms* ⦿ *No Meals* Ⓜ *Waterfront.*

Nightlife

This increasingly busy area is starting to become a place to go after dark.

BARS AND LOUNGES

The Brighton SW1

PUBS | The Brighton is like a bigger and more modern version of your local neighborhood pub. Offering a massive British footprint on The Wharf, this sprawling space has a huge bar and outside seating. Next door to the Anthem, it's particularly popular on weekends or after a show. Sip any of the dozen beers on draft, from sours to darks, feel free to ask the server for a cocktail, or have a watermelon crush or another of the myriad frozen drinks. The pub-themed food menu is chockablock full of British classics like chicken curry and fish-and-chips. ⊠ *949 Wharf St. SW, D.C. Waterfront* ☎ *202/735–5398* ⊕ *www.brighton-dc. com* Ⓜ *Waterfront.*

Cantina Bambina

BARS | Above the Anthem's box office and Water Taxi's ticket office—and just across from the music venue—this ultracasual bar and snack bar has become a favorite of Wharf area concertgoers as well as those just looking for a drink and some spectacular views. Feast your eyes on the long margarita and cocktail list, and grab some small bites at the bar stand downstairs. It gets busy here, so expect to stand during your visit, but that just makes it easier to take in the waterfront views. ⊠ *960 Wharf St. SW, D.C. Waterfront* ⊕ *www.cantinabambina.com* Ⓜ *Waterfront.*

District Winery

WINE BARS | D.C.'s first-ever winery is a unique spot in the heart of The Yards, serving all locally made, small-batch wines that can be paired with dishes in its new full-service restaurant, Ana. Tour the winery to learn how head winemaker Conor McCormack produces his vintages, enjoy a tasting, and then indulge in a meal overlooking the Anacostia River. The menu at Ana consists of tapas-style small bites, with dinner on weekdays and brunch on weekends. The winery also hosts weddings and offers a date-night package for the romantically inclined. ⊠ *The Yards, 385 Water St. SE, Southeast* ☎ *202/484–9210* ⊕ *districtwinery. com* ☽ *No lunch weekdays* Ⓜ *Navy Yard–Ballpark.*

Kirwan's Irish Pub

PUBS | With authentic decor, music, and booze, this pub is about as Irish as it gets in the District. Started by a former Guinness employee, Kirwan's is the place to bask in live traditional music with a good pint on real Irish furniture or at the carved bar. There is plenty of space here with two floors and a full restaurant if you want a good Irish meal before the nightlife takes over. ⊠ *Canopy by Hilton Washington DC The Wharf, 749 Wharf St. SW, D.C. Waterfront* ⊹ *Below hotel, which sits above ground level* ☎ *202/554–3818* ⊕ *www.kirwansonthe-wharf.com* Ⓜ *Waterfront.*

Mission

BARS | With two floors, a gigantic 150-foot bar, and 600 feet of outdoor balconies, Mission is easily the city's roomiest spot for pregame or post-work get-togethers, with the daily happy hour a big draw. Stop in for a glass of wine, beer, Tito's, or even a house margarita, all on tap, and some traditional Mexican mixed with Tex-Mex food. Weekends feature bottomless margaritas. ⊠ *1221 Van St. SE, Southeast*

☎ *202/810–7010* ⊕ *missionnavyyard.com* Ⓜ *Navy Yard–Ballpark.*

Whiskey Charlie

BARS | You may have to search a bit to find this bar, but walk through the lobby of the Canopy by Hilton, head up to the roof in the special elevator, and you'll find a waterfront vista like no other in the city. Munch on some light bites, and choose from the well-curated menu of craft cocktails (go for the Mermaid margarita), all while enjoying a view that stretches from the Capitol building to the Pentagon, or sit inside with floor-to-ceiling windows and sophisticated decor. ☒ *975 7th St. SW, D.C. Waterfront* ☎ *202/488–2500* ⊕ *whiskeycharliewharf. com* Ⓜ *Waterfront.*

MUSIC CLUBS

The Anthem

LIVE MUSIC | The coolest new music venue in D.C. made its home at the helm of The Wharf—and made a splash with the music world's biggest indie and alternative rock acts, even presenting Foo Fighters on opening night. The first midsize venue of its kind in the District (there's a max of 6,000) feels vast and industrial but has elegant design touches, as well as specially angled seats that preclude bad sightlines. Enjoy beer on tap or in the can, cocktails, and homemade Belgian waffles ("Wharfles") before or during the show. ☒ *901 Wharf St. SW, D.C. Waterfront* ☎ *202/888–0020* ⊕ *www. theanthemdc.com* Ⓜ *Waterfront.*

Pearl Street Warehouse

LIVE MUSIC | The 1950s diner–inspired space may make you feel as if you were in New Orleans or Nashville, but walk through a garage door, and you'll find an intimate, modern (there are plugs under the bar to recharge your phone), and lively entertainment space for small bands. A bar links the performance space to the outside alleyway. All seating is first-come, first-served, and some shows sell out; the restaurant is open for dinner on nights when there are shows. ☒ *33 Pearl St. SW, D.C. Waterfront* ☎ *202/380–9620* ⊕ *www.pearlstreetwarehouse.com* Ⓜ *Waterfront.*

Union Stage

LIVE MUSIC | This unique live-music venue is also a popular spot in the neighborhood for pizza, beer, and seasonal cocktails. The Tap Room bar serves 16 beers on tap and 16 in cans, as well as good cocktails, wine, and soft drinks. Downstairs is the music and another bar. Performances here may be by emerging or established talent, but it's an intimate space with exceptional sound and lighting. Whenever there's a show on, you can grab a now-famous Jersey-style pizza with a variety of toppings. ☒ *740 Water St. SW, D.C. Waterfront* ☎ *877/987–6487* ⊕ *www.unionstage.com* Ⓜ *Waterfront.*

🎭 Performing Arts

★ Arena Stage

THEATER | The first regional theater company to win a Tony Award performs innovative American theater, reviving such classic plays as *Oklahoma* and also showcasing the country's best new playwrights. The architecturally magnificent Mead Center for American Theater houses three stages and, after the Kennedy Center, is the second-largest performing arts complex in Washington. Near the Waterfront neighborhood in Southwest D.C., the Mead Center features the Fichandler Stage, a theater-in-the-round seating 680; the Kreeger Theater, a modified thrust seating 514; and the Kogod Cradle, a 200-seat black-box theater for new or experimental productions. ☒ *1101 6th St. SW, Southwest* ☎ *202/554–9066* ⊕ *www.arenastage.org* Ⓜ *Waterfront.*

🛍 Shopping

BOOKS
Politics and Prose

BOOKS | The second of three locations of this well-loved local institution is a go-to shop for travelers staying at nearby hotels or for anyone, really, who wants something good to read while seated on one of The Wharf's many piers. This branch has all the books you could need, as well as ample room to browse or listen to a speaker at an event. It's also a great place to pick up classy D.C.-themed gifts and notecards. Store hours are 10–8 daily. ⊠ *70 District Sq. SW, D.C. Waterfront* ☎ *202/488–3867* ⊕ *www. politics-prose.com/wharf* Ⓜ *Waterfront.*

CLOTHING
A Beautiful Closet

OTHER SPECIALTY STORE | Step into A Beautiful Closet for fair-trade international goods, including jewelry, clothing, home decor, and accessories. All items here are curated by former World Bank staff member Pamela Sofola. If you're in a rush or just can't decide what to buy, request a personalized styling consultation. ⊠ *20 District Sq. SW, D.C. Waterfront* ☎ *301/787–8914, 202/488–1809* Ⓜ *Waterfront.*

GIFTS
Steadfast Supply

OTHER SPECIALTY STORE | Steadfast is the place to get small, unique District gifts. The store carefully curates its inventory from local small businesses and displays each designer's name and story so you know who you're buying from. It's a fun, lively spot filled with items from more than 100 brands, and there's also classroom space for calligraphy and other creative workshops, as well as areas and gifts geared to children. ⊠ *301 Tingey St. SE, Suite 140, Washington* ⊹ *Entrance on Water St.* ☎ *202/308–4441* ⊕ *www.steadfastsupplydc.com* Ⓜ *Navy Yard–Ballpark.*

Willow

OTHER SPECIALTY STORE | Willow is just across the waterfront and a perfect spot to shop before a meal or ballgame with its boutique clothing, jewelry, and gifts. Willow designs its own glassware and a few other small items in-house, while other cards, gifts, and plants are sourced through local companies. There's a great collection of baby items here, too. ⊠ *1331 4th St. SE, Southeast* ☎ *202/643–2323* ⊕ *www.willowstores. com* Ⓜ *Navy Yard–Ballpark.*

HOME FURNISHINGS
Patrick's Fine Linens & Home Décor

HOUSEWARES | Patrick's is a well-known source in Alexandria for upscale furniture, home decor, dishes, and perfumes; its first D.C. branch is now open at The Wharf. Complement your home with top-notch dinnerware and other designer goods from Hermès China, Juliska, Vista Alegre, and Ralph Lauren, among others. Pick up a bottle of perfume or cologne by Carthusia, C.O. Bigelow, or Santa Maria Novella, or take home a luxury candle from LAFCO, NEST, or Thymes. ⊠ *771 Wharf St. SW, D.C. Waterfront* ☎ *202/601–7296* ⊕ *www.shoppatricks. com* Ⓜ *Waterfront.*

JEWELRY
Diament Jewelry

JEWELRY & WATCHES | Diament Jewelry is a unique treasure trove of vintage and handmade jewelry, along with gifts and accessories from local makers. The neatly displayed clothing, candles, paper goods, and accessories lend a high-class feel to this neat, floral-inspired boutique. A large inventory of vintage rings, bracelets, and necklaces invites you to dig for your next favorite treasure, with options ranging from inexpensive bracelets to pricey, one-of-a-kind diamond rings. Follow the shop on Instagram for the owner's latest finds. ⊠ *33 District Sq. SW, D.C. Waterfront* ☎ *347/868–7150* ⊕ *www.diament-jewelry.com* Ⓜ *Waterfront.*

SPORTING GOODS

Pacers Running

SPORTING GOODS | Pacers Running is a perfect fit for the Navy Yard, selling sports and running gear to the Yard's ever-active, outdoorsy clientele. You can get specialty footwear, running togs, and lifestyle gear, as well as active and injury-prevention accessories. ✉ *300 Tingey St. SE, Suite 160, Southeast* ☎ *202/554–1216* ⊕ *www. runpacers.com* Ⓜ *Navy Yard–Ballpark.*

ARLINGTON

Updated by
Barbara Noe Kennedy

⊙ Sights	🍴 Restaurants	🛏 Hotels	🛍 Shopping	🍸 Nightlife
★★★★☆	★★☆☆☆	★★☆☆☆	★★★★☆	★☆☆☆☆

NEIGHBORHOOD SNAPSHOT

TOP EXPERIENCES

Arlington National Cemetery: The most visited cemetery in the country is the final resting place for more than 400,000 Americans, from unknown soldiers, nearly 4,000 Black Americans who were formerly enslaved, to John F. Kennedy and his wife, Jacqueline Kennedy Onassis.

Udvar-Hazy Center (National Air and Space Museum): See the Boeing B-29 *Enola Gay*, space shuttle *Discovery*, and hundreds of other aviation and space artifacts in these immense hangars near Dulles International Airport.

United States Air Force Memorial: Just south of Arlington Cemetery, this memorial honors members of the Air Force who've given their lives in service to the country.

United States Marine Corps War Memorial: Commonly called the Iwo Jima Memorial, it's located just north of Arlington cemetery and is a powerful tribute to all of the marines who have lost their lives in battle since 1775.

GETTING HERE

You can reach Arlington National Cemetery and the U.S. Air Force and Marine Corps memorials by Metro (Arlington Cemetery on the Blue Line, Pentagon City on the Blue or Yellow lines, Rosslyn on the Orange, Blue, or Silver lines) or Metrobus, although there will be some walking involved. You can also get to these sites with a car or via Big Bus and Old Town Trolley tours. Your best bet is to use Metro to visit the Pentagon and 9/11 Memorial (Pentagon stop via Blue or Yellow line). You'll need a car to visit the Udvar-Hazy Center (or take the shuttle from IAD).

VISITING THE UDVAR-HAZY CENTER

A visit to the Udvar-Hazy Center (National Air and Space Museum) will require a good part of a day due to its location; a car is easiest, though you'll probably encounter some traffic. You can also take a shuttle from nearby Dulles Airport. If you're flying out of Dulles, combine a morning visit to the center with a late afternoon or evening departure.

PLANNING YOUR TIME

You can easily combine a visit to Arlington cemetery with visits to the DEA Museum, the Pentagon and 9/11 Memorial, and U.S. Air Force and Marine Corps memorials; it will be a full day and require advance planning for the Pentagon tour.

Discover American treasures, historical attractions, diverse dining, first-class shopping, and eclectic arts and entertainment in the northern Virginia city of Arlington.

Just across the Potomac River from D.C. (complete with easy Metro access), this area offers a great blend of history and urban excitement. Some other noteworthy spots are farther out in northern Virginia, without the Metro access, including some good restaurants in Falls Church.

Spend a day or two visiting Arlington National Cemetery, the Marine Corps War Memorial, the Air Force Memorial, the Pentagon, and the National 9/11 Pentagon Memorial. If you're traveling with kids or just want to ooh and aah over very cool planes and rockets, don't miss the Udvar-Hazy Center in Chantilly near Dulles International Airport. This companion facility to the National Air and Space Museum on the National Mall displays thousands of aviation and space artifacts in huge hangars; you can even watch restoration projects in progress.

◉ Sights

★ Arlington National Cemetery

CEMETERY | More than 400,000 Americans who died during wartime, as well as many notable Americans (among them Presidents William Howard Taft and John F. Kennedy, General John Pershing, and Supreme Court Justice Ruth Bader Ginsberg), are interred in these 639 acres across the Potomac River from Washington, established as the nation's cemetery in 1864. Prior to 1857, the land was a plantation owned by George Washington Parke Custis, grandson of Martha

Washington. Enslaved people built Arlington House, which became the country's first memorial to Custis's step-grandfather, George Washington; the house and plantation were later passed down to Custis's daughter, Mary Anna Custis Lee, the wife of Confederate general Robert E. Lee. Arlington was very much a typical working plantation before it was a cemetery, with 196 enslaved individuals living and working on the property when the Lees inherited it. Beginning in May 1864, the former plantation, which had been seized by the U.S. Army in 1861, became a military cemetery.

Today Arlington is the most famous national cemetery in the country, with an average of 27 to 30 funerals held every weekday and another six to eight funerals on Saturday for people who did not require or request military honors. You can visit dozens of notable grave sites, monuments, and even an arboretum. Sections 27 and 23, two of the oldest parts of the cemetery, are a particular must for modern-day visitors. Fifteen-hundred African American soldiers who fought in the Civil War and the ensuing Indian Wars are buried here, as are over 3,800 nonmilitary African Americans (including many who were formerly enslaved); they are buried in graves marked only as "citizen" or "civilian."

Tour-bus services are provided for a fee every 30 minutes (buy tickets in the Welcome Center or at ⊕ *www.arlingtontours. com*). Wheelchairs and strollers are not

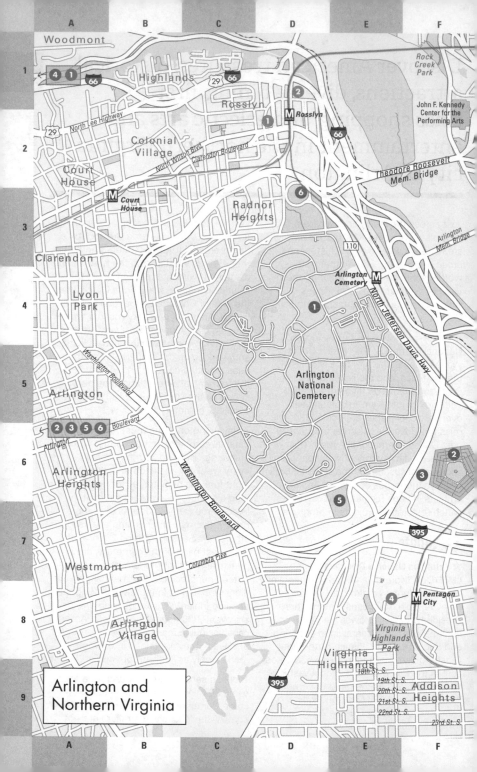

Arlington and
Northern Virginia

Map labels and grid:

A B C D E F
1 2 3 4 5 6 7 8 9

Woodmont

Highlands

66 29 66

Rosslyn

North Lee Highway

29

Colonial Village

North Wilson Blvd

Clarendon Boulevard

Court House

M Court House

Radnor Heights

Clarendon

Lyon Park

Arlington

Arlington Boulevard

Arlington Boulevard

Washington Boulevard

Arlington Heights

Westmont

Columbia Pike

Washington Boulevard

Arlington Village

Arlington National Cemetery

Rock Creek Park

John F. Kennedy Center for the Performing Arts

M Rosslyn

Theodore Roosevelt Mem. Bridge

Arlington Mem. Bridge

110

North Jefferson Davis Hwy

Arlington Cemetery M

395

395

Virginia Highlands Park

M Pentagon City

Virginia Highlands

18th St. S.
19th St. S.
20th St. S.
21st St. S.
22nd St. S.
23rd St. S.

Addison Heights

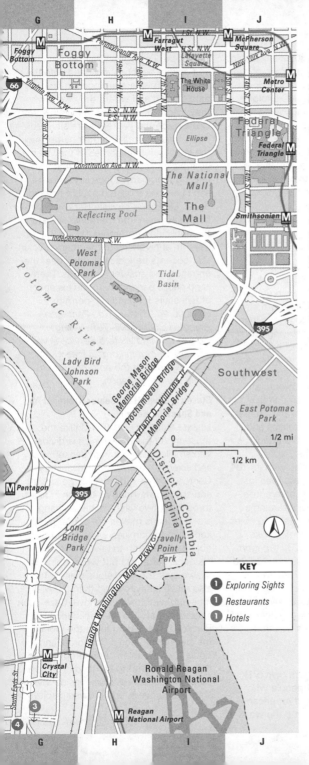

Sights ▼

Restaurants ▼

Hotels ▼

allowed; handicap-accessible vehicles are available upon request. For a map of the cemetery or help finding a grave, download the cemetery's app, ANC Explorer, or use the computers at the Welcome Center. ⊠ *1 Memorial Ave.* ✛ *West end of Memorial Bridge* ☎ *877/907–8585 for general information and to locate a grave* ⊕ *www.arlingtoncemetery.mil* 🎫 *Free; parking from $3 per hr; Arlington National Cemetery tours $17.95* Ⓜ *Arlington Cemetery.*

Pentagon

GOVERNMENT BUILDING | The headquarters of the United States Department of Defense is the largest low-rise office building in the world. Approximately 26,000 military and civilian workers arrive daily. Astonishingly, the mammoth structure, completed in 1943, took less than two years to construct. Following the September 11, 2001, crash of hijacked American Airlines Flight 77 into the west side of the building, the damaged area was removed in just over a month and repaired in a year. In this same area is the America's Heroes Memorial and Chapel, which pays tribute to the civilians and military members killed in the attack. South of the building is the 2-acre outdoor Pentagon Memorial, with its 184 benches commemorating the lives lost on 9/11. Tours of the Pentagon are free and last about 60 minutes, including a presentation and approximately 1½ miles of walking. ✛ *I–395 at Columbia Pike and Rte. 27* ☎ *703/695–5923 Pentagon Pass Office* ⊕ *www.defense.gov* 🎫 *Free* ☉ *Tours Tues. and Thurs. 10 am and 1 pm (though check the website because this may change)* ⚓ *Reserve online through the Pentagon Tour Office at least 2 weeks, but no more than 3 months, in advance* Ⓜ *Pentagon.*

Pentagon Memorial

HISTORIC SIGHT | Washington's own 9/11 memorial honors the 184 people who perished when the hijacked American Airlines Flight 77 crashed into the west side of the Pentagon. Stainless-steel-and-granite benches inscribed with the victims' names are arranged in order by date of birth and where they were when they died. The names of the victims who were inside the Pentagon are situated so that visitors reading their names face the Pentagon, and names of the victims on the plane are arranged so that visitors reading their names face skyward. At each bench is a lighted pool of flowing water. Designed by Julie Beckman and Keith Kaseman, the memorial opened to the public on September 11, 2008, the seventh anniversary of the attacks. Volunteer docents periodically stand near the entrance and answer questions. There is no public parking, with the exception of five stalls for handicap-permitted vehicles. ⊠ *1 Rotary Rd., Pentagon, Arlington* ☎ *800/296–7996 Arlington Convention and Visitors Service* ⊕ *www. pentagonmemorial.org* 🎫 *Free* ☞ *Call 202/741–1004 at the entrance for an audio tour* Ⓜ *Pentagon.*

Steven F. Udvar-Hazy Center (National Air and Space Museum)

SCIENCE MUSEUM | **FAMILY** | Unlike the museum on the Mall, which is divided into smaller galleries with dense history and science exhibits, the Udvar-Hazy Center, its annex, displays large aircraft and spacecraft, hung as though in flight throughout two vast, multilevel hangars. This focus makes the center more appealing for families with kids who may not be old enough to take in detailed historical narratives but will certainly be in awe over the marvelous planes. It is also much less crowded than the Mall museum, with room to move. Gaze upon historic aircraft like the Lockheed SR-71 Blackbird, the fastest jet in the world; the sleek, supersonic Concorde; and the *Enola Gay*, which, in 1945, dropped the first atomic bomb to be used in war on Hiroshima, Japan. Walk alongside space shuttle *Discovery*, and browse displays of

Continued on page 264

ARLINGTON, THE NATION'S CEMETERY

The most famous, most visited cemetery in the country is the final resting place for close to 400,000 Americans, from unknown soldiers to John F. Kennedy. With its tombs, monuments, and "sea of stones," Arlington is a place of ritual and remembrance, where even the most cynical observer of Washington politics may find a lump in their throat or a tear in their eye.

EXPERIENCING THE SEA OF STONES

In 1864, a 200-acre plot directly across the Potomac from Washington, part of the former plantation of Robert E. Lee, was designated America's national cemetery. Today, the cemetery covers 624 acres.

Today, Arlington's major monuments and memorials are impressive, but the most striking experience is simply looking out over the thousands upon thousands of headstones aligned across the cemetery's hills.

Most of those buried here served in the military—from reinterred Revolutionary War soldiers to troops killed in Iraq and Afghanistan. As you walk through the cemetery, you're likely to hear a trumpet playing taps or the report of a gun salute. An average of 27 funerals a day are held here, Monday through Friday. There currently are nearly 400,000 graves in Arlington; it's projected that the cemetery will be filled by 2060.

FINDING A GRAVE

At the Welcome Center, staff members and computers can help you find the location of a specific grave. You need to provide the deceased's full name and, if possible, the branch of service and year of death.

WHO GETS BURIED WHERE

With few exceptions, interment at Arlington is limited to active-duty members of the armed forces, veterans, and their spouses and minor children. In Arlington's early years as a cemetery, burial location was determined by rank (as well as, initially, by race), with separate sections for enlisted soldiers and officers. Beginning in 1947, this distinction was abandoned. Grave sites are assigned on the day before burial; when possible, requests are honored to be buried near the graves of family members.

ABOUT THE HEADSTONES

Following the Civil War, Arlington's first graves were marked by simple white-washed boards. When these decayed, they were replaced by cast-iron markers covered with zinc to prevent rusting. Only one iron marker remains, for the grave of Captain Daniel Keys (Section 13, Lot 13615, Grid G-29/30).

In 1873, Congress voted in the use of marble headstones, which continues to be the practice today. The government provides the standard-issue stones free of charge. Next of kin may supply their own headstones, though these can only be used if space is available in one of the sections where individualized stones already exist.

THE SAME, BUT DIFFERENT

Regulation headstones can be engraved with one of 54 symbols indicating religious affiliation. In section 60, the headstones of soldiers killed in Afghanistan and Iraq reflect the multicultural makeup of 21st-century America. Along with a variety of crosses and the Star of David, you see the nine-pointed star of the Baha'i; a tepee and three feathers representing the Native American faiths; the Muslim crescent and star; and other signs of faith. (Or lack of it. Atheism is represented by a stylized atom.)

Opposite: Sea of Stones; Upper left: Burial ceremony; Bottom left: Changing of the guard ceremony; Right: Coast Guard headstone.

PLANNING YOUR VISIT TO ARLINGTON

ARLINGTON BASICS

Getting Here: You can reach Arlington on the Metro, by foot over Arlington Memorial Bridge (southwest of the Lincoln Memorial), or by car—there's a large parking lot by the Visitors Center on Memorial Drive. Also, the Big Bus Tours (☎ *877/332–8689* ⊕ *www.bigbustours.com*) and Old Town Trolley (☎ *202/832–9800* ⊕ *www.oldtowntrolley.com*) both have Arlington National Cemetery stops in their loops. But only Old Town Trolley offers 7 stops within the cemetary (⌧ *$13.50*).

⊙ Apr.–Sept., daily 8–7; Oct.–Mar., daily 8–5.

⌧ Cemetery free, parking $2 per hr.

☎ *877/907–8585* for general information and to locate a grave.

⊕ *www.arlingtoncemetery.mil*

✗ No food or drink is allowed at the cemetery. There are water fountains in the Welcome Center, and from fall through spring a water fountain operates near the amphitheater at the Tomb of the Unknowns. You can also purchase bottled water at the Women's Memorial.

TOURING OPTIONS

Your first stop at the cemetery should be the Welcome Center, where you can pick up a free brochure with a detailed map. Once there you have a choice: tour by bus or walk.

Arlington by Bus. Arlington National Cemetery Tours leave every 15 to 25 minutes from just outside the Welcome Center April through September, daily 8:30–6, and October through March, daily 8:30–4. The 45 to 60-minute tour includes stops at the Kennedy grave sites, The Tomb of the Unknown Soldier, and Arlington House. Your bus driver will provide basic facts about the cemetery.

Arlington on Foot. Walking the cemetery requires some stamina, but it allows you to take in the thousands of graves at your own pace. On the facing page is a walking tour that includes the major points of interest. Audio tours are available in the Welcome Center.

Above: Arlington National Cemetery

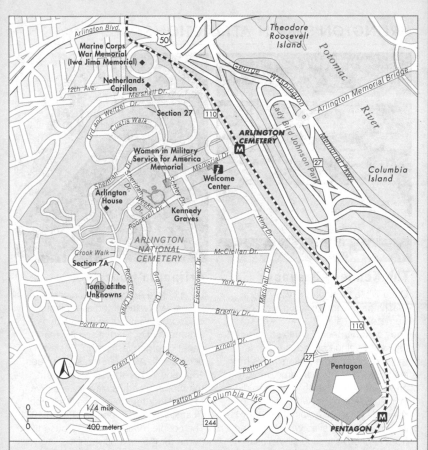

A WALKING TOUR

■ Head west from the Welcome Center on Roosevelt Drive and turn right on Weeks Drive to reach the **Kennedy graves;** just to the west is **Arlington House.** (1/4 mile)

■ Take Crook Walk south, following the signs, to the **Tomb of the Unknowns**; a few steps from the tomb is **Section 7A**, where many distinguished veterans are buried. (3/10 mile)

■ To visit the graves of soldiers killed in Afghanistan and Iraq, take Roosevelt Drive past Section 7 and turn right on McClellan Drive, turn right when you get to Eisenhower Drive, then go left onto York Drive. The graves will be on your right. (6/10 mile)

■ Walk north along Eisenhower Drive, which becomes Schley Drive; turn right onto Custis Walk, which brings you to **Section 27,** where 3,800 former slaves are buried. (3/4 mile)

■ Leave the cemetery through the Ord and Weitzel Gate, cross Marshall Drive carefully, and walk to the 50-bell **Netherlands Carillon,** where there's a good vista of Washington. To the north is the **United States Marine Corps War Memorial,** better known as the **Iwo Jima Memorial**. (1/4 mile)

ARLINGTON'S MAIN ATTRACTIONS

The Kennedy Graves

Once while taking in the view of Washington from Arlington National Cemetery, President John F. Kennedy commented, "I could stay here forever." Seeing Kennedy's grave is a top priority for most visitors. He's buried beneath an eternal flame, next to graves of two of his children who died in infancy, and of his wife, Jacqueline Kennedy Onassis. Across from them is a low wall engraved with quotations from Kennedy's inaugural address. Nearby, marked by simple white crosses, are the graves of Robert F. Kennedy and Ted Kennedy.

The gas-fueled flame at the head of John F. Kennedy's grave was lit by Jacqueline Kennedy during his funeral. A continuously flashing electric spark reignites the gas if the flame is extinguished by rain, wind, or any other cause.

Many visitors ask where Kennedy's son John F. Kennedy Jr. is buried. His ashes were scattered in the Atlantic Ocean, near the location where his plane went down in 1999.

Arlington House

Long before Arlington was a cemetery, it was part of the 1,100-acre plantation of George Washington Parke Custis, a grandchild of Martha and (by marriage) George Washington. Enslaved people built Arlington House between 1802 and 1818. After Custis's death, the property and its slaves were given to his daughter, Mary Anna Randolph Custis, who wed Robert E. Lee in 1831. The couple made Arlington House their home for the next 30 years.

In 1861 Lee turned down the position of commander of the Union forces and left Arlington House, never to return. Union troops turned the house into an Army headquarters, and 200 acres were set aside as a national cemetery. By the end of the Civil War headstones dotted the estate's hills.

The house looks much as it did in the 19th century and a quick tour takes you past objects once owned by the Custises, the Lees, and the Washingtons. The views from Arlington House remain spectacular. ☎ *703/235–1530* ⊕ *www.nps. gov/arho* ✉ *Free* ◷ *Daily 9:30–4:30.*

The Tomb of the Unknown Soldier

The first burial at the Tomb of the Unknowns, one of the cemetery's most imposing monuments, took place on November 11, 1921. In what was part of a world-wide trend to honor the dead after the unparalleled devastation of World War I, an unidentified soldier was interred under the large white-marble sarcophagus. Unknown servicemen killed in World War II and Korea joined him in 1958.

The Memorial Amphitheater west of the tomb is used for ceremonies on Veterans Day, Memorial Day, and Easter. Decorations awarded to the unknowns are displayed in an indoor trophy room.

One of the most striking activities at Arlington is the precision and pageantry of the changing of the guard at the Tomb of the Unknowns. From April through September, soldiers from the Army's U.S. Third Infantry (known as the Old Guard) change guard every half hour during the day. For the rest of the year, and at night all year long, the guard changes every hour.

The Iwo Jima Memorial

Ask the tour bus driver at Arlington where the Iwo Jima is, and you might get back the quip "very far away." The memorial commonly called the Iwo Jima is officially named the United States Marine Corps War Memorial, and it's actually located just north of the cemetery. Its bronze sculpture is based on one of the most famous photos in American military history, Joe Rosenthal's February 23, 1945, shot of five marines and a navy corpsman raising a flag atop Mt. Suribachi on the Japanese island of Iwo Jima. By executive order, a real flag flies 24 hours a day from the 78-foot-high memorial. P703/289–2500

On Tuesday evening at 7 pm from early June to mid-August there's a Marine Corps sunset parade on the grounds of the Iwo Jima Memorial. On parade nights a free shuttle bus runs from the Arlington Cemetery visitors' parking lot.

The Old Guard are not making a fashion statement in their sunglasses—they're protecting their eyes from the sun's glare off the white marble of the tomb.

astronaut paraphernalia, including space food and space underwear! If you want to visit the museum while you are waiting for a flight or connection at Dulles, the Fairfax Connector Bus 983 runs daily between the museum and airport for $2 (SmarTrip card or cash); the trip takes 15 minutes. ✉ *14390 Air and Space Museum Pkwy.* ☎ *703/572–4118, 866/868–7774 IMAX information* 🌐 *www.airandspace.si.edu* 🎟 *Free; IMAX film from $9; flight simulators from $8; parking $15 (free after 4 pm).*

United States Air Force Memorial

MILITARY SIGHT | On a beautiful hillside in Arlington, the Air Force Memorial honors the service and sacrifice of America's airmen. Three stainless-steel, asymmetrical spires slice through the skyline up to 270 feet, representing flight, the precision of the "high bomb burst" maneuver performed by the Air Force Thunderbirds, and the three core values of the Air Force: Integrity first, Service before self, and Excellence in all we do. The spires are adjacent to the southern portion of Arlington National Cemetery and visible from the Tidal Basin and Interstate 395 near Washington. At the base of the spires are four 8-foot statues standing guard, a glass wall engraved with the missing man formation, and granite walls inscribed with Air Force values and accomplishments. ✉ *1 Air Force Memorial Dr., Arlington* ✣ *Off Columbia Pike* ☎ *703/462–4093, 703/695–5923 Pentagon Pass Office* 🌐 *www.afdw.af.mil/about* 🎟 *Free* [M] *Pentagon City or Pentagon.*

United States Marine Corps War Memorial

MILITARY SIGHT | **FAMILY** | Also known as the Iwo Jima Memorial, it is inspired by the iconic photograph taken during the Battle of Iwo Jima in World War II. The memorial depicts six marines raising the current U.S. flag and honors all U.S. Marine Corps personnel whose lives were lost since 1775. It's a 15-minute walk from the Metro station at Arlington National Cemetery, some of it uphill. ✉ *U.S. Marine Corps War Memorial, U.S. Marine Memorial Circle, Arlington* 🌐 *www.nps.gov/gwmp* 🎟 *Free* [M] *Arlington Cemetery.*

🍴 Restaurants

Ashby Inn

$$$$ | **AMERICAN** | If there's a recipe for a perfect country inn restaurant, chef Jonathan Martin and sommelier Stephen Elhafdi have it. Head about an hour west of D.C. into Virginia hunt country, and your reward is extraordinary comfort food. À la carte menu items—like thyme-roasted pork with sweet potato purée or pan-seared chicken breast with mushrooms and lentils—are made with fresh local ingredients and presented in an intimate setting. **Known for:** intimate country inn dining; views of the Blue Ridge; prix-fixe menus with local ingredients. [$] *Average main: $45; $145 for chef's tasting menu* ✉ *692 Federal St., Paris* ☎ *540/592–3900* 🌐 *www.ashbyinn.com* 🕓 *Closed Mon. and Tues. No lunch Wed.*

Chill Zone

$ | **VIETNAMESE** | The Vietnamese dishes at this small family restaurant are made from fresh, organic ingredients—as are their specialty smoothies, bubble tea, and coffee. The expected dishes are all deliciously there, but they're always experimenting with something new, such as Viet shaking beef and salted egg shrimp. **Known for:** creative frappes, smoothies, and shakes; diverse Vietnamese menu including keto options; neighborhood friendliness. [$] *Average main: $15* ✉ *2442 N. Harrison St., Arlington* ☎ *703/270–9466* 🌐 *www.chillzonecafe.com* [M] *East Falls Church.*

★ Inn at Little Washington

$$$$ | **FRENCH** | A 90-minute drive from the District takes you past hills and farms to the English-style country manor that is the site of this well-regarded hotel

Did You Know?

The Pentagon's 9/11 Memorial, dedicated on September 11, 2008, remembers the 184 people who lost their lives at the Pentagon that horrific day (59 aboard American Airlines Flight 77 and 125 inside the Pentagon). The youngest victim was 3, the oldest 71, and their memorial benches are presented in order of age.

restaurant. The service matches the setting, and diners can choose items from two menus: Gastronauts (contemporary endeavors) or Good Earth (vegetarian), both of which have dishes that rotate daily. **Known for:** themed (and pricey) tasting menus; special-occasion dining destination; old English manor vibe. [$] *Average main: $325* ✉ *309 Middle St., Washington* ✣ *At Main St.* ☎ *540/675–3800* 🌐 *www.theinnatlittlewashington.com* ⏲ *Closed Mon. and Tues. (hotel closed Tues.).*

★ Kabob Palace

$ | AFGHAN | FAMILY | Authentic, friendly, and local, the Kabob Palace is open 24 hours a day, seven days a week. The chicken, lamb, and spicy beef kabobs are cooked to perfection and best dipped in chutney sauce and chased with a bite of naan. **Known for:** authentic kebabs; crispy, chewy naan; open 24/7. [$] *Average main: $15* ✉ *2315 S. Eads St., Arlington* ☎ *703/486–3535* 🌐 *www.kabobpalaceusa.com* [M] *Crystal City.*

Ruthie's All-Day

$$ | SOUTHERN | A modern take on Southern dining, Ruthie's offers meat-and-three (or two), meaning diners pick a meat dish and their choice of sides. Most of the meats—running from brisket to salmon to strip loin—are prepared on a smoker or wood grill, while the crisp-topped macaroni and cheese is the most popular side. **Known for:** mushroom scramble and apple pie pancakes for breakfast; not-too-sweet skillet cornbread with honey butter; a spacious patio ideal for families and dogs. [$] *Average main: $25* ✉ *3411 5th St. S, Arlington* ☎ *703/888–2841* 🌐 *www.ruthiesallday.com* [M] *Ballston.*

★ 2941 Restaurant

$$$$ | FRENCH FUSION | Soaring ceilings, a woodsy lakeside location, and a koi pond make this one of the most striking dining rooms in the area. Executive chef Bertrand Chemel's introduction to cooking began with an apprenticeship at a French bakery, and his flair for rising dough shows. **Known for:** romantic date-night dining; gorgeous views; elegant decor. [$] *Average main: $45; $110 for tasting menu* ✉ *2941 Fairview Park Dr., Falls Church* ☎ *703/270–1500* 🌐 *www.2941.com* ⏲ *No lunch. Closed Sun. and Mon.*

Hotels

Across the Potomac, with excellent Metro access and views of D.C., you'll find Arlington County, one of the largest districts in the Washington metro area. Its neighborhoods include Pentagon City with its three popular malls: Pentagon Row, Fashion Centre, and Pentagon Centre; Crystal City with its underground network of corridors linking offices and shops to high-rise apartments; Ballston, home to the Washington Capitals National Hockey League training facility; and Rosslyn, a former ferry landing turned transportation hub for rail, car, and bike. These thriving communities might not offer as much as D.C. proper, but they have everything the weary traveler might need in terms of accommodations, cuisine, and entertainment, sometimes at a more affordable price point.

Hyatt Centric Arlington

$ | HOTEL | If you're feeling energetic, it's just a 15-minute walk to Georgetown over Key Bridge from this solid, over-the-Potomac choice, but if energy is lacking, the hotel is just across from the Rosslyn Metro station. **Pros:** across from a Metro station; runners and walkers can receive trail maps and GPS watches; nice-size rooms. **Cons:** dull neighborhood; not great for kids; not close to any major sights. [$] *Rooms from: $179* ✉ *1325 Wilson Blvd., Arlington* ☎ *855/680–3239, 703/525–1234* 🌐 *www.hyatt.com* 🛏 *318 rooms* 🍴 *No Meals* [M] *Rosslyn.*

Le Méridien Arlington

$$$ | HOTEL | This modern gem, just over the bridge from Georgetown and steps from the Metro, offers stylish and comfortable rooms, many with great views of the Potomac River. **Pros:** convenient to Metro and Arlington cemetery; nice artwork throughout; great views of the skyline. **Cons:** fee for in-room Wi-Fi unless you're an SPG member; no in-room coffeemakers; some rooms are small. [$] *Rooms from: $353* ✉ *1121 N. 19th St.* ☎ *855/516–1090, 703/351–9170* 🌐 *www.marriott.com* 🛏 *154 rooms* 🍴 *No Meals* [M] *Rosslyn.*

Renaissance Arlington Capital View Hotel

$ | **HOTEL** | Spacious rooms, excellent service, and a good on-site contemporary Italian restaurant all add up to an excellent hotel choice outside the city. **Pros:** nice-size fitness center; stunning lobby with dramatic artwork; delightful coffee shop. **Cons:** expensive overnight parking; noise from trains on one side of hotel; a bit of a walk to restaurants. [$] *Rooms from: $200* ✉ *2800 S. Potomac Ave., Arlington* ☎ *703/413–1300* 🌐 *www.marriott.com* 🛏 *300 rooms* 🍴 *No Meals* [M] *Crystal City or Ronald Reagan Washington National Airport.*

The Ritz-Carlton Pentagon City

$$$ | **HOTEL** | **FAMILY** | The feel is more contemporary and casual-chic than what is generally associated with this luxury chain, and it's convenient for both downtown D.C. and Ronald Reagan Washington National Airport, with direct access to the Metro. **Pros:** connected to shops and restaurants; welcome amenity kit for children; 24-hour fitness center. **Cons:** daily fee for Wi-Fi; less luxurious than other Ritz properties; expensive, given the location. [$] *Rooms from: $362* ✉ *1250 S. Hayes St., Arlington* ☎ *703/415–5000, 800/241–3333* 🌐 *www.ritzcarlton.com/pentagoncity* 🛏 *366 rooms* 🍴 *No Meals* [M] *Pentagon City.*

Nightlife

Just across the Potomac, Arlington and Alexandria boast some top-notch bars and lounges—with considerably more parking and less hectic traffic than D.C. Also accessible by the Metro, revitalized Ballston and Clarendon are interesting and enjoyable, though more laid-back, even quiet, places to visit at night.

MUSIC CLUBS

State Theatre

LIVE MUSIC | This is the place to go to see concerts by aging hit makers from the past such as the Smithereens or tribute bands to the likes of Led Zeppelin, Pink Floyd, and Bon Jovi. Attendees have the choice of sitting or standing in this renovated movie theater, which is about 10 miles west of D.C. The popular 1980s retro dance parties, featuring the Legwarmers tribute band, draw locals who like to dress the part. ✉ *220 N. Washington St., Falls Church* ☎ *703/237–0300* 🌐 *www.thestatetheatre.com* [M] *E. Falls Church.*

Performing Arts

Suburban Virginia is home to a number of outstanding performance venues offering Shakespeare, opera, dance, popular music, and more. Arlington's Signature Theatre stages some of the best musical productions in the area and is only a short trip from downtown Washington, while Synetic Theatre, made nationally famous by its production of *Silent Hamlet*, is but a Metro stop away in Crystal City.

MAJOR VENUES

George Mason University Center for the Arts

ARTS CENTERS | This state-of-the-art performance complex on the suburban Virginia campus of George Mason University satisfies music, ballet, jazz, dance, and drama patrons with regular performances in its 2,000-seat concert hall, the 460-seat proscenium Harris Theatre, and an intimate 140-seat black-box theater. ✉ *George Mason University, 4373 Mason Pond Dr., Fairfax* ☎ *703/993–2787* 🌐 *cfa.gmu.edu.*

Wolf Trap National Park for the Performing Arts

ARTS CENTERS | At the only national park dedicated to the performing arts, the 7,000-seat outdoor Filene Center (half of them sitting on the sloping lawn) hosts more than 80 performances from June through September. They range from pop and jazz concerts to dance and musical theater productions. The National Symphony Orchestra performs here in summer, and the Children's Theatre-in-the-Woods, running for seven weeks, delivers 40 free interactive performances, including puppetry, dance, and storytelling. In colder months, the intimate, indoor Barns at Wolf Trap fill with the sounds of musicians playing folk, country, and chamber music, along with many other styles. The park is just off the Dulles Toll Road (Va. Rte. 267), about 20 miles from downtown Washington. WMATA provides round-trip bus service from the McLean Metro stop to the Filene Center during summer events. ✉ *1551 Trap Rd., Vienna* ☎ *703/255–1900 general info, 703/255–1868 ticket info and performance-related questions* ⊕ *www.wolftrap.org* Ⓜ *McLean.*

THEATER

Signature Theatre

THEATER | The Tony Award–winning Signature Theatre company has earned national acclaim for its presentation of world premiere and reimagined musicals, especially those of Stephen Sondheim, as well as contemporary plays. Signature's modern facility has two intimate black-box performance spaces where theatergoers can see Broadway-caliber shows performed with live orchestras 50 feet or less from the stage. ✉ *4200 Campbell Ave.* ☎ *703/820–9771 box office* ⊕ *www.sigtheatre.org.*

Synetic Theatre

THEATER | FAMILY | One of the most distinctive performing arts groups in the Washington area uses music, dance, high energy, acting, and athleticism to transform the works of Shakespeare, Dante, Edgar Allan Poe, and Robert Louis Stevenson into visual theatrics that are guaranteed to leave audiences fascinated. The award-winning theater is tucked away in Virginia's Crystal City, a short Metro ride away from downtown Washington. ✉ *1800 S. Bell St., Arlington* ☎ *703/824–8060 Ext. 117 box office* ⊕ *syenetictheater.org* Ⓜ *Crystal City.*

Chapter 14

SIDE TRIPS TO MARYLAND

Updated by
Akilah Stroman

⊙ Sights	🍴 Restaurants	🛏 Hotels	👜 Shopping	🍸 Nightlife
★★★★★	★★★★☆	★★★★☆	★★★☆☆	★★★☆☆

WELCOME TO
SIDE TRIPS TO MARYLAND

TOP REASONS TO GO

★ **Feast on some crabs:**
Head east to Annapolis on the Chesapeake Bay, and enjoy a Maryland specialty: blue crabs by the bushel (the bib is optional).

★ **"Little America":** With almost every biome (except for the desert) within the state, there is never a lack of something new to do in Maryland.

★ **Explore National Harbor:**
Take in the views of D.C., Maryland, and Virginia from the many hotels, restaurants, and even an observation wheel.

★ **"Charm City":** Shopping, art, architecture, and a sprawling pier are just a few of the things that make Baltimore so special.

With just a bit of planning, any one of these trips can be done in a day or even an afternoon.

1 National Harbor.
Washington's newest entertainment destination is just a water taxi ride away from the National Mall. The biggest draw is the new MGM National Harbor Hotel and Casino, which already accounts for more than 40% of Maryland's total gaming revenue.

2 C&O Canal National Historic Park. The Maryland side of the Potomac River offers dramatic waterfalls, picnic areas, and bike paths. The dramatic and beautiful Great Falls are on the Virginia side of the Potomac.

3 Annapolis. Maryland's capital is a popular destination for seafood lovers and boating fans. The city's nautical reputation is enhanced by the presence of the U.S. Naval Academy. It also has one of the country's largest assemblages of 18th-century architecture.

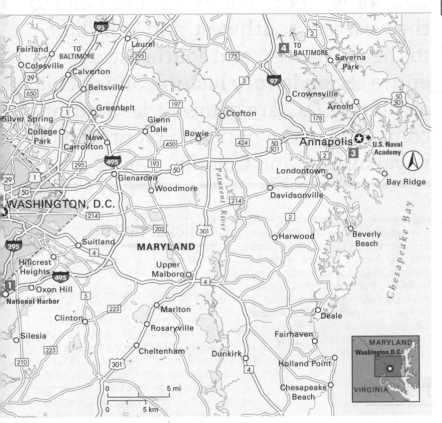

4 Baltimore. Thirty-nine miles north of Washington—a trip made easy by the MARC commuter rail's weekend Penn Line service ($7 each way)—Baltimore's burgeoning restaurant scene has earned national acclaim. But crabs and Old Bay aren't the only things on the menu. A world of fine flavors—Afghan, Indian, Italian, Japanese, Korean, and Spanish, among others—makes it a choice destination for foodies, especially given the outside-the-Beltway prices.

The District of Columbia was carved out of Maryland and Virginia in July 1790 and borders both states, with Virginia to the west and southwest, and Maryland to the north, east, and southeast. The entire region is very historic, and within an hour of D.C. are getaway destinations connected to the nation's first president, naval history, and Colonial events.

In Maryland, you can visit a historic canal that was begun in the early 18th century to connect Washington, D.C., to Cumberland, MD. Another option is to get out on the water in Annapolis, a major center for boating and home to the U.S. Naval Academy. Feast on Chesapeake Bay's famous crabs, then watch the midshipmen parade on campus at the academy. Or you can visit the booming city of Baltimore.

Planning

Getting Here and Around

All of these side trips can be reached within an hour from D.C. if you have a car. Just be aware that parking can be difficult in some places.

Most of these destinations can be reached by public transportation (though in the case of Annapolis, not easily). But Gunston Hall and the sections of the C&O Canal outside Georgetown are only reachable by car.

National Harbor

12 miles south of Downtown Washington, D.C., 2 miles west of Oxon Hill.

National Harbor sprawls across 350 acres of previously abandoned banks of the Potomac River, across from Old Town Alexandria. It's about a 25-minute water taxi ride from the National Mall and provides an alternative if you're D.C.-bound and don't mind commuting. While only one-quarter as tall as the London Eye, the Capital Wheel's 42 glass-enclosed gondolas soar 180 feet above the Potomac River, affording breathtaking views over the District.

Shopping and dining is a mix of big names and successful family-owned businesses.

The new MGM National Harbor Hotel and Casino brings Las Vegas–style entertainment inside the Beltway, while its upscale boutiques and shops, including Sarah Jessica Parker's eponymous shoe store, aim for mass appeal.

To Get To:	By Car:	By Public Transit:
Alexandria	George Washington Memorial Pkwy. or Jefferson Davis Hwy. (Rte. 1) south from Arlington (10 mins)	The Blue or Yellow Line to the King St.–Old Town Metro stop (25 mins from Metro Center)
Mount Vernon	Exit 1 off the Beltway; follow signs to George Washington Memorial Pkwy. southbound (30 mins)	The Yellow Line to the Huntington Metro stop, then Fairfax County Connector Bus No. 101, 151, or 159 (45–50 mins); ferry from Pier 4 (90 minutes)
Woodlawn	Rte. 1 southwest to the second Rte. 235 intersection; entrance is on the right at the traffic light (40 mins)	Bus No. 101, 151, or 159 from Huntington Metro station (45–50 mins)
Gunston Hall	Rte. 1 south to Rte. 242; turn left and go 3½ miles to entrance (30 mins)	No Metro or bus
Annapolis	U.S. 50 east to the Rowe Blvd. Exit (35–45 mins, except during weekday rush hour when it may take twice as long)	Amtrak from Union Station to BWI; MTA Light Rail from BWI to Patapsco Light Rail Station; transfer to Bus No. 14 (2 hrs)
C&O Canal	George Washington Memorial Pkwy. northwest 15.1 miles (30 mins)	No Metro or bus
National Harbor	I–295 South 10 miles (30 mins)	Water taxi from The Wharf (45 mins)
Baltimore	Baltimore–Washington Pkwy. 39 miles (1 hr)	MARC Penn Line or Amtrak train from Union Station (28–60 mins)

GETTING HERE AND AROUND

The easiest way to reach National Harbor is by car via Interstate 295, Interstate 95, or Interstate 495, but keep in mind that neither street nor garage parking is free. Water taxis from Old Town Alexandria, the National Mall, or Georgetown are also convenient. Once in National Harbor, the National Harbor Circulator shuttle provides easy transport along Waterfront Street and between the Tanger Outlets, Gaylord National Resort, and MGM National Harbor Hotel for a onetime cost of $5, good for all-day riding.

TOURS

★ **Potomac Riverboat Company**

BOAT TOURS | **FAMILY** | Jump aboard a cruise ship from National Harbor's dock for a water tour of Mount Vernon, Alexandria, or Washington's monuments and memorials. The trip to Mount Vernon includes admission to the grounds. The company also operates water taxis across the Potomac to even more sightseeing, shopping, and dining options in Alexandria, Georgetown (transfer at Alexandria), The Wharf, or the National Mall. ✉ *Commercial Pier, 145 National Plaza, National Harbor* ☎ *703/684–0580, 877/511–2628* ⊕ *www.potomacriverboatco.com* 🎫 *Round-trip $21.*

[👁] Sights

The Awakening

PUBLIC ART | FAMILY | This sculpture, created by J. Seward Johnson, depicts a 72-foot giant struggling to free himself from the earth and is actually five separate pieces buried in the ground. The statue was originally at Hains Point in Washington but was moved to National Harbor in 2008. Feel free to climb all over the giant; everyone else does. ✉ *National Plaza* ⏲ *Closed Tues.*

★ The Capital Wheel

VIEWPOINT | FAMILY | Stunning at sunset, the nearly 200-foot ascent on this giant Ferris wheel affords views of Alexandria's Masonic Temple, the Washington Monument, and the U.S. Capitol, lasting approximately 15 minutes. Glass-enclosed gondolas are climate-controlled and wheelchair-accessible. Landlubbers can enjoy drinks and Potomac vistas from the Flight Deck bar at the base of the wheel since admission tickets are not required. ✉ *141 American Way, National Harbor* ☎ *301/842–8650* 🌐 *thecapitalwheel.com* 🎟 *$15.*

🍴 Restaurants

★ Old Hickory Steakhouse

$$$$ | STEAKHOUSE | The signature restaurant of the Gaylord National Resort, Old Hickory is perfect for a romantic meal watching the sun set over the harbor or for an expense-account evening of cocktails and fine cigars out on the terrace. The signature 24-ounce porterhouse comes with four sauce choices: béarnaise, bordelaise, green peppercorn, and blue cheese. **Known for:** prime cuts of meat; waterfront views; excellent cheese courses. [$] *Average main: $55* ✉ *Gaylord National Resort & Convention Center, 201 Waterfront St., National Harbor* ☎ *301/965–4000* 🌐 *www.oldhickoryrestaurant.com* ⏲ *Closed Mon.–Wed.*

The Walrus Oyster & Ale House

$$$ | SEAFOOD | FAMILY | Inspired by the Lewis Carroll poem, "The Walrus and the Carpenter," this restaurant is a gem for excellent seafood and views. Come here for a crab cake sandwich or select from the list of fresh, briny Chesapeake oysters in a casual, modern pub setting. **Known for:** all things oysters; patio seating; friendly service. [$] *Average main: $30* ✉ *152 Waterfront St., National Harbor* ☎ *301/567–6100* 🌐 *www.walrusoysterandale.com.*

🛏 Hotels

AC Hotel National Harbor

$ | HOTEL | Loftlike spaces, dramatic art, and lounge seating in the second-floor lobby create a minimalistic atmosphere more like a nightclub than your standard Marriott hotel. **Pros:** outdoor patio and fantastic views of the Capital Wheel and Potomac River; free in-room Wi-Fi; more affordable than most of the other hotels in National Harbor. **Cons:** small closets; expensive valet parking on-site or cheaper off-site self-parking; small fitness room. [$] *Rooms from: $179* ✉ *156 Waterfront St., National Harbor* ☎ *301/749–2299* 🌐 *www.marriott.com* 🔑 *192 rooms* 🍽 *No Meals.*

Gaylord National Resort and Convention Center

$$ | HOTEL | FAMILY | Guests at this larger-than-life resort can dine, shop, get pampered, and even go clubbing without ever leaving the property, which anchors the National Harbor waterfront and, with about a 25-minute ride to the National Mall, provides an alternative to the more expensive options downtown. **Pros:** waterfront location; water taxi to Alexandria and National Mall; full-service spa, fitness center, and indoor pool. **Cons:** downtown D.C. is fairly far; extra per-day resort fee; resort might be too big for some. [$] *Rooms from: $233*

✉ 201 Waterfront St., National Harbor ☎ 301/965–4000, 855/516–1090 reservations ⊕ www.marriott.com ⤶ 1996 rooms ⏾⃝ No Meals.

★ MGM National Harbor

$$$ | HOTEL | The newest addition to the Potomac waterfront at National Harbor is the ultramodern MGM. **Pros:** great restaurants by some of the nation's most celebrated chefs; awesome views from many of the public spaces and rooms; Maryland's most popular gambling venue. **Cons:** might be too overwhelming for some travelers; room rates are high; expensive nightly resort fee. ⓢ Rooms from: $370 ✉ 101 MGM National Ave., National Harbor ☎ 844/646–6847 ⊕ www.mgmnationalharbor.com ⤶ 308 rooms ⏾⃝ No Meals.

C&O Canal National Historic Park

Extends 13 miles west from George-town, including Great Falls Tavern, which is 23 miles northwest of Georgetown.

Although it was a vital link with the country's western territories, rapids and waterfalls along the 185 miles between Cumberland and Washington originally made it impossible for traders to travel the entire distance by boat. Upon completion in 1850, the Chesapeake & Ohio Canal, with its 74 locks, provided an economical and practical way for traders to move goods through the Washington area to the lower Chesapeake, but floods and competition from the B&O Railroad would end traffic less than a century later. The railroad transferred ownership of the canal to the federal government in 1938 to settle a $2 million debt. Since 1971, the canal has been a national park, providing a window into the past and a marvelous place to enjoy the outdoors.

C&O Canal National Historic Park originates in Georgetown and encloses a 184½-mile towpath that ends in Cumberland, Maryland. This relic of America's canal-building era and a few structures are still there.

GETTING HERE AND AROUND

C&O Canal National Historic Park is along the Maryland side of the Potomac and is accessible by taking Canal Road or MacArthur Boulevard from Georgetown or by taking Exit 41 off the Beltway and then following the signs to Carderock. Along the southbound lanes of Canal Road are several roadside spots where you can park and visit restored canal locks and lock houses.

To reach Great Falls Park, take the scenic and winding Route 193 (Exit 13 off Route 495, the Beltway) to Route 738 (Old Dominion Drive), and follow the signs. It takes about 25 minutes to drive to the park from the Beltway.

◉ Sights

Clara Barton National Historic Site

HISTORIC HOME | Beside Glen Echo Park's parking lot is this monument to the founder of the American Red Cross. Barton first used the structure, built by the founders of Glen Echo village, to store Red Cross supplies; later it became both her home and the organization's headquarters. Today, the building is furnished with period artifacts and many of her possessions. Access is by a 45-minute guided tour only, typically offered only on Friday and Saturday. Check the park's website to plan your visit. ✉ 5801 Oxford Rd., Glen Echo ☎ 301/320–1410 ⊕ www.nps.gov/clba ⓢ Free ⊘ Closed Sun.–Thurs.

★ Great Falls Park

NATIONAL PARK | FAMILY | Facing the C&O Canal National Historical Park across the Potomac River on the Virginia side, this

Started as a dream of boat passage to the West, the C&O Canal National Historic Park has a lot to see for 184.5 miles

is where the steep, jagged falls of the Potomac roar into the narrow Mather Gorge, the rocky narrows that make the Potomac churn. No matter the time of year, the views of the falls and river are spectacular, and more than 150 species of birds make their home in and around the 800-acre park. Great Falls Park is a favorite for outings; here you can follow trails past the old Patowmack Canal and among the boulders and forests lining the edge of the falls. There are three overlooks in the park, two of which are accessible to people with disabilities. Camping and alcoholic beverages are not allowed, but you can fish (a Virginia or Maryland license is required), climb rocks (climbers must register first at the visitor center or lower parking lot), or—if you're an experienced boater with your own equipment—go white-water kayaking (*below* the falls only).

⚠ **As is true all along this stretch of the river, the currents are deadly. Despite frequent signs and warnings, there are those who occasionally dare the water and drown.**

Staff members conduct special tours and walks year-round. ✉ *9200 Old'Dominion Dr., McLean* ☎ *703/757–3101* ⊕ *www. nps.gov/grfa* ✉ *$20 per vehicle; $80 for annual pass.*

🏃 Activities

The C&O Canal National Historic Park and its towpath are favorites of walkers, joggers, bikers, and canoeists. The path has a slight grade, which makes for a leisurely ride or hike. Most recreational bikers consider the 13 miles from Georgetown to Great Falls Tavern an easy ride; you need to carry your bike for only one short stretch of rocky ground near Great Falls. You can also take a bike path that parallels MacArthur Boulevard and runs from Georgetown to Great Falls Tavern. Storm damage has left parts of the canal dry, but many segments remain intact and navigable by canoe.

BOAT TOURS
C&O Canal Barges
BOAT TOURS | FAMILY | During one-hour rides on mule-drawn barges along the C&O Canal at Great Falls, costumed guides and volunteers explain the history of the waterway. Run by the National Park Service, the barge rides depart from its visitor center on weekends, from April through October. Check with park service about tour availability. ⊠ *Great Falls Tavern Visitor Center, 11710 MacArthur Blvd., Potomac* ☎ *301/739–4200* ⊕ *www. nps.gov/choh* ⊠ *$8.*

Annapolis

32 miles east of Washington, D.C.

This beautiful city, the capital of Maryland, offers something for everyone. Whether you spend one or several days here, you'll discover fascinating history; exciting sporting, visual, and performing arts events; great dining, shopping, and nightlife; and dozens of recreational activities. There are more 18th-century brick homes in Annapolis than in any other city in the nation, and, because the city is so walkable, it is truly a walk down memory lane. It's also a popular boating destination, and, on warm sunny days, the waters off City Dock become center stage for boats of all sizes. If you love the water, the Chesapeake Bay, and the area's winding inlets, creeks, and rivers provide wonderful opportunities for paddleboarding, kayaking, sailing, or fishing. One of Annapolis's longest-standing institutions is the U.S. Naval Academy, which has been training officers for the U.S. Navy and Marine Corps since 1845. As you stroll through downtown, you'll often see midshipmen in their crisp white uniforms in summer and navy blue in winter. A visit to the Naval Academy campus, to learn about its lengthy and proud history

and get a close-up look at what life as a midshipman is like, is a must.

GETTING HERE AND AROUND
The drive (east on U.S. 50 to the Rowe Boulevard exit) normally takes 35–45 minutes from Washington. During rush hour (weekdays 3:30–6:30 pm), however, it takes about twice as long. Also, beware of Navy football Saturdays.

Parking spots on the historic downtown streets of Annapolis are scarce, but there are some meters for $2 an hour (maximum two hours). You can park on some residential streets for free for two hours, and on Sunday morning from 6 am to 1 pm, most parking is free. The public garage adjacent to the Annapolis Visitors Center charges $2 per hour with a daily maximum of $15. The Annapolis Circulator offers free trolley transportation within the historic area.

TOURS
Walking tours are a great way to see the historic district, and Discover Annapolis Tours and Watermark run historical and ghost tours. Watermark and Schooner *Woodwind* Cruises offer boat trips.

Discover Annapolis Tours
BUS TOURS | Narrated 40- and 50-minute trolley tours, departing from the visitor center, introduce you to the history and architecture of Annapolis. Sights include Maryland State House, WWII Memorial, and water views. ⊠ *26 West St., Annapolis* ☎ *410/626–6000* ⊕ *www.discoverannapolis.com* ⊠ *From $15.*

Schooner *Woodwind* Cruises
BOAT TOURS | Two 74-foot sailboats, *Woodwind* and *Woodwind II*, make daily trips and overnight excursions. Guests aboard the two-hour cruises are guaranteed to see sites like the Chesapeake Bay and United States Naval Academy. Depending on the wind direction and speed, cruisers may also see the Chesapeake Bay Bridge (perhaps even going underneath),

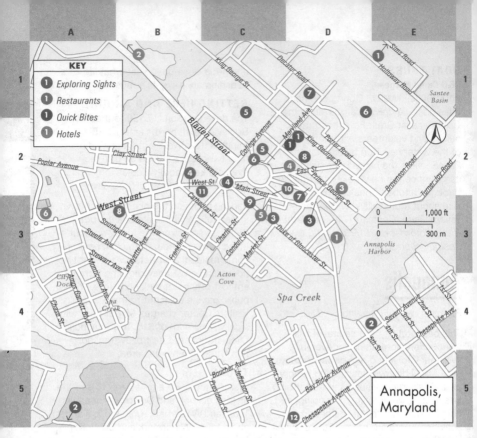

Annapolis, Maryland

Sights ▼

1 Hammond-Harwood House **D2**
2 Historic London Town and Gardens............. **A5**
3 Kunta Kinte–Alex Haley Memorial **D3**
4 St. Anne's Episcopal Church **C2**
5 St. John's College........ **C1**
6 United States Naval Academy **D1**
7 U.S. Naval Academy Museum **D1**
8 William Paca House and Garden.............. **D2**

Restaurants ▼

1 Cantler's Riverside Inn.. **E1**
2 Carrol's Creek Cafe..... **D4**
3 Chick and Ruth's Delly...................... **C3**
4 49 West Coffeehouse, Winebar, and Gallery.... **B2**
5 Galway Bay Irish Restaurant and Pub..... **C2**
6 Harry Browne's **C2**
7 Iron Rooster **D2**
8 Metropolitan Kitchen & Lounge **B3**
9 Osteria 177 .... **C3**
10 Preserve **C2**
11 Rams Head Tavern **C2**
12 Vin 909 Winecafé **D5**

Quick Bites ▼

1 Old Fox Books and Coffeehouse **D2**

Hotels ▼

1 Annapolis Waterfront Hotel, Autograph Collection................. **D3**
2 Country Inn & Suites by Radisson, Annapolis, MD **B1**
3 Gibson's Lodgings of Annapolis............... **D2**
4 Historic Inns of Annapolis................. **C2**
5 Scotlaur Inn **C3**
6 The Westin Annapolis............... **A3**

Thomas Point Lighthouse, and the Annapolis skyline. ⊠ *Annapolis Waterfront Hotel dock, 80 Compromise St., Annapolis* ☎ *410/263–7837, 410/263–1981* ⊕ *www.schoonerwoodwind.com* ⊠ *From $70.*

★ **Watermark**

WALKING TOURS | Tour guides wearing Colonial-style dress take you to the State House, St. John's College, and the Naval Academy on their very popular twice-daily, 2¼-hour "Four Centuries Walking Tour." There's a "Historic Ghost Walk" on weekends. Watermark also runs boat tours, lasting from 40 minutes to 7½ hours, going as far as St. Michael's on the Eastern Shore, where there's a maritime museum as well as dining and boutiques. ⊠ *1 Dock St., Annapolis* ☎ *410/268–7601* ⊕ *www.watermarkjourney.com* ⊠ *From $20* ⊙ *Closed Sun.*

VISITOR INFORMATION

CONTACTS Visit Annapolis & Anne Arundel County. ⊠ *26 West St., Annapolis* ☎ *410/280–0445, 888/302–2852* ⊕ *www.visitannapolis.org.* **Visitor Information Booth.** ⊠ *1 Dock St., Annapolis* ⊹ *Ego Alley* ☎ *410/280–0445* ⊕ *www.visitannapolis.org.*

◉ Sights

Hammond-Harwood House

HISTORIC HOME | Based on the Villa Pisani in Montagnana, Italy, this 1774 home was a Colonial high-style residence. Currently, the museum is working to provide and present greater visibility and documentation about those enslaved at Hammond-Harwood House, including wills and letters. Up to seven women, men, and children were enslaved here in the 19th century, according to census records, and a slavery exhibition documents what scholars and historians have learned about them thus far. There are also exhibits of Colonial art by Charles

Willson Peale and Rembrandt Peale, as well as displays of decorative arts— everything from Chinese-export porcelain to Georgian-period silver. ⊠ *19 Maryland Ave., Annapolis* ☎ *410/263–4683* ⊕ *www.hammondharwoodhouse.org* ⊠ *$10* ⊙ *Closed Tues. By reservation Apr.–Dec.*

Historic London Town and Gardens

HISTORIC HOME | The 17th-century tobacco port of London, on the South River a short car ride from Annapolis, was made up of 40 dwellings, shops, and taverns. London all but disappeared in the 18th century, its buildings abandoned and left to decay, but one of the few remaining original Colonial structures is a three-story brick house, built by William Brown between 1758 and 1764, with dramatic river views. Newly reconstructed buildings include a tenement for lower-class workers, a carpenter's shop, and a barn. Guests can walk around on their own or take a 30-minute docent-led tour. Allow more time to wander the house grounds, woodland gardens, and a visitor center with an interactive exhibit on the area's archaeology and history. ⊠ *839 Londontown Rd., Edgewater* ☎ *410/222–1919* ⊕ *www.historiclondontown.org* ⊠ *$10* ⊙ *Closed Mon. and Tues.*

Kunta Kinte–Alex Haley Memorial

HISTORIC SIGHT | **FAMILY** | The Story Wall, comprising 10 plaques along the waterfront, recounts the history of African Americans in Maryland. These granite-framed markers lead to a sculpture group depicting Alex Haley, famed author of *Roots,* reading to a group of children of different ethnic backgrounds. Here you'll also see a plaque that commemorates the 1767 arrival of Kunta Kinte, who was brought from Africa, sold into slavery, and later immortalized in Haley's novel. Across the street is "The Compass Rose," a 14-foot-diameter inlaid bronze map of the world oriented to true north with Annapolis in the center. ⊠ *Sidewalk* *at City Dock, Annapolis ⊕ www.alexha-ley.com.*

St. Anne's Episcopal Church

RELIGIOUS BUILDING | In the center of one of the historic area's busy circles, this brick building is one of the city's most prominent places of worship. King William III donated the Communion silver when the parish was founded in 1692, but the first St. Anne's Church wasn't completed until 1704. The second church burned in 1858, but parts of its walls survived and were incorporated into the present structure, which was built the following year. Free guided tours are offered the first and third Monday of every month at 10 am and every Wednesday at 12:30 pm. The churchyard contains the grave of the last Colonial governor, Sir Robert Eden. ⊠ *Church Circle, Annapolis* ☎ *410/267–9333* ⊕ *www.stannes-annap-olis.org* ☞ *Free* ⊗ *Closed Sat.*

St. John's College

COLLEGE | St. John's is the third-oldest college in the country (after Harvard and William and Mary) and adheres to a Great Books program: all students follow the same four-year, liberal-arts curriculum, which includes philosophy, mathematics, music, science, Greek, and French. Students are immersed in the classics through small classes conducted as discussions rather than lectures. Start a visit here by climbing the slope of the long, brick-paved path to the cupola of McDowell Hall.

Down King George Street toward the water is the **Carroll-Barrister House,** now the college admissions office. Once home to Charles Carroll (not the signer of the Declaration, but his cousin), the house was built in 1722 at Main and Conduit streets and moved onto campus in 1955. The **Elizabeth Myers Mitchell Art Gallery,** on the east side of Mellon Hall, presents world-class exhibits and special programs that relate to the fine arts.

⊠ *60 College Ave., Annapolis* ☎ *410/263–2371* ⊕ *www.sjc.edu* ⊗ *Mitchell Gallery closed Mon.*

★ United States Naval Academy

COLLEGE | Probably the most interesting and important site in Annapolis, the Naval Academy, established in 1845, occupies 338 waterfront acres along the Severn River. The midshipmen (the term used for both women and men) go to classes, conduct military drills, and practice or compete in intercollegiate and intramural sports. Your visit to "The Yard" (as the USNA grounds are nicknamed) will start at the **Armel-Leftwich Visitor Center.** The visitor center features an exhibit, *The Quarter Deck,* which introduces visitors to the academy's mission, including a 13-minute film, *The Call to Serve,* and a well-stocked gift shop. From here you can join one of the hour-long, guided, walking tours of the academy. The centerpiece of the campus is the bright, copper-clad dome of the interdenominational **U.S. Naval Academy Chapel,** beneath which is buried Revolutionary War naval hero John Paul Jones. You can go inside Bancroft Hall (one of the world's largest dormitories) and see a sample room and the glorious Memorial Hall.

■ **TIP→ Visitors can have lunch on campus either at Drydock in Dahlgren Hall or the Naval Academy Club.** ⊠ *121 Blake Rd., Annapolis* ⊹ *Enter on foot through Visitor Access Center at Gate 1* ☎ *410/293–8687* ⊕ *www.usna.edu* ☞ *Free* ☞ *All visitors 18 years and older must have government-issued photo ID to be admitted. Visitors may not park on campus.*

U.S. Naval Academy Museum

HISTORY MUSEUM | **FAMILY** | Displays of model ships and memorabilia from naval heroes and fighting vessels tell the story of the U.S. Navy. The Rogers Ship Model Collection has nearly 80 models of sailing ships built for the British Admiralty, the largest display of 17th- and 18th-century

Did You Know?

The US Naval Academy, located at the base of the Severn River, covers over 330 acres. It is the only service campus adjacent to a city (Annapolis).

ship models in North America. Kids of all ages will enjoy watching the restoration and building of model ships on the ground level and might even learn a few tricks of the trade should they wish to purchase a model ship kit to build when they get home. ✉ *Preble Hall, 118 Maryland Ave., Annapolis* ✣ *On campus, so government-issued photo ID is required for visitors 18 and older* ☎ *410/293–2108* 🌐 *www.usna.edu* 🎟 *Free* 🕓 *Closed Tues.*

William Paca House and Garden
HISTORIC HOME | A signer of the Declaration of Independence, William Paca (pronounced "PAY-cuh") was a Maryland governor from 1782 to 1785. His house was built from 1763 through 1765, and its original garden was finished by 1772. The main floor (furnished with 18th-century antiques) retains its original Prussian blue–and–soft gray color scheme, and the second floor houses more 18th-century pieces. The adjacent 2-acre pleasure garden provides a longer perspective on the back of the house, plus worthwhile sights of its own: upper terraces, a Chinese Chippendale bridge, a pond, a wilderness area, physic garden, and formal arrangements. An inn, Carvel Hall, once stood in the gardens, now planted with 18th-century perennials. Guests can take a self-guided tour of the garden, but to see the house, take the docent-led tour. Private tours can be arranged. The last tour leaves 1½ hours before closing. ✉ *186 Prince George St., Annapolis* ☎ *410/990–4543* 🌐 *www.annapolis.org* 🎟 *$15* 🕓 *Closed Jan. and Feb.*

🍴 Restaurants

★ Cantler's Riverside Inn
$$$ | **SEAFOOD** | Jimmy Cantler, a native Marylander who worked as a waterman on Chesapeake Bay, founded this local institution 40 years ago. The no-nonsense interior has nautical items laminated beneath tabletops, and steamed mussels, clams, and shrimp as well as a tomato-based Maryland crab soup, seafood sandwiches, crab cakes, and much more. **Known for:** seasonal outdoor dining right next to the water; steamed crabs served on a "tablecloth" of brown paper; a classic casual Maryland seafood experience. [$] *Average main: $35* ✉ *458 Forest Beach Rd., Annapolis* ☎ *410/757–1311* 🌐 *www.cantlers.com.*

Carrol's Creek Cafe
$$$ | **AMERICAN** | You can walk, catch a water taxi from City Dock, or drive over the Spa Creek drawbridge to this local favorite in Eastport. Whether you dine indoors or out, the view of historic Annapolis and its harbor is spectacular. **Known for:** à la carte Sunday brunch; upscale (but not too pricey) seafood specialties; amazing city and harbor views. [$] *Average main: $34* ✉ *410 Severn Ave., Annapolis* ☎ *410/263–8102* 🌐 *www.carrolscreek.com.*

Chick and Ruth's Delly
$ | **AMERICAN** | Deli sandwiches (many named after local politicians), burgers, subs, crab cakes, and milkshakes are the fare at this very busy counter-and-booth institution. Baltimoreans Ruth and Chick Levitt purchased the building, built in 1899, in 1965. **Known for:** giant milkshakes (including a 6-pounder); patriotic decor and a daily recitation of the Pledge of Allegiance; homemade pies and breads. [$] *Average main: $9* ✉ *165 Main St., Annapolis* ☎ *410/269–6737* 🌐 *www.chickandruths.com.*

49 West Coffeehouse, Winebar, and Gallery
$$ | **ECLECTIC** | In what was once a hardware store, this casual eatery has one interior wall of exposed brick and another of exposed plaster; both are used to hang art for sale by local artists. Daily specials are chalked on a blackboard and include a large cheese-and-pâté plate, flatbread pizzas, deli sandwiches, espresso, waffles, soups, and salads.

Known for: live music every night; eclectic coffeehouse vibe; flatbread pizzas, deli sandwiches, and coffee galore. $ *Average main: $17* ⊠ *49 West St., Annapolis* ☎ *410/626–9796* ⊕ *49westcoffeehouse. com.*

★ Galway Bay Irish Restaurant and Pub
$ | IRISH | Step inside this Irish pub, and you'll be welcomed like a member of the family. As would be expected, the corned beef and cabbage and other traditional Irish menu items (along with classic Annapolis bar food like crab and oysters) are fantastic. Known for: traditional Irish grub and hospitality; authentic homemade corned-beef hash; Sunday brunch with live music. $ *Average main: $12* ⊠ *63 Maryland Ave., Annapolis* ☎ *301/263–8333* ⊕ *www.galwaybaymd. com.*

Harry Browne's
$$$ | AMERICAN | In the shadow of the state house, this understated establishment has long held a reputation for quality food and attentive service that ensures bustle year-round, especially during the busy days of the legislative session (early January into early April) and special weekend events at the Naval Academy. The menu clearly reflects the city's maritime culture, but also has seasonal specialties. Known for: political clientele; tasty homemade desserts, such as Oreo cheesecake; champagne brunch on Sunday. $ *Average main: $35* ⊠ *66 State Circle, Annapolis* ☎ *410/263–4332* ⊕ *www.harrybrownes.com.*

★ Iron Rooster
$ | AMERICAN | There's often a line of hungry diners waiting for a table at this comfort-food haven located on the city dock, where the portions are generous, and the service is first-rate. You can enjoy breakfast all day—Benedicts and omelets are top sellers, as are the chicken and waffles and the shrimp and grits. Known for: daily homemade Pop-Tart specials;

Southern-inspired all-day breakfast (including amazingly light-and-fluffy biscuits); long lines. $ *Average main: $15* ⊠ *12 Market Space, Annapolis* ☎ *410/990–1600* ⊕ *www.ironroosterall-day.com.*

Metropolitan Kitchen & Lounge
$$ | MEDITERRANEAN | One of the few restaurants in the city with a rooftop, this establishment co-owned by Annapolis mayor Gavin Buckley takes full advantage of its lovely perch and features live music most evenings. The menu satisfies global palates in a town otherwise known for Old Bay and crab cakes, bringing in a bit of Australian flair from the mayor's homeland. Known for: lamb burgers and traditional Greek salad; one of the few rooftop bars in town; craft cocktails. $ *Average main: $24* ⊠ *175 West St., Annapolis* ☎ *410/280–5160* ⊘ *Closed Mon.*

★ Osteria 177
$$$$ | MODERN ITALIAN | This might be the only local Italian restaurant that doesn't offer pizza or spaghetti. Instead, Osteria serves seafood from all over the world, meat, and pasta made on the premises. Known for: politicians and lobbyists at lunchtime; authentic coastal Italian cuisine; unique pastas. $ *Average main: $38* ⊠ *177 Main St., Annapolis* ☎ *410/267–7700* ⊕ *www.osteria177.com.*

Preserve
$$ | AMERICAN | Jars of pickled chard stems and radishes, preserved lemons, and pepper jelly line the shelves at this lively spot on Main Street run by a husband-and-wife team who both have impressive culinary resumés and a shared passion for pickling, fermenting, and preserving. The chef's roots in the Pennsylvania Dutch country shine through with chicken potpie, pork and sauerkraut, and a Dutch hash and liverwurst sandwich. Known for: varied dishes that highlight unique preservation methods; kimchi and sauerkraut galore;

lots of seasonal veggies. $ *Average main: $29* ✉ *164 Main St., Annapolis* ☎ *443/598–6920* ⊕ *www.preserve-eats. com* ⊙ *Closed Mon. and Tues.*

Rams Head Tavern

$ | BRITISH | This traditional English-style pub serves better-than-usual tavern fare, as well as more than 100 beers—30 on tap—including five Fordham beers and others from around the world. Brunch is served on Sunday, and nationally known folk, rock, jazz, country, and bluegrass artists perform most nights. **Known for:** Maryland cream of crab soup; massive beer menu; live music. $ *Average main: $15* ✉ *33 West St., Annapolis* ☎ *410/268–4545* ⊕ *www.ramsheadtavern.com.*

Vin 909 Winecafé

$ | AMERICAN | If it wasn't for the sign out front, you might think you're at someone's Eastport home, given the charming front porch and well-tended gardens. But walk through the doors, and you'll discover a casually hip and always crowded restaurant serving organic, sustainable, and seasonally focused food that's simply fantastic. **Known for:** crispy pizza with farm-to-table toppings; huge wine menu by the glass and bottle; diverse selection of beers. $ *Average main: $16* ✉ *909 Bay Ridge Ave., Annapolis* ☎ *410/990–1846* ⊕ *www.vin909.com* ⊙ *Closed Mon.*

☕ Coffee and Quick Bites

Old Fox Books and Coffeehouse

$ | BAKERY | With a carefully selected collection of new and used titles, this store is an oasis from the ubiquitous chains, and its café is a local favorite spot for an espresso drink or freshly baked pastry. After a bite, head outside to see the charming Fairy Garden and book house, which is literally made of books. **Known for:** popular meeting spot for locals; coffee drinks made with beans from local roaster, Ceremony Coffee; annual Harry Potter birthday party. $ *Average*

main: $7 ✉ *35 Maryland Ave., Annapolis* ☎ *410/626–2020* ⊕ *oldfoxbooks.com.*

🛏 Hotels

There are many places to stay near the heart of the city, as well as bed-and-breakfasts and chain motels a few miles outside town. Prices vary considerably. They rise astronomically for "Commissioning Week" at the Naval Academy (late May), the week of July 4, and during the sailboat and powerboat shows in October.

Annapolis Waterfront Hotel, Autograph Collection

$$$ | HOTEL | FAMILY | You can practically fish from your room at the city's only waterfront hotel (now part of Marriott's Autograph Collection), where rooms have either balconies over the water or large windows with views of the harbor or the historic district. **Pros:** "feather-free room" available for the allergy sensitive upon request; accessible for travelers with disabilities; complimentary Wi-Fi throughout. **Cons:** some rooms have no waterfront view, some have only partial views; chain hotel lacks charm; parking is pricey. $ *Rooms from: $299* ✉ *80 Compromise St., Annapolis* ☎ *410/268–7555* ⊕ *www. annapoliswaterfront.com* ⇱ *150 rooms* ❑ *No Meals.*

Country Inn & Suites by Radisson, Annapolis, MD

$ | HOTEL | Although this hotel is 5 miles from the historic Annapolis waterfront, there's a free shuttle, and the two-room suites with pullout sofas are perfect for families. **Pros:** reliable and inexpensive option; free shuttle services; complimentary Wi-Fi. **Cons:** distance from the dock; tiny gym; small indoor heated pool can be crowded at times. $ *Rooms from: $145* ✉ *2600 Housely Rd., Annapolis* ☎ *410/571–6700, 800/456–4000* ⊕ *www. countryinns.com* ⇱ *100 rooms* ❑ *Free Breakfast.*

Gibson's Lodgings of Annapolis

$$ | HOTEL | Just half a block from the water, the three detached houses that form this hotel come from three centuries—the years 1780, 1890, and 1980, to be exact—and all the guest rooms are furnished with pre-1900 antiques. **Pros:** conveniently located between the Naval Academy and downtown; free parking in the courtyards; free continental breakfast. **Cons:** cannot accommodate children under the age of eight; two of the rooms share a bathroom; no elevator, although three rooms are on the ground floor. $ Rooms from: $280 ✉ 110 Prince George St., Annapolis ☎ 410/268–5555, 877/330–0057 ⊕ www.gibsonslodgings. com ⇥ 20 rooms ⏺ Free Breakfast.

★ Historic Inns of Annapolis

$ | B&B/INN | Three 18th-century properties in the historic district—the Governor Calvert House, Robert Johnson House, and Maryland Inn—are grouped as one inn, all offering guest rooms individually decorated with antiques and reproductions. **Pros:** beautifully renovated historic properties; within walking distance of activities; lemonade or spiced cider served daily in the Calvert House. **Cons:** prices vary greatly; some rooms are small; $30 valet parking. $ Rooms from: $159 ✉ 58 State Circle, Annapolis ☎ 410/263–2641, 800/847–8882 ⊕ www. historicinnsofannapolis.com ⇥ 124 rooms ⏺ No Meals.

Scotlaur Inn

$ | B&B/INN | On the two floors above Chick and Ruth's Delly in the heart of the historic district, this family-owned B&B is cozy and characterful. **Pros:** a chance to stay above one of Annapolis's landmarks; half off in nearby parking garage; literally in the heart of town. **Cons:** not for those who prefer modern style; rooms are on the small side; no elevator. $ Rooms from: $100 ✉ 165 Main St., Annapolis ☎ 410/268–5665 ⊕ www.scotlaurinn.com ⇥ 10 rooms ⏺ Free Breakfast.

The Westin Annapolis

$$ | HOTEL | FAMILY | About 1½ miles from City Dock, in a rapidly gentrifying neighborhood, this hotel is the centerpiece of a European-themed planned community, complete with restaurants, shops, and condominiums. **Pros:** comfy "heavenly beds"; modern hotel with many amenities; spacious guest rooms. **Cons:** distance from the City Dock; Wi-Fi only free in public areas; lacking charm found in other historic properties. $ Rooms from: $249 ✉ 100 Westgate Circle, Annapolis ☎ 410/972–4300 ⊕ www.marriott.com ⇥ 225 rooms ⏺ No Meals.

Baltimore

39 miles northeast of Washington, D.C.

Baltimore is a city of distinct neighborhoods. While stellar downtown attractions such as the National Aquarium and the Inner Harbor draw torrents of tourists each year, much of the city's character can be found in districts like Hampden (the "p" is silent) and Federal Hill. Baltimore was one of the largest cities in early America, thanks to a protected harbor, which gave it a strategic advantage. Tourism grew dramatically in the early 1980s with the completion of the Harborplace shopping plaza and its crown jewel, the National Aquarium. Further development of the Inner Harbor, including Oriole Park at Camden Yards and M&T Bank Stadium, continued to fuel the city's resurgence.

GETTING HERE AND AROUND

If you are going to Baltimore by car, it's about an hour from Washington, D.C. Parking in the Inner Harbor area, where most tourist attractions are, can be expensive. Fell's Point is usually cheaper.

It's generally easier and faster (and cheaper, considering the cost of parking) to get to Baltimore from D.C. by train. MARC

Penn Line trains run from Union Station to Baltimore's Penn Station several times a day, including weekends, taking about 45 minutes and costing $7. You can also take Amtrak from Union Station to Baltimore Penn Station, but it's about twice as expensive. The Camden Line runs only during commuting hours on weekdays and takes a bit longer, but takes you to Camden Station, which is more convenient to the Inner Harbor sights. You can also take a bus from Union Station, but it generally takes longer.

Once in Baltimore, you can take the free Charm City Circulator shuttle (four bus lines plus a harbor ferry), or, if you are in a hurry, jump in a taxi or ride-share.

CONTACTS Charm City Circulator. ⊠ *1700 Cherry Hill Rd., Baltimore* ☎ *410/545–1956* ⊕ *www.charmcitycirculator. com.* **Maryland Transit Administration.** ☎ *800/325–7245, 410/539–5000* ⊕ *www. mta.maryland.gov.*

VISITOR INFORMATION
CONTACTS Baltimore Visitor Center. ⊠ *401 Light St., Inner Harbor* ☎ *877/225–8466* ⊕ *www.baltimore.org.*

◉ Sights

★ American Visionary Art Museum
ART MUSEUM | The nation's primary museum and education center for self-taught or "outsider" art has won great acclaim by both museum experts and those who don't even consider themselves art aficionados. Seven galleries exhibit the quirky creations—paintings, sculptures, relief works, and pieces that defy easy classification—of untrained "visionary" artists working outside the mainstream art world. In addition to the visual stimulation of amazingly intricate or refreshingly inventive works, reading the short bios of artists will give you insight to their often-moving spiritual and expressive motivations. The museum's unusual,

playful philosophy extends outside its walls, with large exhibits installed in a former whiskey warehouse, an outdoor movie theater, and a 55-foot whirligig twirling in the museum's plaza. ⊠ *800 Key Hwy., Federal Hill* ☎ *410/244–1900* ⊕ *www.avam.org* ⊠ *$16* ⊗ *Closed Mon. and Tues.*

★ Baltimore Museum of Art
ART MUSEUM | Works by Matisse, Picasso, Cézanne, Gauguin, van Gogh, and Monet are among the 90,000 paintings, sculptures, and decorative arts on exhibit at this impressive museum near Johns Hopkins University. Particular strengths include an encyclopedic collection of Postimpressionist paintings donated to the museum by the Cone sisters, Baltimore natives who were pioneer collectors of early-20th-century art. The museum also owns the world's second-largest collection of Andy Warhol works and many pieces of 18th- and 19th-century American painting and decorative arts. The museum's neoclassical main building was designed by John Russell Pope, the architect of the National Gallery in Washington. A $28-million renovation resulted in a new, interactive exhibition space, a renovated visitor's entrance, and a completely reworked contemporary wing. From Gertrude's, the museum restaurant, you can look out at 20th-century sculpture displayed in two landscaped gardens. ⊠ *10 Art Museum Dr., Charles Village* ☎ *443/573–1700* ⊕ *www.artbma. org* ⊠ *Free* ⊗ *Closed Mon. and Tues.*

★ Fort McHenry National Monument and Historic Shrine
MILITARY SIGHT | This star-shaped brick fort is forever associated with Francis Scott Key and "The Star-Spangled Banner," which Key penned while watching the British bombardment of Baltimore during the War of 1812. Through the next day and night, as the battle raged, Key strained to be sure, through the smoke and haze, that the flag still flew

Fort McHenry unique star-shaped fort is commonly associated with "The Star Spangled Banner" written by Francis Scott Key.

above Fort McHenry—indicating that Baltimore's defenders held firm. "By the dawn's early light" of September 14, 1814, he saw the 30- by 42-foot "Star-Spangled Banner" still aloft and was inspired to pen the words to a poem (set to the tune of an old English drinking song). The flag that flew above Fort McHenry that day had 15 stars and 15 stripes, and was hand-sewn for the fort. A visit to the fort includes a 15-minute history film, guided tour, and frequent living-history displays on summer weekends. To see how the formidable fortifications might have appeared to the bombarding British, catch a water taxi from the Inner Harbor to the fort instead of driving. ⊠ *2400 E. Fort Ave., Locust Point* ✛ *From Light St., take Key Hwy. for 1½ miles and follow signs* ☎ *410/962–4290* ⊕ *www.nps.gov/fomc* ⊠ *$15; Annual Pass: $45.*

George Peabody Library

LIBRARY | Known as a "cathedral of books," the five-story reading room is consistently listed among the world's most beautiful libraries. Designed by Edmund Lind, it opened to the public in 1878. Its gilded framework of cast iron and gold showcases more than 300,000 volumes printed from the 15th to the 19th centuries in the areas of archaeology, architecture, history, literature, travel, and art. ⊠ *17 E. Mt. Vernon Pl., Mount Vernon* ☎ *410/234–4943* ⊕ *peabodyevents.library.jhu.edu* ⊗ *Closed Fri. and Sat.*

The National Great Blacks in Wax Museum

OTHER MUSEUM | **FAMILY** | More than 100 wax figures on display recount the triumphs and trials of Africans and African Americans. The wax figures are accompanied by text and audio. Baltimoreans honored include Frederick Douglass, who as a youth lived and worked in Fells Point; singer Billie Holiday; and jazz composer

Sights ▼

1 American Visionary
   Art Museum **F9**
2 Baltimore Museum of Art......... **D1**
3 Fort McHenry National Monument
   and Historic Shrine................. **G9**
4 George Peabody Library.......... **D3**
5 The National Great Blacks
   In Wax Museum **J1**
6 Oriole Park at Camden Yards..... **A8**
7 Walters Art Museum............... **C3**
8 Washington Monument........... **D3**
9 Westminster Burying Ground
   and Catacombs **A5**

Restaurants ▼

1 Ambassador Dining Room........ **D1**
2 Azumi................................ **G8**
3 Charleston.......................... **H8**
4 Cinghiale............................ **G8**
5 The Food Market................... **D1**
6 Gertrude's **D1**
7 The Helmand **C2**
8 La Cuchara **D1**
9 Ouzo Bay............................ **H8**
10 The Prime Rib **E1**

Hotels ▼

1 1840s Carrollton Inn **G6**
2 Four Seasons Baltimore **G9**
3 Hilton Baltimore Inner Harbor.... **B7**
4 Hotel Monaco Baltimore........... **C6**
5 Hotel Revival **C3**
6 The Ivy Hotel **E1**
7 Marriott Baltimore Waterfront ... **G8**
8 Sagamore Pendry Baltimore **J9**

Eubie Blake. To get here from Mount Vernon, take Charles Street north and turn left at North Avenue. ✉ *1601 E. North Ave., East Baltimore* ☎ *410/563–3404* ⊕ *www.greatblacksinwax.org* 🎟 *$15* ⊙ *Closed Mon.–Wed.*

★ Oriole Park at Camden Yards
SPORTS VENUE | FAMILY | Home of the Baltimore Orioles, Camden Yards and the nearby area bustle on game days. Since it opened in 1992, this nostalgically designed baseball stadium has inspired other cities to emulate its neotraditional architecture and amenities. The Eutaw Street promenade, between the warehouse and the field, has a view of the stadium. Look for the brass baseballs embedded in the sidewalk that mark where home runs have cleared the fence, or visit the Orioles Hall of Fame display and the monuments to retired Orioles. Daily 90-minute tours take you to nearly every section of the ballpark, from the massive JumboTron scoreboard to the dugout to the state-of-the-art beer-delivery system. ✉ *333 W. Camden St., Downtown* ☎ *410/685–9800 general info, 410/547–6234 tour info, 888/848–2473 tickets to Orioles home games* ⊕ *www. orioles.com* 🎟 *Eutaw St. promenade free, tour $15.*

★ Walters Art Museum
ART MUSEUM | The Walters' prodigious collection of more than 30,000 artworks provides an organized overview of human history over 5,500 years, from the 3rd millennium BC to the early 20th century. The museum houses major collections of Renaissance, Baroque, and Asian art as well as one of the nation's best collections of Egyptian, Greek, Roman, Byzantine, and Ethiopian works. It also houses Medieval armor and artifacts, jewelry and decorative works, a gift shop, a family activities and arts center on the lower-level, and a café. ✉ *600 N. Charles St., Mount Vernon* ☎ *410/547–9000* ⊕ *www.thewalters.org* 🎟 *Free* ⊙ *Closed Mon. and Tues.*

★ Washington Monument
MONUMENT | FAMILY | Completed on July 4, 1829, the impressive monument was the first one dedicated to the nation's first president. An 18-foot statue depicting Washington caps the 160-foot white marble tower. The tower was designed and built by Robert Mills, the first architect born and educated in the United States; 19 years after completing Baltimore's Washington Monument, Mills designed and erected the national Washington Monument in D.C. After extensive restorations, the monument's lower-level museum has reopened; visitors can climb the 227-step circular staircase to the top and enjoy stunning bird's-eye vistas over downtown. ✉ *Mt. Vernon Pl., Mount Vernon* ☎ *202/426–6841* ⊕ *mvp-conservancy.org/the-monument* 🎟 *$6* ⊙ *Closed Mon. and Tues.*

Westminster Burying Ground and Catacombs
CEMETERY | The city's oldest cemetery is the final resting place of Edgar Allan Poe and other famous Marylanders, including 15 generals from the American Revolution and the War of 1812. Dating from 1786, the cemetery was originally known as the Old Western Burying Grounds. In the early 1850s, a city ordinance demanded that burial grounds be part of a church, so a building was constructed above the cemetery, creating catacombs beneath it. In the 1930s, the schoolchildren of Baltimore collected pennies to raise the necessary funds for Poe's monument. Tours of Westminster Hall (which include the Burying Ground and Catacombs) are offered from April through November every first and third Friday at 6:30 pm and every Saturday at 10 am. ✉ *University of Maryland, Westminster Hall, 519 W. Fayette St., Downtown* ☎ *410/706–2072 tour information and reservations* ⊕ *baltimore.org/listings/*

historic-sites/westminster-hall-burying-ground 🎫 *Cemetery free; tours $5.*

🍴 Restaurants

Ambassador Dining Room
$$ | INDIAN | A Tudor-style dining room in a 1930s apartment building is the setting for superb Indian fare. Go for the classics such as chicken *tikka masala* (grilled chicken in a sauce of red pepper, ginger, garlic, and yogurt) or *alu gobi* (spicy potatoes and cauliflower). **Known for:** outdoor dining in the lovely garden; excellent service; traditional Indian desserts. [$] *Average main: $26* ✉ *3811 Canterbury Rd., Tuscany-Canterbury* ☎ *410/366–1484* 🌐 *www.ambassadordining.com* 🕒 *Closed Mon.*

Azumi
$$$ | JAPANESE | In a town known for its local catch, Azumi's chef flies his fish in daily from Tokyo's famous fish market. Creative takes on Maryland specialties are sure to delight, such as the crab starter, made with tiny Sawagani crabs, which are fried whole and pop in your mouth like buttered popcorn. **Known for:** excellent sashimi, including fresh hamachi; extensive list of Japanese whiskeys; beautiful waterfront views in a luxury hotel setting. [$] *Average main: $35* ✉ *Four Seasons Hotel Baltimore, 725 Aliceanna St., Harbor East* ☎ *443/220–0477* 🌐 *www.azumirestaurant.com.*

★ Charleston
$$$$ | AMERICAN | Chef-owner Cindy Wolf's cuisine has a South Carolina Low Country accent with French roots—and the results are unparalleled. Inside the glowingly lit dining room, classics like she-crab soup and shrimp and grits complement more elegant fare, such as a lobster bisque spiced with curry or wild salmon with avocado. **Known for:** decadent desserts; excellent service; the city's most elegant dining room. [$] *Average main: $79* ✉ *1000 Lancaster St., Harbor East* ☎ *410/332–7373* 🌐 *www.charlestonrestaurant.com* 🕒 *Closed Sun.* 👔 *Jacket and tie.*

Cinghiale
$$ | ITALIAN | The spotlight is on wine at Cinghiale (pronounced *ching-GYAH-lay*), an open, inviting space with tall, wide windows. Enjoy hand-cut pastas such as tagliatelle with tender chicken, greens, and walnuts or lasagna with veal ragù. **Known for:** northern Italian fare; vast wine list of more than 600 bottles; sharp and unpretentious service. [$] *Average main: $22* ✉ *822 Lancaster St., Harbor East* ☎ *410/547–8282* 🌐 *www.cgeno.com* 🕒 *No lunch.*

The Food Market
$$ | FUSION | FAMILY | In the heart of Hampden, on "The Avenue" (36th Street), chef Chad Gauss presents some of Baltimore's most consistently excellent dining with a global reach. Try the Amish soft pretzels with cheddar-cheese dipping sauce as a starter, then move on to coconut green curry or the lamb with spaetzle. **Known for:** convivial atmosphere; popular Saturday and Sunday brunch with huge pours; desserts like Heath bar bread pudding. [$] *Average main: $26* ✉ *1017 W. 36th St., Hampden* ☎ *410/366–0606* 🌐 *www.thefoodmarketbaltimore.com* 🕒 *No lunch weekdays.*

Gertrude's
$$ | AMERICAN | In the Baltimore Museum of Art, this casual yet classy spot cooks up creative Maryland specialties. Crab cakes, served with a variety of tasty sauces, are one option, Parmesan-crusted salmon is another. **Known for:** lovely outdoor terrace overlooking the sculpture garden; a commitment to sustainable Chesapeake cuisine; Sunday jazz brunch. [$] *Average main: $25* ✉ *Baltimore Museum of Art, 10 Art Museum Dr., Charles Village* ☎ *410/889–3399* 🌐 *www.gertrudesbaltimore.com* 🕒 *Closed Mon. and Tues.*

The Helmand

$ | **AFGHAN** | Owned by Hamid Kharzai's brother, Qayum Karzai, The Helmand serves outstanding Afghan fare in a casual yet elegant space. Beautiful woven textiles and traditional dresses adorn the walls, adding color to the simple white table settings. **Known for:** outstanding lamb dishes; vegetarian; the unforgettable appetizer. $ *Average main: $13* ⊠ *806 N. Charles St., Mount Vernon* ☎ *410/752–0311* ⊕ *www.helmand.com* ⊘ *Closed Mon.*

La Cuchara

$$$$ | **BASQUE** | Authentic Basque cuisine is on full display at this lovely restaurant located in the Meadow Mill building: *pinxtos* like ham croquettes with Gruyère cheese, sardines in oil, and fingerling potatoes with garlic aioli are perfect for sharing. The vast space is anchored by a 40-foot chestnut bar, behind which sits a wood-fired grill. **Known for:** duck breast with a honey-Banyuis reduction; homemade breads; friendly service. $ *Average main: $38* ⊠ *3600 Clipper Mill Rd., Hampden* ✣ *Turn into mill complex, crossing wooden bridge, which spans Jones Falls (expressway is overhead). Note: only one car can cross bridge at a time* ☎ *443/708–3838* ⊕ *www.lacuchara-baltimore.com* ⊘ *No lunch weekdays.*

Ouzo Bay

$$$ | **MEDITERRANEAN** | Blink, and you may think you're in South Beach: this trendy restaurant has quickly become the city's most popular, where the suit-and-tie crowd sidles up to the elevated bar or takes a seat on the cushy outdoor terrace. Try the grilled octopus starter, tossed with lemon juice and capers, or the charcoal-grilled whole fish, be it wild sea bass, sole, or snapper. **Known for:** laid-back, sexy vibe; Mediterranean-style seafood; grilled lamp chops. $ *Average main: $35* ⊠ *1000 Lancaster St., Harbor East* ☎ *443/708–5818* ⊕ *www.ouzobay.com.*

The Prime Rib

$$$$ | **STEAKHOUSE** | Bustling and crowded, this luxuriously dark dining room is just north of Mount Vernon Square and a five-minute drive from the Inner Harbor. The leopard-print carpet and live pianist lend a swanky 1960s feel to a place that seems untouched by time, including the meat-heavy menu of steak-house classics. **Known for:** superb prime rib and an even better filet mignon; jumbo lump crab cakes; good but predominately U.S. wine list. $ *Average main: $60* ⊠ *1101 N. Calvert St., Mount Vernon* ☎ *410/539–1804* ⊕ *www.theprimerib.com* ⊘ *Closed Mon. No lunch.*

🛏 Hotels

★ 1840s Carrollton Inn

$$ | **B&B/INN** | This boutique hotel is a series of interconnected row homes that date from the early 19th century. **Pros:** gourmet made-to-order breakfast; complimentary Wi-Fi; impeccable service. **Cons:** free parking is first come, first served; neighborhood can be noisy after hours; small elevators. $ *Rooms from: $275* ⊠ *50 Albemarle St., Baltimore* ☎ *410/385–1840* ⊕ *www.1840splaza.com* ☞ *13 rooms* �◎ *Free Breakfast.*

★ Four Seasons Baltimore

$$$$ | **HOTEL** | The 18-story glass tower rises above the harbor, commanding prime views from each plush and comfortable (albeit minimalist) guest room. **Pros:** hands down, Baltimore's most luxurious hotel; impeccable service; within walking distance to the Inner Harbor and Fells Point. **Cons:** room rates are steep, even in the off-season; expensive valet parking; ongoing construction around Harbor East can be noisy. $ *Rooms from: $499* ⊠ *200 International Dr., Harbor East* ☎ *410/576–5800* ⊕ *www.fourseasons.com/baltimore* ☞ *256 rooms* �◎ *No Meals.*

Hilton Baltimore Inner Harbor

$ | **HOTEL** | The towering Hilton has an unparalleled view of Camden Yards and a skywalk that connects to the city's convention center. **Pros:** connected to the convention center; excellent ballpark views; on-site Coffee Bean & Tea Leaf. **Cons:** rooms are considerably smaller than those at similarly priced hotels in town; it's a chain hotel, albeit a nice one; busy convention hotel generates crowds. [$] *Rooms from: $194* ✉ *401 W. Pratt St., Inner Harbor* ☎ *443/573–8700* 🌐 *www.hilton.com* 🛏 *757 rooms* 🍴 *No Meals.*

Hotel Monaco Baltimore

$ | **HOTEL** | **FAMILY** | This boutique hotel is in the historic headquarters of the B&O Railroad—just 2½ blocks from the Inner Harbor and within easy walking distance of Oriole Park at Camden Yards. **Pros:** a posh downtown hotel at family-friendly prices; amenities include rooms with bunk beds, Xbox consoles; free bike-share program complete with a map of the best downtown routes. **Cons:** the reception area is on the building's second floor; ongoing construction project across the street (former Mechanic Theater); expensive valet parking. [$] *Rooms from: $203* ✉ *2 N. Charles St., Downtown* ☎ *410/692–6170* 🌐 *www.monaco-baltimore.com* 🛏 *202 rooms* 🍴 *No Meals.*

Hotel Revival

$ | **HOTEL** | **FAMILY** | Joie de Vivre hotel group has made a splash in town with its rehab of a historic apartment building, right across from the Washington Monument, offering rooms with wood-laminate floors, brightly colored fabrics, and art reflecting the surrounding neighborhood. **Pros:** free Wi-Fi throughout; historical accents that instill a sense of place; location near the BSO and the Walters Art Museum. **Cons:** area can feel forlorn at night; expensive valet parking; residential-style guest rooms curiously lack desks. [$] *Rooms from: $159* ✉ *101 W. Monument St., Mount Vernon* ☎ *410/727–7101* 🌐 *www.jdvhotels.com* 🛏 *107 rooms* 🍴 *No Meals.*

★ **The Ivy Hotel**

$$$$ | **HOTEL** | Nestled in a century-old brownstone, just a few blocks from Penn Station, this boutique hotel features luxurious appointments such as original art and antiques, a library, billiards room and private interior courtyard, Frette linens atop the beds, en suite gas fireplaces, and heated floors and large soaking tubs in the bathrooms. **Pros:** small but noteworthy spa on-site; attentive staff ensures every need is met; each layout is different; some suites feature multiple levels. **Cons:** very expensive; not pet-friendly; limited privacy in a historic home setting. [$] *Rooms from: $595* ✉ *205 E. Biddle St., Mount Vernon* ☎ *410/514–6500* 🌐 *www.theivybaltimore.com* 🛏 *18 rooms* 🍴 *Free Breakfast.*

Marriott Baltimore Waterfront

$$ | **HOTEL** | The city's tallest hotel and one of a handful directly on the Inner Harbor, this 32-story Marriott has a neoclassical interior that uses multihued marble, rich jewel-toned walls, and photographs of Baltimore architectural landmarks. **Pros:** newly renovated rooms; great location and view; water taxi stop right out front. **Cons:** pricey compared to nearby hotels in the same category; expensive valet parking; staff can be rude. [$] *Rooms from: $239* ✉ *700 Aliceanna St., Harbor East* ☎ *410/385–3000* 🌐 *www.marriott.com* 🛏 *751 rooms* 🍴 *No Meals.*

Sagamore Pendry Baltimore

$$$$ | **HOTEL** | **FAMILY** | The cornerstone of Fells Point has long been the Rec Pier building, once an immigration hub, then later the setting for the TV series *Homicide: Life on the Street*, and now a 128-room boutique gem that has inspired a neighborhood-wide renaissance. **Pros:** stunning infinity pool overlooking the harbor and Domino Sugar Factory; gorgeous

circa-1914 ballroom with original windows and state-of-the-art technology; free Wi-Fi throughout. **Cons:** expensive valet parking; no spa; service can be pretentious. [$] *Rooms from: $500* ✉ *1715 Thames St., Fells Point* ☎ *443/552–1400* 🌐 *www.pendryhotels.com* 🛏 *128 rooms* 🍴 *No Meals.*

Chapter 15

SIDE TRIPS TO VIRGINIA

15

Updated by
Barbara Noe Kennedy

◉ Sights   🍴 Restaurants   🛏 Hotels   🛍 Shopping   🍸 Nightlife

★★★★★   ★★★★☆   ★★★★☆   ★★★☆☆   ★★☆☆☆

WELCOME TO SIDE TRIPS TO VIRGINIA

TOP REASONS TO GO

★ **Get a history lesson:** The sprawling Mount Vernon, the plantation and home of George and Martha Washington, serves as a reminder of the power and complex legacy of our first president—a Founding Father and leader in the American Revolution, and, simultaneously, an enslaver of hundreds of people.

★ **Travel back in time:** Delve into colonial history in Old Town Alexandria, then fast-forward to the 21st century with funky shops, artists' galleries, hot restaurants, boutiques, and bars. Don't miss Alexandria's farmers' market!

★ **Escape to the countryside:** Loudoun County is just an hour's drive away from Washington, D.C.'s hustle-bustle, where you can luxuriate (or hike or bike) in bucolic scenery, go wine-tasting, explore historic sites, and experience small-town life.

With just a bit of planning, any one of these trips can be done in a day or even an afternoon.

1 Alexandria. Alexandria is across the Potomac and 7 miles downstream from Washington. In the 18th century it was a notable commercial port; it's now a big small town loaded with historic homes, shops, and restaurants.

2 Mount Vernon. Sixteen miles south of D.C. is George Washington's beautifully preserved Mount Vernon, the most visited historic house in America.

3 Woodlawn. Woodlawn was the estate of Martha Washington's granddaughter.

4 Gunston Hall. Gunston Hall was the residence of George Mason, a patriot and author of the document on which the Bill of Rights was based.

5 Loudoun County. Wineries and breweries, country villages, and Civil War history await just a short drive away.

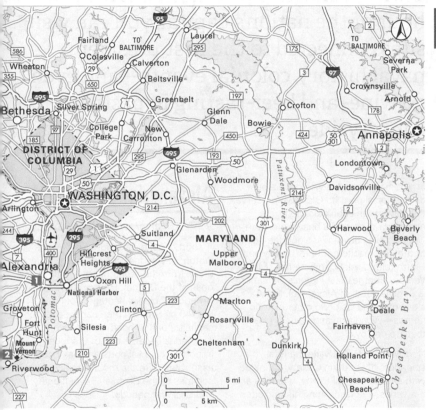

Escape the bustle of the district and dive deeper into the nation's history during a side trip to Virginia. Within an hour of the nation's capital, you can visit sites connected to the first president, naval history, colonial events—and even go wine- and beer-tasting in pastoral countryside.

In Virginia, Alexandria was once a bustling Colonial port. Its Old Town preserves this flavor with cobblestone streets, historic taverns, and a busy waterfront. Cycle 7 miles downriver along the banks of the Potomac to get here, or hop on the Metro for a quick 30-minute ride. Mount Vernon, George Washington's plantation, is 8 miles south of Alexandria. Make a day of it, and visit two other historic homes—Woodlawn and Gunston Hall—that are nearby.

Northwest of D.C. awaits the rural splendors of Loudoun County, sprinkled with exquisite small towns, wineries and breweries, and fascinating historic sites.

Planning

Getting Here and Around

The Metro Silver Line goes as far as Ashburn, just across the county border. But you'll need a car to explore the bulk of Loudoun's country lanes and villages.

Alexandria

8 miles south of Washington D.C.

A short drive (or bike ride) from Washington, Alexandria provides a welcome break from the monuments and the business of the District. Here you encounter America's colonial heritage. Founded in 1749 by Scottish merchants eager to capitalize on the booming tobacco trade, Alexandria became one of the most important colonial ports and has been associated with the most significant personages of the Colonial, Revolutionary, and Civil War periods.

In Old Town, this colorful past is revived through restored 18th- and 19th-century homes, churches, and taverns; on the cobblestone streets; and on the revitalized waterfront, where clipper ships docked and artisans displayed their wares. Alexandria also has a wide variety of small- to medium-size restaurants and pubs, plus a wealth of boutiques and antiques dealers vying for your time and money.

To Get To:	By Car:	By Public Transit:
Alexandria	George Washington Memorial Pkwy. or Richmond Hwy. (Rte. 1) south from Arlington (10 mins)	The Blue or Yellow Line to the King St.–Old Town Metro stop (25 mins from Metro Center)
Mount Vernon	Exit 1C off I–495 (the Beltway) in Alexandria; follow signs to George Washington Memorial Pkwy. southbound about 8½ miles (30 mins). Or go south from Arlington (or I–395) on George Washington Memorial Pkwy. through Alexandria (30 mins)	The Yellow Line to the Huntington Metro stop, then Fairfax County Connector Bus No. 101 (45–50 mins.); ferry from Pier 4, The Wharf (90 mins)
Woodlawn	South on I–395 and I–95 to exit 1766A. Follow Rte. 286 (Fairfax County Pkwy.) to Rte. 1. Turn left and go 5 miles to entrance (35 mins)	Bus from Huntington Metro station to Richmond Hwy./Belvoir stop and then a ¾-mile walk (45–50 mins)
Gunston Hall	South on I–395 and I–95 to exit 163 onto Gunston Rd. (SR 242); the entrance is 5½ miles on left (40 mins)	No Metro or bus
Loudoun County	I–66 to Rte. 267 to US 15 (Rte. 7) to Leesburg (50 mins)	Silver line as far as Ashburn

15

Side Trips to Virginia ALEXANDRIA

GETTING HERE AND AROUND

Take either the George Washington Memorial Parkway or Richmond Highway (Route 1) south from Arlington to reach Alexandria.

■ TIP→ **Stop at the Alexandria Visitor Center at Ramsay House (221 King Street) to get oriented.**

The King Street–Old Town Metro stop (about 25 minutes from Metro Center) is right next to the Masonic Memorial and a 10-block walk on King Street from the center of Old Town.

■ TIP→ **A free King Street trolley operates year-round between the King Street Metrorail station and the Potomac River Waterfront. It runs daily every 15 minutes between 11 am and 11 pm.**

TOURS

A great way to learn more about Alexandria's fascinating history is on a walking tour with Alexandria Colonial Tours or Old Town Experience. All tours depart from the Alexandria Visitor Center at Ramsay House.

African American Heritage Trail

WALKING TOURS | Experience the history of enslaved and freed Africans on this trail along the Potomac River, either in-home on your computer or live on your smartphone. ⊕ *www.alexandriava.gov.*

Manumission Tour Company

GUIDED TOURS | Guided cultural heritage tours highlight Alexandria's extensive African American history. ⊠ *Alexandria* ⊕ *www.manumissiontours.com.*

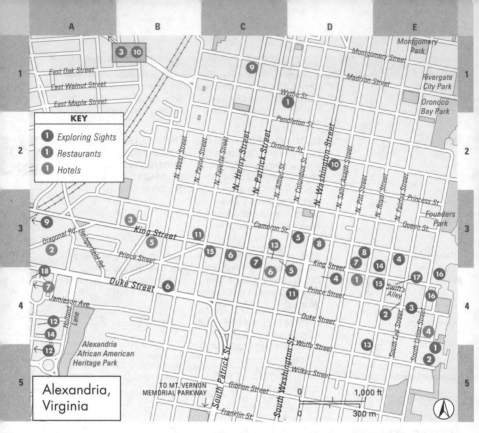

Alexandria, Virginia

KEY

- 1 Exploring Sights
- 1 Restaurants
- 1 Hotels

TO MT. VERNON MEMORIAL PARKWAY

Alexandria African American Heritage Park

0   1,000 ft
0   300 m

Sights ▼

1 Alexandria Black History Museum **C1**

2 Athenaeum **E4**

3 Captain's Row **E4**

4 Carlyle House Historic Park **E3**

5 Christ Church **D3**

6 Freedom House Museum **B4**

7 Friendship Firehouse **C3**

8 Gadsby's Tavern Museum **D3**

9 George Washington Masonic National Memorial **A3**

10 Lee-Fendall House Museum and Garden... **D2**

11 The Lyceum: Alexandria's History Museum **C4**

12 National Inventors Hall of Fame and Museum **A5**

13 Old Presbyterian Meeting House.......... **D5**

14 Old Town Farmers' Market **D3**

15 Stabler-Leadbeater Apothecary Museum... **D4**

16 Torpedo Factory Art Center................. **E4**

Restaurants ▼

1 Ada's on the River **E5**

2 BARCA Pier & Wine Bar................. **E5**

3 Cheesetique.............. **B1**

4 Columbia Firehouse **D4**

5 Don Taco **C3**

6 Hank's Oyster Bar Old Town................. **C3**

7 Kismet.................... **D3**

8 Le Refuge............... **D3**

9 Mason Social **C1**

10 Matt's and Tony's All Day Kitchen + Bar............ **B1**

11 Nasime................... **B3**

12 Sweet Fire Donna's..... **A4**

13 Taverna Cretekou........ **C3**

14 Téquila & Taco **A4**

15 Vermilion................. **C3**

16 Virtue Feed & Grain **E4**

17 The Warehouse.......... **E4**

18 Whiskey & Oyster **A4**

Hotels ▼

1 The Alexandrian Autograph Collection ... **D4**

2 Embassy Suites Alexandria– Old Town................. **A3**

3 Hotel Centric Old Town Alexandria.... **B3**

4 Hotel Indigo Old Town Alexandria.... **E4**

5 Lorien Hotel & Spa **B3**

6 Morrison House, Autograph Collection ... **C4**

7 The Westin Alexandria............... **A4**

VISITOR INFORMATION
CONTACTS Alexandria Visitor Center.
✉ *Ramsay House, 221 King St., Old Town* ☎ *703/838–5005* ⊕ *www.visitalexandri-ava.com.*

👁 Sights

Founded in 1749, Alexandria is known for well-preserved architecture dating back to before George Washington considered it his "adopted" hometown. Alexandria, now a nationally designated historic district, is easily walkable, with historic attractions to discover on every street. Most of the sights are free, though some have a nominal fee. Alexandria is a warm and welcoming place, ideal for anyone from solo travelers to families with small children and pets.

Alexandria Black History Museum
HISTORY MUSEUM | This collection, devoted to the history of African Americans in Alexandria and Virginia, is housed in part in the Robert H. Robinson Library, a building constructed in the wake of a landmark 1939 sit-in protesting the segregation of Alexandria libraries. The Watson Reading Room, next to the museum, holds a vast collection of books, periodicals, videos, and historical documents detailing the social, economic, and cultural contributions of African Americans who helped shape the city's growth since its establishment in 1749. The federal census of 1790 recorded 52 free African Americans living in the city, but the town was one of the largest slave-exporting points in the South, with at least two highly active slave markets. ✉ *902 Wythe St., Old Town* ☎ *703/746–4356* ⊕ *www.alexblackhistory.org* 💲 *$2* ⊘ *Closed Sun. and Mon.* Ⓜ *King St.–Old Town.*

Athenaeum
HISTORIC SIGHT | One of the most noteworthy structures in Alexandria, this striking Greek Revival edifice at the corner of Prince and Lee streets stands out from its many redbrick Federal neighbors. Built in 1852 as a bank, and later used as a Union commissary headquarters, then as a storage facility for the Stabler-Lead-beater Apothecary, the Athenaeum now houses the gallery of the Northern Virginia Fine Arts Association, which hosts free rotating art exhibitions, classes, and receptions throughout the year. The 200 block of Prince Street between Fairfax and Lee streets is known as Gentry Row. ✉ *201 Prince St., Old Town* ☎ *703/548–0035* ⊕ *www.nvfaa.org* 💲 *Free* ⊘ *Closed Mon.–Wed.* Ⓜ *King St.–Old Town.*

Captain's Row
HISTORIC DISTRICT | Many of Alexandria's sea captains once lived on this block, which gives visitors the truest sense of what the city looked like in the 1800s. The houses are now all private residences and reflect the style of the Federal period. While the cobblestone pavement is a replica, it accurately represents the original which, according to local folklore, was laid down by Hessian soldiers taken prisoner in the Revolutionary War. Captain's Row is one of only two streets in Alexandria that is paved with cobblestones. ✉ *100–199 Prince St., Old Town* Ⓜ *King St.–Old Town.*

Carlyle House Historic Park
HISTORIC HOME | **FAMILY** | The Carlyle House offers a rich, nuanced portrait of both American and Alexandrian history. As one of the largest slaveholders in Virginia at the time, John Carlyle established himself as a powerful merchant, city founder, and local leader. Built in 1753 by enslaved people, the house hosted many important mid-18th century figures, from a meeting between General Braddock and royal governors on the French and Indian War to the likes of George Washington, Thomas Jefferson, and Benjamin Franklin for parties and balls. Today, the house serves as a museum where visitors can get a behind-the-scenes look at the history of Alexandria and the Carlyle family (roughly 1753–1780).

Specialty tours and programs focus on other aspects of the Carlyle property's history. ✉ *121 N. Fairfax St., Old Town* ☎ *703/549–2997* ⊕ *www.novaparks.com/ parks/carlyle-house-historic-park* 🍴 *$7* ⊙ *Closed Wed.* Ⓜ *King St.–Old Town.*

Christ Church

CHURCH | FAMILY | George Washington was a parishoner in this Episcopal church, which remains in nearly original condition. (Washington paid quite a lot of money for pew 5—today's pews 59 and 60). Completed in 1773, it's a fine example of an English Georgian country-style church with its Palladian chancel window, interior balcony, and English wrought-brass-and-crystal chandelier. Docents give tours during visiting hours, during which visitors are invited to sit in Washington's box pew. ✉ *118 N. Washington St., Old Town* ☎ *703/549–1450* ⊕ *www. historicchristchurch.org* 🍴 *$5 donation suggested* Ⓜ *King St.–Old Town.*

Freedom House Museum

HISTORY MUSEUM | During a period of the 19th century, one of the South's most lucrative slave-trading businesses, Franklin and Armfield, operated out of this Federal-style row house on Duke Street. More than 3,750 enslaved men, women, and children were held here between 1828 and 1861, en route to cotton and sugar plantations and markets in the deep South. Recently renovated and expanded, the museum has three floors of rotating exhibits that strive to reframe the undertold stories of enslaved and free Black people who lived in—and were trafficked through—Alexandria. ✉ *1315 Duke St., Alexandria* ☎ *703/836–2858* ⊕ *www.alexandriava.gov/freedomhouse* 🍴 *$5* ⊙ *Closed Tues. and Wed.* Ⓜ *King St.–Old Town.*

Friendship Firehouse

OTHER ATTRACTION | FAMILY | Alexandria's showcase firehouse dates from 1855 and is filled with typical 19th-century implements, but the resident Friendship Fire Company was established in 1774,

Alexandria's Farmers' Market ⊙

If it's Saturday and you're up early, join the locals at Alexandria's Farmers' Market, one of the oldest continually operating farmers' markets in the country—open for business since the 1700s. The market is held from 7 am to noon year-round at Market Square (✉ *301 King St.*), a few blocks away from Old Town's waterfront. In addition to incredible produce and flowers, you'll find handmade crafts and prepared foods.

the same year it bought its first "engine." Among early fire engines on display is a hand pumper built in Philadelphia in 1851. ✉ *107 S. Alfred St., Old Town* ☎ *703/746–3891* ⊕ *www.alexandriava.gov/friendshipfirehouse* 🍴 *$2* ☞ *Open 1 Sat. per month 11–5* Ⓜ *King St.–Old Town.*

Gadsby's Tavern Museum

OTHER MUSEUM | FAMILY | The young republic began to take shape through conversations and choices being made in these hospitality spaces, a circa-1785 tavern and the 1792 City Hotel, that comprise today's museum. Named for the Englishman John Gadsby who operated them from 1796 to 1808, the tavern businesses were central to Alexandria's port-based economy, offering places to dine, entertain, and spend the night. A large enslaved labor force made Gadsby's renowned hospitality possible. Notable patrons included George and Martha Washington, Thomas Jefferson, and the marquis de Lafayette. The taproom, dining room, assembly room, ballroom, and communal bedrooms have been restored to their original appearances. Opt for a self-guided tour to dig deeper into early America. A variety of public programs are held throughout the year. ✉ *134 N. Royal*

St., Old Town ⊹ Take the free King St. trolley (runs every 15 mins) to King and Royal Sts., then walk ☎ 703/746–4242 ⊕ www.gadsbystavern.org ✉ $5 ($8 for guided tour) Ⓜ King St.–Old Town.

George Washington Masonic National Memorial
NOTABLE BUILDING | FAMILY | Because Alexandria, like Washington, D.C., has no really tall buildings, the spire of this memorial dominates the surroundings and is visible for miles. The structure overlooks King and Duke Streets, Alexandria's major east–west arteries, and reaching it requires a respectable uphill climb from the King Street Metrorail and bus stations. From the ninth-floor observation deck (reached by elevator), you get a spectacular view of Alexandria and Washington, but access above the first two floors is by guided tour only. The memorial contains furnishings from the first Masonic lodge in Alexandria. George Washington became a Mason in 1752 in Fredericksburg and then became Charter Master of the Alexandria lodge when it was chartered in 1788, remaining active in Masonic affairs during his tenure as president, from 1789 to 1797. Guided tours are included with admission, but you need to make a reservation. ✉ 101 Callahan Dr., Old Town ☎ 703/683–2007 ⊕ www.gwmemorial.org ✉ $18 ⊙ Closed Mon.–Thurs. Ⓜ King St.–Old Town.

Lee-Fendall House Museum and Garden
HISTORIC HOME | FAMILY | Built in 1785, the Lee-Fendall House was home to members of the prominent Fendall, Lee, and Downham families, as well as generations of enslaved and free African Americans. During the Civil War, it served as a federal military hospital. The home's last resident owner was national labor organizer John L. Lewis. Furnishings reflect how the house changed from 1785 to 1969. Highlights include a collection of Alexandria-made furniture as well as a tour and exhibit focusing on the

enslaved and free people who worked in the house. There's also a beautifully restored, award-winning garden, which can be visited without buying a ticket to the museum. ✉ 614 Oronoco St., Old Town ☎ 703/548–1789 ⊕ www.leefendallhouse.org ✉ $7 ⊙ Closed Mon. and Tues. Ⓜ King St.–Old Town.

The Lyceum: Alexandria's History Museum
HISTORY MUSEUM | FAMILY | Built in 1839 and one of Alexandria's best examples of Greek Revival design, the Lyceum is also a local history museum. Restored in the 1970s for the Bicentennial, it has an impressive collection, including examples of 18th- and 19th-century silver, tools, stoneware, and Civil War photographs taken by Alexander Gardner and Andrew Russell. Over the years the building has served as the Alexandria Library, a Civil War hospital, a residence, and offices. ✉ 201 S. Washington St., Old Town ☎ 703/746–4994 ⊕ www.alexandriava.gov/lyceum ✉ $3 (free for Alexandria residents) ⊙ Closed Mon.–Wed. Ⓜ King St.–Old Town.

National Inventors Hall of Fame and Museum
OTHER MUSEUM | FAMILY | Located inside the United States Patent and Trademark Office, the National Inventors Hall of Fame spotlights more than 600 inventors and the greatest technological and trademarked achievements. Browse the interactive gallery of inductees, have a seat in a 1965 Ford Mustang merged with a 2015 Ford Mustang, test your eye for authenticity through an interactive display of authentic and counterfeit products, and more. The gift shop has some truly one-of-a-kind mementos and gifts. ✉ National Inventors Hall of Fame, 600 Dulany St., Old Town ⊹ In atrium of United States Patent and Trademark Office's Madison Bldg., easily accessible from King St. and Eisenhower Ave. Metro stations ☎ 571/272–0095 ⊕ www.invent.org ⊙ Closed Sun. and sometimes Sat. Ⓜ King St.–Old Town or Eisenhower Ave.

Old Presbyterian Meeting House

HISTORIC SIGHT | Except from 1899 through 1949, the Old Presbyterian Meeting House has been the site of an active Presbyterian congregation since 1772. Scottish pioneers founded the church, and Scottish patriots used it as a gathering place during the Revolution. Four memorial services were held for George Washington here. The tomb of an unknown soldier of the American Revolution lies in a corner of the small churchyard, where many prominent Alexandrians—including Dr. James Craik, physician and best friend to Washington, and merchant John Carlyle—are interred. The original sanctuary was rebuilt after a lightning strike and fire in 1835. The interior is appropriately plain; if you'd like to visit the sanctuary, you can stop in the office or call ahead for a tour; a historian is generally there on weekdays. ⊠ 323 S. Fairfax St., Old Town ☎ 703/549–6670 ⊕ www.opmh.org ⚑ Free Ⓜ King St.–Old Town.

Old Town Farmers' Market

MARKET | FAMILY | One of the nation's oldest continually operating farmers' markets has served Alexandria residents since 1753. On Saturday mornings, residents and visitors alike can get fresh meat, dairy, fish, fruits, and vegetables from area farmers. Local artists also sell their work in the bustling Market Square. Stop by year-round. ⊠ 301 King St., Old Town ☎ 703/746–3200 ⊕ www.alexandri-ava.gov.

Stabler-Leadbeater Apothecary Museum

OTHER MUSEUM | Once patronized by Martha Washington, the Stabler-Leadbeater Apothecary is one of the oldest in the country. The shop now houses a museum of memorabilia, including one of the finest collections of apothecary bottles in the country. In fact, they have so many of these original bottles (20,000 in total) that it took six years to process them all. Tours include discussions of the history of medicine as it was practiced at this family-run business for 141 years. ⊠ 105–107 S. Fairfax St., Old Town ☎ 703/746–3852 ⊕ www.apothecarymuseum.org ⚑ $5 ($8 for guided tours of 1st and 2nd floors) ⊘ Closed Mon. and Tues. Ⓜ King St.–Old Town.

★ Torpedo Factory Art Center

ARTS CENTER | FAMILY | Torpedoes were manufactured here by the U.S. Navy during World War II, but now the building houses eight galleries, as well as the studios and workshops of about 165 artists and artisans. You can observe printmakers, jewelers, sculptors, painters, potters, textile artists, and glass makers as they create original work in their studios (and buy their artworks). The Torpedo Factory also houses the Alexandria Archaeology Museum, which displays artifacts such as plates, cups, pipes, and coins from an early tavern, as well as Civil War soldiers' equipment. ⊠ 105 N. Union St., Old Town ⊹ Take free King St. trolley to Old Town waterfront. The Torpedo Factory is about 100 feet from final stop (King and Union Sts.) ☎ 703/746–4570 ⊕ www.torpedofactory.org ⚑ Free Ⓜ King St.–Old Town.

🍴 Restaurants

For centuries, the Founding Fathers and other international dignitaries have dined in Alexandria. Today, you can choose from more than 200 restaurants in all price ranges. During Alexandria's biannual restaurant weeks in January and August, dozens of establishments offer either a $35 three-course meal or dinner for two, and several also offer lunch specials.

Ada's on the River

$$$$ | MODERN AMERICAN | The first thing you notice, whether you're sitting outside on the breezy dock or inside in the window-filled dining space, are the spectacular Potomac River views. But what sets Ada's apart is the fact that most of the dishes touch the grill before leaving the open kitchen—so you have wood-fired steaks and smoked swordfish, but also

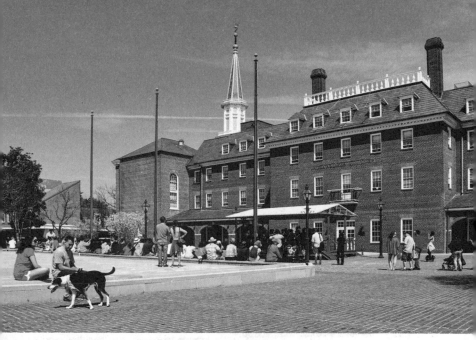

King Street is the heart of historic Old Town Alexandria, Virginia, with lively restaurants and shops.

singed gem lettuce and charcoal-burned brioche. **Known for:** large bar; breathtaking river views. $ *Average main: $36* ✉ *3 Pioneer Mill Way, Old Town* ☎ *703/638–1400* ⊕ *www.adasontheriver.com* Ⓜ *Old Town.*

BARCA Pier & Wine Bar

$$$ | MODERN AMERICAN | Shipping containers floating atop the Potomac River comprise this Spanish-inspired tapas restaurant in Old Town. The lunch and dinner menus feature small plates: *patatas bravas,* ham *croquetas,* and Spanish octopus salad. You can also savor meats and cheeses from Greece and Spain, miniature sandwiches, and more. **Known for:** happy hour; dogs welcome; waterfront views. $ *Average main: $30* ✉ *2 Pioneer Mill Way, Old Town* ☎ *703/638–1100* ⊕ *www.barcaalx.com* Ⓜ *King Street.*

Cheesetique

$$ | AMERICAN | Fans of cheese and wine will fall in love with this adorable retail shop and restaurant. With more than 200 cheeses from local and domestic creameries, a large selection of less

available wines, and an extensive menu that covers every fan favorite from grilled cheese to mac 'n' cheese, visitors will find themselves in cheese heaven. **Known for:** wide variety of both domestic and international cheeses; great wine selections; cheese boards with wine pairings. $ *Average main: $22* ✉ *2411 Mt. Vernon Ave., Alexandria* ☎ *703/706–5300* ⊕ *www.cheesetique.com.*

Columbia Firehouse

$$ | AMERICAN | FAMILY | Built in 1883 in the heart of Old Town and used as an actual firehouse, this historic building now just off bustling King Street houses a popular brasserie with a barroom, atrium, and patio. **Known for:** good staples like fish-and-chips, beef bourguignon, and steak frites; beautiful interior; separate bar menu of seafood and sandwiches. $ *Average main: $24* ✉ *109 St. Asaph St., Old Town* ☎ *703/683–1776* ⊕ *columbiafirehouse.com.*

Don Taco

$ | MEXICAN FUSION | As its name suggests, tacos of every variety are the specialty at this lively spot in the heart of Alexandria's busy King Street. From tacos to rice bowls, burritos, and small plates for sharing, Don Taco's menu will make you crave more than just one item. **Known for:** fun happy hour from 3 pm to 7 pm; large tequila menu; excellent desserts. $ *Average main: $12* ✉ *808 King St., Old Town* ☎ *703/518–8800* ⊕ *www.dontacova.com.*

★ Hank's Oyster Bar Old Town

$$$ | AMERICAN | FAMILY | This classic raw bar is consistently busy thanks to a nice mix of locals and visitors. No doubt it's because the oysters, clams, and lobster rolls are incredibly fresh, and the wine list is great. **Known for:** amazing oysters; non-seafood dinner specials; daily raw bar deals. $ *Average main: $30* ✉ *818 N. Asaph St., Old Town* ☎ *703/739–4265* ⊕ *www.hanksoysterbar.com* ⊗ *Closed Mon.*

Kismet

$$ | INDIAN | A spinoff of the posh Karma Modern Italian in D.C., Kismet offers a new take on Indian food: elevated dishes amid blue couches and booths, orb lights, and a mosaic-tiled bar. The menu follows the seasons, with favorites including red snapper *peri-peri* (hot sauce with red chilli peppers), lamb ghee roast, and tandoori pulled chicken with tartare sauce. **Known for:** relaxed vibe; artful plating; creative cocktails. $ *Average main: $25* ✉ *111 N. Pitt St., Old Town* ☎ *703/567–4507* ⊕ *kismetalx.com* Ⓜ *King St.–Old Town.*

Le Refuge

$$$ | FRENCH | At this local favorite, run by Jean François Chaufour and his wife, Françoise, for more than 40 years, lovingly prepared French country fare is served with beaucoup flavor. Popular selections include trout, bouillabaisse, garlicky rack of lamb, frogs' legs, and beef Wellington. **Known for:** authentic French cuisine with no pretension; three-course prix-fixe lunch and dinner options; tasty profiteroles for dessert. $ *Average main:*

$30 ✉ *127 N. Washington St., Old Town* ☎ *703/548–4661* ⊕ *www.lerefugealexandria.com* ⊗ *Closed Sun.* Ⓜ *King St.–Old Town.*

★ Mason Social

$$ | CONTEMPORARY | The depth of Mason Social's seasonal menu has made it a hit since its opening in 2015. Adventurous eaters will relish options like the marrow burger while those happier with more traditional staples will be delighted with the fried green tomatoes or pan-seared rockfish. **Known for:** brunch; long list of craft cocktails; bone marrow burger. $ *Average main: $24* ✉ *728 N. Henry St., Old Town* ☎ *703/548–8800* ⊕ *www.mason-social.com* Ⓜ *Braddock Rd.*

Matt's and Tony's All-Day Kitchen + Bar

$$ | AMERICAN | Brunch lovers unite over this lively Del Ray restaurant, serving French toast, eggs and waffles, and biscuits and gravy all day long. But there are plenty of other menu items as well, including lunchtime salads and sandwiches, and heartier comfort-fare dishes for dinner, including fried chicken and pork chops. **Known for:** creative menu beyond steak and eggs; fun communal bar; earthy restaurant design. $ *Average main: $20* ✉ *1501 Mount Vernon Ave., Alexandria* ☎ *703/429–4950* ⊕ *mattandtonysva.com* ⊗ *Closed Mon.* Ⓜ *Braddock Road Station.*

Nasime

$$$$ | JAPANESE FUSION | A tiny gem, Nasime serves an exquisite seven-course tasting menu of both traditional and contemporary Japanese flavors. The selections change frequently based on the season and availability of products, but it always includes a wonderful blend of raw, grilled, fried, and baked dishes, plus dessert. **Known for:** stunning, artistic dishes; revolving menu of fresh sushi; intimate seating. $ *Average main: $95* ✉ *1209 King St., Old Town* ☎ *703/548–1848* ⊕ *www.nasimerestaurant.com* ⊗ *Closed Sun. and Mon.*

Sweet Fire Donna's

$ | **BARBECUE** | **FAMILY** | A popular choice for locals, this barbecue joint is known for brisket, daily specials, and some of the best happy hour deals in town. If you're visiting for lunch, get there either on the earlier or later side to avoid the business crowds. **Known for:** barbecue; fast service; happy hour. $ *Average main: $12* ⊠ *510 John Carlyle St., Old Town* ☎ *571/312–7960* ⊕ *sweetfiredonnas.com* Ⓜ *King St.–Old Town.*

Taverna Cretekou

$$ | **MODERN GREEK** | Whitewashed stucco walls and colorful macramé tapestries bring a bit of the Mediterranean to the center of Old Town. The menu takes diners on a trip around Greece—each dish identifies its region of origin, and the whole country is represented. **Known for:** extensive Greek-only wine list; live music on Thursday; romantic canopied garden. $ *Average main: $22* ⊠ *818 King St., Old Town* ☎ *703/548–8688* ⊕ *www. tavernacretekou.com* ⊙ *Closed Mon.* Ⓜ *King St.–Old Town.*

Tequila & Taco

$ | **MEXICAN FUSION** | This popular neighborhood restaurant with funky decor is known for its weekend brunches and freshly squeezed margaritas. Tacos are a mix of traditional like carnitas and al pastor, as well as fun, such as fried chicken and cauliflower. **Known for:** weekend brunch; fresh margaritas; lively atmosphere. $ *Average main: $15* ⊠ *540 John Carlyle St., Old Town* ☎ *703/721–3203* ⊕ *alexandriataco.com* Ⓜ *King St.–Old Town.*

★ Vermilion

$$$ | **MODERN AMERICAN** | Be sure to make reservations because foodies flock here for a taste of its award-winning Modern American cuisine. Vermilion favors locally sourced, sustainable ingredients, though quality trumps local here, so you may find Parisian gnocchi alongside Maryland crab croquettes on this mid-Atlantic menu. **Known for:** casual, hip interior with exposed brick and gas lamps; popular weekend brunch; homemade pastas. $ *Average main: $32* ⊠ *1120 King St., Old Town* ☎ *703/684–9669* ⊕ *www.vermilionrestaurant.com* ⊙ *Closed Mon. No lunch Tues.–Thurs.* Ⓜ *King St.–Old Town.*

Virtue Feed & Grain

$$ | **AMERICAN** | Housed in what was once a feed house in the 1800s (now beautifully restored with reclaimed wood, antique bricks, and glass panes), this lively American tavern serves an all-day menu and weekend brunch, and has a club-like feel on weekend nights. You can sample a wide variety of selections with a seasonal bent, from red wine–braised short ribs and pasta puttanesca to a grilled chicken BLT or a quinoa salad. ■ **TIP→ Make reservations, especially on weekends, because the large space gets packed quickly!** **Known for:** classic farm-to-table cuisine with some spice; a creative pooch menu; late-night menu. $ *Average main: $26* ⊠ *106 S. Union St., Old Town* ☎ *571/970–3669* ⊕ *www. virtuefeedgrain.com.*

The Warehouse

$$$ | **SEAFOOD** | Situated in Old Town Alexandria, the casual yet elegant Warehouse specializes in prime aged steaks and seafood. The historic building that houses it features caricatures of the local gentry on the wall and an antique mahogany bar that's a great place to enjoy a drink. **Known for:** antique mahogany bar; casual elegance; great steak. $ *Average main: $35* ⊠ *214 King St., Old Town* ☎ *703/683–6868* ⊕ *www.warehouseoldtown.com.*

Whiskey & Oyster

$$ | **AMERICAN** | **FAMILY** | While the interior is sophisticated, the atmosphere is casual. The menu boasts, naturally, an impressive selection of whiskeys and oysters. **Known for:** classic and Maine lobster rolls (in season); dog-friendly patio; outdoor dining (weather dependent). $ *Average main: $23* ⊠ *301 John Carlyle St., Old Town* ☎ *703/567–1533*

whiskeyandoyster.squarespace.com Ⓜ King St.–Old Town.

🏨 Hotels

A short train-ride away from Washington, D.C., Alexandria is an excellent option for those who want a quieter stay near the District. Choose from dozens of larger chains or boutique hotels, all ranking highly for atmosphere and service.

The Alexandrian Autograph Collection

$$ | HOTEL | FAMILY | Both business and leisure travelers will enjoy the historic charm of The Alexandrian, just blocks from the waterfront. **Pros:** pet-friendly; 24-hour health center; inner rooms include balconies overlooking the center courtyard. **Cons:** can be noisy; no breakfast on Mondays; expensive parking. Ⓢ *Rooms from: $250* ✉ *480 King St., Old Town* ⊹ *Take free trolley toward waterfront from anywhere on King St. starting at King St.–Old Town Metro* ☎ *703/549–6080* ⊕ *thealexandrian.com* ⤴ *241 rooms* ⧉ *Free Breakfast* Ⓜ *King St.–Old Town.*

Embassy Suites Alexandria–Old Town

$$ | HOTEL | FAMILY | A location across from the Metro station makes this all-suites hotel a convenient base for city exploration. **Pros:** large rooms; free breakfast and evening reception; complimentary fitness center. **Cons:** small indoor pool is often crowded; parking is expensive; popular with school groups. Ⓢ *Rooms from: $270* ✉ *1900 Diagonal Rd., Old Town* ☎ *703/684–5900, 800/362–2779* ⊕ *embassysuites3.hilton.com* ⤴ *288 rooms* ⧉ *Free Breakfast.*

Hotel Centric Old Town Alexandria

$ | HOTEL | This comfortable hotel on King Street, Old Town's main street, melds local history and modern style. **Pros:** near Metro; dog-friendly. **Cons:** complaints of paper-thin walls; smallish rooms. Ⓢ *Rooms from: $200* ✉ *1625 King St.,*

Old Town ☎ *703/548–1050* ⊕ *www.hyatt.com* ⤴ *124 rooms* Ⓜ *King St.–Old Town.*

Hotel Indigo Old Town Alexandria

$$ | HOTEL | At Alexandria's only waterfront hotel, guests can take in views of the river from their rooms or from the restaurant after a day exploring Old Town, a neighborhood marked by cobblestone streets and 18th-century town houses. **Pros:** waterfront views; free Wi-Fi; walk-in showers. **Cons:** expensive valet parking; modern, yet lackluster room decor; poor noise insulation. Ⓢ *Rooms from: $250* ✉ *220 S. Union St., Old Town* ☎ *703/721–3800* ⊕ *www.hotelindigooldtownalexandria.com* ⤴ *120 rooms* ⧉ *No Meals.*

Lorien Hotel & Spa

$$ | HOTEL | Service is top-notch at this casually elegant boutique hotel in the heart of Old Town Alexandria. **Pros:** central to Old Town sights; full-service spa (only one in town) and well-appointed fitness center; elegant interior design. **Cons:** no pool; daily fee for valet-only parking; some rooms are small. Ⓢ *Rooms from: $225* ✉ *1600 King St., Old Town* ☎ *703/894–3434* ⊕ *www.lorienhotelandspa.com* ⤴ *107 rooms* ⧉ *No Meals* Ⓜ *King St.–Old Town.*

Morrison House, Autograph Collection

$$ | HOTEL | FAMILY | Originally built in 1985 in the style of a Federalist mansion for Morrison's wife, Morrison House was later turned into a bed-and-breakfast-style boutique hotel. **Pros:** some rooms have in-room fireplaces; delightful literary theme, including on-site library; live piano music Thursday through Saturday evenings. **Cons:** about a 15-minute walk from Metro and train stations; daily fee for valet-only parking; fee for in-room Wi-Fi. Ⓢ *Rooms from: $255* ✉ *116 S. Alfred St., Old Town* ☎ *703/838–8000* ⊕ *morrisonhouse.com* ⤴ *45 rooms* ⧉ *No Meals* Ⓜ *King St.–Old Town.*

The Westin Alexandria

$ | HOTEL | FAMILY | The staff seems genuinely happy to see you come through the door at this hotel just 1½ miles from the cobbled streets of Old Town Alexandria, and if you don't need or want to be in D.C.—only 20–25 minutes away by Metro—you'll get more for your travel dollar here. **Pros:** complimentary 24-hour gym; free shuttle to waterfront and Old Town and close to airport (though no shuttle); pet-friendly. **Cons:** outside the city; half-hour walk to waterfront; fee for in-room Wi-Fi. $ *Rooms from: $160* ⊠ *400 Courthouse Sq., Alexandria* ☎ *703/253–8600* ⊕ *www.westin.com/alexandria* ⇆ *319 rooms* ⟟⊙⟞ *No Meals* Ⓜ *Eisenhower Ave.*

🏃 Activities

An asphalt bicycle path leads from the Virginia side of Key Bridge (across from Georgetown), past Ronald Reagan National Airport, and through Alexandria all the way to Mount Vernon. Bikers in moderately good condition can make the 16-mile trip in less than two hours. You can rent bicycles as well as sailboats, paddleboards, and kayaks in Alexandria.

Mount Vernon

16 miles southeast of Washington, D.C., 8 miles south of Alexandria.

Once a working plantation in the 18th century, Mount Vernon is an enduring reminder of the life and legacy of George Washington, including his lifelong status as a slaveowner. This historic site features an authentically interpreted 18th-century home, lush gardens and grounds, captivating museum galleries, and immersive educational programs.

GETTING HERE AND AROUND

To reach Mount Vernon by car from the Capital Beltway (I–495), take Exit 1C, and follow the signs to George Washington Memorial Parkway southbound. Mount Vernon is about 8½ miles south. From downtown Washington, cross into Arlington on Key Bridge, Memorial Bridge, or the 14th Street Bridge, and drive south on the George Washington Memorial Parkway past Ronald Reagan National Airport through Alexandria straight to Mount Vernon. The trip from D.C. takes about a half hour.

Getting to Mount Vernon by public transportation requires that you take both the Metro and a bus. Begin by taking the Yellow Line train to the Huntington Metro station. From here, take Fairfax County Connector Bus No. 101 ($2 cash or with SmarTrip card). Buses on each route leave about once an hour—more often during rush hour—and operate weekdays from about 5:30 am to 9:10 pm, weekends from about 6:30 am to 9:45 pm.

You can also take a ferry from Alexandria City Marina and the Wharf in Washington, D.C.

CONTACTS Fairfax County Connector. ☎ *703/339–7200* ⊕ *www.fairfaxconnector.com.* **Washington Metro Area Transit Authority.** ☎ *202/637–1328 customer relations, 202/637–7000 travel information* ⊕ *www.wmata.com.*

TOURS

Spirit of Mount Vernon

BOAT TOURS | FAMILY | You can enjoy a Potomac River cruise and explore George Washington's famous grounds in one trip. *Spirit of Mount Vernon* is the only cruise option that provides a narrated sightseeing round-trip from the Washington, D.C., Waterfront area to Mount Vernon and back. The boats dock directly at Mount Vernon, and it's a short walk up the hill to the estate. Admission to the grounds of Mount Vernon is included in the fare. Cruise goers have three hours to explore Mount Vernon grounds and gardens before embarking back to their original destination. Cruises are offered on select dates from March through October. ⊠ *580 Water St. SW, Pier 4, Southwest* ☎ *866/404–8439 boat reservations* ⊕ *www.cityexperiences.com* Ⓜ *Waterfront–SEU.*

◉ Sights

Whether you're visiting for the day or spending a few days in Mount Vernon, there is much to see and do. George Washington's former plantation is one of the most popular historic estates in the country, averaging over 1 million guests each year. Despite this, there is an air of consistent tranquility, between the vast grounds and a well-organized programming schedule. Take a room-by-room tour of our Founding Father's mansion followed by a stroll through his grounds and gardens. Explore the various outbuildings in which enslaved people ran Mount Vernon's many operations, including blacksmithing, laundry, and cooking. You can learn more about these enslaved people—who represented 90% of Mount Vernon's residents at the time of Washington's death—by visiting one of their living quarters on the property, such as Pioneer Farm. You can also explore the estate by way of interactive shows, tours, tributes, and exhibitions. Mount Vernon also provides a variety of dining options that are suitable for families, large groups, and fine dining alike.

George Washington's Gristmill and Distillery

DISTILLERY | Reproductions of these two operations sit near the Mount Vernon estate, on the sites of the originals. In 1799, the distillery was one of the largest American whiskey producers. Today, using an 18th-century recipe and pro-cesses—thanks to the excellent records kept by Washington—small batches of his whiskey are made and sold here. During guided tours, led by costumed interpreters, you'll meet an 18th-century miller and watch the water-powered wheel grind grain into cornmeal before seeing the grain being distilled. The mill and distillery are 3 miles from Mount Vernon on Route 235 (Mount Vernon Memorial Highway) toward U.S. 1, almost to Woodlawn. General-admission tickets to Mount Vernon include the gristmill and distillery. ⊠ 5514 Mount Vernon Memorial Hwy., Mount Vernon ☎ 703/780–2000 ⊕ www.mountvernon.org ⊒ $10 without Mount Vernon admission ($28 includes admission to Mount Vernon estate) ⊗ Closed weekends ☞ Tours Apr.–Oct.

★ George Washington's Mount Vernon

HISTORIC HOME | FAMILY | The former plantation of George Washington and his wife, Martha, Mount Vernon sits on the banks of the Potomac River about 10 miles south of Alexandria. Washington's great-grandfather, John Washington, was awarded the land grant in 1674 for what would become Mount Vernon. It grew into 5,000 acres with four operating farms by the time the future president inherited it all in 1761. Washington used his wife's financial wealth and hundreds of enslaved people to transform the main house from an ordinary farm dwelling into what was, for the time, a grand man-sion. The red-roof main house is elegant though understated, with quite ornate first-floor rooms, especially the formal large dining room, with a molded ceiling decorated with agricultural motifs.

You can stroll around the estate's 500 acres and four gardens, visiting work-shops, a kitchen, a carriage house, a greenhouse, quarters for enslaved African Americans, and, down the hill, the tomb of George and Martha Washington. There's also a four-acre, 18th-century farm site with costumed interpreters and a reconstructed 16-sided treading barn as its centerpiece.

Throughout Mount Vernon, you can learn about the more than 300 enslaved people who lived here, and whose labor you see all around you. Relevant tours include "The Enslaved People of Mount Vernon" tour and the "Through My Eyes" tour, both of which explore the lives and experiences of the people who lived here and the role slavery had in the life of Washington and how he built and ran this estate.

The exterior of the plantation house at Mount Vernon may look as if it's built of stone, but it's not. It's rusticated pine with sand thrown into the wet paint to give it the rough look of sandstone blocks.

Visitors, especially children, tend to enjoy the Museum and Education Center's 23 galleries and theaters, including hundreds of artifacts, interactive displays, and a 4D theater that brings Washington's story to life. Actors in period dress, General Washington and his wife, welcome visitors at special occasions throughout the year, including President's Day, Mother's and Father's Day, and July 4. ⊠ *3200 Mount Vernon Memorial Hwy., Mount Vernon* ✛ *Southern end of George Washington Memorial Pkwy.* ☏ *703/780–3600* ⊕ *www.mountvernon.org* ⊠ *$28 includes admission to distillery and gristmill.*

National Museum of the Army

HISTORY MUSEUM | The National Museum of the Army, on Fort Belvoir's expansive property near Mount Vernon, isn't just any military museum. It's a state-of-the-art experience that provides a detailed, interactive approach to stories of all U.S. wars, from colonial warfare to the present day, and how they relate to society. A 4D movie details the Army's history, and a cool kids' education center has a fort to climb on and age-appropriate games that teach children about Army innovations, including interstate highways and satellite communications. ⊠ *1775 Liberty Dr.* ☏ *800/506–2672* ⊕ *www.thenmusa.org* ⊠ *Free timed tickets are required.*

Woodlawn

4 miles west of Mount Vernon, 18 miles south of Washington, D.C.

Woodlawn was once part of the Mount Vernon estate, and from here you can still see the trees of the bowling green that fronted Washington's home. It was built for Eleanor and Lawrence Lewis, Martha Washington's granddaughter and George Washington's nephew respectively. Also on the grounds of Woodlawn is one of Frank Lloyd Wright's "Usonian Homes," the Pope-Leighey House. The structure, which belongs to the National Trust for

Historic Preservation, was completed in 1941 at a cost of $7,000 and is one of only three homes in Virginia designed by Wright. Both houses are dedicated to telling the fullest story possible about all people associated with the property, including the enslaved African Americans who worked there.

GETTING HERE AND AROUND

To drive to Woodlawn from Washington, D.C., travel south on the George Washington Memorial Parkway to Mount Vernon; then follow Route 235 to the Route 1 intersection. Turn left on Route 1 and right at the next light onto Woodlawn Road. You can also go south on I-395 and I-95 to exit 166A. Follow Rte. 286 (Fairfax County Parkway) to Rte. 1. Turn left and go 5 miles to the entrance.

Woodlawn is accessible from the Huntington Metro station via a 40-minute bus ride to the Richmond Hwy./Belvoir stop and then a ¾-mile walk.

◉ Sights

The Woodlawn Plantation is a two-part manor that consists of a home as well as a farm complex. It became the first historic site owned by the National Trust in 1952 and is worth the short trip from Alexandria or Washington, D.C.

Woodlawn and Pope-Leighey House

HISTORIC HOME | FAMILY | Two iconic homes on one site are found just west of Mount Vernon. Woodlawn overlooks the Potomac River on lands first belonging to the Algonkian-speaking Doeg people, and then lands of George Washington's larger Mount Vernon plantation. Finished in 1805, the Federal-style mansion was designed for Eleanor and Lawrence Lewis by William Thornton, the architect of the U.S. Capitol. It displays the power and prosperity of America's first ruling class. Anti-slavery Quakers purchased and transformed Woodlawn in 1805. The Quakers and local free Black people

demonstrated that with agricultural reforms and Black landownership, the South could be successfully cultivated without slavery.

Also on the grounds, Pope-Leighey House is a Frank Lloyd Wright Unison home. Designed for the Pope family in 1940, it artfully blends into the landscape. Its innovative design concepts and natural materials create a sense of space and grace. The home is an expression of Wright's radical vision for beautiful, affordable, and more inclusive middle-class housing. To save it from demolition, the home was moved from Falls Church, Virginia, to Woodlawn in 1965 by its second owner, Marjorie Leighey. It's the only Wright house open to the public in Virginia.

Guides and exhibitions at both houses offer insight into the architectural details of both houses, as well as thoughtful narratives dedicated to telling the fullest story possible about all people associated with the property. ✉ 9000 Richmond Hwy., Alexandria ☎ 703/780–4000 ⊕ www.woodlawnpopeleighey.org 💲 From $15 ⊘ Closed Tues.–Wed.

Gunston Hall

5 miles south of Woodlawn, 25 miles south of Washington, D.C.

Down the Potomac from Mount Vernon is the home of another important George. Gentleman-farmer George Mason was a colonel of the Virginia militia and author of the Virginia Declaration of Rights, the model for the U.S. Bill of Rights, which called for freedom of the press, tolerance of religion, and other fundamental democratic principles. Mason was a framer of the Constitution but refused to sign the final document because it didn't stop the importation of slaves, adequately restrain the powers of the federal government, or include a bill of rights. Mason's objections

The National Museum of the Marine Corps is hosted in a glass atrium with interactive experiences.

spurred the movement for the inclusion of the Bill of Rights into the Constitution. This 18th-century Georgian mansion was located at the center of a 5,500-acre plantation. You can tour the home and grounds of Gunston Hall, a National Historic Landmark.

GETTING HERE AND AROUND

You'll have to use a car to get to Gunston Hall because there is no bus stop within walking distance. Travel south on Route 1, past Fort Belvoir to Route 242; turn left there, and go 3½ miles to the entrance. You can also go south on I–395 to I–95 to exit 163 onto Gunston Rd. (SR 242); the entrance is 5½ miles down on the left.

◉ Sights

Not far from George Washington's home lies Gunston Hall, a mansion built in the 18th century for Founding Father George Mason. Many well-known historical figures have set foot on this land. The mansion is now known for its association with Mason as well as its intricate,

unique architecture and interior design. It serves as a museum and is open to the general public.

★ George Mason's Gunston Hall

HISTORIC HOME | FAMILY | The Georgian-style mansion has some of the finest hand-carved ornamented interiors in the country and is the handiwork of the 18th-century's foremost architect, William Buckland, originally an indentured servant from England. Construction of Gunston Hall took place between 1755 and 1758. Buckland went on to design several notable buildings in Virginia and Maryland, including the Hammond-Harwood and Chase-Lloyd houses in Annapolis. It is believed he worked closely with another indentured servant, William Bernard Sears, to complete the house. Unlike other Virginia colonial homes, which tended to be very simple, Gunston Hall was, possibly, the only or one of a few houses known to have had chinoiserie decoration. The interior and the outbuildings have been meticulously restored.

While it is alleged that one of the reasons Mason didn't sign the Declaration of Independence is that it didn't stop the importation of enslaved people, Mason was himself a slaveholder of at least 300 people in his lifetime, many of whom lived at Gunston Hall. While touring the property, you have the opportunity to learn about the lives of some of these individuals, although there is currently not a permanent exhibit focusing on them.

The Riverside Garden currently is being restored; you can view the Potomac from the garden terraces. There are three hiking trails on the 500-plus-acre property. Guided tours are offered daily at 10 am and 11 am, as well as at 1, 2, 3, and 4 pm. ✉ 10709 Gunston Rd., Mason Neck ☎ 703/550–9220 ⊕ www.gunstonhall.org ✇ $10 ◷ Closed 1st 2 weeks of Jan.

★ National Museum of the Marine Corps
OTHER MUSEUM | FAMILY | The glassy atrium of this 120,000-square-foot homage to the military's finest soars into the sky next to the Marine Corps Base Quantico. The design was inspired by the iconic photograph of marines lifting the American flag on Iwo Jima. Inside the museum, visitors can experience the life of a marine. The museum is an interactive experience and has a staggering collection of tanks, aircraft, rocket launchers, and other weapons. There is even a rifle range simulator, where guests of all ages can learn how to hold a laser rifle and practice hitting targets. Service animals are welcome inside the museum, and pets are permitted on the grounds (look for designated relief areas). ✉ 1775 Semper Fidelis Way ☎ 877/653–1775 ⊕ www.usmcmuseum.com ✇ Free.

Loudoun County

The main town, Leesburg, is about 40 miles (or an hour's drive) northeast of Washington, D.C.

Bounded by the Potomac River, the Blue Ridge, and Rte. 7., Loudoun County lies about an hour's drive northwest of downtown D.C., and yet it's a world away. First developed in the 1700s by Germans, Quakers, and Scots, it's all about pastoral views, country roads, and charming villages. You'll find romantic inns, both in the towns and on expanses of farmland, as well as some of Northern Virginia's best restaurants, where award-winning chefs create dishes inspired by the local bounty. Wineries and breweries sprinkle the landscape, offering tours, tastings, and idyllic spots to picnic. You won't find major sights here—but several house museums, a Civil War battlefield, and more whisper about the past. The main town is Leesburg, the county seat, which provides a good base from which to explore this peaceful escape.

GETTING HERE AND AROUND
Leesburg is the hub of Loudoun County. It's about 50 minutes by car from Washington, D.C. Take I–66 and Rte. 267 west to US 15 (Rte. 7). To reach Middleburg, about an hour from Washington, D.C., follow I–66 west to Centreville. Follow Rte. 28 north to Chantilly, then U.S. 50 west to Middleburg.

VISITOR INFORMATION
Loudoun County Visitor Information Center, Market Station (Lower Deck). ✉ 112 South St. SE, Suite 200, Leesburg ☎ 703/771–2170, 800/752–6118.

◉ Sights

The sites may not be major in this quiet realm, but they're fascinating, including two historic manors, a small Civil War battlefield, and a bevy of picturesque small towns.

Aldie Mill Historic Park

NATURE SIGHT | The restored Aldie Mill, built between 1807 and 1809 and once the largest factory of its kind in Loudoun County, epitomizes Northern Virginia's industrial heritage. The twin waterwheels are fully operational, allowing visitors to see grinding demonstrations during guided tours. Aldie Mill also hosts educational programs, teas, and other special events. ⊠ *39401 John Mosby Hwy.* ☎ *703/327–9777* ⊕ *www.novaparks.com/parks/aldie-mill-historic-park* ⊗ *Mill closed weekdays mid-Nov.–mid-Apr.*

Ball's Bluff Battlefield Regional Park

NATURE SIGHT | One of the Civil War's first major engagements unfolded on October 21, 1861, on these wooded bluffs above the Potomac. The Confederates defeated an ill-prepared Union force in a battle that, combined with the First Battle of Manassas, dashed the North's hope for a quick defeat of the Confederacy. The site is now a 286-acre regional park with one of the country's smallest cemeteries and a bucolic trail serenaded by chickadees and tufted titmice. Guided tours and living-history events are offered April though November. ⊠ *Ball's Bluff Rd, Leesburg* ☎ *703/359–4603* ⊕ *www.novaparks.com/parks/balls-bluff-battlefield.*

George C. Marshall's Dodona Manor

HISTORIC HOME | Nobel Peace laureate, Army Chief of Staff during World War II, and architect of the Marshall Plan (which helped Europe recover after World War II), General Marshall lived in this stately home during the most important years of his service to the nation. Faithfully restored to share the Marshall story with a new generation, the historic house and gardens are open for tours. ⊠ *312 E. Market St., Leesburg* ☎ *703/777–1301* ⊕ *www.georgecmarshall.org* ⊜ *$15.*

Leesburg

TOWN | Founded in 1758 at the crossroads of two Native American trails near the Potomac, the hub of Loudoun County retains its historic charm but is totally immersed in the present day. Funky and fun boutiques, coffee shops, stylish bars, and farm-to-fork restaurants housed in historic buildings line its picturesque streets. The interactive Loudoun Museum has rotating exhibits, tours, and talks on everything from the Revolutionary War in Loudoun to the origins of the Virginia wine industry. Leesburg is a good base from which to explore Loudoun's historic sites, small towns, and wineries. ⊠ *Leesburg* ☎ *703/771–2170 Loudoun County Visitor Information Center, 800/752–6118 Loudoun County Visitor Information Center* ⊕ *www.visitloudoun.org.*

Middleburg

TOWN | In the heart of Virginia's hunt and wine country, Middleburg is a welcoming country town that Elizabeth Taylor and Jackie Kennedy (and plenty of other illuminati) have called home. It dates back to 1728 when a cousin of George Washington established a fieldstone tavern on an old Native American trail; that tavern, Red Fox Inn, is still going strong. Boutiques, antiques stores, restaurants, taverns—and a craft distillery—line the enchanting Main Street (US 50), while a bevy of wineries and breweries sprinkle the surrounding countryside. The Middleburg Film Festival is a major stop on the Oscar trail, while in December the town turns into a scene from a Charles Dickens novel, with carolers, actors, and musicians. ⊠ *Middleburg* ☎ *540/687–5152* ⊕ *www.middleburgva.gov.*

Morven Park

HISTORIC SIGHT | This 1,000-acre property and stately mansion was once the home of early 20th-century governor Westmoreland Davis. You can discover the eclectic collection assembled by the Davises on a guided tour of the Greek

Revival mansion, explore the Museum of Hounds & Hunting (also located in the mansion), and visit Mrs. Davis's beloved boxwood gardens. Miles of hiking and horseback-riding trails weave through the grounds, and the Morven Park International Equestrian Center is home to many events and shows throughout the year that are open to the public. ✉ *17195 Southern Planter Lane, Leesburg* ☎ *703/777–2414* 🌐 *www.morvenpark.org* 🎫 *$16* 🕒 *Closed Tues.–Thurs.*

Oatlands Historic House and Gardens
HISTORIC HOME | An elegant estate dating from 1798, Oatlands has terraced gardens and a Greek Revival mansion. The grounds include 8 miles of trails to explore and 4½ acres of terraced gardens for picnics and weddings. Be sure to take one of the guided tours, with themes including contributions of the enslaved people who lived and worked here, history of the gardens, and architecture of the buildings and property. ✉ *20850 Oatlands Plantation La., Leesburg* ☎ *703/727–0670* 🌐 *oatlands.org* 🎫 *$10 (grounds pass), $20 (guided tours)* ✍ *Guided tours must be purchased at least 24 hours in advance* ☞ *Guided tours by appointment Mon.–Thurs.; walk-in tours available Fri.–Sun.*

Small Towns in Loudoun County
TOWN | Two-lane roads—and plenty of dirt and gravel lanes—lace Loudoun County, connecting a bevy of picturesque small towns full of historic charm. Don't miss Purcellville, graced with Victorian homes dating back to 1874 when the railroad came through; Hillsboro, known for its quintessential stone buildings; Round Hill, where wealthy Washingtonians once escaped the summer heat; and Waterford, settled by Quakers and the site of a long-running fall arts festival. Along the way, you'll discover pick-your-own farms, grazing horses, antique shops, breweries, wineries, country B&Bs, and more. 🌐 *www.visitloudoun.org.*

Wineries and Breweries
WINERY | More than 50 wineries and tasting rooms speckle the Loudoun countryside, where you can sample, tour, and picnic. You can't go wrong, but favorites include Chrysalis, which produces wines from the indigenous Norton grape; Willowcroft, Loudoun's oldest winery, occupying a century-plus-old barn; and lively Stone Tower Winery. The county boasts more than 30 breweries as well; some are in towns, but the most interesting are farm breweries such as Bear Chase Brewery and Vanish Farmwoods Brewery—offering rustic beers on bucolic lands and glorious views. ✉ *Leesburg* 🌐 *www.visitloudoun.org.*

🍴 Restaurants

With the bounty of farm goods burgeoning throughout the county, it's no surprise that Loudoun menus feature fresh local items. You'll find everything from roadside stands to white-tablecloth fine dining overseen by award-winning chefs.

The Conche
$$$ | **AMERICAN** | It goes without saying that romance is in the air at this chocolate-themed restaurant, enhanced by low lighting and tucked-away booths. Chocolate may not be used in every dish, but why opt for anything else? **Known for:** romantic setting; the "cocoa flight" of chocolate-infused cocktails; great options for non–chocolate lovers. [$] *Average main: $35* ✉ *1605 Village Market Blvd. SE, Suite J108, Leesburg* ☎ *703/779–1800* 🌐 *the-conche.com.*

The Conservatory at Goodstone
$$$$ | **MODERN AMERICAN** | Part of the romantic Goodstone Inn, which sits on 265 rolling acres near Middleburg, The Conservatory serves exquisite dishes using ingredients literally fresh from the farm. You're in for a treat, with options including Miyazaki A5 Wagyu (a splurge worth every penny), guinea hen with Périgord truffle, and New Zealand

venison with sour-cherry jus. **Known for:** exquisitely presented dishes; beautiful location in nature; attentive staff. [$] *Average main: $82* ✉ *36205 Snake Hill Rd., Middleburg* ☎ *540/587–3333, 877/219–4663* 🌐 *www.goodstone.com* ⏲ *Closed Mon. and Tues.*

Lightfoot

$$$ | **AMERICAN** | Opened in 1999, the Lightfoot occupies a historic bank building, lending traces of vintage architecture to the chic design—the marble staircases are the first tip-off (and the wine cellar is in the old vault). But people flock here for the upscale dining experience, focusing on creative American-style cuisine: lobster and shrimp pasta in rosemary cream sauce; braised pork, shrimp, and grits; filet mignon with horseradish-chive butter and crispy onions. **Known for:** attention to detail; lively atmosphere; live music. [$] *Average main: $30* ✉ *1 N. King St., Leesburg* ☎ *703/771–2233* 🌐 *lightfootrestaurant.com.*

The Restaurant at Patowmack Farm

$$$$ | **MODERN AMERICAN** | Patowmack Farm has been growing produce since 1986, which explains why its ever-changing menu is full of fresh, innovative, thoughtful dishes that follow the seasons. But it's more than that—chef Vincent Badiee approaches his forward-thinking dishes like artwork, in which presentation is just as impressive as taste. **Known for:** spectacular setting; super-fresh ingredients; sending diners home with treats for the next day. [$] *Average main: $145* ✉ *42461 Lovettsville Rd* ☎ *540/822–9017* 🌐 *www.patowmackfarm.com* ⏲ *Closed Mon.–Wed.*

Tuscarora Mill

$$$ | **AMERICAN** | Tuskie's, as locals call it, is a Loudoun institution. Opened in 1985 in historic downtown Leesburg, it occupies a restored 1899 grist mill. **Known for:** creative dishes; attentive service; lively atmosphere. [$] *Average main: $30* ✉ *203 Harrison St. SE, Suite 230, Leesburg* ☎ *703/771–9300* 🌐 *www.tuskies.com.*

Hotels

Whether you're looking for a stately inn in the heart of town, a manor on an expansive horse farm, or a cozy B&B with mountain views, Loudoun has you covered.

Lansdowne Resort

$$ | **RESORT** | **FAMILY** | Perched on 500 bucolic acres on the Potomac, this sprawling resort includes a 45 holes of championship golf, an aquatic center with four pools, and several restaurants showcasing Piedmont and Tidewater cuisine. **Pros:** gorgeous setting; lots of fun activities; great for families. **Cons:** can be loud; dated decor; daily resort fee does not include greens fees or bike rentals. [$] *Rooms from: $220* ✉ *44050 Woodridge Pwy, Leesburg* ☎ *703/729–8400* 🌐 *lansdowneresort.com* 🛏 *296 rooms.*

Red Fox Inn & Tavern

$$$ | **B&B/INN** | The 1728 tavern still offers hospitality to travelers, making it the nation's oldest continually operated inn. **Pros:** 18th-century romance; legendary history; superior service. **Cons:** some rooms have low ceilings; no elevator; only dinner option is an expensive four-course menu. [$] *Rooms from: $300* ✉ *2 E. Washington St., Middleburg* ☎ *540/687–6301* 🌐 *www.redfox.com* 🛏 *22 rooms.*

Salamander Resort & Spa

$$$ | **RESORT** | For the ultimate in understated luxury, Salamander Resort & Spa encapsulates the essence of Virginia's countryside. **Pros:** gorgeous grounds; spa treatments; fun "adult" activities, including painting and horseback riding. **Cons:** food is hit or miss; some complain the service has declined. [$] *Rooms from: $400* ✉ *500 N. Pendleton St., Middleburg* ☎ *540/751–3160* 🌐 *www.salamanderresort.com* 🛏 *168 rooms.*

Stone Manor Boutique Inn
$$$ | **B&B/INN** | Seven romantic suites in an opulent stone house near Lovettsville provide the perfect excuse to get away from it all. **Pros:** gorgeous sunsets; stunning mountain views; luxury suites with fireplaces. **Cons:** some complain of small portions at breakfast; loud if a wedding is going on—ask before you commit. [$] *Rooms from: $300* ✉ *13193 Mountain Rd.* ☎ *540/822–3032* 🌐 *virginiabandb.net* 🛏 *8 suites.*

Shopping

Farms & Farmer's Markets
FOOD | Loudoun is a farmer's paradise, with fresh produce sold at markets throughout the county. You'll find them in nearly every town, along with roadside stands and on the farms themselves—many of which are open for tours, especially during seasonal events such as Halloween pumpkin patches and springtime flower-picking. ✉ *Leesburg* 🌐 *www.visitloudoun.org.*

Activities

Visiting wineries and breweries, picking your own strawberries or lavender, and biking a bucolic rail-trail are just some of the activities offered in Loudoun.

Biking
BIKING | Loudoun's country lanes are ideal for biking. Visit Bike Loudoun (🌐 *bikeloudoun.org*) for cue sheets. The primo ride, however, is the Washington & Old Dominion (W&OD) rail-trail. The 45-mile trail actually begins in Arlington, Virginia, but enters Loudoun County just past mile 21 and ends in the charming town of Purcellville. The 10-mile stretch between Leesburg and Purcellville is especially bucolic. ✉ *Leesburg* 🌐 *www.visitloudoun.org.*

Index

320

Photo Credits

Front Cover: Claudia Uripos / eStock Photo [Description: Washington, D.C.]. **Back cover, from left to right:** Jemaerca/iStockPhoto. Viviane Teles/ VivianeTeles.com. Sborisov/iStockPhoto. **Spine:** Orhancam/Dreamstime. **Interior, from left to right:** Smithsonian Institution and the National Museum of African American History and Culture (1). Cvandyke/ Dreamstime (2-3). Sborisov/iStockphoto (5). **Chapter 1: Experience Washington, D.C.:** Lunamarina/Dreamstime (6-7). Steve Heap/Shutterstock (8-9). Lewis Tse Pui Lung/Shutterstock (9). Orhan Cam/Shutterstock (9). Konstantin L/ Shutterstock (10). Sgoodwin4813/Dreamstime (10). Orhan Cam/Shutterstock (10). Courtesy of washington.org (10). Travelview/Shutterstock (11). Walleyelj/Dreamstime (11). Gary Blakeley/Shutterstock (12). Cdrin/Shutterstock (12). Rena Schild/Shutterstock (12). Bob Pool/Shutterstock (12). Albert Pego/Shutterstock (13). DavidNNP/Shutterstock (13). Lissandra Melo/Shutterstock (13). Sean Pavone/Shutterstock (13). Orhan Cam/Shutterstock (14). Avmedved/Dreamstime (14). Orhan Cam/Shutterstock (15). Camrocker/iStockphoto (16). Stock_photo_world/Shutterstock (16). Sean Pavone/Shutterstock (16). Courtesy of washington.org (16). Steve Heap/Shutterstock (17). Sean Pavone/Shutterstock (17). Ryan Stein Photography 2018 (22). Courtesy of Kramerbooks & Afterwords Cafe (23). Stephen Bobb Photography/President Lincoln's Cottage (24). Romiana Lee/Shutterstock (24). The Peacock Room/Wikimedia (24). Lee Stalsworth/Fine Art through Photography, LLC (24). Nicole S Glass/Shutterstock (25). Andrei Medvedev/Shutterstock (25). Clewisleake/Dreamstime (25). Jon Bilous/Shutterstock (25). Photo.ua/Shutterstock (26). Guillermo Olaizola/Shutterstock (26). Rudi Riet/Wikimedia.org (26). PJames Blinn/Dreamstime (27). Alankolnik/Dreamstime (27). **Chapter 3: The National Mall:** Orhan Cam/Shutterstock (55). Tomwachs/iStockphoto (61). Phototake Inc./Alamy (65). National Capital Planning Commission_wikimediacommons (66). Popperfoto/Alamy (67). Leena A. Krohn/wikimedia (67). Joacim Osterstam/wikipedia (67). Tupungato/ iStock (68). Douglas Litchfield/Shutterstock (68). Chuck Pefley/Alamy (68). Tupungato/iStock (69). Smithsonian Institution (69). diane39/istockphoto (69). Sandra Baker/Alamy (69). Stock Connection Distribution/Alamy (69). Franko Khoury National Museum of African Art Smithsonian Institution (69). faustasyan/Shutterstock (69). David R. Frazier Photolibrary, Inc./Alamy (69). Giuseppe Luciano Crimeni/Dreamstime (69). Smithsonian Institution (70). Vsevolod33/Shutterstock (72). Richard Gunion/iStockphoto (72). William S. Kuta/Alamy (72). Hemis/Alamy Stock Photo (72). Visions of America, LLC/ Alamy (72). Lee Foster/Alamy (73). Alan Karchmer/Smithsonian Institution and the National Museum of African American History and Culture (75). Crimestudio/Dreamstime (81). Orhan Cam (83). Emily Haight/National Museum of Women in the Arts (89). **Chapter 4: Downtown With Chinatown and Penn Quarter:** Prakash Patel/International Spy Museum (92). Courtesy of the Smithsonian's National Portrait Gallery (98). Sean Pavone/Shutterstock (106). **Chapter 5:Capitol Hill and Northeast:** Shawn Miller/Library of Congress (115). Alessio Catelli/Shutterstock (121). kimberlyfaye/Flickr (121). Abbie Rowe/wikimedia. (121). Public Domain (122). Classic Image/Alamy Stock Photo (122). Public Domain (122). Prints and Photographs Division Library of Congress (122). Library of Congrass (123). sborisov/iStockphoto (123). Thomas Crawford/wikipedia (123). Florin1961/Dreamstime (124). Wadester/wikimedia (125). Andrews71/Dreamstime (126). William Penn and the Indians/wikimedia (126). U.S. Senate, 110th Congress, Senate Photo Studio (128). DCstockphoto. com/Alamy (128). SCPhotos/Alamy (128). United States Congress (128). GBlakeley/iStockphoto (130). Devin Dotson/US Botanic Garden (134). **Chapter 6: Foggy Bottom With the West End and the White House:** Tupungato/Shutterstock(145). V_E/Shutterstock (152). Sepavo/Dreamstime (154). **Chapter 7: Georgetown:** Tupungato/dreamstime (163). Rob Crandall/Shutterstock (171). **Chapter 8: Dupont Circle and Kalorama:** Avmedved/Dreamstime (181). Sarah Sampsel/Flickr (187). **Chapter 9: Adams Morgan:** Avmedved/Dreamstime (195). Andrei Medvedev/Shutterstock (200). **Chapter 10: U Street Corridor and Shaw With Logan Circle and Columbia Heights:** Carol M. Highsmith/ (205). Destination DC (208). Chapter 11: Upper Northwest: Hudis/Dreamstime (225). **Chapter 12: D.C. Waterfront:** Tim Brown/iStockphoto (237). Romiana Lee/Shutterstock (243). **Chapter 13: Arlington**: Hang Dinh/Shutterstock (251). Kamira/Shutterstock (257). Condor 36/Shutterstock (258). Sergii Figurnyi/Shutterstock (259). Vario images GmbH & Co.KG/Alamy (259). Kjohnson341/Dreamstime (259). Rzyotova/Dreamstime (260). Ken Hackett/Alamy (262). Rough Guides/Alamy (262). William S. Kuta/Alamy (263). Chris A Crumley/Alamy Stock Photo (263). Jeremy R. Smith/Shutterstock (263). Vacclav/Dreamstime (265). **Chapter 14: Side Trips to Maryland:** Appalachianviews/Dreamstime (269). Jon Bilous/Shutterstock (276). Kirkikisphoto/Dreamstime (281). Christopher Mazmanian/Shutterstock (287). **Chapter 15: Side Trips to Virginia:** Getty Images/iStockphoto (295). Lee Snider Photo Images/Shutterstock (305). Orhan Cam/ Shutterstock (311). Eurobanks/iStockphoto (313). **About Our Writers:** All photos are courtesy of the writers.

*Every effort has been made to trace the copyright holders, and we apologize in advance for any accidental errors. We would be happy to apply the corrections in the following edition of this publication.

Notes

Notes

Notes

Notes

Notes

Notes

Notes

Notes

Fodor's WASHINGTON, D.C.

Publisher: Stephen Horowitz, *General Manager*

Editorial: Douglas Stallings, *Editorial Director;* Jill Fergus, Amanda Sadlowski, *Senior Editors;* Brian Eschrich, Alexis Kelly, *Editors;* Angelique Kennedy-Chavannes, *Assistant Editor*

Design: Tina Malaney, *Director of Design and Production;* Jessica Gonzalez, *Senior Designer;* Erin Caceres, *Graphic Design Associate*

Production: Jennifer DePrima, *Editorial Production Manager;* Elyse Rozelle, *Senior Production Editor;* Monica White, *Production Editor*

Maps: Rebecca Baer, *Senior Map Editor;* David Lindroth, Mark Stroud (Moon Street Cartography), *Cartographers*

Photography: Viviane Teles, *Senior Photo Editor;* Namrata Aggarwal, Neha Gupta, Payal Gupta, Ashok Kumar, *Photo Editors;* Eddie Aldrete, *Photo Production Intern;* Kadeem McPherson, *Photo Production Associate Intern*

Business and Operations: Chuck Hoover, *Chief Marketing Officer;* Robert Ames, *Group General Manager*

Public Relations and Marketing: Joe Ewaskiw, *Senior Director of Communications and Public Relations*

Fodors.com: Jeremy Tarr, *Editorial Director;* Rachael Levitt, *Managing Editor*

Technology: Jon Atkinson, *Director of Technology;* Rudresh Teotia, *Associate Director of Technology;* Alison Lieu, *Project Manager*

Writers: Claire Handscombe, Barbara Noe Kennedy, Akilah Stroman, Jessica van Dop DeJesus

Editor: Angelique Kennedy-Chavannes

Production Editor: Elyse Rozelle

26th Edition

ISBN 978-1-64097-569-9

ISSN 0743-9741

All details in this book are based on information supplied to us at press time. Always confirm information when it matters, especially if you're making a detour to visit a specific place. Fodor's expressly disclaims any liability, loss, or risk, personal or otherwise, that is incurred as a consequence of the use of any of the contents of this book.

SPECIAL SALES
This book is available at special discounts for bulk purchases for sales promotions or premiums. For more information, e-mail SpecialMarkets@fodors.com.

PRINTED IN CANADA

10 9 8 7 6 5 4 3 2 1

MIX
Paper from responsible sources
FSC® C016245
www.fsc.org

About Our Writers

Claire Handscombe is a British writer who moved to Washington, D.C. in 2012 to study for an MFA in creative writing, but also because of an obsession with *The West Wing*. She is the host of the Brit Lit Podcast, the author of the novel *Unscripted*, and the editor of *Walk With Us: How The West Wing Changed Our Lives*. When she's away from books, she's probably checking out a new favorite restaurant with a friend. She updated Dupont Circle and Kalorama; Adams Morgan; and D.C. Waterfront.

After many years as senior editor with National Geographic, **Barbara Noe Kennedy** left in 2015 to fly solo as a freelance travel writer and editor, focusing on destinations, art, culture, food, and adventure around the world. She's watched D.C. grow up into a global city, though her favorite activity remains running on its leafy paths. Her website is barbaranoekennedy.com. She updated Experience Washington, D.C.; Travel Smart; Capitol Hill and Northeast; Upper Northwest; Arlington; and Side Trips to Virginia.

Currently living in Baltimore and working at Towson University, **Akilah Stroman** is a Maryland native who loves to find the best restaurants, bars, and new activities and events in the area. She updated U Street Corridor and Shaw; and Side Trips to Maryland.

Jessica van Dop DeJesus is a widely published travel content creator. She's the founder of the popular foodie travel website The Dining Traveler and author of the coffee-table book, *The Dining Traveler Guide to Puerto Rico*. Her writing has been featured in *Modern Luxury*, Travel Channel , *Washington City Paper, Southern Living,* and Telemundo. She was raised in Guayama, Puerto Rico. Jessica began traveling more than 20 years ago as a young Marine and has traveled to more than 50 countries and lived in six. When she's not traveling, she's at home with her family in Washington, D.C. Follow her on Instagram, Facebook, Twitter, Pinterest, and YouTube @DiningTraveler. She updated The National Mall; Downtown; Foggy Bottom; and Georgetown.